Smile at the world and know that "this Day" is going to be "THE BEST DAY OF YOUR LIFE"

*Tao Porchon-Lynch*

# DANCING LIGHT

# There Is Nothing You Cannot Do!™

Täo Porchon-Lynch in her signature Peacock Pose

# PRAISE FOR TÄO

"One of the most acclaimed yoga teachers of our century, Täo Porchon-Lynch at 96 years is a mentor to me who embodies the spirit of yoga and is an example of Ageless Body Timeless Mind. Like yoga, she teaches us to let go and to have exquisite awareness in every moment."
—Deepak Chopra
Founder of the Chopra Center for Wellbeing and Esteemed Author

"Through her mastery of Yoga and the body-mind-spirit connection, Täo helps us unbind the limits of our human condition in a most gentle and spirit filled way. She is a gift to us all. This book captures her magic."
—Agapi Stassinopoulos
Author of *Unbinding the Heart: A Dose of Greek Wisdom, Generosity and Unconditional Love*

"Täo is a very special woman and I've had the honor of both teaching for and with her, and have had her teachings. The people of the younger generations really have to look at a person like Täo who has weathered so much in her life and has come out the other side still completely pure of Love, Laughter and Light."
—Rodney Yee
Yoga Teacher and Author of *Yoga: The Poetry of the Body*

"I want to BE Täo! What she has done, who she is and the light that's in her eyes. When you say hello to her, she is just so full of Light and Love and mischievousness. I just think she is an inspiration for women and all of mankind."
—Colleen Saidman Yee
Yoga Teacher and Author of *Yoga for Life: A Journey to Inner Peace and Freedom*

"All you have to do is be in Täo Porchon-Lynch's presence to feel the energy of her spirit and the wisdom in her eyes. To have a book which allows us to enter this amazing woman's life is a gift to us all. She is a living example of how we can all learn to live life to the fullest and to truly live from the heart—mind, body, spirit and soul. She is a precious commodity and we are so lucky to understand who she is and how she became that way!"
—Suzanne Steinbaum
Cardiologist, TV Host and Author of *Dr. Suzanne Steinbaum's Heart Book: Every Woman's Guide to a Heart-Healthy Life*

"Täo is a truly remarkable woman who embodies the qualities of a true yogi and possesses a depth of knowledge that is quite rare."
—David Swenson
Yoga Teacher and Author of *Ashtanga Yoga: The Practice Manual*

"All the world has been graced by the presence and independent spirit of our great yoga teacher, Täo Porchon-Lynch. Her fascinating memoir shows us that through the difficulty of her first breath, she learned the importance of breath in all of life, and in yoga. Through the injustices she witnessed in her childhood, she learned the importance of peace. I'm honored to know her and follow in her footsteps."
—Rama Jyoti Vernon
International Peace Mediator, Yoga Teacher and Author of *Yoga: The Practice of Myth and Sacred Geometry*

"Täo has been a role model to all of us who have been practicing yoga since the early 70's. She is a brilliant example of the health and wellbeing that can come with a lifetime of yoga practices. Her grace, compassion, service to the yoga community, and zest for life have inspired me for years, as well as thousands of young souls just stepping on to the yoga path."
—Beryl Bender Birch
Founder, The Hard & Soft Yoga Institute and Author of *Power Yoga: The Total Strength and Flexibility Workout*

"Täo is a true inspiration to one and all. I feel privileged that I have met her. When I look at her life, I think, 'How can one person do it all?' and she says everyone can do it as long as you can harness the power within you! Her nature, spirit and energy are something that I salute."
—Sushmita Sen
Actress and Former Miss Universe 1994

"I feel I am the most fortunate man in this world who has gotten an opportunity to share the stage with a legend like Täo not just once but three times. Each time I danced with Täo I learned new things about myself and my dance. Being with Täo is like being in a class—a class about life and spirit where you grow not only as a dancer but as a human being. I hope I can be a student of this class of Täo forever!"
—Sandip Soparrkar
Dancer-Choreographer, Actor and Humanitarian

"Täo's presence is a life changer for anyone who experiences her movement and wisdom. She is a living example of her own philosophy that "Anything is possible." Yoga is the root of all eastern martial arts. It is the healing and harmony that is essential for life. Täo's approach at 96 makes people realize that there are no excuses to make things happen in your life. Thank you Täo for being a great friend and teacher!"
—John P. Mirrione
Founder, Harmony By Karate and National Stop Bullying Campaign

"I could never imagine that at this age Täo could dance so beautifully. It shows her dedication and commitment for the art. I love the way she has taken care of herself. At 96 years old, she is so fit and beautiful. Her love for the arts is what I feel makes her so alive."
—Hema Malini
Member of Indian Parliament, Actress, Bharatanatyam Dancer and Choreographer

"It has been one of the greatest honors of my career to have the opportunity to create images together that continuously inspire people of all ages, all over the world. Never before have I met a brighter, lighter, warmer, sweeter, kinder human being than Täo. She has inspired countless works of art in our sacred, creative collaborations."
—Robert Sturman
Photographer, Robert Sturman Studios

"The inspiration from collaborating with Täo is second only to being friends with her. Her warm spirit, positive outlook, and heartfelt message of Oneness have enriched my life beyond measure. Congratulations to Täo for all of her life's accomplishments and for deeply touching so many people. I love you!"
—Valerie Romanoff
Composer/Producer, Valrock Music and CEO, Starlight Orchestras

"When I heard about Täo, I never believed that such a person could exist. I was mesmerized to see Täo dance such difficult moves with Sandip Soparrkar. She is an inspiration to all dance lovers. I wish all can live a life like hers and keep dancing forever!"
—Zeenat Aman
Actress and Former Miss Asia Pacific 1970

# DANCING LIGHT

The Spiritual Side of Being
Through the Eyes of a Modern Yoga Master

Tāo Porchon-Lynch
Janie Sykes Kennedy and Teresa Kay-Aba Kennedy

**POWER LIVING MEDIA**
New York

Copyright © 2015 by Täo Porchon-Lynch, Janie Sykes Kennedy, Teresa Kay-Aba Kennedy

All rights reserved. No part of this book may be reproduced, distributed or transmitted in any form or by any means, including photocopying, recording, or other electronic or mechanical methods, without the prior written permission of the publisher, except in the case of brief quotations embodied in critical reviews and certain other noncommercial uses permitted by copyright law. Published by Power Living Media, an imprint of Power Living Enterprises, Inc.

Power Living Media
116 West 23rd Street, Suite 500
New York, NY 10011
212-901-6913
www.powerlivingmedia.com   Email: info@powerlivingmedia.com

Power Living is a registered trademark of Power Living Enterprises, Inc.
There Is Nothing You Cannot Do is a trademark of Täo Porchon-Lynch.

Photo Credits: Except as noted, all images are courtesy of Täo Porchon-Lynch's Personal Collection including the photos provided by students that could not be attributed. A good faith effort was made to discover the copyright holder of each image included. Front Cover and Pages 405, 427 Robert Sturman. Inside Jacket Flap and Pages 455, 460 Eu-nah Lee. Back Cover and Pages 47, 414-415, 417, 419-420, 430-431, 433-438, 441-444, 447-449, 455 Teresa Kay-Aba Kennedy. Pages 6, 20-21, 25-26, 28-29, 33, 38, 43, 73, 119-120, 193, 229, 232, 234, 278, 300, 350: Public Domain. Pages 87, 92, 310: Public Domain / U.S. Government. Pages 94, 99, 147 Guimas. Pages 218-219 Vedanta Society. Pages 263-264, 266-267, 275 Dr. Roman Ostoja. Pages 299, 360 World Education. Page 361 Mary Ellen Kay. Pages 363, 411, 433, 436-437, 438 (bottom) Joyce Pines. Page 367 Susheel Somani. Page 367 Kamini Kaushal. Pages 385, 389 Center for International Dialogue. Page 388 The Jerusalem Post. Pages 407-408 Sandip Soparrkar. Page 413 Judy Rand. Page 427 (bottom) Micahel Taylor. Pages 428, 446-447, 450-455, 458-459 Rafi Abada. Page 429 Andrea Kurtz. Page 438 (top left): Contact Music. Page 430 Chris Lane. Page 439 (bottom) Jaymie Meyer. Page 440: Hudson Health Photographer. Page 445 Janet LeFrancois. Page 457 Megan Kuczynski.

"I Wandered Lonely As A Cloud" by William Wordsworth and "The Brook" by Alfred, Lord Tennyson are used as works in Public Domain.

Library of Congress Control Number: 2015947471

ISBN-13: 978-1-942-51000-0
ISBN-10: 1-942-51000-4

Printed in United States of America

Cover and book design: Teresa Kay-Aba Kennedy
Design Consultant: Molly Heron
Cover photograph: Robert Sturman
Inside flap photograph: Eu-nah Lee
Primary editors: James Scott Kennedy, Jr., Gretchen Robinson, Susan Douglass

10 9 8 7 6 5 4 3 2

First Edition: August 2015

*This book is dedicated
to all of my yoga students,
teachers, and masters who
have inspired me
to write these pages.
I continue to learn
from every one
of them.*

*It is also for
my beloved
homes of India,
France and
America.
All of these places
have shaped my
thinking and experiences.*

*One of my favorite poems I still know by heart
that beautifully describes the dance of nature...*

I wandered lonely as a cloud
That floats on high o'er vales and hills,
When all at once I saw a crowd,
A host, of golden daffodils;
Beside the lake, beneath the trees,
Fluttering and dancing in the breeze.

Continuous as the stars that shine
And twinkle on the milky way,
They stretched in never-ending line
Along the margin of a bay:
Ten thousand saw I at a glance,
Tossing their heads in sprightly dance.

The waves beside them danced; but they
Out-did the sparkling waves in glee:
A poet could not but be gay,
In such a jocund company:
I gazed—and gazed—but little thought
What wealth the show to me had brought:

For oft, when on my couch I lie
In vacant or in pensive mood,
They flash upon that inward eye
Which is the bliss of solitude;
And then my heart with pleasure fills,
And dances with the daffodils.

—William Wordsworth
*I Wandered Lonely As A Cloud*

# CONTENTS

*Opening Poem* — *x*

*Acknowledgments* — *xiii*

*Preface* — *xv*

*Introduction* — *xix*

**Part I   On Peace & War** — **2**

   1   It's a Beautiful Day, Isn't It? — *3*

   2   Feel The Energy Behind It All — *13*

   3   Lift The Veil Of Ignorance — *24*

   4   Boldly Activate Your Beliefs — *39*

   5   Embrace The Twists — *49*

   6   Ride The Waves — *64*

   7   Salute The Sun — *85*

   8   Laugh At Life — *98*

   9   Be A Peaceful Warrior — *109*

  10   Reach For The Moon — *128*

  11   Be Present For Good — *150*

## CONTENTS

**Part II  The Real & Unreal** — **172**

  12  Change With The Seasons — *173*

  13  Come Back To Center — *199*

  14  Let Go — *221*

  15  Begin Where You Are — *236*

  16  Tune Into Cosmic Intelligence — *258*

  17  Say Yes! — *280*

  18  Let Trials Strengthen You — *301*

  19  Honor Human Nature — *317*

  20  Seek Common Ground — *332*

**Part III  Living Light & Truth** — **347**

  21  Feed Your Soul — *348*

  22  Do It Today — *364*

  23  Let Your Spirit Soar — *378*

  24  Dance To Your Own Rhythm — *397*

  25  Live Light & Truth — *409*

*Closing Poem* — *424*

*Photo Album* — *426*

*Author Bios* — *461*

*Glossary & Notes* — *463*

*Index* — *465*

# ACKNOWLEDGMENTS

Thank you first and foremost to Janie Sykes Kennedy and Teresa Kay-Aba Kennedy for being my dear collaborators who helped me make sense of my many stories. Through hours of conversations, they captured my words and pieced them together to display my colorful tapestry of experiences that have spanned the globe. When I wondered who could possibly be interested in a roving epilogue through the many years of my life, they reminded me that I had an important perspective to share.

I met Terri in 2007 when I was teaching a master workshop at Integral Yoga Institute in New York. She did the most beautiful yoga and seemed to light up the room. I had to know her. I found out that she had founded the first yoga studio in Harlem and was doing tremendous work. She since has worked tirelessly on my behalf facilitating my involvement in events like the Newark Peace Education Summit with His Holiness the 14th Dalai Lama and moderating discussions on my life at places like the Pentagon.

Then I met Terri's beautiful mother who has such a warm spirit, as well as being an accomplished journalist. I asked them both to help write this book on Janie's birthday, November 5, 2011, after a workshop they hosted for me in Harlem. A few months later they were able to put aside other projects to dedicate time to me. Despite a few bumps in the road that halted the project, here it is just three years later ready for the world to enjoy. It was a wonderful journey and a monumental accomplishment.

Many thanks to James Scott Kennedy, Jr. for his professional editing, marketing talent and boundless energy while working on this project. It was fun spending time editing in Montego Bay, Jamaica. Thank you also to Sheila Kennedy and Daniel Kennedy for being early readers. I consider all of the Kennedys my family and I am deeply grateful for their love and support.

Thank you to Gretchen Robinson for being an early reader and editor, and for facilitating various events in Rochester and Kansas City on my behalf. Gretchen, Stacy Tucker and Terri facilitated the endorsement from the wonderful Dr. Deepak Chopra to whom I also send gratitude. Thank you as well to David Swenson, Rodney Yee, Colleen Saidman Yee, Beryl Bender Birch, Agapi Stassinopoulos, Dr. Suzanne Steinbaum, Rama Jyoti Vernon, Robert Sturman, Sandip Soparrkar, Sushmita Sen, Hema Malini, Zeenat Aman, John P. Mirrione and Valerie Romanoff for their gracious endorsements. I am humbled by their statements.

Additional thanks to Robert Sturman for the beautiful red dress photo on the cover and Eu-nah Lee for the dust jacket inside photo. Molly Heron, an Integral Yoga teacher and long-time student, helped us refine the book design and formatting for which I am grateful. Sarah Ottino, who participated in my yoga workshop at the University of Delaware, graciously created the line art for the cover drawing. My gratitude also goes to long-time students Lori Schulman and Susan Douglass for their legal work, and Susan for being an early reader and editor.

I am quite honored that this book is being studied as part of the "Women's Wellness & Yoga" course at Converse College in South Carolina. Psychology Professor Janet LeFrancois had the inspiration to include it even before the book was published. The professor and students took time to review an advance copy of the manuscript and provide comments. We are very grateful to Professor LeFrancois and the students including Ashleigh Alston, Jessie Brooks, Amada Byars, Emily Gardner, Kaitlyn Guilbert, Casey Kelafant, Taylor Lamkin, Kathleen Langbehn, Katherine Martin, Madison McKinnish, Courtney Pauley, Sarah Picou, Angelica Rocha-Herrera, Jordyn Richey, Leanne Sandora, Ciara Steele, Abby Sweet, Maddie Tisdel, Paige Vasel, and Joni Ware.

As always, special thanks to Joyce Pines who handles the terrestrial side of my life so I can pursue my spiritual goals, and to my extended family of friends and students who inspire me every day.

# PREFACE

The Dance of Life is inherently a spiritual dance in which we're all invited to participate by the very nature of being given breath. It is our responsibility to show up with passion to experience the wonder in every moment. Täo exemplifies her mantra "There Is Nothing You Cannot Do" and shows us what is possible—that we each can live to our Highest Potential by inhaling life and dancing to our own rhythm.

"Amazing!" "Inspirational!" "Unbelievable!" "Mind-blowing!" Those are the words that have been used to describe Täo. At 96 years old, she danced to rapper Pitbull's sexy song "Fireball" with her 26-year-old partner Vard Margaryan on the television show *America's Got Talent*. They wowed all four judges including Howard Stern, Heidi Klum, Mel B and Howie Mandel, and received a rousing standing ovation. Täo was just doing what she does, being an embodiment of Spirit.

From the moment Täo was born on a ship in the middle of the English Channel, her life has been fantastical, an incredible odyssey through 20th century history with a first-hand experience of events and people most of us only read about. At age 22, she had already marched with Mahatma Gandhi twice and helped Jews escape the Nazis during World War II. She was performing nightly in cabarets during the bombing Blitz in London and was soon to marry a handsome French Spitfire pilot, a member of the No. 340 Ile-de-France Squadron that, among other things, flew cover over Normandy on D-Day. After the war, she became a famous model for designers such as Jean Dessès and then an actress under contract with MGM. That was just the beginning.

Her journey has had peaks of delight and valleys of disappointments, ultimately being a story of resilience and the triumph of Spirit. In the midst of war she found happiness. In the frenetic activity of Hollywood, she felt alone. As the seasons in her life changed, she evolved. When things didn't turn out the way she wanted, instead of being bitter she "closed the book" as her friend Marlene Dietrich advised—and she pressed on.

Acclaimed yoga teacher Rodney Yee said, she has "weathered so much in her life and has come out the other side still completely pure of Love, Laughter and Light." Through Tāo, we see the importance of letting go of attachments and the "story in our head" to be present with what is. We learn that we can "make the sun come out" in our own lives. Her belief of all people being equal, none greater and none lesser, has allowed her to show extraordinary compassion to those around her, as well as walk through the world as a universal communicator for what is right. She is likely the only person still on the planet who marched with BOTH Mahatma Gandhi and Dr. Martin Luther King, Jr.

Her story is a search for Truth, an exploration that started when she was a child and continues to shape her life today. Her philosophical foundation, provided by her uncle in India, was so ingrained that even when she was not thinking of certain spiritual principles she was innately living them. Even when she was not consciously meditating, her state of mind was meditative. Even when she was not sitting to do breathing techniques, she was in tune with her breath sometimes deliberately, other times subconsciously. She may say that she didn't practice yoga for parts of her life. That is because it was second nature and she was "living yoga" in how she approached each day. Throughout her life, she constantly reminded herself of the lessons from her gurus.

She epitomizes the essence of mindfulness, a state of ever-present awareness. For our readers who are yogis, you may notice her innate embodiment of *Ashtanga*, or the eightfold path, as described in the *Yoga Sutras of Patanjali*—how she treats others and herself (*yamas* and *niyamas*), her practice of the physical postures (*asanas*), a deep connection to breath (*pranayama*), an innate control of the senses in relation to the external world (*pratyahara*), her inner perceptual awareness (*dharana*), her constant contemplation on and search for the Divine (*dhyana*) and moments of transcendence (*Samadhi*). She manifests a high level of *sattva*, luminosity or quality of light, in her everyday life perhaps from her decades of yogic living. It radiates out from her eyes, smile and entire being, energizing all around like pure *prana* or Life Force.

Tāo says, "There is so much to do and so little time to do it!" She still has that fearless and fiery spirit as she speaks on peace panels, balances in yoga postures and kicks up her heels in dance competitions. Tāo fully interacts with life and is a manifestation of the concept of *carpe diem*, or "seize the day." She draws energy from the Universe and lives the Oneness that underpins her philosophy. At an age when most have slowed down, Täo is ready for her next adventure and wants to continue to travel the world. With Peter Pan-like endless youth, she says, "In my head I'm still in my 20's, and I have no intention of ever growing up." How did she get this way? That is the value of this book.

Through the lenses of almost a century, Täo is a wellspring of hope that can give each of us an expanded vision of the possibilities in our own lives. We are all in the Dance of Life weaving in and out of spiritual consciousness, searching for how to be present with the wonders of life and maintain harmony of mind, body and Spirit. By witnessing Täo's life, we learn that consciousness evolves through a daily and lifelong awakening and that we can truly co-create our existence by what we put in our mind. Regardless of age, vitality is the spirit you exude and the energy you bring to life. She reminds us that we can continually reinvent ourselves and have many chapters in life as she has—activist, actress, model, producer, wine connoisseur, yoga teacher and ballroom dancer.

The book is divided into three parts. Part I, "On Peace & War," covers Täo's formative early years from 1918 through 1947. It establishes the blueprint of her beliefs from her childhood in India and demonstrates how she put the lessons from her uncle and the great masters into practice during the hardships of World War II and being on her own for the first time. She overcomes obstacle after obstacle and finds her way, including meeting the love of her life.

Part II, "The Real & Unreal," covers her glamour days from the late 1940s through the 1960s. It juxtaposes the glitz and occasional pretentiousness of Hollywood and modeling with Täo's exploration of metaphysics and increasing inner quest to maintain her spiritual center as in the yogic chant, "Lead me from the unreal to the Real." She continues to lift the veil of ignorance we each are under.

Part III, "Living Light & Truth," covers Täo's transformation into a spiritual and wine ambassador from the 1970s through 2015. It starts off on a downbeat with her second marriage and then blossoms into fully teaching yoga, ballroom dancing and the bright light we see today. It assimilates insights from her decades of experiences and teachers.

The OM symbol at the beginning of each chapter represents Divine Energy itself. Täo's two favorite poems, which she recites from memory to this day, are at the beginning and end of the book. She learned them when Noël Coward was helping her improve her English. They speak to nature as the metaphor revealing to us the beauty and dynamism of life. There are over 450 images to greatly enhance the reading, from a picture of Täo wearing a Jean Patou dress and being escorted across stage by Bob Hope to photographs with wine pioneer Dr. Konstantin Frank as they meet to form the American Wine Society. At the end, in an unconventional addition, there is a photo album of significant events and her extended family of friends and students. Although Täo has outlived most of the people from her early years, she illustrates how we can choose to create a vibrant community of loved ones.

We will forever be grateful for Täo and the day she asked us—a mother and daughter writing team—to collaborate on this book with her. It was an unexpected gift, and we have both been transformed by the hours of "sitting at the feet of a master." It has been an honor and a delight, and we are humbled to be stewards of her important story.

The process was like putting together the pieces of a massive puzzle to create a continuous narrative and sincere expression of an epic existence. We let the book organically reveal itself versus trying to fit it into a particular format because Täo breaks all molds. Since she was involved with so many historical people and events, we researched the context of almost every line and found that her recall was precise.

When Täo read her entire story in December 2014, in what we thought was the final round of edits, a flood of additional memories came back. Thus, we extended the writing time so the work would represent exactly what she had in mind. At that time, she also uncovered a treasure trove of new pictures from her archives. As a seasoned writer in her own right, Täo was involved every step of the way until the manuscript went to print. This baby, the book, is hers and we were happy to serve as attentive midwives.

In many ways, *Dancing Light* is a modern *Autobiography of a Yogi*, a manifesto for a new generation of Light Seekers. It takes you on a search for peace, the Oneness behind everything and your exceptional profound Self. As you read, think about your own journey and how Täo's philosophy and reflections can enhance your experience. Be fascinated by her story, witness fearlessness in action and grow from almost a century of wisdom… knowing you too can craft a full and fulfilled "Täo-like" life!

Janie Sykes Kennedy and Teresa Kay-Aba Kennedy
July 2015

# INTRODUCTION

I have always had a curiosity about the nature of things. In fact, nature became my encyclopedia, and through it I began the study of life. I've learned that, for the rare few, enlightenment happens all at once. For most however, it is an unfolding little by little like a seed that is planted and eventually grows into a great sentinel.

When I sat with pen in hand to write a book of my life's adventures, I hesitated. I have always lived in the present savoring the good while believing that "tomorrow" never comes and that yesterday's memories of more difficult times should be washed out of my thoughts. That is why trying to recall my youth and explore the souvenirs of the past is harder than anyone might imagine. There have been some moments throughout my life that didn't always turn out the way I would have liked them to, but I look at them without regrets.

As a child, I was always thinking everyone should have free choice and not accept just what other folks said was "correct living." Stubborn, I travelled the path of what I believed was right. This way of being was encouraged by my beloved uncle in India who gave me key lessons, and under his direction I had an incredible spiritual upbringing. He followed the precepts of the great master Swami Vivekananda and the poet and sage Sri Aurobindo.

My uncle lived by belief in the beauty of Truth and Oneness as Vedanta teaches, "Truth is One, sages call it by many names." The adventures of my early life with him became the path of the road of Infinite Beauty opening up vistas I would never have known. I learned how to tap into the purity and the very essence of life.

My early inspiration from Sri Aurobindo—experiencing his person and studying at his ashram—has stayed in my spirit. He poured through the pages of his extraordinary mind finding beautiful words to match his inner power of Thought. Beyond the pages of poetry, his light even today has brought to Pondicherry people from around the world to live together and share their Oneness.

My uncle's friendship with Mahatma Gandhi affected me deeply. Gandhi roused a whole nation with his belief that freedom without fear belonged to everyone. He wasn't scared to be in prison or go without eating day after day to become a symbol of hope. Experiencing the 1930 Salt March with him was extraordinary. He has decorated the walls of my mind throughout my life. Through his example, I became more fearless and resolved to stand up for freedom and what was right.

My aunt in France showed me, as did Gandhi, that one person could make a difference and that women could be as brave and enterprising as men. During World War II, she devised a clever way to hide Polish Jews in cement wine vats to help them escape. She had a sense of fearlessness that I admired. Running our family vineyard in the Rhône Valley, my aunt shared with me her love and knowledge of wine. During my eight months with her, she taught me to honor and treasure this great "nectar of the gods" as I later became friends with wine pioneer Robert Mondavi, published the *Beverage Communicator* newspaper and was a co-founder of the American Wine Society.

The great French General Charles de Gaulle gave a call to rally for the cause of France and Europe and inspired me to deepen my commitment to the Resistance. During the dark days of World War II, his radio addresses in June 1940 rang out against the evils of war as it spread across the world and thousands of young Frenchmen rose to fight for freedom. Later, I would work with the great French hero Joël Le Tac and willingly risk my life to help Jewish people and others who were being persecuted escape the atrocities of the Nazis.

People who saw Oneness in all surrounded me. My many teachers—Swami Prabhavananda, Dr. Roman Ostoja, Maharishi Mahesh Yogi, B.K.S. Iyengar and K. Pattabhi Jois—added new layers of wisdom. My studies of the *Bhagavad Gita* and the writings of Helena Petrovna Blavatsky in Paris expanded by mind. Two incredible women, Mataji Indra Devi and Dr. Welthy Fisher, inspired me to stretch myself even further and to fully embody being a yoga teacher, film producer and giver of Light.

All of these Masters have been a part of my life and what they have stood for has played a significant role in my search for Spirit and Truth. They made me realize the power of a smile and the knowledge that, if I believed sincerely, the answer to my problems would clarify the darkest moments and lighten the path to solutions. I came to believe something good would happen even with the worst calamities, and that you must go out and do, not just talk.

I traveled across the world experiencing the outward beauty of modeling for esteemed designers such as Jean Dessès, Elsa Schiaparelli, Jeanne Lanvin, Jean Patou, Coco Chanel and Marcel Rochas, as well as the inner beauty of writing, producing films and teaching yoga. It was my search for Truth that helped me face the mystifying phases of acting in the cinema of life. It allowed me to find answers in the beauty of nature that surrounded me, seeing that which is possible with the Life Force. It gave me clues to understanding the gift of life.

I had a sweet and wonderful handful of friends who entered my story at various times. I cherish my talks with the great writer Ernest Hemingway in Sancerre after the war. My clique in Europe—Maggy Sarragne, Guimas, Marlene Dietrich, Noël Coward, Bobby Helpmann and Maxim's owner Louis Vaudable—brought me immense joy. My Hollywood friends—Johnnie Raven and his partner Dick, Mary Ellen Kay, Cesar Romero, and those from the Charity Players such as Ginny Berndt and Frances Tolman—opened my eyes to new experiences and were my angels in a foreign city. Great writers and scientists like Aldous Huxley, Gerald Heard, Christopher Isherwood, Frederick Manchester and so many others were on a similar path searching for the spiritual side of being at the Vedanta Society in Los Angeles.

I bless these people who walked along with me on the search for Truth, including expert teachers, such as Beryl Bender Birch, David Swenson, and Rodney Yee, who taught early on in my own yoga Teacher Training programs and for the Yoga Teacher's Association I co-founded. I am grateful for the inspiration of people like Rama Jyoti Vernon who was a pioneer in using yoga for international peace discussions. I've had the pleasure of sharing my thoughts on a peace panel with Nobel Laureates His Holiness the 14th Dalai Lama, Jody Williams and Shirin Ebadi, and other notable people including Dr. Deepak Chopra.

Occasionally, I have seemed to swim in a strange path of enlightenment, a state of Divine Bliss or self-realization, what we call *Samadhi* in yoga. I felt the Oneness with all. Then, I was brought face to face with the ignorance of the world such as experiencing the hatred toward Blacks and Jews in 1940s America. It reminded me of when the Colonial British called me "half-breed" for being half-Indian and half-French. At times my own actions channeled me into hazardous directions and possibly inescapable situations. Whenever things seemed to go wrong, I tuned into my "Inner Diary"—to the great Masters, nature and my teachers—to open up the path I should take and then I continued the sacred Dance of Life.

Now, at 97 years old, I am expected by many to know the secrets of life. What I know is that life is a dance of mind, body and Spirit—the grand dance of Eternal Energy. At times it is an Argentine tango, an intense and highly coordinated exchange, other times it is like the Cuban cha-cha-cha, stepping forward and back. Certain moments it can feel like the jive–a fun, uninhibited lightness of being. Sometimes you play off of your partner and other times it's your solo. Always it is working with the energy that is within you. No matter how dizzying life can be, sometimes you may even feel like you're spinning out of control, you have the power to turn things around.

What you put in your mind materializes in your life and deeply affects how smoothly the Spirit can dance. It is in that moment of union, the coming together of the individual Self with the Universal, that the dance becomes Divine. You experience what we call *yug,* or *yuj,* in Sanskrit—unity of mind, body and Spirit—that is yoga and the Oneness of life. Despite potential missteps along the way, in those special moments of harmony you are floating like a magical Viennese waltz.

Even though I was named the Oldest Yoga Teacher by Guinness World Records in 2012 and have won over 700 First Place Awards as a competitive ballroom dancer since I started at age 87, my story does not begin on the yoga mat or on the dance floor. I grew up in the disquiet of the world, and had a very real and human journey. Yoga has always been a part of my life and my being and yet this book is not really about the physical practice. It is about life, the dance of the Spirit and my search for Truth and Oneness.

It seems like I came out of the womb asking questions like, "Why am I here? What am I supposed to be doing? Why are so many people suffering?" From my childhood, I was searching and my search continues every day. My eyes remain open to all that is.

As I tell my story and uncover my souvenirs, I seek to share lessons and insights to enhance the present experience. No matter what has happened in the past, I wake up each morning knowing that this is the best day of my life! This is my meditation for the day.

Whatever problem and seeming calamity faces you, know that the answer will be a better solution than what you expected. Whatever you have in your heart—smile. Don't look down, don't look backwards, and don't procrastinate. Do it today. Dance to your own rhythm and let nature be your encyclopedia showing you the wonders of what is possible in the Great Forest of Energy. There is nothing you cannot do if you harness the power within you—for you are not the doer, you are the instrument!

# DANCING LIGHT

*Part One*

# On Peace & War

Even when the outside world is at war, you can come back to your natural state of peace. When you settle down into a quieter way of being, you will free the Life Energy from the captivity of the mind.

CHAPTER 1

## It's A Beautiful Day, Isn't It?

I grew up in a time of war and yet peace has always been in my heart. I guess it was my *dharma*, something deeply rooted in my being.

I was born toward the end of World War I. Millions upon millions had been killed and national borders were being redrawn. Countries and empires had fallen including Russia, Germany, Austria-Hungary and the Ottoman Empire. It was estimated that upwards of fifty million people died as a result of the 1918 flu pandemic.

In the midst of this turmoil, my mother, a Hindu girl from the royal region of Bihar, and my father from the French colony of Pondicherry fell in love.

Her home was a land in the north, full of rivers and forests sprinkled with Buddhist temples. It was the seat of the ancient "Golden Age of India," a high point of cultural creativity, philosophical enlightenment and incredible achievement in science, astronomy and mathematics, including the decimal numeral system and the concept of "zero"—a new view on the meaning of "nothing."

My father's home was La Côte d'Azur de l'Est or the "French Riviera of the East," a southern coastal territory with white sandy beaches and sparkling blue waters. Once an ancient Roman trading destination, it had a lively mix of Tamil and French cultures and yet the picturesque charm of an understated beach town.

Both my parents grew up in India, but two worlds and many miles apart. Theirs was a story of defiance. In those days you didn't marry into another race. The British Colonials, in particular, didn't like that, but if the French were in love, it didn't matter what others said.

The war was drawing to its final end and I was told my father, who had joined the French-Canadian army in England, was returning from service to reunite with his beautiful wife. She, seven months pregnant with me, was crossing from Cherbourg, France to Southampton, England to meet him.

They must have been ripe with anticipation of their first baby on the way, a likely mix of joy and trepidation. My father's brother had served in the Indian army and they were planning a jubilant reunion before my father took us, his wife and unborn child, to our new home in Canada. He had immigrated there and had purchased a horse ranch in the western province of Saskatchewan, an inland prairie with tempestuous weather.

My debut on August 13, 1918 seemed like my way, to be in a hurry, ready to experience it all. I was born on a ship in the middle of the English Channel two months too soon. I can imagine being vigorously rocked in my mother's protective womb and ushered into this world by the oscillating movements of the Atlantic Ocean. As I inhaled deeply with my first breath and cried my welcome, sadly, my mother struggled feebly and let out her last breath.

Breath is life. It opens the door to the creation within us. It connects us to the Universe—to every plant and tree, to every inhabitant between earth and heaven. As you see, my first breath was both joyous and tragic. Any time a baby is born there is the wonder of potential. Who will he or she become?

> *Breath is life. It opens the door to the creation within us.*

Beginnings sometimes mark the ending of something else like when the caterpillar disappears into the butterfly. Obviously, I was impatient to make an entrée into this world but why did my mother have to die when I was born, to pierce the scene with an event of sadness?

The place of my turbulent beginning seemed to foretell my high-spirited life of constant travel and adventure, and the ebb and flow of contretemps and delight. I would revisit these waters many times during my underground escapades for the French Resistance and later as a model and actress.

When the ship arrived in Southampton with a premature baby and his wife dead, my father must have been devastated. This new life that they had planned had been shattered. He must have endured the war with the hopes of a normal existence and now that was gone.

As I started my life's journey, my father must have been trying to comprehend the reality that he had lost his wife while also struggling with thoughts of how he could care for an infant just a few days old. He had to make some tough decisions right away.

My father's French-Canadian regiments were lining up to return to Canada while my uncle's Indian regiments were preparing to transfer back to India. What had been the possibility of a cheerful greeting and farewell between brothers had become an overwhelming crisis. My father's plans had changed instantly.

Stunned and saddened by the loss of his beloved, he asked himself and his brother, "How can I take this tiny newborn to the plains of Saskatchewan to live on a horse ranch with no one to feed or take care of her?"

My uncle, who was married and returning home to Pondicherry, offered to solve the monumental problem. Although he could do nothing about the incredible pain of loss, he had a solution for how this sweet little girl could be cared for and loved. He offered to take me to India where he and his wife would raise me until I could be with my father.

And so the die was cast. Several weeks later, I received the precious heritage of belonging to the most amazing family not just in name but also in full spirit. It would become one of the most beautiful souvenirs of my life. Sometimes calamities breathe possibilities of beauty and unforeseen gifts.

> *Sometimes calamities breathe possibilities of beauty and unforeseen gifts.*

The ill-fated circumstances of my mother dying while giving me life may have started me on my spiritual journey and my feeling of Oneness with the Universe long before I knew the path I was on or had words to express it.

My beginning set me on a certain course. Was it destined? Perhaps the future realms of my life were meant to take place on the warm enchanted beaches of India and not the blustery land-locked plains of Canada. Even now, I get chills thinking of that. I cannot stand the cold. I love the feel of sunlight on my skin.

Pondicherry, on the Bay of Bengal, was the perfect backdrop for my youth. I now believe I showed up on this earth in the right place at the right time to the right family though the world sometimes wanted me to tell a different story.

*Old Pondicherry, French India.*

People seem upset when they find out that my father gave me up at birth. But I know he made the best choice he could by allowing his brother and wife in India to raise me.

I would often get asked whether I felt sorry for myself growing up without my mother or father. They would say, "Oh, don't you miss them?"

My response would be, "No, honestly I can't say I do because I didn't come in contact with them."

If they had been on the next street or town it would be different, but I didn't know them. I was very lucky to be with my wonderful uncle and aunt. They treated me as their own. I had a good home and a better family than most people ever get. I learned early on to cherish good fortune instead of lamenting what could have been. Most of all, I think there was a reason why I was brought up by my uncle, an extraordinary man who would share, shape and bring meaning to my life.

The 97 years that followed were impressed by his philosophy and kindness. Like the seeds of nature sprout into beautiful flowers, my inner self took root in this wonderful atmosphere and opened up like dawn spreads itself across the globe to answer the many questions of why I was on this earth.

***

The story of this book then should really be about him, Vital Porchon. I called him "oncle," French for uncle. He held himself straight, a vestige from his army years. Not very tall, he was grand in my eyes and influenced almost every detail of my childhood. A Frenchman with a cheerful heartfelt smile and a good sense of humor, he was always full of fun. My uncle had a way of making the spirit of all those around him feel light.

My earliest childhood memories are of the joy of waking up and anticipating the adventures of each day, exploring nature or playing on the beautiful nearby beach. My uncle set the tone of our home. He never seemed to wake up angry about life or say, "I can't do that." Instead, he always had something positive to offer.

He would start each morning with, "It's a beautiful day isn't it?" That was his inclination. We are each inclined to a disposition. Some people wake up anticipating doom, others expect good. I learned from my uncle that we can choose to see the good.

> *We can choose to see the good.*

He laughed with everybody. I never saw anyone who wasn't smiling around him or patting him on the back. He could get anybody to do practically anything. He had that special quality. He never seemed to be afraid of anything because he didn't believe in fear.

If he said he was going to do something, he would do it. You knew where he was going and what he stood for. He always took the time to share with me his special beliefs, "If you believe in something, do it if it's good. If it's not good, back away until you know what's right and wrong."

Every single day, my uncle gave me something to think about. He never would let me make fun of anybody. He would say, "Stay away from criticism of other people. Always remember: never look down on anyone, never ask anyone to understand you, always try to understand them. And if you don't like them it's not their fault, it's yours. Try to think good and let everything else go. Know that every single thing on this earth pulsates with the same heartbeat as your own." I was fascinated by that thought.

One day, I had my ear to the grass and my aunt asked me, "What are you doing?"

I innocently replied, "I'm listening to the grass grow."

In disbelief she said, "What do you mean, listening to the grass grow? That's nonsense! Who puts this in your head?"

She went to my uncle exclaiming, "You know, I think she's crazy. She is getting all of these weird things in her mind."

Smiling with his usual good-hearted nature my uncle imparted some of his wisdom to my aunt, "She's not crazy, she's right. That piece of grass had to have power to come through the earth. There's energy in the grass. It has a heart like you have a heart. Everything comes out of the ground such as our food. When you stop breathing, you go back into the ground. You disintegrate. So, as I believe there is a God in everything, I believe he's right inside of you beating with your heart."

He wouldn't let anybody push anything on me, even my aunt. She was Indian and unlike my uncle in many ways. She had become a strict Catholic and was very focused on making me into a "good girl" which I appreciate more now.

Although my aunt was of different sorts, I admired her for a lot of things including the good manners she taught me. She would say, "Don't sit at the table with your elbows on it!" Although I don't have too many souvenirs or memories that stand out about her, etiquette and how to be a lady are things that helped me as an adult and have remained with me.

My uncle was open to anyone searching for spirituality and the inner reality. His openness fueled my curiosity. I seemed to absorb a way of being from him without even realizing it. For example, he didn't believe in waste. He would say, "Never put on your plate more than what you can eat. If you can eat it, please eat it. If you can't, don't throw it away because we can give it to somebody who hasn't had any food today."

If I didn't eat something, he would take it out to somebody in the street. He also respected all living things and would say, "Don't kill anything."

Once a British family invited me to "high tea." It was a cultural tradition that was popular with the English aristocracy. They gave me these dainty little sandwiches.

Curious, pointing to what I thought was a special treat, I asked, "What's inside there?"

My British hostess answered, "Sardines."

I wondered out loud, "What are sardines?"

Pointing to a bowl filled with goldfish, she shocked me with her answer, "Sardines, they're like goldfish."

I went home and cried, "They killed those poor little goldfish. They gave me goldfish to eat!"

I couldn't face any food for at least eight to ten days and had to be given liquids to survive. Since then I haven't been able to eat meat or kill anything.

My uncle's compassion came through in everything he did. I had an *ayah*, a nursemaid, who took care of me. Her parents had arranged for her to be married off when she was twelve years old. When her husband-to-be died unexpectedly, she was caste off, abandoned and thrown into the street.

My uncle took her in and treated her as part of the family, giving her a home and education. She wasn't a servant but more like a daughter and an older sister to me. I think she came from the same area as my mother.

My ayah was already a teenager when I was a baby. Hearing her tell others that she was my ayah, I began to call her "Ayah" and never changed that. She actually helped to name me.

When my uncle took me as a newborn to India, I was yet to be officially named. When I was born on the ship, England became my place of birth and a nice British couple gave me their name for the identity papers as a temporary solution since my mother had just died. I was born at a time when identity was critical to life and death. As it still is today, in some places people were being persecuted simply for where they were born and what culture they claimed.

Eventually, I was given the perfect name, Täo Andrée Porchon. Ayah came up with the name "Täo." I don't think she realized it but in Indian astrology, having a "T" at the start of the name indicates a strong spiritual belief and the ability to make prophecies. In Chinese philosophy, Täo means "the way or path," and "the energy of nature." It also is the symbol for long life.

> Täo means "the way or path and "the energy of nature."

Andrée is a popular French name meaning "brave." My full surname, Porchon de Sanglier, indicates that my ancestors in France were keepers of the forest where the wild boar lived. My name was perfect in foreshadowing my future–my love of nature, constant search for Truth and decades of soul-stirring experiences.

Ayah would look after me most of the time. At the start of the day, she would bathe me and help me dress. She did not rush as she daily brushed my long jet-black hair. I was often not a willing participant. Almost every day she would have to tap me on the shoulder and say, "Stop moving!"

I would often say to her with excitement, "I just want to go to the window and feel the cool morning breeze kissing my face." I was ready to get outside and explore the world.

She would say, "Täo, you don't have to rush, you have plenty of time."

Without uttering one word, I often thought about the things I could do on the beautiful new day. I would smile silently and think, "No, I don't have plenty of time, there are so many things happening outside that I want to see. I don't want to miss a moment!"

Once I was dressed to Ayah's satisfaction, I would cheerfully greet my aunt and uncle and hastily enjoy a small breakfast with my family. When I was not in school, a day of adventure would begin.

In the late afternoon and again in the evening, Ayah would bathe and massage me. I was really pampered. Ayah always spoke her mind and made sure I wasn't too spoiled. She would tell me when I did something wrong which was often.

My uncle instilled in me a sense of freedom and curiosity that sometimes got me in trouble. For example, we were fairly well off and had many servants. There was someone to clean the floor, someone to prepare the food, and so on. Since it was so hot in India, we had one servant who worked this big ceiling fan. It wasn't one that you put on with electricity like nowadays.

His job was to pull a thick long rope up and down to make the fan go around. He would sit there all day doing that and sometimes he would fall asleep. Once I crept up and tied the rope to his ankle. I wanted to see what would happen. When he awoke, he tried to run after me but fell over because his foot was bound. I was naughty like that.

When I was at school I was a little devil and couldn't stay still. I had to get up constantly. In fact, one time, I even brought a very real-looking toy mouse to class. One of the nuns, Sister Veronica, got on a stool and started screaming. She put me in a corner with a hat on my head like I was a dunce.

Although I was often shy with people I was always completely comfortable and confident with life. I was a willful child and would do what I wanted to do. Instead of walking straight, I had a dance in my step. I liked to tiptoe and would go up on the balls of my feet. People would look at me and wonder what I was doing. I didn't really care. I liked the feeling of pressing in and feeling energy in my feet long before I knew anything about yoga or dance.

I never owned a doll. I was considered a strange child more fascinated with nature than playing with other children, and this set me apart from them. I didn't really have a special childhood friend but I drew others to me. They seemed to like me and were always joyfully requesting, "Tell us a story!"

I loved storytelling. That's the only time that I wasn't shy with others. Sometimes I'd make something up and other times I would talk about where I had been with my uncle or about nature. To me the world was filled with wondrous energy and delights.

My uncle never laughed at my questions and always had some wonderful explanation to satisfy my curiosity. For this reason, I was in tune with nature and felt that both on earth and in the heavens the pulsation of life was written into all things and all beings.

The children thought the stories I was telling them were fairy tales. When I explained that the grass had the same heartbeat as we did, they seemed fascinated and wanted to believe that to be true. They thought that fairies came out of the grass, and so, I was always telling them little fantasies.

That annoyed my aunt and we would have these verbal dances. Once, she said, "You're getting mixed up with all these children. They're beneath you."

I didn't believe that and responded defiantly, "No one is beneath me.

If I can make them laugh and we can talk, we talk. They taught me how to go fishing."

I don't think I ever saw my aunt more shocked and bewildered, "You mean you've been in the water? You're going to get killed. Did you take off your clothes?"

With a sassy smile I replied, "Well, I didn't take off my underwear."

Quite appalled, she reprimanded me, "Oh, that's terrible! You're supposed to be covered up."

I guess I was always making movies in my head and looking for the next marvel. When I saw people climbing coconut trees, I tried to climb them. My aunt would say, "You're not supposed to!"

She was always telling me what I was not supposed to do. It stayed with me all of my life. I decided that I would always do what I want to do if I believe in it. Don't tell me what I cannot do. Only tell me what I can do, and I'll go from there.

*Don't tell me what I cannot do. Only tell me what I can do, and I'll go from there.*

Beginnings matter but does your beginning seal your destiny or simply set a direction? Is your journey predetermined? Maybe it was the manner of my beginning that set me on my search or perhaps the search is why we are here and we all eventually come to these fundamental questions.

Whatever your beginning, I believe you can choose the direction of your story at every turn. You can jump in the dance or sit it out. You can speed up or slow down. It's all about finding your own rhythm. Anticipate the adventures to come. Start each day with joy and wonderment. It's a beautiful day, isn't it?

CHAPTER 2

## Feel The Energy Behind It All

Life is the primary teacher. Look all around. You will see trees that are hundreds of years old and they are living together. None of them are the same. Yet, they are all part of this Great One, a Forest of Energy. By observing nature, you can feel the Life Force that pulsates within the heart of every atom and tap into the wisdom of the ages.

*By observing nature, you can feel the Life Force that pulsates within the heart of every atom and tap into the wisdom of the ages.*

It's like the sound of OM, which represents the Oneness of life and the energy of the soul. Where do you think Amen came from and so many of the words that indicate peace? Ah-men, Sha-lom, Sa-lam, all of them came from the sound of OM. It is the first sound of the Universe, containing all other sounds, words and languages. It is a reflection of Absolute Reality, without beginning and without end. It is Divine Energy. When you feel it within you, nothing's impossible because it governs the whole of everything. If you simply observe nature you can learn about its essence. We feel, commune and participate with life's energy.

Given my mischievous ways, my family took me out of school and brought in people to educate me. Eventually, I took the French exams. I passed them with high marks and earned the certificates, but my real education was on the railroads. Those were my best childhood memories, traveling with my uncle. Like the sound of OM, those journeys expanded my mind beyond the bounds of Pondicherry into the expansiveness of the world. I learned to love and respect the Oneness in all people.

My uncle designed, constructed and repaired railways and was very well known. From the jungles of Africa to the steps of Siberia, from Hanoi to Yan'an in China, he was instrumental in making rail travel possible across continents. As I joined him, he opened the door to pathways that would lay the foundation for my life. I had a freedom most young people didn't have because he took me everywhere.

My aunt would say, "You're taking her all over the world. Aren't you afraid of taking her into the jungle like that?"

Oncle would just smile. When we encountered new people, he would say, "They're not different from us. They're the same. They have a lot of things we can learn from. The farmer may not be able to read or write but he knows more about farming and his field than we do. So don't ever think that you're better than he is. You may think he's illiterate but you know nothing about farming so you're illiterate about that."

He prompted me to be an explorer, "Täo, you must go out into the world. Maybe you don't understand their language, but they have a language just as good as yours. Look for the good and something beautiful will happen. You'll hear beautiful languages spoken. You'll see a smile on someone's face."

*Look for the good and something beautiful will happen.*

My uncle appeared at ease everywhere and seemed to be born with an understanding of other people. When he built the tracks, he would go from one small village to the next, opening up trade and transportation routes and meeting people along the way.

In each place, he would train a new group of men. When they finished laying the rail in their area and earned enough money, they wouldn't go on to the next village with him so he would have to start again. It must have been very frustrating but he never complained or got angry.

Although my uncle had an interpreter in each town, he had no trouble with languages. He insisted that I try to learn a little of the language of the places and people we visited. His motto was strongly adhered to: "Never ask anyone to understand you, learn their language."

When we were going to different countries, he'd say, "Learn first of all the verb."

"What's the verb?" I would ask.

He explained, "The verb is the action of speech, the energy behind the thought of people. It shows you how they think. Learn the verb even if you don't know any other words. Learn that and you will be able to make contact with people. You will be able to go anywhere and be with anyone. It will put you on the right path and you will find Oneness with them."

My uncle must have been good at what he did because he was known everywhere. The British would often call him to help on very important rail lines. When the Trans-Siberian Railway had trouble, he was brought in to Russia to help. We went to Massawa on the east coast of Africa up to Addis Ababa in Abyssinia, which is now Ethiopia.

Somaliland had various sides: Italian, French and British. He worked on the line linking French Somaliland to Addis Ababa. He taught me some Swahili. I even found myself sitting on a seven-foot-tall Watusi warrior's shoulders learning to swivel my head around, and then how to do some African dances. It was funny. To this day, I still love the natural rhythm and energy of African movements.

***

I was always very intuitive. One time, Ayah and I joined my uncle when he was designing a train line from Hanoi to Yan'an. Hanoi was the capital of French Indochina and Yan'an was in the newly created Republic of China. Indochina was where Hanoi and China almost meet. As usual, I was having a delightful time soaking up the energy and moving with the rhythms of another culture as my uncle continued to give his sage advice.

Oncle obviously had a lot more work to do and decided to send Ayah and me back to Pondicherry. He planned our boat trip home to go to Calcutta and then down to Pondicherry with a stop in Rangoon, the bustling center of activity in Burma, now called Myanmar.

Burma is nestled in next to India, China, and what are now Bangladesh, Thailand and Laos. At that time, there were a lot of Indians and a potpourri of other Southeast Asians, Chinese and the Burmese people. Like many places in that region, it had a magical feel, a mix of lavish gardens, beautiful lakes, magnificent temples and other interesting buildings. I had never been to Rangoon but after we got there, almost suddenly, I felt I knew all about the city.

Ayah checked us in a hotel and we decided to start right away to explore this unusual and very busy place. On the boat we had heard people talking about some great sites and we were ready to find them. I thought, "This is going to be fun."

I could tell that Ayah liked being in charge. To show her seniority, she gave her first order with great authority, "Täo, go and get a taxi."

Beaming with excitement of a new adventure, I quickly started walking and responded, "We don't need one."

Stopping me immediately with her hand on my shoulder to keep me still, Ayah looked at me shaking her head and chided in disbelief, "What do you mean we don't need one? You've never been here. How do you know?"

Ignoring her question I simply repeated in my best matter-of-fact way, "No, we don't need one."

Baffled that I was so insistent, Ayah spoke very firmly, "Go and get a taxi!"

Exasperated that I wasn't minding her, Ayah stopped a taxi and told him where we wanted to go. Using a term of respect for an upper class woman, he replied, "Memsahib, you don't need one!"

Ayah gave me a very strange look and without another word, she took my hand and we began to walk to our destination. I kept trying to tell her that but she didn't believe me. It ended up that we didn't need the taxi. I just knew what we were looking for was right there.

The next day we got up to go into the market from our hotel. Ayah asked in her firm, but caring manner, "Täo, go and get a tonga bicycle to take us to the market."

Again, I shook my head pointing as I spoke, "We don't need one. The market is just down there."

Astonished, she replied, "But you've never been here. How do you know?"

She would not believe me so she asked a local who was passing and he promptly answered, "Oh, just down there Memsahib. Turn here, turn there, it's about one hundred feet. You don't need transport unless you want us to help carry your fruit."

The man pointed out where the market was located which was where

I had already told her. I could see that Ayah was getting more and more perplexed by my knowing so much, and so, I didn't say another word about it.

We were supposed to stay for three or four days, but Ayah was so bewildered by me that we were on the next boat to Calcutta. She was anxious to get us home to the safety of Pondicherry.

On our return trip Ayah didn't ask me any more questions. She just kept looking at me with the same love and protective concern as always, and yet, I could tell that she was puzzled. I sat quietly with a feeling that Ayah was wondering if I was a magician with the ability to know things and make things happen! I smiled inside knowing that there was nothing strange about my knowing. When you feel a connection to all that is, you know what to do. You just know.

> *When you feel a connection to all that is, you know what to do.*

\*\*\*

When I wasn't traveling, I liked to go along the beach and listen to the music of the sea—the ocean's orchestra with its clashing waves, rushing waters and hypnotic humming. Once, in yet another one of our verbal dances, I had commented to my aunt on the beauty of the music of the sea. Shaking her head, she gave me one of her usual incredulous replies, "It's not making music!"

I reflected and stood my ground, "Yes, it is. If you listen carefully, you will hear its movements. You will feel whether the tide is angry with the sea or whether it's at peace as it comes in nice and softly. You can tell what it's going to do. Every day it's different because every day the air is different."

She thought I was nuts. It was just the opposite. I was learning to tune into the soul within nature.

I once experienced a tidal bore in Calcutta. It is a force of nature that occurs in relatively few places across the globe. One is in the Bay of Bengal, the largest bay in the world. There is another in the Bay of Biscay. The tide comes in with great force, with a powerful roar and a mountain of water like the waves of a tsunami.

When it was about to come, we heard a whistle and ship bells ringing to warn everyone. People rushed out to ready their boats for the onslaught of water. Some wanted the water to carry their boats upstream to various villages. The clamor and scramble of everyone to secure themselves and their belongings may have seemed scary to some but the tidal bore I witnessed was a breathtaking sight and deepened my respect for nature.

Pondicherry was absolutely magical when I was growing up. As I look back, sometimes I wonder if it was a figment of my imagination, but it was real. It was a quaint little town that would make you think you're in France. There was an Old World feel with columns, courtyards and gardens. The buildings weren't very tall, though they stood out with a mix of pastel colors and natural wood. The beach was the real oasis, flat and golden, speckled with shells and there was a clean fragrance in the air.

You could see a few houses right by the bay and fisherman with their huge baskets. Often you'd see a man standing on a tiny floating platform. It looked like he was walking on water. He'd have a little cage and maybe catch one lobster to sell. There was a *joie de vivre*, or joy of living, that was very French.

Yoga seemed to creep into my life. I knew absolutely nothing of what it stood for or that its foundation was breathing from your inner self. I was eight years old when I was captivated as I watched the jubilance of a group of young boys scarcely older than me on the beach making beautiful shapes with their bodies. They were from a nearby school.

It excited my being. I followed every movement with great pleasure. I thought I was learning a new game and I was even more excited because I could do many more movements than they could. What was also great was that the teacher did not chase me off the beach. It seemed they almost allowed me to attach myself to the group.

That day, thoroughly breathless with delight, I hurried home to tell my uncle and aunt about the exciting morning I spent with this new game. In my excitement, I tried to demonstrate some of the movements.

My aunt was shocked and very strictly exclaimed, "Nonsense! That is not a game. That is yoga! It's unladylike. That's not for girls." Obviously flustered, she demanded that I not continue. She thought I was becoming too much like a tomboy. It was a period in India when girls didn't do yoga.

Oncle tried to make her stop her ravings, "She's just a child. Let her enjoy all that makes a spiritual impression on her life."

While I didn't want to concern her, I also didn't want to give in so I said, "It was beautiful, Auntie, and if boys can do it, so can I." And so I did.

The matter was sealed. From the beginning of each day, the game took place. I became very good at it and would find a place to hide trying to do my own lively version. Looking back, I know that yoga seemed to radiate within from then on without my receiving instruction.

At the time yoga didn't mean a thing, just play, but it lit the flame that would burn brighter as time went on. It was something I would need as I became more swept up in the Dance of Life. As I reflect, I realize that my uncle was teaching me the philosophy of yoga, and without knowing it I was learning the *asanas*, or postures, on the beach during my playtime.

Still, my uncle would tell me when I was becoming too much of a tomboy for my aunt's liking though he wouldn't stop me. I would try to copy everything boys did, from yoga to riding a bicycle backwards. I liked the freedom boys seemed to have.

Most all of the experiences of my childhood were guided and protected by my uncle who was deeply involved in his own spiritual discovery. He welcomed our long conversations as we traveled the rails to his job assignments. I had so many questions about people and nature, and what I was supposed to do with my life. Many people would have been dogged by some of my questions, but that was never an issue for him. I was allowed to voice my opinions, discuss them and experience the wonders around me.

Now I realize how important my uncle's work was in expanding the rail system. The rail lines were central in bringing people together. My education and travels with him gave me an international understanding and a feeling that despite differences in look and language, we were all equal and part of the Great One.

*** 

One of the most memorable experiences of my childhood happened in 1928. My uncle had a railroad mission that was going to take several months in Darjeeling, a town in the Indian state of West Bengal where the British would go to escape the summer heat.

On this occasion, he was going to be working on the Darjeeling

Himalayan Railway with its old miniature steam engine that to this day still chugs uphill. It had broken down so they brought my uncle in to fix it. It was a funny-looking toy-like train that ran along very narrow tracks through the hills. That train is now a UNESCO World Heritage Site.

*Darjeeling Himalayan Railway, or "Toy Train." My uncle was called in to fix it in 1928. It is now an UNESCO World Heritage site.*

My uncle took me with him on this trip because he didn't want my aunt to convert me to Catholicism. I had already been sent to a convent school and my aunt was becoming a bit fanatical. I was still young and since my mother had been Hindu, my uncle thought it was important that I choose what I believe in and not have one religion ingrained in me.

My aunt said, "Oh, but she needs…"

He interrupted her, "No, no, no. Even in Hinduism they say, 'At every age I come back. All Truth is One, there are many paths. Sages call it by many names. All of them are right. Whatever is yours, you don't have to change it. If you're doing it, your path will lead you to the top of the mountain as well as the other one.'"

He felt strongly that I should find my own Truth and spiritual path, that I should understand the energy behind it all and choose my practice.

He said, "When she grows up and has enough intelligence to find out her own roots, she can then make up her mind. She will have had enough experiences with us to learn what she wants to do."

That's why I was able to travel so much with my uncle. He was rather afraid to leave me under my aunt's influence. Ayah wasn't on this trip with me because I was going to be taught and cared for at a very nice convent school.

*Your path will lead you to the top of the mountain as well as the other one.*

Darjeeling offered one of the most breathtaking views with the majestic Mt. Kanchenjunga, the third highest peak in the world, soaring over the town. Sometimes it looked like the great peaks were commanding the immense blue sky. Even though I was trying to get accustomed to the great heights, I loved Darjeeling right away.

*Mt. Kanchenjunga, the third highest mountain in the world. It is part of the Himalayas located both in Nepal and India. You can get a beautiful view of it from Darjeeling.*

The harmony of all of nature was everywhere, especially the little zoological park filled with animals and beautiful flowers that clung to the sides of the mountain slopes. It sparked me with joy to listen to the growl of the snow leopard and roar of the Siberian or Bengal tigers that seemed to make the earth tremble. For hours I could watch the funny little monkeys swing from branch to branch as they seemed to laugh at nature. I felt that I could almost reach out and feel their heartbeat mix with mine.

I'll always remember the night I stepped out onto the veranda and looked up into the night sky. It was filled with stars that were so close it seemed I could pluck them out of the heavens. As I looked into the galaxy, with the moon lighting up the snow-clad peaks, there was an ethereal music coming from them as countless shooting stars seemed to slip by.

I loved watching the stars and talking to them. I made up my mind that I too would travel across the globe. Without further thought, I felt I was put on this planet to fulfill my destiny, whatever that may be, and I began to talk to the stars.

"Stars, you light up the sky as though you are having a good time up there. Are you as interested in me as I am in you? Will we ever get to know each other?"

Suddenly, I heard the sweet tone of Sister Ignatius as she laid her hand softly on my shoulder asking, "What are you doing out of bed?"

Excitedly I replied, "I'm so wanting to talk to the stars. Will we ever be able to talk to each other? I want to know if they are as interested in me as I am in them. They are so beautiful. Do you think they are talking back to me?"

With both hands, she turned me around gently and replied warmly, "They're God's little guardian angels trying to protect everyone. They're looking down to see that everything is all right."

I had my own thoughts on it, "But it's not all right. Some don't like it up there. They are shooting away out of the heavens. Why do some stars stand still while others seem to journey through the sky? Where are they going? Will I ever get to meet them?"

"Maybe they're needed in another part of the world." She smiled, "Questions, questions. Time to go to bed."

"Hmm," I wanted to know more.

Smiling, she said again gently, "Questions, questions, questions."

I persisted, "Do you think I will ever fly up there and get to know them?"

Eyes sparkling as if she had the inside scoop on a big secret, she responded softly, "Täo, put your head on the side like this. See the stars writing in the sky? Can you see the T?"

"Yes, but what does it mean?"

She said the most beautiful thing that has stuck with me all of these years, "It's T for Täo. T for Travel and T for Truth and when you grow up, you will be doing everything you want to do. Now, bedtime."

I'll always remember Sister Ignatius and she was certainly right. Truth has been my constant beacon, and my life has been rich with travel. My uncle instilled in me a belief that became my mantra, "There is nothing you cannot do."

Wherever you are you can experience the richness of this world. You don't have to be riding the railroads or traveling to far away places. Walk the path in front of you. Listen to the sound of the birds. Look up into the sky and watch a flock of geese in formation streak across the heavens. Feel the heart beating within you. It is advertising the beauty of your being. Know that it is within every creature, every atom. The tiniest insect, a blade of grass—everything in this Universe pulsates with the same energy of creation. It is the wonder of living. This is the Oneness and the energy behind it all.

*The tiniest insect, a blade of grass—everything in this Universe pulsates with the same energy of creation.*

CHAPTER 3

# Lift The Veil Of Ignorance

*Guru* means "teacher" in Sanskrit. It is someone who helps to remove ignorance. In yoga philosophy, ignorance or *Avidya*, is at the root of all suffering. It makes us blind to our true nature and the Oneness of all. The master sheds light on the darkness in the student's consciousness by sharing stories and spiritual wisdom, as well as opening our eyes to the world around us and within us. My uncle was my first guru and, without realizing it at the time, Pondicherry was my spiritual academy. I was learning individual steps to the sacred dance, which I would put together much later.

> *In yoga philosophy, ignorance or Avidya, is at the root of all suffering. It makes us blind to our true nature and the Oneness of all.*

It was one of those places south of Madras, now known as Chennai, where people used to come to escape the British. The French welcomed everyone and would give them asylum. You saw a lot of foreigners and Indians from different parts finding respite in this coastal colony. To me, it was the land of great spirits—Swami Vivekananda, Sri Aurobindo and Mahatma Gandhi. All three had stepped foot in Pondicherry. My uncle's openness and belief in Oneness drew him to these men. His profound influence on me prompted my own search to learn more about these spiritual giants. Their stories influenced my life and my path.

Although Swami Vivekananda died before I was born, his impact on me was strong because my uncle studied and lived his principles. I learned as much, or more, from my uncle's stories as I did later from books.

Vivekananda was from a very rich family and was on the track to study law like his father. He then heard people talking about this incredible man, Sri Ramakrishna Paramahamsa, the great spiritual leader who is said to have gone into *Samadhi* at nine years old. Samadhi is a state of superconsciousness or Divine Bliss. In Raja Yoga, it is the most advanced state of self-realization and the eighth limb of the royal path. As the ancient text of the *Yoga Sutras of Patanjali* says, "It is the state devoid of differentiation between the knower, knowable and knowledge." It is the culmination of meditation.

*The great spiritual leader Sri Ramakrishna Paramahamsa and his wife and spiritual partner, Sri Sarada Devi or Holy Mother.*

Still called by his given birth name Narendra, Vivekananda was fascinated by a person who could attain such a state of enlightenment so he went to meet him. It's said that when he got there Ramakrishna declared, "He's arrived." Those around him said, "Who has arrived? There is only a man coming in here." Ramakrishna said, "I know. I can feel the grass being trodden on. The person I'm expecting is coming." That was Vivekananda, as he was later named. He was so intrigued by Ramakrishna that he eventually left everything else behind and became his main disciple.

Vivekananda traveled around India and the world teaching Vedanta. Vedanta is a Hindu philosophy that says that Truth is One. It's the Life Force. It's the Oneness with all people. You're not different from me and I am not different from you. We are together. There's only Oneness. It doesn't matter what path you take to get to the top of the mountain. Only when you get to the top of the mountain can you see everything as a whole. It's true, if you've ever climbed a mountain, as you move upwards you only see one side of it. When you get to the top, you see all sides and all directions.

> *If you've ever climbed a mountain, as you move upwards you only see one side of it. When you get to the top, you see all sides and all directions.*

This message of Oneness is what Vivekananda shared in his famous speech to the Parliament of the World Religions event in Chicago on September 11, 1893. As the story was told to me, he had managed to get on the program and when he walked in the room, people were apparently fighting over religion. One man said to another, "You killed Christ."

*Swami Vivekananda, credited with bringing Yoga and Hinduism to the West. My uncle followed his teachings of Vedanta which heavily influenced me.*

Vivekananda, with his orange turban on his head, bowed and began his speech with, "Sisters and Brothers of the same God!" Just from his presence and those words, the 7,000 people there gave him a standing ovation for two minutes. He had instantly captured their attention and hearts and calmed the crowd.

"Truth is One. Sages call it by many names. You don't have to change your religion. For all paths lead you to the top of the mountain. All paths lead you there." There was a big sigh and everyone sank with more ease.

*Vedanta says that Truth is One. It's the Life Force. It's the Oneness with all people.*

He continued by saying, "It fills my heart with joy unspeakable to rise in response to the warm and cordial welcome which you have given us. I thank you in the name of the most ancient order of monks in the world… I thank you in the name of the millions and millions of Hindu people of all classes and sects."

In talking about Hinduism, Vivekananda said, "We believe not only in universal toleration, but we accept all religions as true." He also quoted from the ancient text, the *Bhagavad Gita*, "Whosoever comes to Me, through whatsoever form, I reach him; all men are struggling through paths which in the end lead to me."

His talk was brief but it made a lasting impression. The story became a part of Chicago's history and is said to be the introduction of Vedanta and yoga to the Western world.

Vivekananda became famous in America and elsewhere. Everybody wanted to talk to him. He had a great sense of humor and was incredibly intelligent. And yet, he knew how to simplify things so the everyday person could understand. He was well known in India. He became an ardent supporter of the poor and an advocate of providing service to the needy. In relation to Hinduism, he believed that freedom to learn the Truth should be a practice available to everybody regardless of caste.

His nationalistic views made him not well liked by the Colonial British. Many say he influenced both Sri Aurobindo and Mahatma Gandhi in his spiritual teachings and his opinions on a unified India. His lessons on Raja Yoga said that "each soul is potentially divine" and that our goal is to manifest that. Wherever he went, his message of the understanding of Vedanta and "Truth is One" became the anchor for the beautiful teachings of Oneness for all people across the globe. My uncle lived by his teachings so they became a part of my life.

\*\*\*

Just around the time I became aware of yoga, Sri Aurobindo, who had been imprisoned by the British, established an ashram in Pondicherry. An ashram is a place where a spiritual leader goes to retreat and where people live together in peace. It is usually in nature. Sri Aurobindo introduced the spiritual practice of Integral Yoga, which focuses on transforming one's being to be in harmony with the Divine.

*The Sri Aurobindo Ashram in Pondicherry, India as it is today.*

Sri Aurobindo was an incredible poet and wrote the most beautiful things. He was different than Vivekananda in this way. Aurobindo wrote more for the elite who could understand him. His writings may have seemed a bit esoteric for the everyday person. I loved it though and still have many of his little books in French. I have used them so much they are now falling apart.

When Sri Aurobindo talked, people would gather around him. However, he wasn't so interested in making a big thing out of it. His interest was in writing. Mirra Alfassa, originally from Paris, was his main disciple. She became the spiritual guide of the ashram community and was known as The Mother or Holy Mother—a name of respect like with Sri Sarada Devi. At the very beginning, there was a small group that grew to about a hundred people living there. They were all making things and sharing the money to live.

When we returned to Pondicherry from our travels, I would attend the Aurobindo Ashram. My uncle was very close to the Swami and I would go for walks with them along the beach as they discussed the Vedas, the ancient Sanskrit scriptures and writings. Many foreigners visited my uncle, who was extremely well liked and versed in various languages.

*The great poet and sage Sri Aurobindo and The Mother.*

As more and more people flocked to Pondicherry to see Sri Aurobindo, there were no real hotels to house them. So, there at the frontier, right at the beginning of customs, a small settlers village sprung up called Aurobindoville, or Auroville. It still is an incredible place to visit, separate from the actual ashram.

I heard that not too long ago someone had suggested making Auroville into an established city. Many don't want that because they feel that it would change the whole reason why they are there, ordinary people living together in Oneness sharing everything.

\*\*\*

My uncle was always bringing people whom he thought were spiritual to our home. Often they hadn't eaten so he would give them food. My aunt didn't quite like all that he was doing. She felt that he was too open. That wasn't quite her style. He became friends with all of these different people and she didn't really approve.

One day, I went to see a yogi. Thousands of people were going to see him. My aunt was very much against it. It was funny because she got extremely upset and told a Jesuit priest that I was "listening to a naked fakir."

A fakir is a man who does black magic and he usually wears a *dhoti*, which looks like a skirt, instead of pants. In some traditions they are considered holy men, but to call someone a "fakir" can also be derogatory like a street beggar. That is how my aunt meant it.

Showing disdain, she continued, "She's out there listening with a big crowd of people. It's terrible."

The priest responded, "If she had looked behind her she would have recognized somebody that she knew."

Aroused by curiosity, she quickly asked, "Who?"

With a smile and a little twinkle in his eyes, he said, "I was there."

My aunt was shocked.

That's why I like Jesuit priests. They are open.

Soon my aunt was in a panic. Many Indians were visiting my uncle from British states. My uncle would go away for several days to the chagrin of my aunt who insisted it was dangerous business. She would exclaim, "Why? Why?"

He just smiled and said, "I believe in their freedom as I believe in mine. The world is changing."

Every day was filled with exploration and delight. I'll always remember one special day when I returned home from my adventures. I walked in and saw a strange little gentleman who was visiting us. He was wearing a white dohti that was very clean.

I figured he was one of Oncle's new friends. I stood captivated in the doorway mesmerized as I watched my uncle bringing in all of these people and introducing them to this man. I was very still trying hard to figure out why people kept coming in front of him and touching his toes. I had never seen so many surround someone who looked more like a holy priest than an important official.

I was told that this funny-looking little man was Mohandas Gandhi or "Mahatma" as people called him, which is an honorary name meaning "great soul." I soon learned from Oncle that he was a great man of vision and love for all people and his country—India. The more I found out about him the more I wanted to know.

I realized later that Oncle was influential in bringing Mahatma Gandhi to Pondicherry at that time. They were friends, and my uncle followed him because he believed in what he stood for—Truth, nonviolence and the Oneness of all people.

Three weeks after that encounter, my uncle told my aunt that he was going away for a couple of weeks. She had a fit when he said he was taking me with him.

Then he told me, "Pack up and don't bring any fancy things and fine clothes, just some clean underwear and some tops. I'm taking you across the country. Don't think you're going to stay in hotels or visit people, because you're not."

In the days that followed, our house was filled night and day with foreign Indians, but I could get no clue of what was going on.

Suddenly, my uncle told me to get a good night's sleep as I wouldn't be getting much for a long time. My interest was piqued with anticipation of a new adventure. Eagerly, I asked, "Where are we going?"

A warm smile crept across his face as he assured me, "Don't worry. We don't discuss this in front of your aunt."

My eyes must have twinkled as I thought, "We are going on a secret expedition." I could hardly contain my excitement.

I didn't know where we were going. I was very curious, but it was clear that I shouldn't ask any more questions. I just listened and went along with him with great expectations. We took the train for hours, and as usual, Oncle let me sit near the window where I could see the wonderful sights of nature. If I had not been so preoccupied with the amazing panorama of the countryside, I think I would have exploded with expectancy.

Along the way, people were coming in from all directions, Lahore in the north and from south and east like us. For the Bombay people, it wasn't too far. Trains and buses were packed. People on camels were crossing over. There were lots of elephants being used to cart big things in those days. It seemed that waves and waves of people speaking different Indian languages were congregating from every part of India.

We went from Pondicherry to Madras, the shortest part of the trip, and then the long haul northwest over to Hyderabad where a lot of people got on. After a long night and day with people hanging onto the doors as the train rolled on, we finally reached Gujarat just skimming the desert of Rajasthan.

My uncle took my hand as we got off and we began walking to an area where we joined some others who had assembled. Oncle finally told me, "We are here to march."

He explained to me that the march was to the Dandi salt flats where for centuries Indians had taken salt out of the sea for their food. Now the British were prohibiting them from collecting or selling it and were imposing a heavy salt tax, and forcing Indians to buy the salt.

Salt was something that all people used and the tax was too high for the everyday person. India's poor particularly suffered under the tax.

The British Colonial laws were very restrictive in so many ways. To my eleven-year-old ears, it just didn't seem fair. Salt was given by God from the ocean for all people.

I was even more excited about our quest when Oncle said, "We are going to march on the road that will convey 'FREEDOM OF INDIA' to the world."

We joined the march with Mahatma Gandhi. To my surprise, as we walked silently passing through villages and towns, more and more people joined us until there were hundreds of people. As we walked further, the number grew and there were thousands, and then tens of thousands marching with us.

My mind was racing. It was unbelievable!

If I were not there, no one could ever describe it to me. Day after day, not only men but also families of women and children were walking in silence in this spectacular caravan.

People stopped walking only to take care of basic needs, food or drink. Despite imminent danger, they continued the march. I was grabbing hold of my uncle in case I lost him. There was hardly a place to move. You couldn't get two cars past on the road because there were all marshes around us.

British soldiers lined the route trying to prevent people from marching, shouting, "Long Live The Queen!" and "Long Live Her Majesty!" as they fiercely struck and wounded the passers-by with their clubs.

I couldn't believe what my eyes were seeing all along the way as the soldiers indiscriminately beat the marchers, forcefully knocking them down badly injuring some while killing others.

Those who were able calmly got up from the ground, often wounded, and quietly continued walking paying no attention to the soldiers. Some stopped to care for those who had been beaten down, but the majority kept the march moving down along the narrow strip towards the flats.

I held on to my uncle's hand tighter than ever in my life. Tears ran down my face as I saw people falling to the ground in pools of blood. Bleeding in silence, the marchers kept going, none crying out except those in pain upon being violently struck, yet none retaliated.

Until then, I didn't know such cruelty existed. How would I know about it when all that I had seen or been taught was respect for others and the Oneness of all?

*Mahatma Gandhi leading the 1930 Salt March. I still remember that experience vividly.*

I noticed that some of the British soldiers started to watch in awe. A purposeful aura permeated the whole scene and many soldiers stopped attacking the crowd. Some seemed astonished as they watched the groups of French and non-Indians marching among the crowds. Overall, the police beatings were relentless on the marchers but they were careful not to strike these foreigners.

The magnitude and brutality of the march brought hundreds of the international press to the scene and they captured the inhumanity as this remarkable story unfolded. The press filmed and photographed the horror of the scenes along the march. The whole world could witness the despicable actions being taken by these Colonial British on people who were nonviolent in every way.

The images of that day are still vivid in my mind. My memories of the feelings are just as strong. While making a film in India years later, I visited the beach nearby with Clement Baptista, a famous Indian documentary filmmaker with Hunnar Films. He had a home there where we stayed. Recalling those moments of savagery left me unable to walk along the beach because it brought back so much inward pain. I asked him if we could leave and go back to Mumbai after only a couple of days.

I must say that there are also good memories that will be with me forever. All kinds of people crammed together around Gandhi as they continued to move forward. My spirit was imbued with excitement because I felt inside that we were a part of a great pursuit. It was an extraordinary scene.

The atmosphere was charged and it penetrated the soul as millions marched across deserts to the beaches. With every step, the whole country was being transformed into one of the most beautiful and symbolic examples of spirituality that has ever presented itself on this earth. For always across the world, it is a symbol for all who seek freedom, that good is more powerful than the evils of killing.

It not only lit up the heavens, but also played a part in the meaning of freedom to this day. I have traveled the dark pages of the history of wars and believe that by avoiding violence, we open the gateway to Universal Peace. That is what Mahatma Gandhi taught and demonstrated.

That same power infiltrated the marches of Dr. Martin Luther King, Jr. If, from time to time, we encompass our lives with the song of freedom, we open to new chapters and penetrate the whole of life with the true meaning of religion and Truth. My uncle was right in saying, "This march conveyed 'FREEDOM OF INDIA' to the world." It's a freedom deserved by all.

I learned later that my uncle wanted me to experience that momentous journey. He had taken me with him to join Mahatma Gandhi on what became known as the Salt March. It was an unprecedented demonstration of *satyagraha*, Gandhi's principles of nonviolent protest. In Sanskrit, *satya* means "truth" and *agraha* means "force." Gandhi was an indomitable force of Truth as he set out to protest against the British salt monopoly and spurred a collective call for freedom.

In the many years since then, I have reviewed in my mind and told others about that historic event. The march began on March 12, 1930 from Mahatma Gandhi's home base in Gujarat, the Sabarmati Ashram in Ahmedabad, to the Dandi Salt Beach. It started off with a group of seventy-eight select people and along the way tens of thousands joined in walking south to the coast.

That day in Dandi when Gandhi picked up salt from the sea, the air was electric. There was such a great sense of pride and dignity among the many who were there. This man had quietly yet defiantly broke the salt law through his simple act of producing salt without paying the mandated salt tax. He inspired many others as millions across India in other coastal towns followed his lead and made salt.

As a young impressionable girl, the image of the women there stuck with me. There were two notable women among the marchers who knew my uncle and I would meet again many years later, Dr. Welthy Fisher and Dr. Durgabai Deshmukh. When Dr. Deshmukh was with Gandhi as a teenager she was illiterate. Later, she became a Member of Parliament and started Andhra Mahila Sabha, a school to help women and children. Dr. Welthy Fisher also did tremendous work for women's literacy and, at Gandhi's request, eventually founded Literacy House and World Education.

I didn't understand the importance of what was going on, just that there were people everywhere following this little man and taking beatings for it. I get goose bumps thinking about it today. Gandhi looked so fragile, yet he was so powerful going through all of that. The power came from his strong beliefs and his courage to take mindful action. He showed people that if you believe in something, you have a purpose in life. Even if you starve and go to prison, no one can hold you down.

*If you believe in something, you have a purpose in life.*

After the Salt March, there was a new problem looming for the British—the campaign to boycott imported British cloth in favor of Indian homespun cotton. This greatly helped Indians in the textile industry. Their textiles were now being imported to Britain.

The sudden surge of Indian textiles caused problems with loss of work in the Lancashire milling areas. In an effort to stop imports in the country, Britain imposed a new tax on Indian cotton and silks. Even with the tax, Indian textile imports still cost less than those made in Britain.

Gandhi was in London for the Round Table Conference in 1931 and decided to visit the mill areas of Lancashire where poor British workers were suffering due to the boycott. He wanted to explain India's case to them and show that the same problems beset both countries and their workers.

He was warned by the police not to go there since many workers had lost their jobs and were angry. Gandhi went anyway. In his dhoti, he talked with the British workers who were mainly women. Instead of being angry, they welcomed him with cheering hurrahs. These poor workers saw him as a man devoted to helping those in need.

Gandhi had confronted the colonial rulers in ways that average Indians could understand and be a part of—the Salt March and the boycott of British cloth. Both of these civil disobedience campaigns were successful and put great pressure on the government, and so the British viceroy opened talks with Gandhi. The salt campaign shattered the legitimacy of British control and rallied the Indian people to the cause of independence, which eventually came in 1947.

Gandhi's commitment to freedom and equality showed us how one person could have an effect on so many and be the impetus for change. We don't have to simply wait for things to happen. We can do something.

*We don't have to simply wait for things to happen. We can do something.*

\*\*\*

Gandhiji, as many call him using the "ji" as a form of respect, is one of my heroes. His push for equality became ingrained in my being at an early age. My personal experience with discrimination made his teachings more real to me.

Today the British are pleasant but in those days the Colonials were a different class of people. Certain wives of soldiers arriving in India with little education suddenly found themselves living a new style of luxury with five or six servants and thought they were the aristocracy of England. They tried to look down on Indians by bringing an atmosphere of what they considered was "high class" into the way they lived.

They even looked down on Indians who were more intelligent and far more educated than they were. They decided to dominate every occasion and keep the more glamorous Indians in their place. I would run up against these Colonials and get so disgusted with them. They looked down on people, something I was always taught not to do.

I greatly admired Bengali poet Rabindranath Tagore who in 1913 was the first Indian citizen to be awarded the Nobel Prize for Literature. The British Crown bestowed Knighthood on him in 1915, but in 1919, he renounced it and the title "Sir" in protest of the Jallianwala Bagh massacre when the British Indian Army fired upon a group of nonviolent protesters.

Many Colonials didn't like the fact that I was half-Indian. I was considered a "half-breed." People could see that I was different because of my long jet-black hair. I would wear it Manipur style with the chignon on the side, particularly when I dressed up. When I went into British areas they didn't want to let me in the hotels.

That was one of the few instances I would see my uncle get upset. He would insist they let me in. If my uncle had not been well known, I would have really caused some trouble. This is probably why I relate so well to people who are being treated as inferior. It makes me incensed! I had learned and knew in my heart that all people are equal.

I think the middle class Colonials were frightened by some of the Indians because the Indians were so refined. That's why I think India liked the French and acknowledged them in the country. The French helped with the freedom marches and mixed with everyone. They also had a sense of humor and always thought of India as having something beautiful whether it was the clothes, spices or the surroundings. Think of what an Indian woman can do with a piece of colored cloth!

***

My constant questions of why I was on earth magnified with each year and through this incredible man, my uncle, I met wonderful people whose paths crossed my own opening and revealing the Oneness of life. I marched with Gandhi a second time a few years later.

The essence of his spirit has stayed with me and continues to be a source of inspiration. I have a big drawing of Gandhi in my living room today. It has been around the world with me from India and France to Hollywood and my home in New York. As I look up at the image, it reminds me of Gandhi's principles and his peaceful and courageous nature.

Nowadays when you go to Pondicherry there is a majestic statue of Gandhi at the Place de La Republique overlooking the beach. It survived the tsunami that hit right up to Madras. When I was growing up, the statue didn't exist, but I was fortunate to have met the man. Gandhi, like my uncle, brought into my life the belief in freedom and the knowing that we could break the boundaries of ignorance. The marches and words of this great, saintly man made me more fearless.

Despite the dismay of watching people fight or turn against each other, I learned to believe in the goodness that can surface. I learned that collectively, like nature had shown me, we could live together like the magnificent trees of the forest that have stood through a thousand years sharing the earth.

*Statue of Mahatma Gandhi in Pondicherry.*

As I look back, I realize my true treasure in life. Although my family was well off, my real riches came from an abundance of experiences. I didn't have a child's life like most, playing with dolls or with friends. We had a big garden in the back that was beautiful but most of the time I skipped around playing on the beach on my own or was out on a trip with my uncle. I was comfortable with myself. I began to live the code of the mantra he taught me, "There is nothing you cannot do."

My spiritual academy was indeed Pondicherry, a unique gathering place of great leaders. I have had many gurus that helped me experience my true nature, some that were around me like my uncle and Gandhi and later dear Swami Prabhavananda, and others I studied like Swami Vivekananda. Gurus can be found all around us. You may have direct access to them or their philosophy may live in their writings and teachings.

Look around for the gurus in your own life. Your guru might be an actual teacher or a grandparent. Study the masters and that which you think is good. Most of all, take time to meditate on your true nature. Consciousness has a guise. When we control *vritti*, the mental fluctuations or racing thoughts disturbing the mind, the veil of ignorance is washed away.

*Consciousness has a guise. When we control vritti, the mental fluctuations, the veil of ignorance is washed away.*

CHAPTER 4

# Boldly Activate Your Beliefs

Nature doesn't hide itself. It springs out at you unapologetically. Each flower expresses what it is meant to be. It doesn't hold back. The peaceful pale blue of the hydrangea greets you as courageously as the assertive deep red of the rose.

*When something special is in the air, don't procrastinate.*

My character was molded under the guidance of my uncle who taught me when something special is in the air don't procrastinate. You have to at times be bold. This is one of the things I admired about Gandhi. He would emphasize taking action. You can make bold remarks but are you acting on what you believe?

Gandhi managed to entwine his philosophies with other great men like the younger Jawaharial Nehru whom he mentored and would later become India's first Prime Minister. He was another one of my uncle's friends. Both Gandhi and Nehru believed in India's freedom and that all religions could live under the same heaven. They both had great vision and took action. They both were beacons of light for me.

Years later in 1939, I had a rendezvous with my uncle who had been at one of his meetings with Gandhiji in Ahmedabad. My uncle decided to take me to visit Bombay where he had arranged to meet up with several of his engineer friends who were directors in the Port of Bombay.

This busy seaport town was bustling with commerce, educational pursuits and all kinds of people. In this very interesting and lively environment we could get the latest news of what was happening in the outer world.

We met at our usual place, the famous Wellington Club, where our conversation was as it was often at that time about the possibility of war and what it might do to shipping through the Suez Canal.

I listened a little bored with all this constant talk of war but noticed they seemed more serious this time. Things seemed graver as we discussed the news that another war was breaking out.

The Germans seemed to be moving in everywhere. Hitler had already conquered and occupied what were Hungary and the Czechoslovak Republic. Now, he had started to move into Poland. It even looked like he was trying to move into Egypt from the Mediterranean. It seemed as if the Germans were coming around in a circle. We talked about the possibility of who would be next—France?

My uncle had just returned from French Somaliland where he had completed a job on the railroad. It was near Italian Somaliland where there were a lot of Italian troops at the time. He told us that it was rumored that Mussolini might be bringing troops back to Italy secretly with the idea that if the Germans invaded France from the north, he could invade from the south.

What really caught my attention was when my uncle made a remark that he had heard news that Mussolini had ordered an Italian ship, the *Victoria* of the Lloyd Treistino Line, to pick up a contingent of Italian soldiers from Italian Somaliland.

The ship filled with Italian troops was docking in Bombay in the next few days and many rumors were running riot as to why the soldiers were being shipped back to Naples and Genoa.

Curious, I asked, "Where are these places?"

My uncle chuckled and asked, "Are you contemplating taking a cruise?"

His friends teased, "With so many handsome young men on board, they will all fall in love with you!"

Interest in soldiers was the furthest from my mind, however, I playfully returned their banter, "And why not?" With a bit of mischief in my voice, I added, "If Naples or Genoa is anywhere near a port in France, I can go and visit my aunt." I was interested in my family in France I had never met.

Everyone laughed and the subject was changed, but somehow I could not get the idea out of my mind.

My uncle had already checked to find out if the rumor about a ship was true and he found that the *Victoria* of the Lloyd Triestino Line was definitely docking in Bombay Harbor from Africa on its way to Naples.

If war broke out between Germany and Great Britain, the British government promised to give India back if the Indians would send their regiments under the British flag. Many were trying to get Gandhi to support that approach but some didn't believe the British would keep that promise.

If the pending war wasn't dangerous enough, my uncle said that we should be very careful because he heard there was an outbreak of typhoid fever. I was innocent to the potentially devastating effects of typhoid and news of the Italian military didn't mean much to me. However, when I heard that Lord Tennyson's famous cricket team would be on the ship, it started a whirlpool of thoughts in my mind. Cricket was the most popular sport in India and Lionel, Lord Tennyson had captained the Hampshire and England teams. I was intrigued at the possibility of meeting him. Years later, I would learn by memory his grandfather's poem, "The Brook" by Alfred, Lord Tennyson.

My uncle said something that turned my curiosity into conviction and started me on a new path. He was talking about news that Canadian troops were already arriving in England. It was murmured that some French Canadians would be sent to guard the Maginot Line in France.

The Maginot Line was the great Defense Wall built by the French to protect them against an invasion from the German frontier. France had been invaded from that frontier during World War I. It was a long wall of concrete forts to serve as a barrier between Germany and France in the Alsace-Lorraine region.

Oncle mentioned that he had received news that my father had decided to join the French Canadians to help. Although we seldom spoke of him, I asked if he would be amongst them. Laughingly my uncle replied, "It is certain that my brother will get involved."

With that I blurted out, "Then, I'm going to France because I have to meet him." It was an instant decision. I'm afraid I'm like that. When I say I'll do something, I do it.

For a moment, no one at the table spoke. I had just turned twenty-one and I guess it seemed strange that I was running right into the war, but my uncle never stopped me from doing anything I wanted to do so he said, "If you believe in it, then okay."

Oncle thought it would be good for Ayah to accompany me since she had been a constant companion throughout my childhood. She didn't really want to leave her home of India, but she agreed to go with me on this new adventure. I liked the idea of having her with me since we were very close.

We immediately began to make plans. Ayah prepared and helped me gather my things. I packed some saris, shoes and one evening gown. My uncle said with amusement, "You probably will not be wearing too many of those saris in France." I'm sure he was also wondering what I was going to do with an exquisite dress in the middle of a war.

Ayah and I were to stay with my aunt who had a small vineyard in the Rhône Valley that had been in our family for several generations. Unlike my father and uncle, my aunt had not lived in India. She was older than her brothers and I understood she was entirely French in all of her ways.

My uncle said, "My sister is a stick in the mud and very serious. You don't know her and I'm not sure you'll like her. She'll probably like you though because you're different. In any case, I'll let her know you're coming."

Oncle had a Scottish friend who had spent thirty-six years in India, most of those years as a bank manager in India for the National Bank of Scotland. We learned that he had retired and was going to board the boat and return to Scotland. After my uncle talked with him, he promised that he would keep an eye on us.

Two days later I boarded the *Victoria* of the Lloyd Triestino Line with Ayah and went sailing into a new life. I found out later that it was the last passenger voyage of that great ship. She became a troopship in 1940, and then was torpedoed and sunk in 1942.

\*\*\*

Although my uncle had said it, seeing a lot of young Italian military on board was not quite what I expected. Most were suffering from the typhoid fever epidemic so we were told not to talk with them and to keep away. Roped off from the rest of the passengers and closely guarded, the rather decrepit looking group of uniformed young men hung over the bows. I learned that typhoid is the kind of illness where all your hair could fall out and you could die.

Ayah and I managed to get a cabin with an Italian girl a little bit older, and she caught it right away. Instead of sleeping in the cabin, my uncle's friend, Scottie, suggested we sleep on deck and we did all the way through the Suez Canal. Little did I know at the time that the disease had likely penetrated my body and would affect me later. For now, I was taking in the journey.

*Victoria of the Lloyd Triestino Line. I was on the last passenger voyage in 1939. She became a troopship in 1940, and then was torpedoed and sunk in 1942.*

We left India behind and crossed the Indian Ocean to the Arabian Sea that was peaceful but hot with intermittent monsoon showers. The rain was welcomed but interrupted the serene calmness as we crossed the Gulf of Aden.

We were making our way past North Africa. The first part of the trip seemed familiar to me since I had been to French Somaliland with my uncle. Now, we were going up the Red Sea past the Arabian Peninsula and the Nubian Desert. We would be heading north past Egypt to the Mediterranean Sea.

I didn't mind sleeping on the deck in the open air. Actually, I had a wonderful time listening to the music and singing from the soldiers on the other deck. During the early hours, before it was too hot, I had fun trying to play table tennis with the handsome young men of Lord Tennyson's famous cricket team. They were on their way to London to play against Cambridge University. They wanted me to join in but my game was a complete disaster. I could not hit a ball straight and it went all over the place. They were quite amused.

Scottie was funny. I had met him previously in Calcutta and he could certainly make me laugh. His French was with a Scottish accent, something you simply had to hear to realize how strange it sounded.

When we got to Port Said, an Egyptian city north of the Suez Canal, he said somebody was trying to get him to try out some opium. With his wonderful Scottish brogue, he explained, "I've been thirty-six years in India and I've never taken the stuff, but I guess I should try it before I get off this boat for Scotland. So *Be Sure and Begorrah*. I'm about to go on a spree!"

I didn't know whether he was kidding or just wanted to get rid of me. However, when we docked at the port for a few hours, he went off to try some dope.

Unfortunately, the spree didn't go over so well. The following morning, when I didn't see him, I went down to his cabin and all the staff and others were laughing hysterically. From within the cabin, Scottie was loudly raving and swearing blue murder, violently sick with what sounded like stomach gas.

When he came out, I approached him and asked, "What happened?"

He exclaimed loudly, "Never touch the stuff! Never touch the stuff!"

I wanted to know, "Why? What happened?"

Still looking drained, he explained, "They gave it to me and I thought it would make me feel good, a kind of high. Instead, it made me violently sick. Now I've got this awful diarrhea."

Laughter continued.

As we neared our destination and entered the final crossing of the Mediterranean, we made a deal that I would meet him one day at the Overseas Bar on Princes Street in Edinburgh, Scotland and we would have a drink together there.

So far the trip seemed like a fun voyage. We had hit the Mediterranean Sea and were crossing toward the west coast of Italy. I had never been this close to Europe.

Crossing the Mediterranean was rough. It became cooler and the sky was overcast. Talk about the recent Polish invasion by the Germans and what they were doing to Jewish people and those who helped them, sent a chill up our backs. I didn't know much about that since no one spoke about the Jewish in India, but it made me curious. People were wondering what the Germans would do next. It seems that those in France felt comparatively secure with the Maginot Line guarding the eastern frontier but the instability of the rest of Europe still created tension.

I wanted to go below and learned that the young girl with whom we were to share our cabin was taken off the ship with the Italian soldiers to be transported to a hospital. No one else was allowed ashore. The ship continued en route to Genoa.

The *Victoria* was scheduled to go on to Marseille where we were going to meet my aunt, but suddenly it was announced that all passengers would no longer be going there. Instead, without any explanation, they put us all off in Genoa near the frontier between Italy and France. The Italian military stopped all communications and ships going further to Marseille.

Here a crowd of people anxiously waited for some of the passengers but we were guided immediately into a closed section surrounded by police. We were then divided and without a word marched with our baggage to a train from Genoa to Monaco.

There was a short halt at the frontier. Just when we got to the docks, we saw little hovels, like makeshift markets. For some reason, unknown to me, people flocked to buy wines and raspberry fruit cordials. Ayah stayed with the baggage. Thinking it was rather fun, I decided to go and buy a present for my aunt.

When I returned to the platform, chaos reigned. The platform was crowded with worried people. A French steward transferring the people across the frontier said he would help me get news to my aunt in Antibes, but he wasn't absolutely sure that the train would get that far.

Scottie was packed on another train to Marseille and we bid each other adieu. We laughingly repeated our promise that if I ever came to Scotland to contact him at the Overseas Bar on Princes Street in Edinburgh.

Speaking French with his wonderful Scottish accent, he promised, "We will have a *burra peg* or *chota peg* in souvenir of our adventure," meaning a double Scotch or small Scotch whisky.

Years later I did get to Scotland but did not find Scottie.

I never could fathom how the French steward who was helping us managed to get news to my aunt. Luckily, she was informed at the vineyard when the train would arrive and she managed to get news back that she would be there.

We eventually took a train across to Antibes where she had an olive grove and she was there to meet us. I didn't know how we would find each other but she recognized me. I guess I was easy to spot wearing a sari with Ayah in her sari by my side.

My aunt took us to the family vineyard in the Rhône Valley. It was near Carpentras on one side and Châteauneuf-du-Pape on the other, an area famous for its wine. She instantly made us feel welcome. In her seventies, my aunt was tall, a little gaunt and very French, nice but stern.

I soon saw her as this incredible woman who was used to bossing people around. I suppose she had to learn to be the boss since she took over the running of the vineyard when she was only a young girl. It had been in the family for hundreds of years and it was important to her that she kept it going.

Every day as I learned more about my aunt, I became more intrigued. I soon began to call her "Tante," which is "Aunt" in French.

Tante seemed to have so many projects in her life. The olive grove in Cap d'Antibes was one of her big loves and took a lot of her time. It was also so interesting to learn about the house she had on the west coast where she took care of every kind of homeless animal.

It was her love and knowledge of wine that most amazed me. She talked about wine not just as a drink to be consumed, but as a cultural gift of God to know more about. My aunt certainly transformed my life and taught me to honor and love this great nectar of the gods.

***

My aunt had two big beautiful poodles. They would knock on the door and she'd say, "Entrez." They would open the door, come in and then wait for her. She would then say, "Maintenant, fermez la porte." Then, they would turn, shut the door and come inside the room. They were obviously well trained.

If they sat where she did not want them to, she would say, "Non, vous ne vous asseyez pas là. Qu'est-ce que vous faites?" meaning "No, you don't sit there. What are you doing?" They would then go to where they were supposed to be. One was always right next to her feet. It didn't matter where she was going they never seemed to leave her side. They seemed to know everything she taught them and were very friendly dogs.

As a Catholic, Tante couldn't get over the fact that I was not

Christian. She insisted on putting a picture of the Virgin Mary over my bed. Although I didn't consider myself Hindu by religion, I enjoyed the many stories such as those of Ganesh. Ganesh, with its protruding belly and big elephant head, is considered the remover of obstacles and the giver of wisdom. The necklace I always wear now is a silver Ganesh and is more than a hundred years old.

*This is in my home today. Ganesh is the statue in the middle.*

I often saw a lot of different people working at the vineyard talking with a foreign accent. I had never seen anybody who looked like them before. Some of the men had locks of hair on the side of their head like long side burns. They seemed to disappear into the night. When I asked about them, my aunt said, "They are working on the harvest. They are immigrant workers picking grapes."

On several occasions I saw people slink into the vineyard at night and lock themselves among the fermentation vats to hold meetings. Since I knew little about vineyards, I had no reason to question her. She was also taking journeys to Marseille and Cap d'Antibes saying it was to oversee her small olive grove. One time when she was supposed to be going to Marseille, I noticed her train ticket was for Montpellier, west of Marseille towards Spain.

I saw her talking to several women with a foreign accent. When I inquired about them, my aunt made a funny excuse and I became more intrigued. What was she up to?

One day she said to me, "Go up to the priest in the village above and pick up a parcel of clothes for me."

I asked, "For who?"

"None of your business! The priest will know what you're talking about."

I went without asking any more questions. When I came back with the clothes I gave them to my aunt. Later, she apparently received some bad news and told me she was going on a trip south. I didn't dare ask what it was all about but I knew something serious was going on.

That is when I saw the man, woman and two children. The man put on a priest outfit that he seemed embarrassed to wear, and his wife had on a nun's robe. It was so strange to see.

At this point, I couldn't refrain from asking why they were staying with us and wearing those clothes to harvest. I said jokingly, "You better be careful or someone might think you're hiding them."

My aunt became a little cross, "One day you may need the help of others." Then, she laughed, "Anyway, no one would question an old woman like me."

I wondered why she was going away with this family and whether they were the Jewish people I had heard about. When I asked my aunt about them, she simply said, "They're having trouble. You will never have any conception of what these people have gone through. If you've suffered as much as they have, you wouldn't mind helping them."

I would soon witness the depths of my aunt's bravery. She had the kind of boldness that made me believe even deeper in my mantra, "There is nothing you cannot do." She seemed to be driven by a greater purpose no matter how risky. That made an impression on me and I could see I was somewhat like her. I suppose my decision to leave the safety of India and go right into the war was rather daring.

The power of belief can fuel great action. It can wash away fear and give you the courage to step out. It's like learning to tango. It may seem daunting at first but once you understand the pattern and feel the music, you have the confidence to express yourself. If there is something in your heart that is good, then it's meant for you. If you believe in it, don't hesitate. Boldly activate your beliefs.

> *If there is something in your heart that is good, then it's meant for you. If you believe in it, don't hesitate.*

CHAPTER 5

# Embrace The Twists

In yoga, twists wring out toxins and energize the spine. They stimulate the *agni*—digestive fire that allows us to transform. They are said to awaken the *kundalini*, a power that makes contact with the earthly forces and moves upwards into another level of consciousness.

*Twists stimulate the agni—digestive fire that allows us to transform.*

If performed with the link coming from within, the source of energy to our bodies is one without a second with the ceaseless motion of creation and in touch with this inner energy that heals us physically and mentally.

The twists and turns in my own life were increasing my flexibility to deal with challenges. I was learning with each day how to tap into that innate strength, a foundation that had formed from my youth and my uncle's teachings. I didn't realize then how much his influence on my thinking would save me time and time again. War either breaks you or makes you resilient. I wasn't accustomed to breaking.

The tension was building up because the conversation between the British and the Germans was going nowhere. The Germans were apparently holding it up because they wanted the British to believe that some resolution was still possible but in reality they were getting ready to invade.

One morning we awoke with a shock that seemed to cut through our breathing. The dawn of that new day brought news that choked our senses. It was so unbelievable. It left us with a blank starkness that seemed to seep throughout France.

It was May 1940. The Germans had taken everyone by surprise and invaded us from the north. The famous Maginot Line that everyone had expected would be a barrier against any invasion did little to help the soldiers guarding it and had been for the most part bypassed.

The Germans had outwitted the French and British by coming south through the northern part from Poland and down through the neutral areas of Holland and Belgium into France. They had come through the Ardennes Forest. It seemed as though the whole of France was completely trapped. The unexpected hit us with disbelief. The invasion through the north shattered us all.

As the catastrophe unfolded, we began to hear how incredibly the world was shaken by the news. Everyone was overwhelmed when they learned how many of our troops had rushed to find boats to make their escape under the biggest bombardment from the Germans at Dunkirk. It was unthinkable to find out that our troops didn't have the arms to retaliate. Everything seemed unreal.

Thousands lost their lives. Thousands were taken as prisoners and shipped to enemy camps or shot. The horror of defeat left people stranded. Many French and British were caught in the Dunkirk area surrounded by German soldiers and bewildered by the sudden offensive.

Those who could managed to cross into England. There were hundreds of people from Belgium and Northern France trying to get across the Channel, but not much help was coming to France from the British High Command that was busy with their own defensive.

Winston Churchill had just been made Prime Minister. He had not been a friend of India and Gandhi, and he didn't seem very interested in helping the French. The British were focused on getting their boys back.

Many tried to escape across the straits of Dover to Great Britain. Those who managed to get a boat to cross the Channel between France had little or no arms and arrived in England sure that the invasion would not stop there.

The massacre of the British and French armies was a striking blow to the Allies. Fighting and death had become real. The news raged across the country that WORLD WAR II HAD STARTED—this time in earnest.

\*\*\*

It was one of the few times I was scared. As the realization of the horror sank deeply into my being, I asked trembling, "Do you think my father might have been killed with this onslaught?"

My aunt, always facing a tragedy with an indomitable spirit of defiance, replied, "Nonsense, child! Your father is a great soldier and, if he is there, he will know how to get his regiment to safety."

We knew that the French-Canadians were being put at the Maginot Line but we didn't know if my father was actually there.

As time passed, we heard more and more tragic news. The Vichy government in Central France became the hub of talks. The grim news spread across the country that France had capitulated to the Germans.

The Vichy government and the Germans divided France into two sections. Germans would occupy Northern France north of Vichy, and the Southern Zone from Vichy south would remain unoccupied for the French.

The Germans were more interested in getting across the Channel to England. By building up the North they could invade. Splitting France into two zones made it possible for them to move ahead with their plans.

Now the people who had escaped and were just starting to settle in had to flee again. Also, there were big groups of French coming from the occupied zone that needed protection.

My aunt was horrified that her beloved country had been invaded and that France had given in to the Germans. Even the unoccupied zone was filled with fear.

The Germans were shipping hundreds of young people to work on constructing roads if they were not being put in concentration camps. I realized how dangerous it was. A dark cloud hung over France. The images and memories of this time are still clear to me after so many years.

Fear was prominent in people meeting each other on the street or conversing about who might have been taken prisoner. Fear had never been a part of my experience growing up and I

*Once fear captures you, it can cripple you.*

didn't want to welcome it now. Once fear captures you, it can cripple you.

Many people were fleeing from the north and flocking south since the Germans hadn't infiltrated the southern zone. That didn't last long though. Italy wanted a part of France and there was news from the Italian-French frontier that Mussolini was getting his troops together and was going to invade France from the south.

When Hitler saw that Mussolini was intent on invading France from the south that brought a new threat of Germans moving further down to block the escape routes.

Germans started to slowly infiltrate the southern zone despite their pact with Vichy. Pretending non-interest, they were coming in twos and threes looking as if they were on holiday. They were seen moving in even though it was still considered unoccupied. They didn't want it to look like they were going to take over.

In all directions, the Germans were spreading out like a cobweb throughout France, particularly on the highways going south and to Marseille. They wanted to bring their ships in and take over that great Mediterranean seaport.

Many people had been trying to flee from the port of Marseille and escape to North Africa, to Morocco and Algiers. Now the seaport was becoming more and more vulnerable. Although the underground was getting more organized to get people across the Mediterranean, the roads were becoming more and more dense with Germans blocking the highway to freedom. Everything was becoming more dangerous in the unoccupied zone.

With dangers lurking all around us, Ayah was getting more nervous. I found it difficult to help her control her fears. "Why did you make me leave India?" was the phrase I would hear over and over again.

She asked my aunt, "Why can't we get a boat back to India?"

My aunt told her, "You can't get through the Mediterranean Sea. I'm afraid you won't be able to go back for a long time. The only way is down the African coast out of England."

So now she knew she was stuck.

For a passing moment I thought, "I wonder if I could find my father..."

\*\*\*

My aunt began watching me carefully and particularly Ayah when the Germans were around. She didn't want us to be questioned. We really didn't know what was going on. However, without realizing it, we could have given information to get her in trouble.

Ayah was kind of outspoken and my aunt would have to "shush" her by putting her hand up meaning "not another word."

If the Germans asked, "Did you see somebody here?" she would most likely say, "Yes" or something else risky. She didn't know what they were asking about. They would not be asking outright, "Have you seen people around who don't belong here?"

None of this seemed to frighten my aunt.

One day, I saw German soldiers arrive and begin to inspect the area. My aunt seemed to be courteous by asking, "Would you like to have a glass of wine?"

Not knowing her intentions, I was a bit confused when I saw her being so nice to them. I thought, "Why is she giving them a drink when we don't like them?"

I saw her graciously give the soldiers a glass of wine and then they left without looking around too much.

My aunt looked at me and winked.

It suddenly struck me what she was up to. How brilliant! I knew she was into more than winemaking!! Later that day, it became even clearer.

My aunt had emptied one of the large cement wine vats used to age wine and placed a carboy, a type of container of wine inside with a tap on the outside so that if Germans or others came snooping around, they would never know that there were people hiding inside. This made it possible for her to turn on the tap and have the wine freely flowing.

When she learned that the Germans were on their way to her vineyard, she gathered the people she was hiding all together, got them in the vat and cautioned them, "Don't even breathe if you can help it. No matter what I do, such as turning on the tap, don't move."

At that time, I didn't even know there were people hiding inside of the vat right under the noses of the Germans. The people inside must have hardly been breathing out of fear of the deadly outcome of getting caught.

My aunt had devised a way to hide people until it was safe to get them to Marseille where they would be able to cross over to North Africa or Spain. It was quite creative and she was fearless.

After the soldiers left the vineyard, people came in from the underground and I saw the people my aunt had been hiding getting ready to be moved.

Furtively, groups of small families or friends were being separated to make their escape easier. I noticed that they were picking up a couple of people I knew. I watched, listened and learned that they couldn't move them all en mass. It had to be done little by little, this person connected to this one and the next person connected to someone else. It had to be planned carefully so families could be moved together.

The pieces of the puzzle I had been trying to put together for months were now almost in place.

I probed my aunt for some answers. At first she refused to talk about it.

Since I had observed how relaxed and charming she appeared when so much was at stake with the soldiers, I asked, "Aren't you scared?"

With a slight shrug, she nodded confidently, "Oh, no. I'm 72. They think I'm a helpless old woman. Why would anyone suspect me, an old lady, to be capable of doing anything so dangerous? As long as they keep thinking that, we can do a little work."

I began to learn the whole story. She had begun helping Jewish refugees who had fled the Nazi invasion of Poland. She had become furious with Hitler's invasion into Poland and the stories that were circulating about the atrocities towards the Jewish people there. Many were trying to escape.

At first they were going to Belgium, but the country was not really letting them in anymore. A friend of my aunt, a doctor from the Jewish hospital in Montpellier, confided his plan of action to bring Polish Jews to the South and help them across to North Africa. She decided to help.

When she started, the South was still unoccupied by the Germans so the people she was helping did not have to hide. They would just work in the vineyards until she could get them to Marseille or her olive groves in Cap d'Antibes, but sometimes she would have to take them to the wine cellar just to be safe if Germans were around.

I discovered that the secret meetings were often to enlarge or quietly change the escape line. I know now that she was very tight-lipped because she didn't want to involve me in work that could be life threatening.

At the beginning my aunt was working primarily by herself. She knew one person in Marseille who was her link to get people on boats and out of the country. There were also a couple of priests and nuns up in the hills trying to help people. The priest and nun outfits I collected that day were for an Orthodox Jewish family coming through.

I learned that more and more women were forming an underground chain. I was amazed at how a staunch Catholic like Tante was not only showing sincere concern, but was also risking her life every day to help the Polish Jews.

When the Germans started coming south, she knew that to continue she had to devise a clever way of concealing people. That's when she started using the wine vats.

Now that I had more understanding as to what was happening, I was more intrigued than terribly scared. I wanted more and more to help her. Sometimes I would get in the way of some of the things she was doing and ask, "Is there anything I can do today?"

We didn't really talk about what was going on. She felt the less said was better. If ever I was caught, I would know very little.

I would go shopping and it would be really to give a little note to a person to give to someone else that we were writing to pick up someone else. It was undercover and that's why it was called underground work.

My aunt would say, "Give this to the woman at the baker shop." I would innocently go along.

This went on for a while. It felt good to be a part of it. However, there was so much tension and every single day there was more and more. When there were one or two Germans at first, now droves were coming in. Almost every day they were coming to our vineyard. It was interesting that even the poodles didn't like them. The Nazi soldiers were looking at me, asking all sorts of questions. I stood out because of my saris and Ayah.

Sometimes my aunt would insist that we hide, saying, "You should not be wearing your saris. You're asking for trouble!"

Finally, more insistent, she asked, "Why can't you be more civilized and wear Western clothes?"

Mildly resisting I responded, "Well, I don't have any."

"We'll go and buy some," she firmly concluded.

I didn't really understand the gravity of the situation, but I could sense her growing concern. We were hearing things from people who were underground further west and north. We were inundated with strange, scary stories about so many atrocities such as the Germans finding people and shooting them all. It was almost as though we were being suffocated by all of the horrible things that were happening.

We were beginning to know there was no such thing as an unoccupied zone anymore. It was almost filled with Germans. They knew that people were trying to escape but they also wanted to prevent Mussolini from coming in. They wanted the seaports for themselves—Antibes, Nice, Monte Carlo and anyplace that had a port.

People were trying to escape with even more desperation across the Mediterranean in any boat they could find. You couldn't cross over on eastern side because of the Italians. If Mussolini couldn't have southern France for himself it seemed like he wanted to at least share it.

Nearly all the men were taken away. Not many people realize that the women were becoming the big heads of the underground. It wasn't just my aunt. Nobody gives full credit to the women. They were just as brave as the men.

My aunt was in contact with the underground in Paris. You have to realize how many hundreds of miles away that was. The network was all over in places like Avignon and Châteauneuf, and all the wine countries going north. A lot of them were hiding people if they could. The wine season was a good cover to help people trying to get to the south or west coast. I don't think they were doing what my aunt was doing and hiding people in vats.

The fear that was accumulating in the south was why there was such a force of underground people trying to help. Even in Vichy, some of the underground people stayed up there so they would keep in touch and know more of what was going on. They were actually Free French. The French underground was secretly being developed much more during that time.

There were also among the French people those who were spying for the Germans. Some people thought right away, "I'm going to be on the winning side." You had to be careful what you said in public.

Those in rural areas like the Dordogne and the mountains like the French Alps would use a hiding place called the *Maquis*. The word itself can be translated as "bush." People would "Maquis" under a tree or bushes to hide themselves. A lot of men who couldn't leave their family, like farmers and those who made cheese, would hide in that way.

The Maquis also came to symbolize the underground, particularly groups of rural resistance fighters. They were upsetting the Germans. They would find a place to hide and use it to taunt the Germans and try to sabotage their efforts. They would help people escape and blow up railways if a train was coming with Germans. They were everyday people trying to do what they could.

The seeds of patriotic thought were becoming prevalent. One of the most significant moments was when this extraordinary man, General Charles de Gaulle, called to French across the world to unite after the Battle of France—not to give in but to keep the fight up. Even though the Germans had defeated the French forces, he said:

> "...The war is not limited to the unfortunate territory of our country. This war is not over as a result of the Battle of France. This war is a worldwide war... Whatever happens, the flame of the French resistance must not be extinguished."

It was June 18, 1940 when he gave that speech on the BBC. He gave a similar speech four days later that was distributed as "A Tous Les Français." It captured the attention of French everywhere. He said:

> "France has lost a battle! But she has not lost the war... This is why I invite all Frenchmen, wherever they may be, to join me in action, in sacrifice, and in hope. Our motherland is in lethal danger. Let us all fight to save her! LONG LIVE FRANCE!"

I've heard it so many times and it always brings me to tears. To this day, it gives me chills and makes me proud. After that, people from around the world flocked to his side as French colonies joined him. That's when so many pilots were trying to get over to England to unite with the efforts.

That's how the Free French Movement came into being. Later, it was called the Fighting French or the Free French. It was the real start of French resistance to Nazi occupation. Right then Vichy decreed that General de Gaulle was a traitor to France and he was going to be shot. They had put a bounty on his head.

I thought General de Gaulle was an incredible man. He pulled people together. When he started to talk, I immediately wanted to become involved but my mind was now focused on finding my father. I was hoping I could find some way to escape.

*General Charles de Gaulle's "A Tous Les Français" speech on June 22, 1940 after the main speech he gave on the BBC radio on June 18, 1940. I've had this plaque for so many years and it still makes me proud.*

There were more and more Germans looking at me strangely and asking where I came from. My aunt was getting more alarmed because of the increasing questions about me. She wanted to continue her work with the underground, but couldn't use me as much. She was concerned that because of me they would begin to check everything more carefully.

One day my aunt beckoned me to come to her. Instantly, I knew she had something life-changing to tell me. "You better leave because it's getting too dangerous."

I wasn't stunned or shocked because I had been there about eight months and the Germans were closing in. The horrors of German occupation were becoming more violent. It was not always easy to know who was in the underground and who would turn you in.

She felt it was time for Ayah and me to leave, and I really wanted to find out what had happened to my father and those guarding the Maginot Line. I almost felt a sense of relief thinking I was getting away from the fear that was permeating the unoccupied zone of France. My charmed life in India didn't prepare me for this new reality.

What had happened really started to sweep the nation. The stark truth was realized. France was occupied and words were not enough to find a solution. The war was on and France was being influenced more and more by the Nazis.

My aunt decided that the best course for Ayah and me was to try to escape to England. We couldn't take a boat going through the Mediterranean because it was blocked off. Little by little Marseille was no longer safe. The only way was to cross over the Channel and link up with the northern underground.

We tried to find news of my father and his regiment but everything was in the throes of fear. Even so, my aunt seemed impossible to frighten. After a close call, she insisted that now was the time for us to go. Her argument was also that if my father was alive, it is now I should try to find him.

My aunt informed me that she was leaving for Saint-Jean-de-Luz to arrange and start a hospital for animals. She was gone about a week, but returned in a hurry and announced, "It's time to go!"

She urged me to leave most of the clothes I had brought from India behind, but I refused. I hardly wore Western clothes and I was just as proud of being Indian as I was of being French. My aunt arranged for Ayah and me to travel as lightly as possible and said we must wear European clothes. In spite of her objections, I packed as much as I could in my case—shoes, saris and all.

My aunt used her underground network to coordinate the details. She had arranged for Ayah and me to take a train to Paris. From there, we were to meet someone and he was to arrange for us to travel to Trouville, a little village in Normandy.

Giving strict instructions, she said, "Here are tickets which will take you to Lyon and then to Paris. Get off the train in Paris and go to this address. My friend will arrange the next part of your journey and try to give you safe transport to the coast. Hopefully, you will get a nice fisherman who will take you across to England."

She insisted giving a farewell warning, "Take Ayah with you and leave straight away. Follow the instructions exactly. Don't deviate. Don't stay in Paris. Go straight to Trouville. Be very careful. Don't talk to anybody. You don't know which side they are on or listening to. This is no time to be openly friendly."

We were told not to discuss with anyone anything about her and the wartime. She did not want to give away her own secret of sheltering Jews. She couldn't risk us coming in contact with traitors who thought that by siding with the Germans they would keep themselves free.

With a warm hug from my aunt, I was off again on a new journey with Ayah, who was afraid and continued to ask in despair, "Why did you make me leave India?"

***

The journey to Paris was uneventful. The people on the train appeared tense. An atmosphere of foreboding was prevalent and seemed to hang in the air and in the bodies of the travelers. Hardly anyone exchanged a word, and even if someone did, it was a hushed whisper as though scared it would fall on the wrong ears. Not many people seemed to be traveling north.

When we stopped in Lyon in east-central France, a lot of Germans boarded the train. A couple of them looked in on our compartment then moved on, but an even larger group followed pushing their way onto the train. Some were polite while others did not add to the atmosphere by being braggadocios. Although we could not understand their conversation, the reaction of the passengers was either a grim smile or nod while others pretended to be involved in reading or asleep.

*Enfin* Paris! Finally, we arrived. It was so beautiful, yet the laughter had gone out of the people. It felt like a dark cloud hung over the city despite the blueness of an incredible fall sky. The taxi we took was plying its way through the streets and then pulled to a halt before a big iron gate on Avenue Raymond-Poincaré.

We unloaded and rang the bell. On the corner, I noticed a small bouquet of flowers on the ground. Thinking someone had dropped it, I started to point it out to the taxi chauffeur. Just at that moment, a group of German soldiers kicked it away from the corner and started laughing as though they were engaged in a football match. The driver signaled me to be quiet.

Our gate was opened and we entered into the courtyard. Friends of my aunt came down to greet us. They had caught the action and quietly remarked that I would see several flowers propped against walls or corners of streets where someone had been shot. They quickly welcomed and ushered us into their home.

Although it would have been nice to stay longer in Paris, I know my aunt said not to and her friends told me it was getting more dangerous. They seemed worried that I was not alone, but with a brown Indian girl. I was told to rest and that our tickets to Trouville had been bought.

I tried to interject, "Wouldn't it better to go to Calais since it is the nearest cross over La Canal de la Manche?" referring to the English Channel.

Still almost in a whisper, they explained, "All the major cities along the coast down from Belgium are filled with German regiments."

I looked at the tickets he gave us and they were for Trouville, a small town not far from the famous spa area of Deauville, the place where all the casinos were like Las Vegas today. It had been a playground for the ultra chic.

Trouville was where the fishing people lived. It was a much easier exit point. My aunt's friends told me I was sure to make contact with one of the fisherman there who could carry us across to England.

They said, "The fishermen are helpful by taking people across the English Channel. If pilots are shot down, they rush over to rescue them. If they are still alive, they try to get them back over to England."

The following morning, after having a good night's rest and a nice meal with my aunt's friends, we were taken to the Gare Saint-Lazare, a big railway station. Loaded with our baggage, we boarded the train along with a young mother and her two children, a girl and a boy about four and five years old. There was also a stiff-looking old French gentleman probing his way through the corridor and found his place in the same compartment with us. He helped with our luggage and we settled quietly beside him.

On the next part of the trip, there seemed to be more German soldiers on the train. They were walking up and down the corridors.

Some of them saluted me. After all, I was an attractive young woman and they were young men. Some of them were very handsome in uniform and a lot of them tall.

My seatmates were nice enough but not too many of them talked. Most tried to keep to themselves. Even though the trip seemed peaceful on the surface, there was an underlying feeling of stress. From time to time, a group of German soldiers would break into a song and the others would join in.

Alive with energy and delighted by the train ride, the children darted from one compartment to another. The mother was fearful not to anger the two German guards who were in our nook. I laughed at the antics of the children and tried to calm the mother by inquiring where she was off to. She explained she was on her way to her home in Lisieux and that her family had apple groves and made Calvados, a type of apple brandy. She was going back to help them.

The rather staid looking gentleman beside me heard me getting into a personal conversation. He seemed afraid of where it was going and jerked out of his reverie. He pressed my hand trying to stop me from adding more. Ayah looked at me with a frightened face.

Unaware of the politics of war, the children were fascinated by the soldiers' uniforms. The soldiers seemed to have heard nothing of my talk and appeared to really enjoy playing with the children. I realized that I had made a gaffe, but obviously did not get the true inference. I turned and tried to engage the old gentleman.

"And you, Monsieur, why are you traveling?

He replied almost crossly, "I am returning to my home which has been bombed."

He remained silent as the train rattled on keeping his eyes on the children and Germans as he pretended to read his newspaper. A little later the train pulled into Lisieux and the family got off, the children waving in a friendly manner to the two German soldiers.

Then, a funny little lady entered our compartment and sat next to me. She was very talkative and asked me, "Where are you going?"

Being naïve and not having learned my lesson, I was very cocky and tried to be clever, or maybe not really thinking at all, I said, "I'm going to find a boat and cross over to England."

Under the circumstances, it was a very foolish response. A shudder went through the cabin at my stupidity.

The little old gentleman sat up straight and almost went white. He gently nudged me as to say, "No, no, hold your tongue."

So I then said, "I'm just making fun. I'm really on holiday."

The gentleman quickly chimed in about the weather as to block my words. Some German soldiers popped their heads in from the corridor and briefly talked with the two soldiers in our compartment. Fortunately, they hadn't heard me or, if they did, their French wasn't good enough to understand. They just smiled and returned to the corridor.

While the soldiers' attention was caught in conversation, the old gentleman pressed a piece of paper into my hand. Curious, I got up and went to the toilet to read it. It simply said, "Go to the Poisson Heureux, a little bistro on the shore, and meet me there."

When I returned, my compartment was silent for the remainder of the journey except for this chatterbox, the little lady who talked nonstop more for herself than for the rest of us.

Soon our train pulled into the little station of Trouville. The German soldiers were surprisingly polite helping me with my baggage as the train came to a complete stop. Jokingly saying in perfect French, one said, "Only a woman would travel with so much luggage!"

I just smiled and nodded, "Thank you."

The soldiers descended and were met by an officer. They filed into a line and were marched off.

Ayah was a mess. Her mantra, "Why did you make me leave India?" became constant and was putting a drain on both of us. As much as I could, I tried to have an air of nonchalance, saying "As soon as I find my father, everything will be all right." That did little to calm her nerves.

Life is full of twists and turns. You can either flow with them and draw strength from your center, or resist and spin out of control. Sometimes an unexpected twist may seem scary. You do not know what is around the turn. Stay present and embrace the new energy. Often, from the lenses of hindsight, you will realize that it opened up your life in a whole new way.

> *Life is full of twists and turns. You can either flow with them and draw from your center, or resist and spin out of control.*

## CHAPTER 6

## Ride The Waves

W ater has an illusory quality. Sometimes it is opaque and other times it is clear. It is fundamental to existence—in our bodies and in the world—reminding us of our connection to everything and everyone. The ocean teases and dares you to jump in even though there may be sea monsters lurking. It can be very easygoing and flowing, yet can sweep you up in an instant. If you go against the tide, it can be hard to swim. So, sometimes you simply have to ride the waves.

*Sometimes you simply have to ride the waves of life.*

As we stepped off the train, I could see that Ayah was really worried now as she looked at me for what to do next. Someone nudged me. It was the little gentleman pointing the way off the platform. As he smiled, he nodded and asked unexpectedly, "Are you happy to be back in Trouville?"

Also with a smile, I replied, "I don't know."

He then asked in a whisper, "Are you really serious about wanting to get to England? I know you're laughing about it but somehow I get the feeling that you're serious."

I was a bit stunned by the question since I had been warned about not trusting anyone, but somehow, I knew deep within that I could trust this man. He could have been a spy but I took the risk and answered, "Yes, I am. I have to find a fisherman who will take me across the Pas-de-Calais."

He hastily inquired, "Well, if I help you get a boat, will you do something for us?"

"Us?" I wondered, but without hesitation, I nodded, "Yes."

He then shook my hand with the note in it. I thanked him with a slight nod and then he moved off away from us. We just followed a couple of others out of the station. Finally, I looked at the note. Written in French, it read, "If you are serious, go to a little bistro in the port around seven o'clock."

I noticed a porter in front of the station and asked him the way to a nice hotel near the beach where we could get something to eat. Then, nodding to the gentleman, we headed for the hotel. We were hungry and tired from having had two long trips by train with very little food. We now had hours before we could circulate or find the bistro address on the note. We were glad to wash up and rest a while.

It was a complicated time with the hatred that was going on. While resting a bit in the hotel, I reflected on the German soldiers playing with the two little children on the train. The children didn't know who they were and they didn't hate the soldiers because they were German. They were just looking up at them and the young men were holding them and tossing them up in the air. The children thought that was great but the poor mother was sitting there holding her breath hardly daring to speak.

The soldiers were probably not even thinking about them being French. For those moments, they were just two young men who were enjoying being human without the thoughts of war and two young children enjoying the fun.

After just a little rest, we were very hungry. Both being vegetarians, we had only munched on some cheese and apples at the hotel. I decided we should go to the bistro. It was almost evening by that point and the little space was filled with Germans eating. A man sat us in a corner and we ordered a baguette.

Suddenly, I noticed the man from the train. He smiled a warning and signaled to eat slowly. I could tell he wanted us to wait a bit until the bistro was empty. I knew we needed to be careful.

After a while he came over to our table for a little chat as though we were old friends. We talked about the weather and he said, "The evening will be good for fishing. What do you have in mind to do in Trouville?"

We continued a bit with small talk. The proprietor of the restaurant changed our table nearer to the kitchen away from the soldiers. We learned that he was a retired professor and we chatted about Normandy's apple season.

I realized he was also trying to interview me as to what my intentions were. "Why have you brought your friend here? Deauville is a much more exciting town."

I caught the direction of the question and played along, "I was not exactly looking for a casino!"

The Germans finished their meal. As the place emptied, the man turned quietly and chastised me, "That was a little dangerous remark you made on the train."

Finally, when the Germans had left, he pulled us into the back and said, "If you will help us we'll help you get a boat."

My curiosity and joy at the prospect of really being able to accomplish so quickly what seemed to be an impossible task made my heart beat fast. I agreed, "Of course, but what can I do?"

"We would like you to go and buy some wine and cheese, and a couple of baguettes from the boulangerie. Tell them 'neuf heures.' They will understand. Don't ask what it is for."

He smiled at me as I looked at him with increased curiosity. He took my hand and continued, "A little fishing boat is anchored near the pier for them to unload their catch. Don't pay any attention to them. On the rocks, you will find their fishing nets. Hide the items among the nets and go back at nine o'clock onto the beach right near the pier. There is an abandoned boat on its side. Get underneath it and stay there the night. Don't parade around because everywhere is filled with Germans. Stay under the boat. When you hear a whistle then you can get up, but don't talk or make noise."

I didn't know quite what to think and simply nodded. The instructions were precise. I knew we had to be careful.

Poor Ayah was going out of her mind. She didn't like the plan. Shaking with fear, she said once again with greater desperation, "Why did you make me leave India? What's going to happen to us now?" This was nothing like our fun adventures in India.

I still didn't know what we were really doing but we followed his directions and went to the bakery. I saw the gentleman from the train in the back with somebody. He was apparently moving about orchestrating everything.

The front was full of Germans. He looked at me and shook his head to say, "Not now." So, we simply had some tea. When the soldiers eventually moved out, the man took us through the kitchen and gave me further instructions. Most of all, he advised, "Try not to talk to anyone."

Well of course, as soon as we got outside, one of the Germans who said hello to me on the train was looking over at me curiously. So, I went over to him and said, "Allo!"

Trying to speak French, he asked what I was doing, "Qu'est ce que vous faites?"

Casually, I replied, "Je voudrais nager." I told him I was looking to see where I'm going to go and swim.

I wasn't sure whether he really understood. I think he was just trying to be friendly since nobody would talk to him. Smiling as a young man does with a young woman, he nodded as to say, "That's nice." Then, he rejoined his group and we slipped away.

I didn't really know what to do next or where to go so we wandered down to the old pier. We had another close call, for suddenly behind us a truck drew up. I turned and recognized another one of the German soldiers who had been on the train. He obviously recognized us too and asked in broken French, "What are you doing here?"

I waved to him and tried to make easy conversation. Pointing to the ocean, I smiled back and replied, "Isn't the ocean beautiful?" Thinking it was a good idea to remain social, I talked briefly about the little port and the weather. He really didn't understand, but touched his cap and started unloading the truck. A couple of other soldiers marched by chanting their song to ensure the town's occupants knew they were taking over.

I could feel Ayah tense up. Western clothes were making her feel uncomfortable and fear was getting the best of her. She was becoming more and more agitated, so I knew I'd better be careful.

Even as a child she had thought I was too impetuous and that my uncle gave me too much freedom. Some unknown destiny seemed to govern my enthusiasm to live without fear.

We were beginning to feel tired again from our journey and wandering around trying not to be conspicuous was difficult. I had hidden the bread and wine among the piles of fishing nets on a rock as instructed. We also hid our cases under an overturned boat that was lying precariously on its side. Now, we needed to conceal ourselves during the remaining hours.

We almost bumped into a German patrol that was engaged in a lively song recital. I was grateful when they didn't notice us as we passed into a small alleyway. We knew we had to hide quickly or we would certainly arouse suspicion.

Our hiding place was very cramped and so close to the fishing nets. The stench seemed to penetrate the whole area and almost suffocated us. Poor Ayah was practically overcome. I was having a hard job trying to prevent her from betraying our position by weeping and complaining with her new mantra, "Why did you make me leave India? Why did you make me?"

Annoyed, I whispered, "Tais-toi," a slang expression that means "shut up." I couldn't believe she was being so noisy and added in French, "Shush, the Germans are going to come and take us prisoner if you don't be quiet!" I felt bad having to be so stern but the situation required it.

We could hear the soldiers marching in the distance. The three hours dragged on and dusk started to fall. A few dimly lit lights reached us from the quais. We tried to sleep, but it was impossible. Ayah continued to sniffle. Worse of all, she began to cough. I had to keep putting my hand over her mouth to quiet her. To be fair to her, it was damp and somewhat cold.

We stayed under the smelly fishing boat until at least eleven o'clock at night. Although I really didn't know what I was doing, I knew deep inside of me that things would be okay.

I felt like stretching my legs, but was worried that Ayah would give us away if we changed position in any way. Suddenly, I felt rather than heard movement and people coming towards us. Soon, they passed close to our shelter. I gripped Ayah firmly to prevent the slightest movement that might give us away.

More people moved towards us, carrying between them what appeared to be a large bundle. As they neared us, a tiny jet of light from a small torch distinguished that it was not a bundle but they were carrying their companion.

I realized it was time to show ourselves as I heard a soft whistle.

Hearing our movement, one man stopped short in his tracks and came towards us cautiously with gun drawn. Some of the others started to run. I stood up dragging Ayah to her feet and cautiously pointed where the cache of wine and bread had been hidden.

Without a word he signaled us to follow him. It seemed like ages passed as we picked our way towards the sea trying to dodge different piles of fishing nets and gear. We arrived at a huge bulk and I was finally able to distinguish it to be a fishing boat.

A rickety plank squeaked as we followed it precariously onto the boat. Ayah was stumbling and I tried to maneuver between holding onto my case and helping her onto the boat. The man signaled me to throw my case away, but I stubbornly hung onto it refraining from arguing.

As we stepped down into the boat, in the dim light I found that the shadowing forms of about nine young men surrounded us. We joined them. They had the bread and wine I bought which was to feed us. Ayah started talking again and our contact quieted her, "Shush!"

I couldn't make out their whispering, but since I could determine it wasn't German, I was fine with it. The fisherman pulled up an anchor. I almost fell over as the boat slightly rocked as he pushed an oar into the water and paddled away from the shore. He and his partner silently paddled us out to deeper water. The soft plugging sound made us all hold our breaths for a few moments as we speechlessly moved out into the ocean.

Cramped, yet feeling fortunate to be moving away from the shore, I caught myself with a bit of cheerful anticipation that my adventure had just begun. Ayah kept complaining bitterly that she should not have let me coax her into leaving India. She kept talking and making noise until one of the men said, "You know, Miss we'll throw you overboard if you don't stop talking!"

I'm not sure if Ayah even understood what he said, but she certainly understood his tone.

A slight breeze seemed to wipe out the stressful past hours and the awful fishy odor that saturated our clothes. I heard one person administering to the injured man while I recognized the voice of another man as being the gentleman from the train.

The sea was calm albeit the darkness of night made hardly visible the forms of the people crowded aboard. The soft chugging of the boat seemed to tranquilize everyone and almost take the fear out of the atmosphere. Even Ayah seemed to calm down.

A couple of hours passed and I was becoming stiff. I tried to stand up but was almost pushed over board as we jerked. A young man whom I could identify from his uniform as being a pilot pressed me into the boat. He motioned me to stay down and quiet.

Abruptly, a chill went through the group as the barely perceptible sound of another boat pierced the darkness. Softly a ray of light lit up our boat for a brief moment and our fisherman responded with a flash. I could just perceive the outline of a small craft that advanced on us like a fierce bird. It reached us and cast a heavy line to our boat and brought it alongside. The engines stopped.

Quiet but authoritative orders were given to the fisherman who immediately handed over the injured man. It was hard to make out the uniforms. All we could hear was someone speaking French with an English accent.

Ayah was already beginning to mutter, "How am I going to get on that?"

I barked, "Tais-toi!" in a quiet but stronger tone.

A short discussion took place between the men, and before we could hardly take a breath, we were helped aboard and the engines started up.

It was a small motor torpedo boat that seemed to speed across the English Channel with wings. I felt a curious anticipation the closer we got to England. Although hiding under the old smelly fishing boat was no fun, the motor torpedo boat ride was a thrill.

Speeding through the water I thought, "This could be intoxicating under different circumstances—if we were not in danger of being caught by the Germans." I sensed a strange camaraderie with others who were trying to escape.

Not even an hour had passed when it seemed as though out of nowhere the dark outline of a coast came into view and we moved toward a large dock. It was in a location that was somewhat difficult to see. They apparently didn't want anybody seeing clearly who was coming in or going out.

Suddenly, the whole wharf was alive with uniforms. Almost before we could make out what was going on, they were unloading our group onto the dock and swept them all—except for Ayah and me—out of sight.

One of the officers wanted to take my case, but I hung on tightly not about to let go. I hadn't traveled half across the globe to be without my only possessions.

When I moved forward to leave the boat, I was signaled to stay in place. In the dim light, the sailors looked at Ayah and me with amazement—one Indian woman, and one Eurasian girl.

They took us through some kind of tunnel. I didn't know where we were. We ended up at what seemed like a checkpoint.

The British didn't want to let us in. There was quite a stir as I tried to ask in bad English, "Have I arrived in Angleterre?"

The only answer was a polite command, "Papers please."

I couldn't quite understand. They didn't seem to be welcoming. A young officer asked me for our papers again. It must have been clear that I didn't understand because he repeated adding "passport."

I thought, "Ah, yes. That I can produce," so I passed him our passports.

He looked at me strangely and motioned for us to sit down. Then, he called through to someone. I could see him agitated repeating. "French passport from India."

Within a few moments, another officer who appeared to have a higher rank reached the scene followed by an escort of two Special Service police. They searched our luggage.

What appeared to be bothering them was that our passports were French, but I had a case full of saris. They didn't know what to think about Ayah and me. We didn't seem to fit in anywhere.

"You are from India?" the officer asked.

"Yes."

"Both from India?"

"Yes."

Sounding very military, the young officer asked, "Why do you not have a British passport?"

I looked up at him in amazement and replied, "I am from French India."

Thinking we were in trouble, Ayah muttered something in Tamil.

The man was getting agitated as he pushed her aside, "There is no French India."

I couldn't figure out what he was talking about when he added, "What city in India?"

"Ah," I breathed a sigh. I think I finally understood, "I am French from Pondicherry."

He muttered something to one of the Special Service policemen who disappeared. He himself turned his back on us scrutinizing our passports. Then, he motioned us to sit down again and wait.

Very tired and starting to get angry at their treatment, I found myself pacing the floor. When they reappeared at the door, I rushed out and said, "Canada... I have come to England to find my father. He is a Major with the French-Canadian Regiment."

His face softened and a smile of relief crossed his lips. He turned and ordered something from his *aide-de-camp* and within a few minutes this other official was making sure we were given tea.

With a more assuring tone, the senior officer said, "I will contact Canada House in the Westminster area of London. That's where all the Canadian soldiers meet."

I heaved a sigh of relief. The stress of not getting anywhere and being probably taken for a spy crossed my mind. What was going to happen next? What were they going to do with us? The war was now heating up and the military police in this area were on the lookout for spies. Everybody was escaping and there were a lot of people coming through saying that they were fleeing.

Just then two female soldiers appeared and took Ayah and me by the hand. They led us off to a waiting car. We were transferred to a lively barracks filled with women in uniforms and then taken to a small dormitory. Here we were told by one of them who spoke French to lie down and rest.

I tried hard to get more news from them, but was fatigued as the warm tea and cookies make their way into my body. It was useless to worry, better to rest and maybe everything would be clearer when we awoke.

I don't know how many hours passed but we were suddenly awakened by one of the women bringing us towels and showing us to the bathroom. My habitual attitude in life to laugh at everything came back and I started to whistle, to the chagrin of Ayah.

"How can you be so cheerful? We don't know where we are going."

I just smiled.

So, under the veil of night, we had arrived on the shores of Dover. We were apparently at the foot of the majestic Dover Castle. I later found out this was the place where the rescue at Dunkirk was orchestrated. Secret tunnels under the castle played a role in evacuating survivors in what was known as Operation Dynamo.

*Dover Castle. Secret tunnels under the castle played a role in evacuating survivors in what was known as Operation Dynamo. This picture is from decades later.*

After we washed up, we were taken to a car where one of the young soldiers drove us to the Dover Railway Station. He gave me instructions on how to get to Canada House once we arrived in London. I was curious about Britain's capital city. Ayah was beginning to calm down.

When we got to the train, we found two seats. In my normal manner, I smiled at everyone who entered the carriage but was a little shocked to see no one return the greeting. My uncle had taught me to smile at the world. The power of a smile can radiate an energy of peace.

*The power of a smile can radiate an energy of peace.*

I got up and decided to move out of the atmosphere of gloom. Walking down the corridor, I bumped into a young soldier who smiled back and told me that he was going on a very quick leave to see his family.

His military post was high on the famous White Cliffs of Dover. He had been stationed there since the Battle of Dunkirk and told me he may only get a few hours with his family.

He gave me some tips about air raids just in time for me to experience my first one. As he explained what could happen, instantly I was caught off guard by the loud high-pitched wailing of sirens. He told me "Everybody calls it 'Weeping Willie.' That is a warning of enemy planes approaching."

As soon as the sirens started, the lights in the train's corridor and carriages turned off. Looking almost petrified with fear, some people quickly pulled down the blinds while many others scurried out in a panic. Grimly, I staggered as I tried to return to my carriage when the skies lit up and the train slowed down.

The young soldier calmly suggested we stay inside so we took his advice. We heard the British ground guns firing and from the train window, we soon witnessed an enemy plane on fire falling from the night sky. Fortunately for us, the plane was shot down before it could hit its target—our train. There was a strange silence. After that, we only stopped once on the way to London. Once again, I was entering a whole new reality. It looked like we escaped the Germans in France yet ran right into a front line of the war!

\*\*\*

When we arrived at Waterloo Station, the weather was damp and chilly. I couldn't wait to have something hot to drink but before we could get to a café, the bombing started again. "Where to go?" I thought. We crouched close to the wall.

Ayah was in the throes of a complete nervous breakdown and tried to get closer to the shelter of the doorway, asking me with shudders, "What are we going to do? Where will we stay?" I hadn't really thought about that.

Huge fires blazed and blanketed the streets everywhere around Charing Cross. For the first time in my life I did not know which way to turn. Where were we going to stay?

As though answering my prayers, a taxi stopped and a voice with a deep cockney accent asked me, "Where do you want to go lady?"

I could hardly splutter out, "I don't know, somewhere to stay the night. We don't know London. Somewhere not dear."

"Okay, jump in."

He turned down a shabby little street, stopped at a doorway, and London welcomed us into its darkest bosom. As the bombs were shattering the sky nearby, a woman peered through the door and I paid her five shillings for only one narrow bed.

I know I asked for something not expensive but when I looked at the cramped and dismal space I almost said no, but the taxi driver who had waited assured me gently, "Tomorrow you can find something better."

He smiled and with a parting goodbye, we went into the room. We fell asleep without undressing and hugged each other as the discordant and jarring sounds of the bombs continued for the remainder of the night.

I tried to console Ayah with, "It will be better tomorrow." I could hear my uncle's voice in my head, "Try to think good and let everything else go."

> *Try to think good and let everything else go.*

The next morning I found that we were a bit fortunate. The room was in the vicinity of Leicester Square, not far from Trafalgar Square where Canada House was located. We awoke to hear young men singing, a more cheery sign of the dawn of a better day. The dawn radiates the song of new beginnings so I was hoping this would be ours.

As I went from our little room to the hall looking for the bathroom, I found that I had to wait on line to wash up. There was this cupboard-type room that had the only toilet and sink. I could not wait to leave the place and find Canada House.

I went downstairs to buy some food. Ayah was still asleep. I asked for fruit and juice and heard a burst of laughter at my request.

With a slight accent that was obviously not British, a young man explained, "You are in the wrong country."

Another chimed in with a weary type of amusement, "No mangoes, no oranges, just apples."

I wasn't sure what an apple was like, so I took a piece of toast for Ayah and one for myself. When I asked for more butter, one young man informed me, "butter is rationed," whatever that meant.

I returned to our room and found that Ayah was now awake, hungry and groaning. All of my life in India, Ayah had been the senior one in charge. Now the roles were reversed and I felt the responsibility of looking out for her.

Canada House was a beautiful building looming over Trafalgar Square. The people were courteous, but couldn't understand why I had come there.

Several hours went by and then I was allowed an appointment with a charming women official who promised to help me. After she took the history of my life and the fact that I was searching for my father who was with the French-Canadian Regiment, she started to understand my predicament.

*The dawn radiates the song of new beginnings.*

She asked where I was staying and suggested a place. Realizing my meager money, she inquired to her staff where we might go.

Since we didn't have very much English money with us, we had to be careful. We took a little room just behind Piccadilly Circus in Covent Gardens, not too far from Canada House. It was on the eastern edge of the West End not far from Soho, an area where there were a lot of foreigners.

Ayah had a fit because we shared a toilet with all these boys and other people. It was all we could afford. To have a bath, you had to get some water and boil it yourself. It wasn't the nicest area or room but at least it was a step up from the first place. It was certainly far from the luxury of our home in India. I began to appreciate my childhood much more.

\*\*\*

I became friends with the two young men who had teased me about my search for tropical food. To my delight, they lived in our new building on the same floor and were both from Malta, in the middle of the Mediterranean.

One was Francis de Salva Hall. I don't remember the name of the other boy. It's funny. As years go by, if you try to think of some of the people—those even you knew well—you may not remember their names. You might not remember what they wore. You may not even remember what they really looked like. But you are likely to remember their energy, the essence of who they are.

It was great to have my two new friends because they were much fun. We used to walk along and laugh because none of us could really speak English. We would get so mixed up on everything. When I saw something that had "sale" on it, I thought it was dirty since that is what *sale* means in French.

It took a little bit of time to get on with the British. In those days they wouldn't talk to you about anything. They would sit very proper and snobbish. If you smiled, they ignored you. Now, they've changed a lot but when I first arrived during the war, I didn't like England at all. I thought, "My goodness, what a country! I can't get out of here fast enough!"

I checked in with Canada House every day to see if they had found my father's regiment. I learned that the Canadian troops had joined in to support the British Expeditionary Forces. They had been sent in first. My father was with what they called the "Defense with the French Canadians." Many of them were in Aldershot and Bramshot, which was the military area of England. I explained the best I could, "I need to find out if the soldiers escaped and where they are now. I need to find my father."

The woman at Canada House assured me that she would help if she could, but reminded me that a lot of people had been hurt and had lost their lives in Dunkirk. She told me what I had learned before leaving France, "They thought that the Maginot Line would stop the Germans, but the Germans didn't come that way and they came in so fast that they caught the Allies off guard."

She advised me to be positive and I was yet, I didn't know whether my father was injured or killed so I kept checking in. I wondered if I would ever see him.

At that point, the bombings were starting to come more fiercely. As the days went by, Ayah became more and more sick from fear. I was worried about her. I realized that I couldn't drag her through my life's journey. I didn't mind me being in trouble but I wanted her to be okay and have food and shelter. The war was on and she couldn't get out to go back to India. No ships were running.

I inquired with Canada House to see if they could help her get a job. They said that some of the people were moving away from the bombings, from London and the big cities to Devonshire and Cornwell. They were trying to get as far away as possible and needed help taking care of their children.

They found a family going down to Ilfracombe in North Devonshire who was looking for a nanny. Sadly, I suggested Ayah take the job where she would be safer. With a long hug, she was gone to stay with the family. I knew she would be all right.

\*\*\*

It was a strange time. I was simply trying to get used to London. I would go to Canada House and just sit there. I didn't want to wander around too much because I didn't have much money to go and buy anything. I was trying to think about what to do. I really didn't know. I was just laughing at myself saying, "You got yourself into this and now you get yourself out of it!"

To make matters worse, the water in England made my gums soft and my teeth were slightly moving. I had such a toothache and my gums were hurting so I went to this Italian dentist in not a very nice area of Covent Gardens.

He said he couldn't treat me unless I paid upfront. The amount was practically every bit of money I had brought with me, but the pain was becoming excruciating and I knew that I must not get sick or incapacitated. I paid him and made an appointment for the next day.

When I went back to hopefully bring relief to my teeth, his office was closed and I saw military police standing outside the door. When I tried to enter, I was told that the man had been taken into custody because he was a spy.

Completely shocked, and finding that I too was being questioned, I tried to get them to find the money I had paid in advance. Since they had been watching this Italian dentist for a long time, they believed me but they couldn't get my money back. Everything had been confiscated.

It seemed that my whole world was falling apart. I was twenty-one years old and had never worked in my life. I had been somewhat spoiled in India. I didn't know how to work. I was more innocent really than a twelve-year-old because I had always been with my uncle. I never learned anything to make money.

My English wasn't very good and now I was alone with no money. The two boys I knew were talking about joining the army and Ayah was gone. The shock of being alone for the first time in my life was not helped by the weather. I had heard that the British weather was not the most desirable, but actually experiencing it was enough to crush my spirit. I was yearning for the sun and sand.

I really didn't know what to do quite frankly. A cup of tea at Lyons Corner House in Piccadilly and I was left with only a couple of shillings and my landlady after me to pay for the room. I started to laugh and said to myself, "You left the safety of India. You were able to escape France and now look what you got yourself into! Now what are you going to do? What would Oncle do?"

I remembered him saying, "There is God in everything and he's right inside of you beating with your heart." I felt that the best thing I could do was to simply know that things would be all right.

I took a walk along Shaftesbury Avenue near where the famous theatres were located, going towards Piccadilly. I had one bar of chocolate and a shilling in my pocket, and no money to pay my rent. Nothing. Almost immediately out of the blue I heard a passerby who stopped and approached me asking, "Don't I know you?"

"Oh dear, what next?" popped into my mind. With a quizzical look and watching her closely, I responded with some hesitation, "I don't think so."

The stranger was a very pretty young Indian girl and as she stood there facing me and smiling, I thought, "She looks so very Indian, like the many beautiful Indian women I now missed seeing on the streets."

In a mix of English and Hindi, she continued, "Weren't you in Calcutta two years ago?"

Surprised, I quickly replied, "Yes."

Seeing my surprise, she added, "Well, weren't you at the Oberoi Grand?"

Now curious, I felt delighted to answer, "Yes, I was once."

She explained, "You were with a gentleman at the Oberoi Grand Hotel having a meal. I was in the cabaret and had just come off from doing a show at the hotel during the dinner hour. When I came off the floor, my dress got caught in the chair of the gentleman with you. He was so nice and helpful."

"Yes, that was my uncle."

She continued, "Later, I watched you doing Indian dancing *bharatanatyam* on the floor, laughing with him. I thought you must be a dancer."

I was surprised, "How do you remember all that?"

"You were doing such beautiful hand movements."

As I listened, the clouds of gloom seemed to evaporate and the souvenir flashed back to the incident. I was just dancing with my uncle, nothing special.

With a happy smile at finding someone so pleasant so far from my country, I almost flipped. Before I could say anything she asked, "Can we have a cup of tea together? My name is Surah."

"I'm Andrée," the name I started to use when I came to Europe. Realizing that I was penniless, I felt a little choked adding, "I'm very sorry. I'm a little broke."

Showing concern, she asked, "What's wrong?"

Somewhat embarrassed, I told her what had happened.

"Oh, please," she insisted. "Come, I live quite close and I miss India so much. Won't you join me?"

I could hardly believe my ears, unable to talk, only to nod, "Yes." This special moment in life seemed to verify that when everything seems hopeless, good can happen even in the worst calamity.

*When everything seems hopeless, good can happen even in the worst calamity.*

Surah was like an angel saying, "I'll get you a job. I'm doing a show in a nightclub here. I'll introduce you. The owner had a big nightclub in Paris and so he speaks French. It will be helpful to you."

Hopeful, but still a bit unsure of myself I asked, "What can I do? I've never done anything in my life really. I have no idea."

Assuring me that she could help, she replied, "Well, I'll introduce you. I know you can dance."

"The only thing I know how to do is the Indian dancing."

Confidently, Surah said, "Well, if you like to, you could dance with some of the people who come into the nightclub."

Surah was very sweet and had me come and stay with her. She even advanced me money and I went back to my room in Soho to collect my things and pay the rent. Things seemed to be falling into place.

I ran into my Maltese friend and happily told him I had found a job and a place to stay. He, in turn, was in a frenzy packing because he had joined the British overseas army.

So we bid farewell and parted. I was getting used to goodbyes. I moved in with Surah and started along the new route in my path of life.

\*\*\*

I had one dress that was made in Bombay, the evening dress that had made the journey with me from India to France and now England. So I had something to start with.

My job was hardly the kind I had anticipated, a dance hostess at the Havana Club in Piccadilly. Our nickname for the club was Cubanola.

I treated it as a joke, but I needed a job badly. The owner was charming and the club had an international flavor. He had spent time in Paris and had many friends. I didn't like dancing though with some of the clientele. He kept telling me I should try not to be too "high hat."

One night I was introduced to a very sweet old gentleman in his eighties, Mr. Moore, a friend of the boss and the very rich owner of the famous makeup house Potter & Moore's Powder Cream.

Intrigued by my accent, he started to be a constant visitor to the club. Every evening he asked me questions of my background in India and how I came to be in London.

Sitting at his table one night, he said, "What are you doing dancing in a nightclub? You were brought up to be a lady. Why are you in a job like this?"

With a growing sense of responsibility, I answered, "It's easy to say but I have to be able to pay my rent. I don't know what else I can do."

He tried to convince me to give it up, but I needed the money to survive. So, Mr. Moore talked with his friend, the owner, and he finally gave in, "Well, we could put her in the chorus."

Surah had also been asking to get me in the chorus. She had already assured him, "I've seen her dance. She can dance very well."

Sorry to say, my chorus efforts were not a success either. I was not used to wearing such scanty costumes. I had what the French call "a lot of people on the balcony," yet they put me in a tiny brassiere made of big beads. It hardly lodged my bust.

Unfortunately, I was doing the show and everything spilled all over the place, wooden beads rolling in all directions. I couldn't help but laugh.

Everyone thought it was part of the show and were laughing and clapping. The owner wasn't too pleased because the show literally went to pieces!

He said, "I'm afraid you're not good for chorus."

I thought, "What now?"

*Picture of me performing during World War II wearing a similar brassiere I had on that fell to pieces at the Copacabana nightclub! I wasn't used to wearing such scanty costumes.*

My purpose for coming to England to find my father seemed to elude me. One day though, about three months after arriving in London, a woman from Canada House called me and said, "Andrée, you have to come down here right away. I'll be waiting for you."

With a pounding heart and a racing mind, I left immediately to meet her. I kept thinking, "Will I come face to face with my father? What will I do? What will he do?"

I kept telling myself, "I know in my heart it's going to be good news and he will be alive and healthy."

When I reached Canada House, she took me by the arm and we rushed to Waterloo Railway Station. On the way, she explained why we were in such a hurry.

Practically running in, we saw the Canadian Flag flying over the entrance to the platform with smaller flags and notices on each carriage of the train.

I learned that the train was filled with Canadian soldiers who had been hurt in Dunkirk and were being shipped back to Canada. I thought, "Oh no, my father cannot be wounded on this train."

The departure time caught my attention and my heart pounded even more as I quickly glanced at the station clock. We didn't have much time. I saw that the train should be leaving now!

We hurried towards the train and in the midst of those who appeared in charge, stood a chic-looking Major to whom I felt an instant connection. With commanding urgency, he showed that he was definitely in charge as he waved us out of the way, calling "LADIES, PLEASE MOVE AWAY."

The woman from Canada House identifying that he was definitely my father began shouting back, "MAJOR, I'M BRINGING YOUR DAUGHTER!!"

Emphasizing her words as she pointed to me standing next to her with her hands cupped around her mouth, she repeated loudly, "DAUGH-TER." She was almost screaming trying to be heard over the noise of the army assembled next to the train. Magnifying the syllables of each word, she continued shouting loudly, "THIS IS YOUR DAUGH-TER. I'M BRING-ING YOU YOUR DAUGH-TER!"

Suddenly rigid, it seemed the Major was prevented from saying anything as though he had stopped breathing at the incredible story being relayed in front of him. He looked at me and I looked at him.

As we took a step towards each other, breathlessly I tried to form his name but at that very moment over the loudspeaker, the command was given "ALL ABOARD!"

We didn't get to say anything. Almost instantly, the train seemed ready to leave the station.

Stripped of speech we leaned towards each other as the command was repeated, "LAST CALL! ALL ABOARD!"

The remainder of the regiments and those in charge without further delay boarded the train while other latecomers jumped into the rear wagons.

It seemed for a moment the earth stood still as my father's eyes searched my every feature. I thought I saw a glimmer of a smile in his eyes. The Major hesitated, refocused, then abruptly came to attention, saluting me and jumped aboard. Almost immediately the doors clanged shut.

As the train slowly started to move, he could hardly wave goodbye as it passed in front of me. Almost stupefied, I stood alone on an emptying platform until the young Canadian woman took my arm and steered me away. Neither of us could talk. There were no words.

Empty silence penetrated the scene like a flash of lightening—like a misty cloud blocked even our breath as though there was no beginning, no answer to our meeting. No words could possibly suffice or be uttered to break through this mist. It was as though I was walking in a trance. I left the station and closed another chapter of my life. I never saw my father again.

London certainly didn't agree with me at first. No warmth from the British. No Ayah. No father. I waited so long and that was it. I had thought that when I found my father my life would be different. Now, I was truly on my own in a very strange land. To some our brief encounter may seem tragic, but I believe it was as it was meant to be.

The journey of life is all wrapped up within our minds, it can be dark or light. I could dwell on the past or lament about a lost future. Instead, I chose to move on thankful that I had that moment. I had learned from my uncle to be open to the wonders in each moment. If not, you miss them forever. You have to be present and flow with life.

*The journey of life is all wrapped up within our minds, it can be dark or light.*

Despite being confronted with the dim light of war and the ups and downs of those first few months, there were moments of meeting up with incredible beauty buried among the debris as doors opened for me at the exact right time. I was filled with a joy-like wonder and was encouraged to not let despair take over. I knew everything was going to have reason.

The waters were not always calm, but I was beginning to see a new reflection of my Self. I came to London looking for my father and instead I found my first career, some guardian angels on my path and a growing circle of friends. I was learning to ride the waves of life. As my uncle always said, "Look for the good and something beautiful will happen."

CHAPTER 7

## Salute The Sun

The blackest darkness of night covers the earth with a seemingly impregnable blanket of stillness. Then, the light comes and reminds us that everything is alive. Every morning throughout India different variations of *Surya Namaskar*, the Sun Salutation, are practiced.

*No matter how dark it gets, one little burst of light can illumine your pathway.*

The Sanskrit word *surya* means "the sun" and *namaskar* means "to bow to" or "to adore." It is a graceful celebration of the sun preparing us for the day. This salute taps into *jnana*, our higher wisdom and the light within.

No matter how dark it gets, one little burst of light can illumine your pathway. It is important to greet your day with gratitude. Even if the external sun is not visible in the sky, you can make the sun come out in your own being.

The London days were dark and got even darker as September came. My own energy kept expanding and contracting like the counterbalance of the Sun Salutation. It was limbering me up for the challenges ahead.

It was nearly five o'clock in the afternoon. As I was preparing to go to the cabaret, I heard someone call out, "They're doing a big show in the sky!"

I quickly ran outside to look. It was the first time I had seen such a beautiful formation of planes, so many planes together. Everyone just stood and gazed in amazement at the spectacle.

It is hard to even imagine now, but there were hundreds of airplanes flying in different unbelievable formations over London. It must have been several minutes before we realized that this was an enemy attack.

Suddenly, we saw objects being released from planes coming to earth like a deluge of oversized drops of black rain. Only seconds passed before we saw terrific flashes of light and heard the overwhelming sounds of bombs hitting their targets, destroying buildings and killing people.

In what seemed like no time at all, there were ferociously burning fires that blinded our eyes and confounded our senses. People were grabbing the hands of children and loved ones, running to find cover and safety. London was being bombed more fiercely than anyone had ever seen.

Hitler was beginning his massive bombing Blitz that was his attempt to bring London into submission and to weaken the morale of the people. The German planes were not even shot at in the beginning, even as they crossed over the straits of Dover.

After that first daylight bombing, it became a nightly Blitz that lasted from September 1940 to May 1941 every single night. During the day, people bravely tried to go and do their work. As soon as five o'clock came, everyone would disappear off the streets. Many people rushed down to hide below the ground in the underground train stations.

The planes would fly over when it was getting dark and start bombing. Sometimes the first "Weeping Willie" sirens would come on from Dover. I guess the Germans felt they were safer to attack at night than to be in the open daylight where they could be spotted right away and shot down by British guns.

The Nazi planes would fly over London dropping bombs of destruction and death. Then, there'd be more planes coming in that would fly over Manchester and then try to get to Liverpool and Hull. Hull, which is on the eastern coast facing the ear of Germany, was hit very badly. So many buildings were being flattened every night and thousands of people lost their lives. The planes were coming from all directions, from everywhere.

Once the Blitz began it was difficult for anyone to sleep easily at home. People spent most of their nights in air raid shelters. I would not go there. Many others went to the London Underground, using the train stations as bomb shelters. People would ask me why I didn't go there to hide. I wasn't interested.

My habit of deep breathing made it impossible for me to endure the stench of people's body odor as they crammed side by side on the platforms and even on the tracks after the trains had stopped running for the night. I could more easily bear the smell of bombs and burning devastation above ground for at least there was some air to breathe.

I also felt the satisfaction of bringing some relief from the stress of war to others by just a simple dance. So I faced the risk of bombings every night.

*People taking shelter in London's Underground station during the World War II bombing Blitz. I didn't take this picture but this is how it was—men, women and children side-by-side every night. The fear was palpable and the stench was unbearable.*

In the midst of the external fires, there was something exploding inside of me. One day without any warning, I had this sudden terrible pain in my stomach.

Somebody asked, "Are you pregnant?"

I answered, "No." I was actually still a virgin. Baffled and bewildered, I replied, "I don't know what it is."

He put his hand on my abdomen and said, "Whatever it is, it's going to burst. We have to get you to Charing Cross Hospital. With all the bombing they are not letting anybody in but we have to try."

Chaos was everywhere. Bombs were being dropped, buildings were on fire, people were running to find safety. Despite everything, my friends managed to get me to the hospital and were able to find a doctor who quickly examined me. I was in a life-or-death crisis. My appendix had burst and it could be fatal unless treated without delay. I later learned that when this happens infectious materials spill into the abdominal cavity and cause serious inflammation.

With a grave sense of urgency, the doctor told his staff to prepare me for surgery right away. I heard everything they said and I knew I was in extreme danger. Despite the continuing pain, I felt thankful that I was in a place with a doctor who could operate on me to save my life.

Right at that very moment, a bomb hit the hospital. The chaos that we had seen on the streets as they rushed me there, was now inside and all around me. Since they couldn't operate, the doctor quickly put clamps on me to stop the poisoning of my system. While he was hastily doing this, there was a frenzy of movement and voices right in the area where we were. I could hear crashing walls, and with little delay, I felt the hot blaze of the burning hospital.

In the midst of this great turmoil, I forced myself to open my eyes a little. I saw doctors, nurses, all of the hospital staff, as well as others, helping patients who could not help themselves. Lying still unable to move, I could hear the pandemonium of people talking, giving directions, rushing and running to get everyone out of the burning building. It was bedlam beyond the imagination.

Not knowing what would happen to me and the other patients, I soon heard that they had started bringing buses without any seats to transport us. Before very long, they rolled me out and put me with the others, lying down on the floor of the bus.

*In times of crisis, it helps not to panic. It's important to focus on breath which is life itself.*

I was taken to a tuberculosis hospital where the nurses didn't know what to do. They saw these clamps and thought they'd better take them out. It was horrible! The appendix burst open again and the infectious materials were no longer confined.

I didn't immediately know what they had done, but I sensed the alarm and desperation of the nurses around me. They were running around trying to get a doctor who knew something to help my situation because all of their doctors focused on tuberculosis.

They had to wait until they got doctors from other places. I was just lying there with my eyes closed focused on my knowing that everything was going to be all right.

Finally a doctor was found who performed emergency surgery and saved my life. That is why I have this scar down the middle of my stomach even today. In times of crisis, it helps not to panic. It's important to focus on breath which is life itself.

This wonderful gentleman, Mr. Moore, found out that I'd had surgery and was in the hospital. To cheer me up, he sent ladies from a shop over with a whole load of dresses and clothes for me even though I couldn't do any dancing for a while.

He had instructed them to parade the clothes in front of me and let me choose anything I wanted.

Half of my clothes had been destroyed in the bombings so he sent me an entire wardrobe. All of the nurses were gathering around in amazement. I chose one dress and they were trying to make me take more.

Although I was touched by Mr. Moore's generosity and caring, I explained, "I can't take more. I can't afford it."

Enjoying the excitement of my all-expense-paid private fashion show, a nurse exclaimed, "Oh, you're not paying for it. He's a millionaire."

"I don't care if he's a millionaire. It's nice of him to send them but I don't like the idea of taking more than I'm supposed to."

Now that I was out in the world alone, I found myself going back to my uncle's philosophy when I had to make a decision. In this case I remembered his words, "You don't need to take more than what you need." I thanked Mr. Moore and let him know that I was grateful for just that one.

*You don't need to take more than what you need.*

Although so much went wrong, it always turned around. I never let anything get me down for too long. For instance, the water really got to me when I first arrived and like I have said it affected my gums and teeth. Perhaps it was the harsh water or a delayed reaction to typhoid fever that had impregnated my system on the boat, but one day my long hair started to fall out.

I didn't really have time to be upset since I had begun dancing at the club again. As for the loss of my hair, I did everything I could to cover it up. I started to wear a big turban. I also had a big Spanish hat, a sombrero. Darkness could fall but I tried to be my own light, knowing that the solution would come.

One day I went into a Boots Cash Chemist in Piccadilly and saw a tin of coconut oil. I started putting it on my hair and scalp. Within two weeks it started to grow. Although my hair was never the same, I still love coconut oil and juice.

> *Darkness could fall but I tried to be my own light, knowing that the solution would come.*

Things from nature have wonderful healing properties. I was beginning to once again tap into nature's encyclopedia. Perhaps it would open up a way.

The severe bombings continued and I was obliged to go back to dance hosting using that lovely evening gown from India that had survived. It was a little too chic for the job, but it was all that I owned besides the dress from Mr. Moore. Although I did not like my job, I'd rather be a dance hostess in a nightclub than go to the air raid shelter or the Underground.

Countless nights after performing, I'd come home and find that many of my clothes and things didn't make it. I'd come in and find only one shoe left. All of London was on fire.

The London Underground was bad enough during the initial air raids. During the Blitz it was absolutely unbearable. People would bring a towel or something to lie on. They were sleeping on the platforms and anywhere they could find a spot—adults, children and babies on top of each other. They crammed in one by one right next to each other side by side. You had to find a place to squeeze into. I couldn't take it. To get on a train, you had to walk your way through it. When the train shut down for the night, many people even moved onto the tracks.

\*\*\*

Mr. Moore, who had taken on the role of being my protector-friend and guardian, continued trying to convince me to get out of cabaret work but I was determined to be able to take care of myself.

He then suggested something that ended up changing my life, "If you have to do nightclub work, you should become a star. Use your talent to put together a more glamorous show."

He insisted that he would help me and I should go and stay with his sisters in Bournemouth until I was ready. I didn't know what else to do so I said, "Well, that's nice."

It was a couple of hours away from London on the southern coast of England. The estate was magnificent and quite beautiful. His sisters were two charming old ladies who were also gracious.

I appreciated their hospitality but, after a short time, I told Mr. Moore I must go back to London. I felt I must learn to take care of myself and so I said to him, "This is all very nice and everything but I don't want you to just take me over. I have to be able to earn a living. I'm not going to live off of people and I'm not made to scrub floors. I have to do something that comes from me, from within."

He tried to convince me to stay longer talking about what might happen to me on my own. I think he underestimated how persistent I could be. My aunt in India fortified my will by always telling me what I was not supposed to do. I was developing a deeper conviction to always focus on what I can do, not on what I cannot. I lived that way as a child, and now as an adult, I was more consciously embodying my mantra, "There is nothing you cannot do." Life can sometimes distract you from what you already know, but the wisdom is there inside and you can always come back to it.

*Life can sometimes distract you from what you already know, but the wisdom is there inside and you can always come back to it.*

After a little while, Mr. Moore gave in and said, "I'm going to find someone who can help you become a star. I know just the right person."

He had helped me find a nice apartment near Madame Tussauds Wax Museum in Regents Park on Duke Street. Within a short time, he put me under the guidance of a very charming young man who seemed to know everyone in British high society circles. He wasn't an agent but I always thought of him that way because he did everything and more than a truly good agent would do. He was a high society man himself with money and so many contacts.

Mr. Moore seemed pleased with the possibilities of changing my life, "We've got to do something about her. This little girl dances so beautifully and she does Indian dancing and everything."

Assured and without hesitating, this new young molder of my career suggested, "Why don't we first get some lavish costumes together?"

Although I was fiercely independent, this time I really welcomed the help. As I was selecting these gorgeous outfits, creative ideas were racing through my mind on how to choreograph my first show.

In a few months, with a great deal of fertile thinking and hours of practice, I opened up in one of London's most elegant nightclubs. My first show was a big success. I had designed, choreographed and had given my first professional performance.

Right away, other clubs were asking about me. Mr. Moore asked my new high society "agent" to act as sort of a guardian, making sure I was treated right and didn't get into trouble. As the bombing seemed to get worse, I continued my cabaret work.

Although I was still not making much money, I became very popular because I wasn't afraid to perform through the bombings. More people began to ask for me as I appeared in more clubs.

It was difficult to move around at night because of the strictly enforced mandatory blackout, when all sources of light had to be blocked out to prevent the Nazi pilots from finding a target. Most clubs were underground and offered some safety.

*London during the World War II bombing Blitz.*

Night after night, I listened to the not very distant booming sounds of bombs tearing buildings apart and destroying lives. I walked through the darkness going from one club to the next one often only lit by crackling flames of fires, street after street.

Despite my thoughts about people who may, at that very moment, be caught by those awful bombs, I knew I had to keep on walking to do the only thing I knew how, and that was to perform with joy and bring some relief from the fears of war.

Even with everything bombed out, I liked walking through the streets and squares. One day I was coming from Canada House and went into a small vegetarian restaurant in Leichester Square.

As I looked around I wasn't sure if I would find a seat. The place was full of people. This charming couple motioned to me and the man said, "Sit down with us."

So I joined their table. Even with my poor English, we began talking. The gentleman seemed very impressed by my family background and intrigued by my accent.

It turned out that he was the Australian-born film producer Gordon Wellesley. Among other things, he had written the novel *Report on a Fugitive* that became the award-winning film *Night Train to Munich*. We became friends.

He took me down to Elstree Studios in Hertfordshire, less than a half hour from London. Elstree was London's "Hollywood" with its studios and the excitement of film production. It was only about fourteen years in existence when I first went there.

Now, with an 87-year history, Elstree has been the studio of choice for many legendary producers and directors from Alfred Hitchcock to George Lucas and Steven Spielberg. It's been called the birthplace of *Star Wars* in film production and some of the most famous films in the world. Back in 1941, Elstree opened up a whole new experience for me.

Gordon got me a small part in a film with Conrad Veidt who had been in *The Spy in Black*. It wasn't very much, only to come and say something in French. I never saw it but it started me doing films there. Pockets of light were revealing new possibilities.

It was through Gordon that I got a part in the movie, *The Thief of Bagdad*. He introduced me to producer-director Alexander Korda. He had done many films and was married to a girl from Calcutta, half-Indian and half-French like me. His brother was director Vincent Korda.

Alexander was making *The Thief of Bagdad* with Sabu, the little boy-actor from Mysore in Southern India. Sabu had been in the film *Elephant Boy*, based on Rudyard Kipling's book, *Toomai, of the Elephants*. He was becoming popular. It was nice because we could speak Hindi together, something I didn't get the chance to do very often.

The actress that was playing the golden idol in the movie had to have her whole body painted gold. You could only keep it on about twenty minutes then you had to take it off. Her skin kept breaking out and she quit. Even though she was well known and I wasn't known at all as an actress, they gave me the job.

I didn't have to talk which was good because I still couldn't really speak English. They saw that I could do these Indian hand movements and liked them. They made me wear these long claws on top of my nails when I killed the Maharaja. You could see my eyes but you wouldn't recognize me very much in gold paint. I didn't care because I needed to make some money. I also played in *French Without Tears* in Piccadilly and was in several musicals.

This is when I met Michael Wilding who later married Elizabeth Taylor. I would go out with him sometime and have a drink. I appeared with him in the film *Sailors Three* that also starred Tommy Trinder and Claude Hulbert. I only had a small French part but by this time I was well known because of my nightclub work.

I also met Guimas around this time. I don't remember his first name since we always called him by his last name. He was a Frenchman who escaped to England. I later found out he was part of the Free French and had been at the French Embassy, which was really General de Gaulle's Free French Headquarters. He was always filming everything that was happening with General de Gaulle and everybody else. They didn't know quite what to do with him so they gave him a sailor's uniform. He knew a lot of celebrities and notable people because he was always taking photographs of them. It was nice to begin to make friends.

*My dear friend Guimas in his sailor's suit in the early 1940s.*
*He was a photographer and part of General Charles de Gaulle's Free French.*

Even in the throes of the war, nightclubs lit up my life and it was a very busy time for me. Mr. Moore was pleased by my success and delighted he was able to help. There were hundreds of cheap dives I could have resorted to performing in. He did not want me to descend into those. Instead, he gave me access to the most exclusive venues frequented by people who still had money and those in charge of regiments.

As my cabaret performances started to receive rave notices, I found myself a star at five of London's most famous nightclubs. Instead of rushing into the Underground, people followed me from one nightclub to another and the clubs were filled.

I appeared in The Coconut Grove, which was one of the big ones on Regent Street as well as the Copacabana. The Nut House was where you saw everybody under the sun. The Cabaret Club was a very snooty club. Then, there was the Wellington Club in Knightsbridge.

My number would take half an hour and I would do a couple of dances. Then, I would take off for the next club. They were all right there in Piccadilly.

Almost nightly, I would be asked the same question by someone, "Aren't you afraid of walking every night through bomb-shattered London?"

My answer was always the same, "No."

I hadn't realized that anyone was truly following my performances but I started to become famous. I had moved to the upscale cabarets and developed friendships with many celebrities. Surah and I kept in touch and she would come to see me perform.

In one nightclub, I met an interesting American foreign war correspondent, Quentin Reynolds. His column "Darker London" was relaying to the American people all of the horrors of the Blitz including the fires that were destroying famous areas like Piccadilly.

While taking a look at how those nightly bombing assaults were affecting the people, it seems he began to follow me. One night after my performance, he came over to me and introduced himself. He was impressed by how I braved the bombing without fear and filled each cabaret every night with people who would follow me from one club to another.

People were intrigued that I wasn't afraid of anything. They also liked the relief they experienced by escaping from the fear of war as they lost themselves in my performances.

Quentin was very nice and introduced me to so many people. Once he invited me to socialize with him and an American journalist from Chicago named Jim Evans who had come to London to film the arrival of bomber planes from America. Since the British didn't have a lot of big bomber airplanes, and the bombing continued to get worse, they were getting some planes from America.

Jim was doing the publicity on it and Quentin said we had to celebrate this momentous event. We were at this club that stayed open for him even though it was supposed to be shut down to the public during the day. As we were sitting there talking, they were trying to teach me about "Pimm's." I didn't know what a Pimm's was, but I soon found out that it is a classic British cocktail that is almost as much a tradition as a cup of tea.

The original Pimm's was made with lemonade, ginger ale or fruit juices and was mixed with gin. By the time they were teaching me, there were a number of variations: Pimm's #1 is with gin, Pimm's #2 with scotch, Pimm's #3 with brandy and Pimm's #4 with rum. I didn't like the drinks very much but I was enjoying the company.

I was sitting on this stool and found out I was a little rickety. The drinks were having an effect on me so I sat for an extra half hour breathing deeply so no one would know that I was slightly inebriated. Although I enjoy wine to this day, I like to have my senses about me. Even though it was a lesson well learnt, it was nice to get away from the chaos outside and just talk and have some distraction from the war.

It was a big affair to have bomber planes coming from America to help the British. Along with the actual planes, they brought in members of the Lafayette Flying Corps, a group of American pilots who flew as volunteers for the French during World War I. There was a big party being thrown for these older pilots at a hotel in Charing Cross. That's where I met Lady Cavendish, Fred Astaire's older sister.

I had been invited to do a show to greet them. Hélène Lavarre, whom I met in the cabaret, was also invited. She used to sing French songs in a nightclub as well as songs made popular by Fred Astaire. We did a lot of shows together and became very friendly. Her real name was Hélène Foufounis and when she was ten years old a member of Greek royalty lived with her family in Marseille when they were in exile.

So many people were at this party. Hélène and I noticed a lively, vivacious woman. I didn't realize that she was also slightly inebriated, but she was so much fun. She was Fred Astaire's sister Adele, who had married Lord Charles Cavendish of Devonshire and had moved to Ireland.

Since she was born in America and had worked in Hollywood, she had come to London with the heroic old timers of the Lafayette Flying Corps to show her support as a celebrity.

Little did I know that several years later I would meet her brother in Hollywood and then decades later be teaching yoga and dancing at the Fred Astaire Dance Studio bearing his name. The over 700 First Place Awards I've now won have been in Fred Astaire Dance Competitions.

That night with Lady Cavendish, people around us said to me, "Now, when she asks you to come and have a drink, only drink Champagne. She doesn't get drunk on Champagne. She gets drunk on everything else." So anytime I saw her, I did.

One night, after severe destruction, Quentin was amazed that I still didn't miss my club appearances and, despite the dangers, people were still following me.

The next day he called me "Brighter London" in his article entitled, "Lighter London–No Darkness or Fear Wages as They Follow Her." Afterwards, he said, "I'm here to write about Darker London, but since you've been around, it's Brighter London."

My uncle's favorite expression in crisis or where there seemed to be no solution to a problem was, "Face it knowing that nothing's impossible for all the power of the Universe is right inside of us and as we tune in, it will bring the solutions one seeks to the problem."

He was right. There is usually some light in the midst of darkness. You have to be present to see it. Fear will cloud your vision.

All of the trauma I was living through and all of the danger that closed in during the night could not repel my belief that a solution lie close by. I told myself, "Let this only be a chapter of the path that leads me to be conscious of the true meaning of life." Each new day brings hope that can penetrate gloom. The sun always breaks through.

*Each new day brings hope that can penetrate gloom. The sun always breaks through.*

CHAPTER 8

# Laugh at Life

L aughter, like breath, taps into your essence within. It is a deep diaphragmatic inhalation that allows your energy to shift. It can wash out negative thoughts and fears which fill our mind, body and spirit with poison. It can trigger a more positive feeling. If you can make light of a situation while still doing what you need to do, then it will be all right. You don't have to be too serious, even in serious situations.

*You don't have to be too serious, even in serious situations.*

The bombing became really fierce and I hated it. I still wouldn't go down below and hide in the Underground like most people. I preferred to be working, and I starred in various theatrical productions.

It seemed like the Blitz was going on forever. To make things even worse, one day I was home and the savage bombing had already started long before dark. Without warning I heard the planes flying over and it seemed within minutes I could hear bombs as they were hitting their targets.

Lying in my bed listening, suddenly one of the bombs came straight through my window, zoomed right over my head, blasted through the wall on the other side of my room and crashed into the next house. This was one of the rare occasions I was petrified. It stunned me for a few minutes.

It was unbelievable how the bomb blew up on the other side and didn't touch me. I was very lucky. The whole of my wall was opened up. If the bomb had come a little lower it would have hit me. Very thankful,

I gathered my things and went to perform in all my cabarets knowing that I had to say goodbye to this apartment near Madame Tussauds and find another place to live immediately.

My agent-friend was right there to help me and I moved to Hamilton House. Lady Hamilton had been Lord Nelson's girlfriend. The building was beautiful. It was a place for diplomats and celebrities on the corner of Piccadilly and Hyde Park.

There, I met a lot of dignitaries and extremely exciting people such as Bobby Helpmann and Margot Fonteyn from Sadler's Wells Ballet, a predecessor of the Royal Ballet. Guimas knew them and introduced me. Margot became the prima ballerina of all time as Dame Margot Fonteyn. Bobby was an Australian dancer who became an international ballet star, choreographer, actor and director. At that time, he was one of British ballet's premier male dancers. Years later, in 1968, he was Knighted and became Sir Robert Helpmann.

*Guimas with the Sadler's Wells Ballet. He was taking pictures of them and they pulled him on stage to be in one.*

I knew a lot of Canadian pilots who would come and see my shows. The Canadians were the first to go over right at the beginning of the war. There was one young man we called "Big Chief." I never knew his name. He was a fantastic Canadian squadron leader. He used to come up with his boys to Hamilton House and play pranks. They would move all of the statues and everything, put them outside my door and slide down my banister. It was one of those funny things in life.

I laugh sometimes about the good memories in the midst of such destruction. My agent-friend was nice and introduced me to everybody, including Noël Coward who was a famous composer, singer, playwright, actor and director. He was also a friend of Guimas and Bobby.

Noël had seen me in *French Without Tears* and thought I had a nice voice. He was pretty funny, especially when he tried to teach me English.

One time he asked, "You don't like the person over there, do you?"

I responded, "I don't know him."

Ostensibly, attempting to teach me the art of English conversation, he instructed me to go over and tell this man, "You are an insalubrious object of abject despair."

"What does that mean?"

He brushed off my question, "Never mind."

He had me practice it a few times and then greet the man with it. Naturally, the man was not too happy. Noël was indeed a prankster.

On another occasion, he instructed me to go to a man and say, "I presume that you're presumptuous but precisely incorrect and your sarcastic insinuations are too obnoxious to appreciate." It delights me that I can still remember that. I didn't know what it meant, I just loved it. I couldn't say anything else except, "Hello, How are you? Thank you. I am dancing tonight. Yes." What Noël taught me stayed with me all of my life. I don't know how useful it was, but I've never forgotten it.

I eventually became Noël Coward's protégé. It was through him that I met and became friends with Marlene Dietrich. She was so nice. I first called her Mademoiselle Dietrich but she thought that made her sound old. So, in her unbelievably classy style, she insisted, "Darling, do call me Marlene."

This was the beginning of lifelong friendships for me. We would go out together. They would come and see me in performances.

One time, Marlene, Bobby, Noël, Guimas and I were in a taxi going down Bond Street, a very exclusive area where all the money people were. There were all these girls standing on the corner in these beautiful mink coats. They were prostitutes.

Marlene exclaimed in disbelief, "They have a mink as expensive as mine!"

Noël responded with a chuckle, "Yes, but you wouldn't do what they do."

Showing indignation, Marlene said, "Vat you mean? I can do anything!"

Noël jokingly countered, "I dare you."

Marlene looked at him, smiled coyly, got out of the car and went to the corner.

Almost immediately, this funny little man came along and we could see him saying something and sort of moving his hands signaling her to move ahead.

Marlene's eyebrows went up while gesturing with her hands. Shaking her head in shock, she looked as if she was saying in her way, "Vhat you mean? You're insulting me!"

We couldn't understand exactly what was happening but she abruptly turned and came back to us.

Everybody was in hysterics. With great interest, Noël inquired, "What happened?"

Displaying exasperation, she said, "He wanted me to walk in front of him and he only wanted to pay me a pound. My legs are insured for a million dollars!"

We all laughed. The taxi driver laughed so hard he couldn't even drive for a while. Laughing was an elixir to the perils of war.

When I received a small part in a film, Marlene and Noël decided to throw a party for me at the exquisite Berkeley Hotel right on the corner of Piccadilly and Berkeley. The area is famous for the song "A Nightingale Sang in Berkeley Square."

Delighted to be in such a beautiful hotel, I was grateful to have friends treat me so wonderfully. Marlene, with her sophistication and elegance, was absolutely incredible. She was so much fun. I tried to imitate her even to the way she curved her eyebrows. I still do it. It's never left me.

I wanted to make myself beautiful for this event. I bought a long cigarette holder. Although I didn't know how to smoke, I wanted to make an entrance. As I walked down the stairway, much to my chagrin, I slipped and was caught by several people at the bottom of the stairs.

Embarrassed as I was, Marlene tried to make me laugh as she said, "Oh Darling, 'vhat an entrée! I must use that in my next film." With that, everyone laughed and put their arms around me.

The Blitz was bad enough but what was really horrible was when they started dropping the delayed time bombs. Those bombs wouldn't go off right away. Not knowing if you would walk into a blast, people were afraid to go down certain streets. The time bombs were nearly everywhere, and dangerous.

It was not easy getting around so I walked a lot. One day I walked down to Oxford Street and the streets were bring sprayed with bombs that made getting to the club dangerous. In the midst of the sounds of bombs I began to hear singing.

I looked back and saw that a taxi was coming slowly down the street and it was the driver singing loudly with a heavy cockney accent, "Old Man Moses is Dead. Old Man Moses Kicked the Bucket," over and over again. Suddenly, the taxi drew up close to me and the driver shouted out, "Op in."

Startled, I reacted, "I beg your pardon."

In a voice as non-threatening as he could muster, he repeated, "Op in."

I stated emphatically, "I don't have any money to pay you."

Looking at me sincerely as his voice quavered, "It doesn't matter. You're walking as though you're scared of nothing and I need you in my car. I'm scared out of my life. I'll take you wherever you want to go."

I took him up on his offer saying, "I just have to go down to Oxford Street, then onto Regent Street where I am going to the Copacabana."

Pleased to oblige and without hesitation, he beckoned me, "Good, op in. I'll take you there."

I hopped in his taxi and he started singing that funny song again, "Old Man Moses Kicked the Bucket, Old Man Moses is Dead" trying to avoid streets that had time bombs. We had to go over and around a long way because there were so many scattered unseen time bombs in the rubble and on the streets. He continued on safely. When we arrived, he told the people at the club, "She ain't even scared of the bombs!"

As the Blitz continued, I worked more. Theatres tried to stay open across the country. People felt safer in a big theatre than in their homes. They would rush to the Lyons Corner House, for example, since it was such a sizable place right on the corner in Piccadilly. It was the biggest one that stayed open during the Blitz. Everyone from the nightclub would come for coffee, tea or dinner.

They thought they were safer in there because it had huge walls and was high up on Piccadilly Circus. I found that to be a bit odd since the really big theatres were prime targets to be hit.

Some of them were actually safer because they had underground cellars and things like that. Unfortunately, bombs hit several of them. Many of the ceilings and roofs were completely battered. It was cold and the theatres were without heat. People seemed to need entertainment and would come anyway with their blankets.

In addition to my cabaret performances, I began to combine some vaudeville work at theatres that were not too far away from London. This could work for me because I could travel back in time to appear in the clubs at night. For instance, I'd wash up and leave at 5 p.m. and take the train to Aldershot a couple of hours away and then come back by 12 a.m. to do five nightclubs in one evening. Then, the next morning I would be ready to work on films at Elstree Studios during the day. In reflection, it seems like I never slept.

I had the reputation for not being scared of anything. Like my aunt in France, I didn't believe in fear. I didn't really think about it. Fear blocks your inner light and weakens the positive energy flow.

*Fear blocks your inner light and weakens the positive energy flow.*

People couldn't get over the fact that I was not frightened by the air raids. They would say, "There's a French girl who is not scared. It's amazing! She goes and entertains the troops on the Cliffs edge."

I was the star in various theatrical productions and also went down to a theatre in Dover to do a show every other week. I did this for almost a whole year. The owner, Mr. Armstrong, actually said I kept his place open. He liked having me there because I brought in everybody. It became the stronghold of the people on the Cliffs.

Dover was military-zoned in case of an invasion. He couldn't get anybody else to come because it was a protected zone and quite dangerous. You had to have a permit to go into it because, after Dunkirk, they really expected the Germans to invade.

During my first trip to Dover, I learned about the troops there. Someone said, "These soldiers have not seen a show or anything, can you do something?" They apparently had no entertainment and needed some kind of relief.

So, in between shows at Armstrong's theatre, I would entertain the troops along the White Cliffs of Dover. I decided I would take a couple of costumes and simply climb up there. I would put on these little tiny shorts or something just to go up and then I would change. I received special permission to go to these camps since they couldn't come down to the theatre. I'd do a show at their barracks.

One time I decided to do an American Indian tom-tom number. I would walk along the Cliffs with my drum. I didn't get paid. I just thought that I had to do something.

I would try and bring other girls with me to join the show and make it more exciting, but most were afraid. Hélène joined me once.

Sometimes the military guys would take me up there in a jeep. They also had these little torpedo boats and it was funny how they would fight about whether the Air Force was going to help me or whether the Marines would.

There was this enormous policeman in Dover who used to meet me at the train station. We called him "Tiny Tim." He couldn't get into the Army because he was over seven feet tall. They said everybody would see him since he would certainly stand out.

He was always waiting and would say, "Oh, my wife just loves you. You do such a nice show. She says that it is the greatest pleasure she has. You make everybody so happy."

Smiling, I would give him tickets for the performance.

I learned what to expect. When I would hear sirens someone would call out loudly "Weeping Willie." Then, we would see a whole formation of German planes coming towards us on their way to London to start bombing. Right away, all along the edge of the Cliffs, our machine guns would begin firing up into the sky shooting down Nazi planes.

One evening, as usual, the theatre was crammed full of soldiers and sailors. I was on stage doing a number when Mr. Armstrong came rushing in and anxiously announced, "Stop the music! Stop the music! A time bomb was dropped in front of the door and I don't know whether it is a good idea to be here. We can take you out through the back door or we can stay here and find out what's going to happen."

I had on this Tahitian dress that I had made of cellophane to do a Hawaiian sort of dance on the stage and a little sailor shouted from the audience, "If she can go on in that suit, we can stay here and watch."

It was good because if we had gone out we would have been blown up. Another time bomb went off about two minutes later and blasted the door in the back of the place. Then they all were fighting to buy me a drink between acts.

I always remember this little soldier in Dover shouting out as one of the funniest things that happened. Although there was constant danger and trouble, we could find a way to laugh. We could find fun and momentarily forget the war around us. Inherently, we all seem to know that laughter is healthy, even though in those days no one was talking about the release of endorphins. Joy knows no fear.

It was a special time for me because I was busy doing what I could to help entertain the soldiers and regular people find some escape from the stress that was all around us. Some people think that was courageous, but since I wasn't afraid, you can't call it that. I was just doing something I felt could help others. If you start thinking about it and put fear into your mind and you still do it, then you're courageous. I never let it get that far. I'd just go right on and do it. It made me feel good that I could do something to help.

\*\*\*

One night a group of Naval Officers invited me to go to a party they were having on their new gunboat. I had never been on a military vessel. It was prohibited. I wasn't supposed to be there since it was against all the rules. Despite all of that I felt great. I had bought my first fur coat because it was so cold and I was enjoying the evening. Now I wouldn't buy fur given the harm to the animal, but I hadn't really thought about it then. There are also many more warm options today.

While we were having a nice party, the tide was rising and the wind started to howl. It looked like a bad storm was coming. The gunboat was not locked down properly and was rocking from side to side.

When they were seeing me off the boat, the boy who was to get off to hold on to me fell in the water. He was a Naval Officer, but I could see he was having difficulty swimming. I instantly jumped in to help him. I couldn't really swim either. My high heels came off because there was no way to keep them on and my coat was heavy.

They got me out of the water and I was drenched. They put one of their big Navy coats on me and got me back to the hotel, my makeshift home. My coat was soaking wet and I put it in the boiler room. The fur went crispy. It was a mess! With good humor, my friends nagged, "Look at how much you spent on that fur coat. Look at it! An animal wouldn't even wear it."

Three weeks later, I went back to Dover to perform. I was downstairs where they served drinks and someone came over with a letter. It said I had to appear at Naval Headquarters. Suddenly, as if perfectly timed, military police came to the theatre, handed me a court order. Without the usual warm smiles I'd grown accustomed to receiving they said, "You have to come with us."

I didn't know what I'd done wrong really. Puzzled, I responded, "I have my papers."

Sternly and looking straight ahead, one of them stated, "No, this has nothing to do with that."

Somewhat disturbed, I thought, "What did I do? My goodness, I'm going to have trouble."

The court order said that I had to appear in front of the Admiral. I remembered that I wasn't supposed to be on that gunboat and started to get a little nervous.

They took me to the dock where I saw the new gunboat that was the scene of our party. Along the pier there were Navy officers and lines of sailors in their uniforms, standing very tall, staring straight ahead. Although I was looking at all of the boys that I knew, they had such serious expressions on their faces and were trying not to look at me.

"This was certainly not going to be a party," I thought.

I was taken to stand in front of the Admiral. It felt like I was in court, like he was the judge and I was the guilty party. Then, I began to hear one Naval officer attempt to say something in French but I could hardly understand.

It translated to "… and the wind was blowing and the sea was rough. Our greatest naval rescue has been a damsel in distress. It was the day we rescued Andrée from Admiralty Pier."

Then someone asked, "What is the verdict?"

Right in that moment I realized that this was a big joke. Not getting my English right, I had called the dock "Admiralty Pier." I think everyone realized at that moment that I had caught on to the delightful charade as I relaxed with a big sigh of relief and turned on an unbelievable smile.

With a slight twinkle in his eye, the Admiral handed me a quart of milk and told me it was my job to name the ship "The Distress." My joy and exhilaration could not be measured as I hit the boat like they do when they christen a ship with Champagne.

All of my stern faced Navy friends broke out laughing. It was hilarious. For the remainder of the day, the high spirits of these soldiers in the middle of war electrified the air with merriment. When I first got there, I really thought I was in trouble and it ended up being wonderful fun.

***

It was an interesting time because the theatre tour took me all over the place. It wasn't always safe taking the trains to the various productions. As soon as the bombing started, the trains would stop. Instead of going to the outside of London, they would just go as far as they could underground. Sometimes the bombings were so severe the train would be canceled so I would get a motorcycle ride back to the West End.

On one occasion, coming back from Yarmouth on the East coast near the sea one time, a bomb hit our train and we had to abandon it on the outskirts of the city before we even got to the East End. It was eleven o'clock that night and I was coming back. I was going to get off the train and then get an Underground to Piccadilly Circus for my evening performances at the different clubs.

With me were two comedians traveling back to London and Michael Doyle, son of the famous Irish boxer Jack Doyle. Jack was one of the biggest boxers in the world at that time. Michael was a singer. We had just completed a vaudeville show where Michael's beautiful voice and Irish songs had been a pleasure to all audiences.

We had no idea where we were. There were fires in all directions and many roads were blocked. Everyone was terrified and at a loss as to what to do. The throngs of people trying to rescue their belongings were not inclined to stop and give us directions. They were all scared.

A kindly fireman pointed, "Not sure you can get through Mum."

The comedians asked, "Now what do we do?"

I said, "I've got to get back. I have a show to do. In fact, I have several shows to do so let's start walking."

One comedian exclaimed, "Walking in this?!"

I replied, "Well, what are we going to do? Where are we going to hide?" These were men telling me what we couldn't do. I was only interested in what we could do.

So I said to Michael, "Go between them, take their hands and start singing."

Looking at me as though I was out of my mind, he exclaimed, "Singing!"

Shaking my head yes, "We're going to sing as we go along. We just need to ask directions to the straightest road."

So we started singing and walking through the streets with blazing fires on both sides of the road. It was not just one building but all of them on fire all the way along. Some people were throwing things out on the street from their homes trying to save their stuff.

Between the debris and my high heels I got off to a rough start, but we made it through the rubble. Little by little, holding hands, Michael singing Irish songs and me French, we tried to keep the humor alive for even the comedians had no feeling for comedy.

Dodging pit holes and barriers, it took us another couple of hours to reach the West End. The two comedians were so scared they stopped in the first place they could which wasn't on fire. Michael and I continued. It was 4 a.m., the bombing had stopped and the clubs were starting to close. We arrived at Lyons Corner House in Piccadilly, which was still open.

We were a mess covered in soot. My heels were ruined. It was impossible! I was carrying my clothes in one hand looking very dirty. We welcomed a good cup of tea and then rushed to our homes hoping that no disaster had befallen them. To my joy, I had just enough time to go home, wash down and catch a train to the studio to begin filming at 6 a.m.

I learned from observing Gandhi and my aunt in France that you have to look fear in the eye and say, "You know what? You're transitory. I don't believe in you." The death that stalked every street could still not dispel the beauty that nature and my new friends brought into my life and heart. Real friends can help you see the light around you. I could face the horrific disasters that left the whole of London in a blaze of ruins. Together, we could choose to see the good in our moments and laugh at life.

*Real friends can help you see the light around you.*

CHAPTER 9

Be A Peaceful Warrior

My twenties brought an explosion of activity. Although I was used to adventure from traveling the rails with my uncle, this was a different kind of energy. It was intense with the possibility of being consuming. I was learning about the reality of war and the world around me.

That period in my life reminds me of the legendary warrior Virabhadra, an incarnation of Shiva. In yoga, when you want to build endurance and stamina, you go into *Virabhadrasana II*, or Warrior II. It is one of the standing postures that invites you to tap into deep wisdom and inner strength. You have to stay present with the breath while keeping your *drishti*, or gaze, focused on the horizon otherwise you can lose your balance. As the war continued, I had to find a way to keep my center and find a bigger purpose.

*You have to stay present with the breath while keeping your drishti, or gaze, focused on the horizon otherwise you can lose your balance.*

For eight months, the Blitz decimated London killing thousands. Although I was working around the clock entertaining and bringing some relaxation to soldiers and others, I thought, "There's a war going on and I'm not doing enough for it." My cabaret work was not enough. Yes, I was going along the Cliffs of Dover to entertain the troops but I wanted to do more. I heard about other people doing incredible things to help and I felt dissatisfied.

One day at Lyons Corner House in Piccadilly, I saw a bevy of beautiful girls from the Windmill Theatre surrounding one of the most handsome young Frenchmen I had ever seen. Though I tried, I could not decipher what regiment or squadron he was in.

As I watched, fascinated and amused by all of them trying to get a date with him, a Captain from Free French Headquarters, interrupted the joyful flock and without further ado this mysterious man took leave of the girls.

My friend said softly, "That's Joël Le Tac."

"What regiment is he connected with?" I asked.

My friend, amazed at my interest, replied, "He is with Carlton Gardens, General de Gaulle's Headquarters. He disappears now and again and you won't see him." Then, he laughingly added, "Sometimes you can catch him at Le Petit Club Français, Olwen Vaughan's club. All the French meet there."

*At Le Petit Club Français in London during World War II. The Cross of Lorraine is on the wall. My dear friend Guimas is standing far left, Burgess Meredith is in the center. The others are a man from French Headquarters and two unknown women.*

Besides meeting other French people, something else now intrigued me about the famous rendezvous club on St. James Street.

I decided to check it out and was delighted by what I found. Le Petit Club Français, the little club of France, opened a whole new world for me. It was there that I met other French refugees and got to know so many who had also escaped to England.

On entering the club, I immediately noticed the French Flag and the Cross of Lorraine proudly displayed. The cross was a sign of support for the Free French, a symbol of pride for all French to show their feelings for the movement. Many French wore a Cross of Lorraine as I started to do soon thereafter.

*I'm wearing the Cross of Lorraine in London around 1941 to show my support for the Free French during World War II.*

The walls of the club were posted with flyers but the one that my eyes focused on was an enormous ear with a message in French and English, "Shush! Even the Walls Have Ears." This was to prevent people from talking about any war happenings. In case there were any spies they would not receive news about people trying to escape.

I realized that several important people from Carlton Gardens often came to the club. It was also the gathering place for many pilots, film and theatre stars like Broderick Crawford, Charlie Chaplin and many other notables. Whenever I was there, I felt like I was in France. I thought, "Maybe it is here that I will find out more. I really want to get news about what is happening to my aunt."

It became more and more my haunt and so my young agent-friend found me a room to rent close by on Jermyn Street. I always tried to stay where I didn't have to walk very far. It belonged to the Duke and Duchess of Gloucester, Princess Marina.

My new place was near Carlton Gardens and Le Petit Club Français. The apartment was nice but it wasn't without its perils. One day, I walked into my building and noticed the two high-class uniformed men standing at the door talking. I went up to my room and saw a flash of light and a bomb near the window. I called out downstairs and tried to tell them what I had seen. They came up, but the bomb had rolled further out.

They couldn't find it so they thought I was seeing things. They pondered pleasantly, "Oh, you know Miss, you must be very careful. We know it's very hard for you not to think you're seeing things."

The next morning the police and other people were there trying to locate the time bomb. They eventually found it. I was lucky because it hadn't gone off in the night while I was sleeping.

I couldn't think too much about the dangers around me. I had to keep moving forward. My place was also near a club where famous musicians gathered and played into the night, often until five in the morning. No matter how bad the bombing was, the club was always filled with young French pilots who assembled for the few hours that they were off duty.

French jazz violinist Stephane Grappelli, who founded The Quintette of the Hot Club of France with Django Reinhardt, could be seen there. I would meet Django later on in France.

I met a number of Americans there, including the famous bandleader Glenn Miller and dashing actor Clark Gable. Drummer Gene Krupa could often be seen leaning on the railing of the upper balcony caught up in the music.

I made friends with Olwen Vaughan. I think her grandfather was from Liverpool but she had lived most of her life in France and knew the area in the Rhône Valley. She loved France and missed going there. That's why she started Le Petit Club Français.

She said she spent more time in France than she ever did in England. I started to help Olwen as I tried to find out how I could become involved in the war. Olwen was the one who told me that the Germans were now throughout France.

She knew how to get things done. For example, you couldn't freely get food. Everything was rationed. You would get a small piece of butter for the whole week. You were allowed so much and not any more than that.

So, she would go in the country and pick up things like eggs and say, "This is what we're going to have tonight." It was based on what she managed to get. She would go off and pick up lamb from someone who killed his sheep. Then, she would make the food with a French cook. It was clever.

\*\*\*

I would see Joël from time to time at Le Petit Club Français, but then he would disappear for several weeks. It was difficult to get information since no one would talk about the war, but I knew I had to find out how I could participate.

Carefully, I had to choose someone to test—someone who I did not believe to be a spy for the Germans. Still, I could not know for sure. It was risky.

Even so, I took the risk and said, "Well, you know I'm fed up. I'm doing nothing for the war. Yes, I'm entertaining the troops but that's really nothing. And my aunt is almost killing herself. They might shoot her or something for what's she's doing."

After that, I had a sense I was being watched in the French Club but nobody came up to me. One gentleman would pose questions here and there but that was it. I was getting more frustrated thinking, "How do I get back? I'm going to go back to France. I have to do something." I wanted to be actively involved in the Resistance activities like my aunt.

One day, I took an even bigger risk and mentioned how my aunt had been helping the Polish Jews escape, something she had warned me against revealing. Suddenly this young man came up to me and said, "Is your aunt Porchon de Sanglier?"

"Yes." That is my family name.

"Do you know what she does?"

I nodded, "Yes. That's why I escaped to England."

"Do you know other people in France?" he asked.

"No, not really. I came here looking for my father."

That was the extent of that exchange.

Then, one day, there was something about a boat off of Penzance with fishermen from Brittany and a German submarine grabbed hold of them. I learned that the fishing boat had been traveling back and forth bringing people over.

That reminded me of my aunt's dangerous work so, within earshot of the man who had been questioning me, I said, "You know, maybe I could get back to France."

It made me think about how I boarded the *Victoria* of the Lloyd Treistino Line two days after finding out it was docking in Bombay. I could be impulsive if I believed in something.

For the first time I was seriously approached by Joël and another older man. They seemed to be measuring me up. Was I someone flaunting ideas or even a spy? They posed hundreds of questions about the occupation in various parts of France. How much did I know? Did I have any connections with my aunt, or any underground subversive groups?

Although said casually, I knew it wasn't when Joël asked, "Have you ever contemplated going back to France? Are you aware that your aunt is no longer in the Rhône Valley but in Saint-Jean-de-Luz?"

Obviously, my suspicion that they had put me under surveillance was true. I supposed they realized that I was sincere about getting involved with more serious work and the theatre was a good cover up. No one could cross over from Dover or any of the coastal towns. They were being bombed and were heavily guarded. With my work in the theatre, I went twenty-eight weeks to Dover. I would go to places like Portsmouth, where soldiers were congregated without problems.

We went on talking and little by little he would bring somebody else and they would ask me questions. Afterwards, Joël came to me and asked, "Are you really serious?"

"Yes, I am," I answered without hesitation.

"Then, I will show you what you have to do and what not to do, and how to react when the Germans are around."

Working underground in the Resistance was extremely dangerous. I had a greater appreciation for my aunt's work. We had to go through training to lessen the chances of being caught. We were required to know about dressing, cigarette smoking, and the way food should be eaten. For example, the Germans would know an American right away because Americans had a habit of cutting food with their knives and forks differently from the British or French.

When we were crossing over, we had to make sure even our clothes had no marks saying where they were bought. We could not smoke. A French person usually smoked with the cigarette dropping down. The British smoked differently.

We were going over with fishing boats and so if we were caught the Germans would know right away where we were from by the British money in our pockets or tickets for travel on a bus or train. We went through strict training and all of these things were pointed out to us.

During the war, I didn't use the name Täo. It was an unusual name that could be linked to my family. I used my middle name Andrée only. Even the pilots were changing their names.

I was very excited about getting involved. Joël immediately began to prepare me for my first crossing. "Well, you're going to be in the theatre in Portsmouth. That's good. It's very close to Charmaine and nobody knows you down there. Remember you must cut the labels out of the clothes you're wearing. No tickets in your pockets. No British money, just a few francs."

He continued, "We have a cargo of stuff that we're trying to get across and we don't have the planes yet to drop it. There is a fishing boat going over there." Joël added almost warmly, "And if you can, make contact with your aunt, she is one of our head liaisons going through the Pyrenees to San Sebastian."

I felt a wave of chills because this was amazing news for me to hear about her. I soon found that we were greatly needed at that time because they didn't have enough planes that could fly over and drop things. The planes were too small to do much good and if they dropped guns, the ammunition could blow up.

That began my underground work from London. I found it hard to contain myself and keep my mind free of activity. The expedition would be canceled if I took it too lightly. Joël was to be my partner and teacher. He would go in one direction and I would go in another. We would just go off together on the boats and we would know where to join up again.

On my first crossing, my mission was to transport the cargo in the fishing boat, as well as French money. The money was brought over from England to be given to our network of Resistance workers so they could pay off people. They needed to be careful and watch out for spies that could even be amongst them. I got in there and found that they really needed the money as well as other things.

I felt so excited at the prospect of seeing my aunt in Saint-Jean-de-Luz. Joyfully we hugged and I thought, "How wonderful it is to be in the arms of a loved one." It seemed like it had been so long. I could tell that she felt the same way.

We began to talk and it was like we had been together all of the time. I remembered my days with her in the vineyard. She was just laughing and acting as if all was normal. The reason for her flight was the Germans had found out about her underground work and closed in on her at the vineyard. She was lucky a friend warned her and helped her escape just before the Nazi soldiers moved in to capture her.

This did not deter my audacious aunt. She escaped and crossed over to the other side of the Atlantic, near the Spanish frontier. It didn't take her very long to devise a new plan to set up an underground station. She found out that the German soldiers were patrolling with police dogs there. Since she understood a lot about dogs, she came up with another clever way to help people escape.

She opened an animal hospital and graciously offered to board the dogs for the German soldiers when they were not patrolling with them. In no time she had set it up so that she was receiving extra food coupons that she used to buy food for the people she was trying to get across the border.

Smiling, she told me how the Germans would come in and say to her, "Oh, you take such good care!" She would be lovingly patting the search dogs. She knew that if they found out what she was doing, they would be even crueler to her because she had tricked them. She and those she was protecting would be captured, put in concentration camps, tortured or possibly killed.

I was amazed as she told me how she was able to hide people right under the noses of the German patrol. She explained, "When the dogs are left with me, I patiently work at introducing the people to the police dogs and the dogs to the people. That way the dogs don't bark around them."

As I listened, I felt proud of my shrewd and fearless aunt. I had learned in the vineyard that she was determined and relentless when she committed herself to something in which she believed. She was a good role model for me because she always seemed to find a way to get things done.

My aunt seemed proud of my underground work. She thought it was "perfectly right." I learned first from my uncle and Gandhi, and now from my aunt that if you believe in something and it's good, don't hide it from yourself. Instead, do something about it, especially if it can help others.

I returned to London feeling satisfied about a successful first mission and, of course, about spending some time with my aunt.

***

I continued my theatre performances and hanging out with my friends at Le Petit Club Français. One day I was asked, "Do you know Paris?"

Curious about the question, I replied, "Not really very well. I've only been there once."

"Well, there is a group of people underneath Paris and we're trying to get them out slowly. Are you scared?"

"No, I'm not scared. Why should I be scared?" I answered with confidence.

"Well, this mission is extremely dangerous."

Without hesitation I declared in a strong serious voice, "I can do it." I knew now I would be working directly with people helping them like my aunt.

Soon the time came for me to go to Paris to be in a theatrical production, *The World is Round*. I used that performance as an opportunity to join up with the people we were hiding in caves under the city.

My mission was to get the people out safely from the dark underground place. I had to move them to boats carrying potatoes that were being brought into the city. They would be concealed while being transported to a safe destination. I felt a warm thrill that I might soon play a vital part in the war. So many people risked and gave their lives for the concept of "freedom."

I was constantly made aware of the penalty of my actions if caught—

torture, concentration camp or death. The same would happen to the people I was trying to help and any family member they could connect with us. It was no longer an exciting event but one fraught with danger which seemed to sink into my most inner being. I did not take my responsibility lightly.

When I got to Paris and met up with my contact, I was told that we were going to the tunnels and without much talk we began walking. I didn't know what to expect, but I knew I had to follow directions and be alert. As we walked, I saw German soldiers with their highly trained search dogs patrolling the area looking for anyone who was trying to escape or anyone they thought looked suspicious. Paris was dangerous for young French soldiers because if found, the Germans put them in camps working to make roads.

Against the backdrop of the majestic Notre Dame Cathedral, my contact and I continued walking as if we were good friends going for a stroll.

To my surprise, we entered this very old restaurant in a building that went back to Roman days. It was a quaint, little place no bigger than a small room in a home. Everybody was crowded in so tightly we could hardly move through the people. I followed as we squeezed our way slowly through the crowd and went through another small room below the main floor where they kept all their supplies. It went under the river Seine.

On a level below that supply room we came upon steps. It looked as if it was barred off like no one had touched it for centuries, but it was leading somewhere. That's where we entered one of the tunnels under Paris. The Germans apparently didn't realize it was an entrance. It was this unobtrusive little restaurant that nobody would ever suspect. I thought, "How will I get the people I am to transfer through this crowd?"

Using a flashlight to see, I followed my contact. We just kept moving along deeper and deeper into a network of dark creepy catacombs under the streets of Paris. I went far down into the damp cold bowels of the city. I never allowed fear to enter my mind. I knew that what you put in your mind materializes, so I needed to keep my mind clear.

*What you put in your mind materializes.*

*Catacombs under Paris.*

Many of the people in the caves were transported into Paris in potato boats that were bringing in food and other supplies from the south of France and everywhere. People were arriving from places like Alsace-Lorraine. They'd come into these underground tunnels because they thought they could escape much easier from there. It wasn't true but they came in there anyway out of desperation. A lot of the Jewish people in particular had no money left to escape on their own and were in dire need of help.

As we moved closer to where the people were waiting, I thought, "This is where I will actually have to get the people out to safety."

It was so horrible down there. Being among all of the ancient filthy debris of hundreds of years and smelling the stagnant underground water almost took my breath away. All of that stinky stuff had been thrown in those tunnels for centuries including millions of bones of the dead of Paris. It had the reputation as the "world's largest grave." We were walking through it all.

At last we were almost there. Then suddenly, I nearly gasped as my eyes adjusted to the area ahead crowded with children, women and men waiting and depending on me to transfer them. As we got closer I saw some of them sitting on the floor and some of them standing with a few candles dimly lighting the area.

In the center, I saw a man doing movements with his hands, his body and his face. He was telling a story to entertain them without making a sound. I learned that it was young Marcel Marceau doing pantomime.

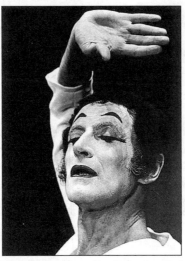

*Marcel Marceau years later after he became known as the "master of silence." I met him when he was much younger.*

Marcel was trying to keep everyone from going mad. He knew how devastating it was living down there, hiding, hungry with no lights or anything, having nothing to do but think and be fearful of the unknown. Since everything had to be done in silence, Marcel started doing his speechless performances to bring some relief from the fears and despair of hunger and darkness.

I watched and had tremendous respect for him. I learned later that at the beginning of the war, Marcel had to hide his Jewish origin and change his name from Mangel to Marceau. When his family was forced to flee their home, his father was deported to Auschwitz where he was killed. Both Marcel and his brother, Alain, escaped to Paris and were committed to their work in the French underground.

They helped many children escape and many people change their names as well as identities by making up papers for them. Whether they were Jewish or French they would make them younger on their new papers. During his lifetime, Marcel Marceau became the world's legendary mime. He moved audiences without uttering a single word and became known as a "master of silence."

After his performance that night, my natural instincts were to try to cheer the people up as I was doing in cabarets in London. However, I kept my responsibility in mind, realizing the importance of my mission in the horror of this scary deathlike atmosphere. I remembered what I had to do was to keep these people safe and alive. I told the group why I was there and gave them instructions that must be strictly followed for me to move them to safety.

There were many entrances to the nearly three hundred miles of tunnels and caves under Paris and some of them were open and some were locked. For the transfer, I was directed to an exit that was very close to the Seine River where I noticed a church on the right hand side. A lock had been placed on that entrance to the tunnel so it looked as if it was secured. The German soldiers didn't realize it was open and that's how we were able to slip out unnoticed and I was able to go back in after each transfer.

I could only take out a few people at a time. They were so scared that they were shivering. Along the sides there were soldiers with their dogs. We had to get to the boats that were waiting for us. With every move I made, I thought, "I cannot let these people die." At twenty-three years old, I had these people's lives in my hands.

We made it to the flat boats that were loaded with wood and coal that they were bringing in to supply heat to Paris. Some boats had food. I was able to get the first group of people on the first boat safely. We were wrapped up in potato sacks and told to lie on our tummies. The potato sacks would camouflage the smell of the people from the dogs.

As we were traveling down the Seine to our destination, German soldiers were patrolling along the river listening for anything suspicious. We didn't dare move, stretch or do anything once we were wrapped in the sacks. A cough or loud breath could mean death. We knew our lives depended on absolute silence. We had no guns or other weapons to defend ourselves if we got caught.

When we would get to a certain point someone else would take over and I would get out of the boat and return. This way, we could get people to safety or out of the country. In the words of the mission, we had "transferred the people over." I repeated this operation until all of the people had been transferred and my mission was complete.

On each return to the tunnel I was so aware of the passengers whose faces showed only too well the horrific terror and problems they had encountered. The real horrors of war were ever present.

***

At that time people didn't realize that there were mostly women in the French Resistance. As I had learned in France with my aunt, women were the ones left to do most of the underground work since the young men had been taken.

On some missions, we would pretend we were socializing. Sometimes we would go through Bordeaux vineyards and drink wine knowing there would be somebody hiding there hoping to meet us. It was dangerous. We kept transferring and getting in and out along the riverbank. In that way, we could stay close to the shore and do more pickups. As I learned earlier from my aunt, the power of women was often underestimated. The Germans weren't quite as suspicious of a beautiful lady walking arm and arm with a man or chatting with other women.

As I was getting deeper into the Resistance, I continued my performances in England doing cabaret, vaudeville stage and theatre work. No one knew what I was doing. They would think I was just off doing theatre in another town so it appeared normal if I wasn't seen for a few days. I wouldn't get involved in much talk about it in case I was under surveillance. I always met my contacts in different places.

It was my nature to make the best of situations. Especially at this time I would reinforce constantly to myself how my uncle started each morning with, "It's a beautiful day, isn't it?"

I was in a show in Manchester and the theatre had been bombed. Half the ceiling was blown out. The show was *Chinese Follies* and it had a French Can-Can in it. It was freezing so every day when they were practicing the chorus I would get behind them and try to follow it. I did what they were doing to keep warm since I only had one dance in the whole show.

One day most of the girls became sick. Out of twelve girls, only five were left. They thought they were going to have to cancel it. They lamented, "This is terrible! How are we going to do it? We can't just put five girls on and call it a chorus. We don't know what we're going to do. We tried to get other people to join us but nobody wants to come and do it on the middle of the stage."

The stage was beaten up so much that it made it hard for the chorus line to move around. The manager, Cyndi, was in a frenzy. I offered,

"You know Cyndi, I think I know the routine. If you like I'll do it with them."

Interested, he asked, "You really think you can?"

He saw me do it and conceded with some relief, "Okay, you will save us making it at least six girls but you have to wear a wig."

I questioned that, "With all my hair I have to wear a wig? It's impossible!"

He insisted, "No, no, no. You have to wear the wig."

All of the girls had to wear these heavy black wigs and on top of the wigs they had this Chinese pagoda headdress, like a big spiral. My own hair was long enough to hold the headdress without the wig but the director insisted. When I bunched my hair on top it was like a big chignon. So I had the wig on top of the chignon and the Chinese headdress on top of that.

I went on stage and was really into what I was doing. I wasn't even thinking about the audience or anything. I was gaily dancing intent on getting all the moves right. I was trying to remember the routine so I wouldn't spoil it for them.

Suddenly, I heard shrieks of laughter. I couldn't figure out what it was so I didn't pay too much attention. The whole place was roaring hysterically. I thought, "I don't know why they think it's so funny."

I kept dancing, not looking at myself. Then, my own chorus started to choke with laughter. One girl dashed off stage and then another.

Finally, I was the only one left on stage. I looked over at one of the girls at the side of the stage and she pointed at my stomach. I looked down and saw that the extra wig had slipped under my chin and was hanging like an enormous beard. The people laughed so hard, the comedians refused to go on after me.

They argued, "We can't follow that. She spoiled our act!"

Every time they tried to put someone else on stage, people would say, "Send her back on! Send her back on!"

I guess I just wasn't supposed to be in the chorus.

They were a bit cross with me. They thought I did it on purpose. I didn't. I didn't even know!

The show was a big sellout. Despite the cold and everyone arriving with blankets, the theatre was packed because of the story of the bearded lady.

After three shows, the *Chinese Follies* went off and was replaced by a gypsy musical. We tried to find humor even in the midst of the fierce bombing.

***

In addition to Dover and Manchester, I went to Bridlington on the coast as well as Hull and Liverpool. The Germans were bombing the dickens out of these places almost as bad as London. From Liverpool, I crossed over to Dublin. I was so fed up with the bombings in England, I happily said yes to going to Ireland. It was supposed to be neutral ground.

At the theatre in Dublin, I was playing a gypsy girl with a musical comedy group. I did a number of those. After one of the shows, I wanted to send some cards off to my friends in London and to my family in India. Given the war, I wasn't really sure that my correspondence would even get there but had to try to let my uncle and aunt keep up with me.

As I crossed over the road, a taxi came out of nowhere and hit me. I was in terrible pain as the car was lifted off of my shoulder. Fortunately, it appeared to be just a bad bruise. They wanted to put me in the hospital.

I practically begged, "I can't speak English. Don't leave me here. I truly don't understand these people's Irish English."

Even though I was hurt, I got on a boat and continued on the tour in our last show playing the gypsy role.

At the next theatre back in Liverpool, I was doing a dance number with the tambourine. With the shoulder injury, I was raising my arms high above my head and tears were rolling down my face. I guess it must have seemed like I was really acting the part. The truth is that my shoulder was hurting so badly. Still, I wasn't going to let them put me in the hospital, so I endured it. I didn't want them to leave me alone where I didn't know anybody.

After the performance, I received a standing applause and people from the audience came to me saying, "You are such a fine actress."

I smiled and thanked them, but in my heart I knew that I wasn't acting at all. I was hurting. That's when I gave up theatre, as far as moving around in what they call vaudeville-type theatre. I got out of that.

At one point in England I was in a show in Aldershot, very near

Southampton. One night row after row of German planes passed overhead dropping bomb after bomb destroying everything. It was awful. The theatre had to close down and people were scrambling to get out of town and away from it.

There were four girls in the chorus of the show who had no place to stay so I took two of them to stay in my room at my hotel. I was able to get all four of them shelter but thought, "Now, what to do with them?"

Two of them were redheads and two were blondes, so I conceived an idea. Offering some assurance I said, "I'll tell you what, I will make a little show with the four of you. That way you'll have a job. I'll have two blondes and two redheads, and I will be the brunette."

So I spent all my money setting it up. I tried to teach them swing and different things. I had them with fans dancing and making a display around me, as well as doing Latin dancing even though they didn't know anything about it.

They were not the best dancers but I found a very nice Trinidadian bandleader, Edmundo Ros, at one of the clubs. He had a Latin dance band and later became very popular and quite celebrated in England. I put a show together with the girls playing maracas as they danced.

I wasn't formally trained in any of it. I made it up as I went along, allowing the energy and creativity to come from within me. It was like when I used to tell stories to my little friends in Pondicherry. I was simply communicating from within.

In that show, I had a hat and a brilliant red sequin dress with a train behind me so it was sexy as well as funny. Everywhere I went I had something in my show that brought fun and relaxation to the people.

I was actually using this show so I could go to a theatre near Portsmouth and cross over the Channel from there for underground work. I couldn't cross over from Dover or any of those other places because it was too dangerous. It was so heavily guarded in that vicinity.

At the end of the show I told the girls I was going to visit friends and crossed over to Saint-Brieuc, a little town in Brittany. There I was able to complete my mission. Even the girls were not suspicious as I constantly disappeared. I would do all of these things without them suspecting me. Caution was of upmost importance in case they had spies with us. I later found out they did.

I was careful. I was in the theatre as far as they were concerned or probably with a boyfriend. I was an actress so whatever silly things

I would put on or did, nobody suspected even though I may have someone with me when I reappeared.

I made several successful crossings to France, but on the last one someone turned my partner and me in. Fortunately for me, I left about ten minutes before they came and so I managed to escape back to England with my group. Sadly, Joël was not as fortunate.

I learned at the end of the war that the Germans were so cruel to him. They pulled out all of the nails in his hands and feet, and injected him with tuberculosis. He was sent to a concentration camp and was tortured. They were trying to get information out of him.

What they did to this gorgeous young man made everyone very sad. He was imprisoned for over three years and endured it all. Joël Le Tac was a true French patriot.

You never knew what really happened since so much was done in secret during these times. However, we suspected that there was a young man spying on us in London that let the Germans know what we were doing. He was from Alsace-Lorraine and was always trying to join us in Carlton Gardens. I wondered why he was constantly following us around.

I didn't know why but I never liked him. I just had this bad feeling about him and used to try and avoid him. He was always very officious, you know. "Oh Andrée, so nice to see you. Where are you going now?"

I would quip, "I'm going to be in this theatre."

"Oh, so you're still doing theatre work?" would usually be his response.

Annoyed, I would answer, "What do you expect me to do? I don't know how to do anything else."

It is still strange to recall the way he was always asking questions like, "Where did Joël go and when is he returning?"

At first, I denied knowing Joël. Later, I would answer cheerfully, "Oh, Joël has a rendezvous with a girl."

Afterwards someone told me that he'd actually killed his own twin brother who was pro-French. He'd come over on his brother's name and managed to be a spy in London. After Joël was turned in, he disappeared. I never saw him again in England.

*If you reach deep inside, the answers will be revealed.*

At the end of the war you would hear a lot of stories. Whether they were true or not, I didn't know but this is what was said. I still get an unsettling feeling talking about him even now. I get goose pimples and my hands go cold when I think of his possible role in hurting my friend Joël.

When Joël got caught, I had to stop. It was not safe for me to return to Paris and I was barred from making more expeditions. I couldn't go back because they would have identified me. They knew he had partners but they didn't know who they were.

The first two years in London had been sort of frantic. So many things were happening. I first didn't know what to do and then I had quite a lot to do. I had fun with the theatre and film work, and found greater purpose with the French Resistance.

Although there was intense danger during this war, I know I found strength and inspiration from my beloved uncle, my revered family friend Mahatma Gandhi, my fearless aunt, and the great General Charles de Gaulle. My underground partner and teacher, Joël Le Tac was heroic and gallant and inspired me with his absolute, single-mindedness of purpose. He was a great man.

I was reminded to face life without fear and to look to each moment knowing that the worst problem can be solved. I learned not to dwell on the darkness of life, but know that every cloud can be swept away. Like the sun after a storm makes the sky look its bluest and the rainbow signals the end of a storm, so the Infinite is all-powerful. If you reach deep inside, the answers will be revealed. At times, we all have to take on the warrior spirit, facing the battlefield of life with courage, grace, determination and a peaceful heart.

*At times, we all have to take on the warrior spirit, facing the battlefield of life with courage, grace, determination and a peaceful heart.*

CHAPTER 10

## Reach For The Moon

One of the most beautiful visions is a wolf howling at the moon. It is a form of communication, often when seeking a mate. It is a call of the wild, a connection of earthly and heavenly bodies. It's like the standing yoga posture, *Ardha Chandrasana*, or Half Moon. It balances the calming force of the moon with the fiery energy of the sun. It is the harmony of two energies coming together as one like the love between a man and a woman. Up until this point, I had not experienced true romantic love. I now know that regardless of distance, circumstances or time, love is the force that brings everything together.

*Regardless of distance, circumstances or time, love is the force that brings everything together.*

Right in the midst of the war I met my stepsister Kaye one day at Canada House. She had grown up in Canada where I might have been if my mother had not died giving birth to me. When I was looking for my father, the people at Canada House had found her as well.

Our father had told her about me so she had been hoping that one day we would meet. She had an older sister, Irene, who had come over to England with the United Nations. In Canada, my father apparently had married their mother who was a widow. She already had the two girls so he became their stepfather. Even though Kaye was my stepsister, I became close to her.

Kaye explained how she came to England, "When I saw my sister come over I put my age up and joined the Canadian Army. I was just a teenager when they put me on to operate the radars."

She was located in the area north of Cambridge. One of the big military zones of defense was Cambridgeshire where radar gave warning of enemy planes crossing the Channel. The Canadian squadrons were also stationed there. Kaye had been on that radar when the planes first came in for the bombing Blitz.

Meeting Kaye brought another sense of levity to my life. It was so incredible when she started coming to London. She liked dancing and would bring a dress with her. She'd leave the camp with her uniform on and then change when she came to stay with me. She was tall and not particularly pretty but when she walked in everybody would look at her. She was so elegant and a lot of fun. I met her sister Irene much later, but didn't get to know her well. I also found out that I had a brother but never got to know him either.

My circle of friends and family was expanding. Despite the war, the power of love captured my attention. I was twenty-three years old and had been in London a couple of years. It was the spring of 1942 and I had been booked at the Wellington Night Club in Knightsbridge, at the corner of Hyde Park and Piccadilly where Hamilton House became Kensington. I was starting a new show with my four girls, the two redheads and two blondes. We were going to do a Tahitian dance using the Hawaiian-type skirt I had created from cellophane. Since I didn't have straw, I had flowers all around it. My show with that costume was a hit! Soldiers would often come see me perform.

We had been hearing about a great squadron of French pilots coming to England that was stationed near London. Many had escaped from all parts of France and others had come from French colonies around the world. In any case, they kept coming in and eventually they had their own squadron and so the Ile-de-France RAF Squadron 340 was formed.

I had met several of them and had heard through Guimas about the incredible air battles they fought against the Germans. Winston Churchill wanted them to serve under the British squadrons as he had done with the Polish pilots. He also wanted everyone to wear British uniforms. However, these extraordinary pilots from Biggin Hill chose to have their own uniforms and to fight under General de Gaulle. They said, "No, we're here and we're fighting. Like General de Gaulle said, 'This is a world war' and we're going to be there identified with France."

*Massat, head of the Ile-de-France 340 Squadron, and another member pose by a Spitfire fighter plane that proudly displays the Cross of Lorraine. Lower photo: Massat is in the cockpit.*

That's why we started to see them in their dapper French uniforms. They were such devils in a good sense. They were gallant and lionhearted. You have to be to think, "I'm going to go off to another country and fight." It's bad enough if it's in your own country. You have to be brave.

It was so incredible. I used to almost choke with pride and a bit of reverence to see them come in their custom-made uniforms. They were not like ordinary soldiers. They stood out and looked very stylish. I had seen so many men in uniform, some handsome and some not so much. It was the first time I had seen them all looking so chic.

They walked with a strong sense of self-respect and dignity. Some of them who had escaped France didn't even have any other clothes with them. Many spent their last shilling to have these special uniforms made on Savile Row, a street in Mayfair in central London. Even today, it is known for its tradition of fine tailoring.

One day at the Wellington Club, a fabulous group of these Free French fighter pilots from the Ile-de-France Squadron walked in. They were quite a spectacle in their new uniforms. A young French pilot named René Mouchotte brought this dashing group to the club to see my new show.

*René Mouchotte and fellow pilots of the Ile-de-France Squadron.*

After the performance, the pilots were standing on the steps coming down into the club, which was below ground. The young Frenchmen were happy being with such beautiful girls so I introduced the girls to the pilots. Soon only one young man was standing there very peaceful with a big smile on his face. I thought, "That's the most handsome man I've ever seen in my life!"

I said to him, "Well… to whom do you want to be introduced?"

Laughingly, he said, "I'm looking at her."

I turned around to find the girl he wanted to meet, but instead, I saw another pilot who said, "His name is Yvan. We call him 'Pop Off' because he suddenly yodels when he goes into a battle with German pilots."

Another friend cut in and said without even a short pause, "That's typical of Pop Off. You'll never get a straight answer from him, but when he knows what he wants, believe me, you're stuck."

Interested and puzzled, I asked, "What does he want?"

His face lit up with a broad smile and said, "He wants you! He wants to be with you!"

"Oh!" I said quietly as a feeling of enchantment filled my being. I turned back to face this dashing pilot and saw him standing there looking at me with a smile so tender I fell in love in that instant. I felt my heart throbbing with excitement as he introduced himself as Yvan.

I said, "I am Andrée."

That was the beginning of my first love.

*Yvan Moynet in his wonderful 340 Ile-de-France uniform. He was a Free French Spitfire fighter pilot and became the love of my life and husband.*

I was very proud because Yvan really was handsome. He wasn't very tall, not much taller than me but like my uncle he always made me laugh and absolutely had no fear. He didn't like a lot of flashy things. He was really unassuming.

When he got a little bit sick and was in the hospital, I went to visit him. Some of the others were teasing him saying, "The girl with that Indian accent is always smiling. She's always smiling."

Being from Pondicherry, I spoke French with an Indian accent. I only realized how strange that must have sounded to the French when I went back to Pondicherry many years later and heard a tonga driver speaking with a similar accent.

They would also tease me because I didn't eat meat. It was nice for these poor boys because I would give them my ration ticket. I didn't eat things that I had ration tickets for such as the meat and sweets, like sugar. I hardly ate anything, usually just fruit. I didn't eat anything that was killed, particularly after my goldfish experience when I was a child.

Once, though, they took me to Prunier's famous fish restaurant. I said, "Fish, I don't eat fish."

They said, "Oh, this is not fish, you'll see."

So they gave me an oyster. I liked it and for the next three weeks I'd go and order a dozen *huites*. They thought that was a big joke on me.

Yvan and I had so many things in common and many of the same ideas. He was brought up in Hanoi, the capital of French Indochina at the time. So we used to talk a lot about that. I would share stories from India.

Given how we both grew up in the colonies, we were not typically French. Although he was not a vegetarian, he was used to a lot of fruits and vegetables, which were hard to get in England during the war. Since we were both from the tropics we shared a love of warm weather. Like me, he couldn't stand the cold.

When we got to know each other we found out that his father had also connected with my uncle on that railroad from Hanoi to Yan'an in China. We didn't know that when we first met. It's funny how things happen. His mother had been back in France for a long time so I didn't know much about her at first.

The love affair that developed with Yvan was exciting. I got a big job to entertain at the theatre in Dover and was staying at a hotel there.

Every time he got some leave he would rush down and spend a few hours with me.

One day he was leaving me to go back to his plane and he looked out of the window as the train was moving off and said, "Oh Cherie, on va se marier la semaine prochaine," which meant, "Oh, by the way, we're getting married next week."

Not sure I heard him correctly, I responded, "Qu'est ce que tu as dit?" meaning "What did you say?"

Smiling, throwing me a kiss and waving, he responded, "On va se marier. Au revoir."

Then, the train took off. It seemed a miracle had entered my life. I was so happy.

A couple of weeks later when Yvan returned, we got married in a small ceremony in Brighton. He had to get approval. I was supposed to do something for a Canadian squadron. This one squadron had a big painting of me in my cellophane Hawaiian skirt on all their planes. They had taken it from one of my photographs. That was certainly one way to distract the Germans! The Canadians were really funny and quite wonderful.

My friend "Big Chief," who used to come up with his boys when I lived in Hamilton House and play pranks, came down for the wedding. We had become such friends that he was the best man for Yvan, and one of our witnesses. He said, "Now you take care of her because she is special. Otherwise our whole squadron will be after you!"

***

Yvan was part of an important squadron. The Free French No. 340 Ile-de-France Squadron RAF flew defensive patrols and fighter sweeps. General Charles de Gaulle visited the squadron in England. I was honored to once again be associated with the great General de Gaulle.

Despite the war, every moment with Yvan was wonderful. We had the greatest time when we were together, but that didn't last too long. He would stay with me a little bit and then would have to go. I was getting used to being a pilot's wife. His squadron was everywhere. They were never in one place very long.

*General Charles de Gaulle visiting the Ile-de-France Squadron in England.*

Yvan had a sense of humor despite the danger. He would say, "You think I'm worried to be in the clouds with the Germans? I yodel when I'm up there flying."

His friends would say, "There goes Pop Off. The Germans are going to think they're in the wrong country."

Yvan's squadron was soon transferred to Scotland due to the influx of German activities there. A lot of German submarines had been seen along the Scottish coast. Submarines were starting to come into the harbors from the North. Some said that the Germans might try to invade Great Britain from Scotland rather than across the English Channel.

The Ile-de-France Squadron was moved just outside of the capital city of Edinburgh to the funny little village of Drem. Outside of Drem was a big airport called RAF Drem or Royal Air Force Drem, which was used for air defense. There they were watching the Channels on the eastern side while others were safeguarding the west coast of Scotland. The Nazis were trying to find a way to creep in and our boys were keeping watch.

*A member of the First Free French 340 Ile-de-France Squadron with his plane.*

Yvan and two other boys were shipped to Prestwick near Glasgow on the southwest coast. I don't know why they sent him to Prestwick first when the squadron went to Drem. I left everything in London, all my things, and went to join Yvan.

We eventually made some friends in Prestwick. There was one funny lady who liked me. She used to call me, "The Wee French Lady" in a real deep Scottish accent. She would say, "You don't like meat but he will like this sausage," talking about Yvan. "Can't get sausage often in here so you give it to him. I saved some for him." She was so helpful. She couldn't get over the fact that I ate so little and didn't eat meat.

Yvan received orders to go to Drem and bought a car to take us across. He had confidence in everybody and was sold a car that didn't go very far. It broke down along the way. We finally made it to Drem and joined the other members of his squadron.

We found that Drem was on rations that were so small we couldn't find much to eat. Some of the boys would go out and try to shoot rabbits. They would bring one back and cook it. I didn't particularly like that they were killing innocent animals but I understood that they needed food to eat. They needed the energy to fight.

There was an odd doctor from Marseille. One night we were all sitting and talking and he was saying to me, "I just miss my horse meat."

I said, "Horse meat! You don't eat horses do you?"

He said, "In Marseille, we eat horse flesh." Since there was so little food they started to eat horses. Survival during the war was often difficult.

I had the strangest experiences in Scotland. When we first arrived in Drem, we were staying at the house that our friend Pierre and his wife shared with another pilot and his wife. At the beginning, we had no bedroom. It was a big house, so we slept in their library. During the night books and things were hitting us. It was weird. Yvan slept through it but I didn't. I got hit by one of them.

We were always sitting and talking. One time I said, "Somebody just came in. I heard the door."

Pierre said, "No, you couldn't have. It's locked. If it is, it must be Andre." He was the only one who was not married in the group.

Someone said, "No, Andre went to bed."

I said, "You know. I'm sorry but there's something bizarre about this house. It's evil." Even now I get shivery remembering it. So, Yvan and I moved out to another house around the corner.

Yvan was the cleanest person that I ever met in my entire life. He couldn't stand dirt. He would clean it up right away. He would take a bucket of ice water and wash. All the others would shout loudly, "Throw that cold water away. Put it on you but take it away from us! We don't want it. It's too cold. Ice water to wash with! Ugh."

When we would go into the ordinary hotels at that time there were no tissues. Only the best hotels had toilet tissues. When we were in a hotel with tissues, I would see him come out with his pockets bulging. He always made me laugh.

One day, going up the steps of where we were living I heard in a heavy Scottish accent, "dirty foreigners."

I thought, "The only foreigners that are here are us. Yvan would carefully clean the tub before and after a bath. Why is she calling us dirty?"

She continued, rolling her "r's" in her strong Scottish lilt, "I've had my bathroom for thirty-five years and I've never used it and he's using it all the time!"

I thought that was pretty funny. I don't know what she was using her bathroom for but she wanted us to use just a bowl with a big jug. We were supposed to use that to wash with?

One day a girl in our group staying at the previous house came dashing in and said, "Please come over. Lindsay is in a terrible state."

Knowing Lindsay was pregnant, I was concerned and asked, "What happened?"

She said, "Pierre went off to fly and she was staying in bed. Suddenly, she felt something tapping her on the leg. She opened her eyes and saw a woman standing at the end of the bed. She thought she might be dreaming so she shut her eyes."

Even though she was in the land of ancient folklore and hauntings, she didn't believe in ghosts.

She continued explaining, "Lindsay opened her eyes and the woman was standing next to her. With that, she hopped out of bed—big and pregnant—and dashed into my room yelling, 'There was a woman at the foot of my bed!'"

That was such an odd occurrence. We didn't quite know what to think about it.

The grass on the back lawn of the house was getting tall so Pierre would go out and do some cutting. One day he stumbled upon a big plot in the middle of the lawn. We found out that it had been a burial ground from when people had been massacred.

No wonder it had an eerie energy. I can feel things like that. I'm glad we had moved away from that house. Sometimes you get in those places where they have lived a long time like in Scotland and you experience supernatural things pierce the atmosphere.

I like adventures, but that was a bit too mysterious. I was rather happy when we got the news Yvan's squadron was being moved out of Scotland down to Perranporth in Cornwall, southwest almost near Penzance just south of Devonshire. That was our new home, right on the other end of the United Kingdom.

Unfortunately, Lindsay lost her baby. That mystifying energy in Scotland seemed to put a dark cloud over her when she gave birth in Perranporth. It was so sad.

\*\*\*

We had been in Scotland for about three months and now we were back in England. I couldn't believe I was actually happy to be back. It was the end of 1943 and the Ile-de-France Squadron was being called on to take to the skies again.

The war was hard on love in many ways. A lot of these pilots were getting married to girls and they were right away having babies. They'd come back with a lot of nerves and everything, and then run over to their family very tired. The pilots flew the Spitfires all day with hardly a rest between the flights.

*Members of the Ile-de-France Squadron. Yvan is on the left.*

It was stressful to the woman and not really fair to the children. If the man got shot down the woman was suddenly left with no money coming in from the French government to help them.

That's why we didn't want to have children. At that time, I thought, "I can't bring a baby into the world with the war. I can't be pregnant and have my husband fighting Germans in the sky worrying about me and whether he is going to get back or be shot down." For me, it would be bad enough for him to be shot down without me being pregnant. So I wouldn't let it happen.

Yvan said, "I don't really believe in just getting married to a girl and putting her to bed for sex. I want more than that." So, it was different. I tried to be with my husband as much as possible, but I wouldn't allow myself to get pregnant even though nearly everybody else was.

Whenever a pilot escaped to England, it was a rule not to discuss his background with anyone outside the barracks. Even with Yvan, I knew little about him except we were both from French colonies and that his father and my uncle were both involved with railroads. We talked about our childhood and growing up in similar climates and such, but not about our adult lives. I never told Yvan about my underground work.

Often Yvan would bring a friend from his squadron to have dinner with us. One night, it was a charming pilot named Marcel. He looked too young to be a pilot but nobody questioned him. A little sheepish about his background, all he would say was he escaped from Normandy. He seemed to have little understanding of English and was following the rule to only speak French.

Once Marcel began flying on missions as a Spitfire pilot, the others saw what he could do and he became well liked. He was known to be fearless for his bold and daring offensive efforts in destroying German planes. He had been sent to join the Ile-de-France Squadron after completing his training at RAF Biggin Hill, the first airfield to claim a thousand enemy planes destroyed. Today, on the lawn in front of St. Georges Chapel at Biggin Hill Airfield there is a full-size replica of a Spitfire plane.

*Ile-de-France Squadron. Yvan is on the ground on the right. Marcel is sitting on the wing.*

It was clear that Marcel was proud to be in the Ile-de-France Squadron. As the months passed, he became a close friend eating and spending more time with us. Yvan took him to the cabaret club where I was appearing and I introduced him to a friend of mine named Rita. She was a beautiful singer and I got her a lot of jobs. She introduced me to some of the people singing in the big bands.

In no time, Rita and Marcel fell madly in love. We would tease him, but he only had eyes for her. Every time he could get a ride from Biggin Hill, he never left her side. There were countless stories and couples like Rita and Marcel falling in love in the midst of war. Some of them made it, some didn't.

The combat was no longer just over the English Channel, but bombs were being attached to the nose of the Spitfire planes. This very dangerous feat saw many pilots blown up. As the war grew more intense, and the pilots were out on more and more dangerous missions, many did not return. Yvan didn't like to talk about it.

There were also boys who had no wives and they used to come to our place to eat. It was at this point that I really and truly learned to cook. They'd go down to Penzance when they had a few hours free where many French fisherman were escaping or helping others escape used to congregate. They would bring all of the pilots different fish.

The pilots would come back and who would they ask to cook? Me! I knew nothing about it. I hadn't the faintest idea how. I'd seen people do it. Yvan would say, "There is never a dull moment. Everybody wants to come and have food with you. You never learned to cook but you know everything. Where do you find all the things that go in and give it taste?"

I used to walk along the sides of the road along the hedges, there were hardly any trees, and taste plants and pieces of grass. If it didn't hurt me, I would bring it back and put it in some food to make it taste different. All of the other wives of the pilots would say, "We don't understand. Where do you find all this food? Are you doing the black market?"

I responded, "No, first of all I don't eat meat. I give my coupon to you for meat and then find things in nature."

Once I ate a plant that I found and got boils all over me. Underneath my arm, and the back of my leg something started to rise up. I was a little scared because it had poisoned me.

Looking at me laughing and shaking his head, Yvan asked, "What did you do now?"

No matter how dreary the day, even if he'd come back sad because one of his friends had been shot down, he said I made him laugh. I kept his mind free.

I lost so many of my shoes and other things in the bombings, I actually ran out of shoes. I would find items on the beach that had been washed ashore and make things. One day I found cork on the sand. I took it home and made myself shoes that were high enough for my taste and then painted them. It was ridiculous. Yvan was in hysterics. I couldn't wear the English shoes. I thought there was nothing smart or fashionable about them. I also loved high heels because they're in direct contact with the energy of life. I would make Yvan laugh about so many things.

*Yvan taking a break between flying.*

It made me happy to be in nature. I would press the ball of my foot into the earth like I did when I was a child. I felt more connected to the Oneness in all, the Divine Energy that governs the whole planet.

Sometimes I would walk along the sands and try and find things like clams and mussels. I had to be careful because the tide would come in and cut me off. Once I almost got stuck. The water came around where all of the mussels were and it was getting higher and higher. I thought, "I better get across before the water gets me. I can't swim across there."

I had to wade through the water holding my things high above my head. Luckily, I got out.

The tidal bores in Pondicherry prepared me for even the biggest waves. I wasn't scared but I did have a sense of reverence for the power in nature.

I would come back with my catch, usually clams, and say to Yvan, "Invite your friends over. We have a whole lot of clams. I know they'll eat them." I wouldn't eat them but I knew they would. Our house, which was really a room in a hotel, was sort of the place where everybody gathered.

At that time, we weren't in real apartments. We would be wherever we could find a room. You have to know that houses, even big houses in England, often only had one toilet and one tiny little bathroom. If you were in a hotel you would go down the corridor to it and have to share it with the other rooms.

*\*\*\**

From Perranporth the pilots were suddenly going out flying every day—every single day fighting an air battle. A lot of the American and Canadian pilots were also flying into that area. The High Command started to move squadrons southeast into a military zone. Travel was severely constricted and you needed special papers to enter this controlled region. You couldn't get in anywhere in Aldershot and Bramshot. More and more severe air battles were guarding the ground forces.

*Members of the Ile-de-France Squadron with a Spitfire fighter plane which was considered one of the most famous planes of World War II due to its superior speed, firepower and agility. This gave the British a critical edge over the Germans.*

It was very stressful. I had been married for less than a year and had given up my own work in shows to be with Yvan in Scotland and then in Perranporth. Now, he was being transferred again.

The wives were not allowed to go with their husbands so I went back to London to simply wait. Yvan told me that the pilots were sleeping in tents and sleeping bags.

Although wives knew something serious was happening, pilots were not supposed to say anything about what was really going on. They didn't want anyone to give out information. Even Yvan wouldn't tell me what was in the works.

I began watching every plane that landed like all of the other women and wives. Every day we were holding our breath fearfully counting the planes coming back, each woman wondering whether her love was in one of them or not.

After just two days of being back in London, the Americans were arriving there. We noticed that many American soldiers were wearing their medals when getting ready for combat. Although Yvan had many medals, he wouldn't wear them. General de Gaulle had made an announcement to all French soldiers saying, "Nobody should wear their medals. When we get back to France then maybe you can put them on, but until then no medals." So, they didn't do it.

Kaye was coming to see me a lot in London about this time, and I would get all of these phone calls. I would answer the phone and hear a man's voice say, "I'm so and so, and I'm looking for Kaye to go dancing."

On one occasion, I received a call and a man said, "I'm coming into London. I want to dance with Kaye."

Trying to speak English, I asked, "Who are you?"

"Who am I?"

"Yes, who are you?"

"Is Kaye there?"

"No."

He then said, "Just tell her this is her boyfriend."

Surprised, I questioned, "Boyfriend?"

Wanting to know how she could get in touch with him, I asked, "How did she meet with you?"

He responded, "Just call General Eisenhower's headquarters."

He concluded by saying pleasantly, "Tell her to cancel all of her appointments."

When Kaye arrived, she told me about him and that he was General Eisenhower's *aide-de-camp*, an officer who was a confidential assistant to the General.

Kaye was a lot of fun and she would come every time she could. During one of her visits, Kaye told me that Irene was now with UNRRA, the United States Relief and Rehabilitation Administration, which later became a part of the United Nations. It was a relief agency for the victims of war and provided food, fuel, clothing, shelter, medical and other basic necessities and essential services.

\*\*\*

The weather in England was always cloudy, clammy and dark. It already made the atmosphere depressing. Now, a cloud of anxiety and apprehension was looming. A sort of climatic fear seemed to be spreading across the country. The atmosphere was so heavy it could strangle your lungs.

Sometimes even as I think about it now, it literally takes my breath from me all these years later. The quality of your breath can indicate your current state of being. If it is shallow and irregular, then something is wrong. It's a sign to come back to center.

I realize now that, although I was not practicing physical yoga postures, breath was my foundation. It was my pulse beat and my barometer. Right at that moment, I knew something serious was brewing. There was a murmur that we were preparing for D-Day, an extraordinary combat attack to beat the Nazis.

We all seemed to be on pins and needles waiting, not knowing exactly what to expect. Everyday people were listening to their little radios for any news on the war, but even then the news was concealed. Nobody was allowed to talk about it, even amongst themselves. Everybody gathered waiting for the invasion to happen. We were all waiting, waiting, waiting almost every minute.

The momentum seemed to grow. A huge army was gathered coming from all parts of England. Airports filled with anti-aircraft guns were prepared for the fight. The Allies were readying to prevent the Germans from crossing the Channel.

Then, we heard the incredible news. D-Day had arrived—June 6, 1944. It sort of silenced everyone. I found out later that it was supposed to be the day before but the weather had delayed it.

Hundreds of ships filled with Allied troops were amassed between Great Britain and the French coast. Spitfires were prepared to locate targets and guide the gunfire of the ships. There was such intensity. I wondered about Yvan. He was in the middle of this dangerous activity. I really felt as though I was going to simply explode.

Every time a plane came in or a bomber flew over there was a sense of anticipation. At one point, I saw something like twenty bombers cross over the sky towards France. I was relieved to know they were not enemy planes. They were our Allies.

Somehow the Germans got news of the intended invasion of the French coast. The battle of sky and sea was massive as the Allies tried to reach the beaches of France.

If we heard a wailing, we knew the Germans were trying to come in across England but they were being stopped or shot down. We could see the Allied planes and Spitfires blazing through the sky. Everybody would hastily dive into air raid shelters.

The horror was unbelievable as hundreds were shot by German guns that were amassed along the coast line. Everyone on both sides witnessed the horror of war, hate and destruction.

The Free French Forces joined in on the D-Day invasion, flying cover for the landings on the beaches of Normandy in France. It was a tremendous show of force—the British, Americans, Canadians, French and others coming together.

So many more boys lost their lives. All I could do was wait for news from Yvan. Now I look back with pride that he played such an incredible role on that important day. Guimas said he took a picture of General de Gaulle on a boat looking at France on D-Day.

Guimas was simply remarkable taking photographs of what was happening. That's how he ended up filming D-Day when it happened. Later I asked, "How could you get this photograph of all of the French soldiers advancing? You had your back to the enemy."

He said, "Well, as long as I couldn't see them I wasn't afraid."

With his back to the enemy, he was filming all of the French boys dashing out. He was extraordinary. He later filmed in Indochina before the Americans came into what is now called Vietnam. He was always in the middle of the action.

*General Charles de Gaulle in England in June 1944. Image taken by my dear friend, Guimas. He said de Gaulle was on a boat in the English Channel looking at the French coast on D-Day. All around were soldiers invading against the Germans.*

Right at this momentous time, our friends Marcel and Rita were married. There was now hope that the war was coming to an end.

Soon after D-Day, General de Gaulle set foot on French soil after being exiled for four years. They still tried to kill him but he was so brave as he walked towards Notre Dame Cathedral without fear. He was the very magnificent symbol of France.

In his speech to the French he said, "Paris outraged, Paris broken, Paris martyred, but Paris liberated!"

After that, the Germans launched another attack on Normandy and General Eisenhower sent in paratroopers from America.

It was a great day in August 1944 when the Allied troops marched through Paris signaling its liberation. I knew soon we would be going home, if not to India, it would certainly be to France.

*** 

It wasn't quite over though. The Ile-de-France Squadron and the other squadrons in the south of France continued to support the efforts. The high of General de Gaulle being back in France was met with the low of watching every plane again.

Nightclubs were still filled with people seeking some levity. Yvan, like many of the French pilots, loved jazz and swing. It was during the time of all the big bands. Whenever we got the chance and Yvan was not flying, we would go to the nightclub and listen to some music. The Nazis were against jazz and the British seemed indifferent.

The famous bandleader Glenn Miller would come in uniform. He had actually come to see me perform and was really nice. He had joined the United States Army Air Force Band.

His band entertained the troops and would play with some of the people that were there in the clubs. Other musicians, like the famous drummer Gene Krupa, would come. I met some of them previously but didn't really know their music well. My husband, though, could name every single jazz musician telling me who played what and who was in which orchestra.

We were there the night Glenn Miller disappeared. We went to a club east of London. René, who first brought Yvan and the other Free French pilots into the Wellington Club, was with us. The next day Glenn Miller flew off and nobody knows what happened after that whether he was shot down or what. His plane apparently vanished somewhere over the English Channel.

It was still a stressful time. So many pilots were being shot down during the Battle of the Bulge and each time my fears for Yvan grew once more. I lost many friends.

Yvan received news that his brother, whom he had lost contact with when the war started, was in England in an adjoining squadron so we were worried about him as well. I was lucky that Yvan came home to me. So many young men didn't. One day, Marcel did not return to base. His body was never recovered. Rita was devastated.

Joy and sadness seemed to intermingle. One day, Yvan returned home with a big smile on his face. The young man with him was his brother who had been in the French Air Force at the beginning of the war and had escaped to North Africa. Waiting for a new squadron to be formed, we had the pleasure of having him with us for a couple of months. After that he was killed.

I received the sad news that my aunt in France died right after D-Day. Although I had spent less than a year with her, she made a lasting impression on me. I admired her fearlessness and desire to help people. Our beautiful family vineyard had apparently been destroyed by the Germans, and when I went back years later it had been built over. In her will, my aunt left her assets to causes related to nature and animals. I'm glad I saw her that time in Saint-Jean-de-Luz. She knew I had her resilient spirit and would be okay. She never met Yvan, but I'm sure she would have liked him very much.

There were so many dark moments during the war. Being in love made everything seem a bit brighter. The exhilaration of love transcends almost everything. Love helps you experience life. It is a shared journey, part of the sacred dance. It is like the tango. Even when your partner is leading, your energy still has to come from within so you can do your part and express your Self. As your steps become coordinated, the dance becomes more beautiful. No matter what the surroundings, war or other distress, the beauty of love can bring immense light like the moon brightens the night.

> *The exhilaration of love transcends almost everything.*

CHAPTER 11

# Be Present For Good

The Eternal Energy springs across the Universe and is there for us and is within us. It is in the vast heavens, which vibrate in every atom and the breath that puts life into every entity on this planet. There is good all around us. It is meant for us to tap into. We simply have to be present to see it and receive it.

*There is good all around us. We simply have to be present to see it and receive it.*

Although Paris had been liberated, the war was still really bad throughout the northeastern part of France, which was not completely liberated. Champagne, northeast of Paris, and Strasburg, on the German frontier, were still under enemy control. They were going northeast to Belgium, Holland, Denmark and all the way across to Germany. The southern part of France was liberated.

Our military was in Paris and the American soldiers were there also, but the wives of soldiers were not allowed to go yet. Even though Paris was free, we had to wait several months.

Once Yvan was able to land his plane in the airfield of Paris, the first thing he did was to shop for me. He was loaded down with presents. He bought me twenty-four pairs of earrings and every imaginable kind of perfume and underwear, including this beautiful silk nightgown.

He had the funniest story of his return with my gifts. Since he brought back to England more than he was supposed to, he wore the silk nightgown under his clothes in order to not pay customs. Unfortunately, it fell down below his pants. The officers didn't know what to think! He was so serious by nature but could certainly make me laugh.

About the lingerie, Yvan's friends teased him saying, "How did you know her size and what she likes?"

He answered, "I know my wife!"

He came back laden with presents from Paris.

As the months went by, I was still entertaining the troops in London. There were a lot of bombers coming in. Dover was still a dangerous zone and you couldn't go through. London was packed with people.

Then, I had a miscarriage and Yvan didn't want me to work. He felt I should take care of myself. Losing the baby was very sad and not performing after starting up again was a big adjustment.

***

The war was still on but Paris was free. Yvan was already there. I was happy when he called me up and told me the wives could come to Paris. He said that we should buy two bicycles. Cars were hard to come by.

We were finally going home, repatriated back to France. It was a country I knew only briefly when I stayed with my aunt and when I worked in the French Resistance, but I was still excited. I was half-French and would soon live like a real Parisian.

I said goodbye to my friends such as Noël, Guimas, Marlene, Bobby, and Surah. Some who had been based in London were scattering. My agent-friend was going up north in England to where he was originally from. I think Mr. Moore was going to stay with his sisters in Bournemouth. Yvan suggested that I bring Rita with me so she could try and make contact with Marcel's family. There were other military wives trying to make it to France.

The train leaving London was packed. A lot of people were trying to get back to France and Belgium. There were officers from Scotland Yard at the station trying to keep it orderly. They were going around looking at people when they went through. There were so many trying to get back home. I was happy to begin a new chapter of our lives.

We didn't quite know what we were going to do in Paris. We had no real place to stay. The military had taken certain hotels for the soldiers and put us in them but it was a temporary thing. I wasn't worried though. Things always seemed to work out. You never know how the pieces of your life will come together. You simply have to remain open and optimistic.

Since I had become well known in the best cabarets in London and had been in several movies, I almost immediately got a small part in a revival theatrical production of La Terre est ronte with Pierre Fresnay. I got it last minute when they were changing the cast. It was a play that opened while the war was on. Yvan saw how excited I was to be working again so he supported it and was happy for me.

> *You never know how the pieces of your life will come together. You simply have to remain open and optimistic.*

I felt that if I kept in my mind that good would happen, it would. I was getting into the conscious practice of calling up my "Inner Diary" for guidance, lessons I had learned from nature and the great Masters. I could hear my uncle say, "Look for the good and something beautiful will happen."

Rita kept looking in vain for Marcel's family. We knew he had a sister so I helped in the search.

\*\*\*

As life seemed to be settling into a routine, the war finally ended. One day, I was walking along the Champs-Élysées and a woman in uniform came up to me with her arms extended like she was about to hug me. She said, "Oh, you're the very person that we need so badly."

Confused, I asked, "What do you mean? I don't know you."

Still caught up in the moment of having found a solution to a problem, she continued, "Yes, but you entertained our troops in London. I saw you there. You dance and were at the theatre up on the White Cliffs of Dover. During the war you used to climb the Cliffs to entertain the troops. Everybody talked about you."

I would go places that were offbeat even for the English.

Reflective and curious, I inquired, "Yes I did, but what has that got to do with me now?"

With enthusiasm, she explained, "I'm with the Women's Auxiliary Corps of the American Armed Services. We are called WACs for short. We have over 2,000 girls in hotels in Paris and we don't know really what to do with them."

Although I didn't understand all that she said, I had heard about the WACs and wanted to know more. I continued to listen with great interest as she continued, "Many of the duties that these dedicated women had during wartime no longer exist and they want to remain in the WACs. We've heard that the Germans are now as far away as Salzburg so we think the war is almost over. We need to send the girls out but we've got to find out what they can do. We need somebody to come and help us put together some shows. Are you free for a job?"

Confident that I could do the job, I immediately said, "Yes."

She gave me the details for how to start. I would be showing an American General the performances I came up with for his approval. I was excited about being asked to train the girls how to entertain the troops. It would give them work and at the same time they would be going out to boost the morale of the soldiers.

I hurried back to the hotel to give Yvan the news. About to burst with excitement, I was so happy he was still in our room. On seeing him, I blurted out, "Yvan, I have been hired for an important job!"

Without pause, I cheerfully began to tell him the story of my unusual encounter on the Champs-Élysées.

Yvan was always encouraging saying, "You are so very talented and I know you can do this." He held me in his arms and kissed me. We decided to celebrate.

I had a chance to meet some of the American girls who had been put up at the best hotels in Paris. They were shipped in from England because it was too expensive to stay there. Even though there were some language barriers, I knew we could find a way to communicate. When I went to the bathroom, I noticed something I thought was so funny. They were using the bidets to put their ice and other stuff in. It really wasn't for that purpose.

I decided to tell them an amusing story that the French would have fun telling their American friends. There was this American couple that had just gotten married and was on their honeymoon at this little hotel in Paris. The owner was very proud of his hotel and so he graciously showed the couple their room.

The bride looked in the bathroom and saw the bidet. She joyfully said to her husband, "Oh Joe, look at the little bath to wash the baby in."

The hotel owner quickly responded, "Oh, no Madam. Not to wash the baby in, to wash the baby out!"

We all laughed. I could see that they had a great sense of humor and felt even more strongly that I would be able to teach them to bring laughter and fun to the war worn soldiers.

My mind started racing with planning the project. I wondered, "What can I teach them?" I began to reflect on all of my encounters with American soldiers and remembered that during my time in England, I learned how to swing and jitterbug.

I smiled inside as I thought about an American pilot who said he knew "a French girl who could out dance them all." He got his whole squadron to come to London and they had a bet on it. He made money off of me but I didn't know what he was doing at first. We became friends and they taught me how to swing and jitterbug. I liked the free-flowing improvisational feel of the dance.

Also I had heard all of the American boys, particularly from the South, calling each other "Joe." They would say, "Hi Ya Joe!" They were calling all of the girls "Chicks." I decided that it would be a good idea to make the troops laugh a little bit so I created a jitterbug wedding.

I met with some of the girls and was given a place to rehearse. We had loads of fun preparing the performance to show the General.

Since I couldn't find any flowers, I used a huge cauliflower and put a ribbon around it to look like a bouquet. Then, I had one girl pretend to be the bride and another girl pretend to be the man and someone behind to marry them. It went something like this:

"Will you take this Chick to be your wife?"

And the orchestra and everybody went "A tick, tick tick—a tick, tick, tick."

"Will you take this Joe to be your man?"

The orchestra and everybody again would do "A tick, tick tick—a tick, tick, tick."

"Now you're married I wish you joy."

"First a girl and then a boy."

Then everyone went into a jitterbug.

The General laughed so much he actually pee-peed in his pants. He didn't dare stand up. He approved, "You have to take that chick with you to Salzburg."

One of the girls asked, "What should we call her? Will they let her in?"

The General jovially commanded, "Get her a uniform so she can come with us and put 'Special Service Company' here," pointing to my left shoulder. "Also, try to wrap her hair up as much as possible."

All the girls in uniform had short hair and my hair was very long so they rolled it up.

Yvan enjoyed my show as well and didn't make a fuss when he learned I would be going with the WACs to Austria where the training was to take place. He still had duties as a pilot so I went with his good wishes for success.

I had been on all kinds of boats but had never been on an airplane before. So, my first flying experience was in a parachute plane, the kind where we were facing each other on seats made especially for paratroopers who were ready to jump. As you can well imagine, the seats were not made for comfort, but there were no complaints. We just wanted to get to our destination safely.

When we got to Salzburg, the Germans were still in the barracks so we were held up a bit. As the Germans moved out, the American girls moved in. They wanted me to stay with the officers but I said, "No, if I'm teaching the girls, I want to be with them. I can't speak very good English. I have to be with these girls so we can get to know each other. In this way, we may understand each other better."

So I stayed with the girls there. We had a lot of fun. We had to first find clothes and everything for the show. I went with them to get things in Salzburg. I don't know how much help I was. I only knew a few things in German like "die Maus ist grau und die Großmutter ist alt" which means "the mouse is grey and the grandmother is old."

The girls tried to make me feel comfortable by giving me everything that had French on it, such as French toast, French mayonnaise, French fries. They were so funny and really nice. That's where I ate my first doughnut. I had never seen a doughnut before. They had a doughnut machine and I was fascinated by it.

The shops were full of French butter and cheese because the Germans had taken so much from France. They would just come and collect what they wanted.

I was delighted when I was taken to the Salzburg Festival Hall, the huge theatre and stage where I would be teaching the girls and where they would be performing. At that time I didn't know the history. I was told that we were using the site of the internationally renowned annual

Salzburg Festival. It was available because the Germans had canceled the festival the year before.

I learned that the festival continued during most of the war, but suffered some major losses of key people and talent. In 1938, the German occupation of Austria meant that several top artists would not, or could not, work in Austria because they were Jewish including Max Reinhardt who was one of the founders of the festival and anti-Fascist Arturo Toscanini. I also learned that Salzburg was Mozart's birthplace. Working in such a beautiful, historic and creative place was great incentive to create some fun shows.

I wondered, "What else can I teach them?" I saw somewhere that Americans liked to ice skate. I didn't really know much about it but decided to make one of the shows about that. In that show, I had all of the girls do a number that looked like they were skating across the stage and tumbling in the snow. It was loads of fun to watch.

I spent a month working with them on different acts and giving them ideas about creating their own shows when they reached their assignments. The girls were then prepared to go out to take over the USOs, the United Service Organizations. They were sent off to different regiments that were scattered all through Europe such as Austria and Hungary, wherever Germans had been.

Yvan and I missed each other and I was ready to return home to Paris. It was perfect timing since Yvan was coming in from flying in Lyon.

I hadn't been back home in Paris very long before I was invited to be in *Images of Israel* at the legendary landmark Parisian concert hall, Salle Pleyel. I was the only person in it who wasn't Jewish. It was quite an honor. They asked me to join it because they knew that my aunt did so much to help people escape the Nazis, and that I had worked with her during my stay at the vineyard.

I never exposed the work I did helping people escape the caves of Paris, not even to Yvan. That part of my life was a secret for many years as I'm sure it was with many women who worked in the Resistance.

The shows I mounted for the WACs were so well received by the troops that I was asked to return and train even more girls. They pleaded, "Come and help us some more."

So I went back through Vienna where the Russians were coming in. They kept looking at my Special Service Company badge and holding us up. Even the American soldiers there didn't know really what it meant. I always seemed to cause or be in these unusual situations.

In any case, I worked another month training the new group in Bad Gastein close to Salzburg, one of the places where the famous German generals would go to as a resort. The girls and I found the Alpine town to be relaxing. We especially enjoyed breathing the pure mountain air and unwinding in the hot springs.

I got to know the girls. One said, "You have to come to America. We have to stay in touch with each other." I liked her very much so we started corresponding.

***

After Bad Gastein, I was offered an opportunity to go to Saint-Brieux in Brittany to do a modeling show. Somewhat reluctant, I revealed, "I've never done anything like that before."

My friend replied with assurance, "Don't worry. There will be pretty dresses. You'll be fine."

So, I figured, "Why not?" That began my modeling career based in Paris.

Since I had "a lot of people on the balcony" and a seventeen-inch waist, I was quite shapely. I also had a somewhat different look being half-French and half-Indian. With the modeling, I could travel a little bit and I liked that. Yvan was proud of me.

I became friends with one of the furriers who had a very elegant shop. He used to sell these beautiful fur coats including minks and everything to the British. He put me in one of his shows. He was the number one fur man in Paris.

One day he inquired, "You're going to England aren't you?"

"Yes," I answered with what I have been told is my signature smile. I was planning on seeing my special family who had given me their name when I was brought into England at the death of my mother. I had reconnected with them during the war. Whenever I could, I would try to visit them. I wanted to bring them food that was still rationed there. Meat was a big delicacy so I brought them cheeses and steaks, or a roast. I was looking forward to seeing them this time, and was going to pop in to see Olwen Vaughn as well.

The furrier asked, "Would you do me a favor?"

"Well, yes of course."

He needed someone to take a fur coat over there.

I agreed, "I'll take it over for you."

He wondered, "But can you go through?"

Always optimistic and still very innocent to the ways of the world, I nodded and assured him, "Yes." I didn't really know what I was getting into.

It turned out I was carrying the fur so that my friend wouldn't have to pay the premium. I didn't know that you had to pass through the police and everything.

My friend said that if I was questioned by the police I had to say the fur belonged to me. Although he told me about this before I left Paris, I still did not understand all of the implications.

I took one over and on arriving in London right away a British officer came to me and said, "Hello! You're back!"

Somewhat surprised, I asked, "Do I know you?"

He boasted with a real cockney accent, "Yes, I'm from Scotland Yard. I was there when you were repatriated. Nice to have you back. I won't forget that smile!"

I smiled warmly as I thought, "My goodness! I'd better be careful!"

A few weeks later back in Paris, my furrier friend asked me if I would do it once more. Of course I said yes! So, on my next trip, I took the fur off and gave the coat to the people with my case. Then, I went directly over to the policeman and said, "Hello! I'm back." I thought it was better to be bold than to try and sneak by him.

When I look back, I see the risks I took but didn't think much of them at the time. On reflection, I see that I really didn't know what I was doing and was used to helping people when I traveled.

Those first few months in Paris were strange but fun. The stresses of the war were over and the soldiers were all waiting around wondering what to do, whether they could get a job. I was rediscovering Yvan. It was glorious. We were enjoying a somewhat normal married life for the first time. Joie de vivre filled the air.

I also fell in love with Paris with Yvan by my side walking along the Champs-Élysées, going to the clubs to listen to jazz and riding bicycles up to visit Yvan's mother to the north of Paris near St. Cloud. St. Cloud is one of the places the Germans gave orders to blow up but she made it through.

Her home was in a village called Garches, one of the suburbs surrounding Paris. It was about half an hour if we took the train. We could get a train from near there and then would have to walk a couple of miles. A lot of times we took our bicycles but it was all uphill. I wasn't too keen on that but we started to see her quite a bit. She liked me very much and treated me like a daughter. I realized that I missed the feeling of having a family, of not being alone.

*\*\*\**

I saw my old friend Marlene Dietrich again. We'd had so many good times in London and now she was in Paris. She was having a love affair with French actor, Jean Gabin, who had been in the Free French Forces.

During this period, she was going back and forth to Hollywood to take care of her husband Rudolf Sieber who was sick. She seemed to love him but it was not like a passionate love affair. Marlene was also helping their daughter who was just beginning her acting career entertaining the troops as Marlene did.

Marlene had a terrific sense of humor. Honestly! She was not like the Swedish starlet Greta Garbo who had an air of "don't touch me." Garbo was beautiful and alluring but would go out wearing the most outlandish clothes. She would say, "I want to be alone," but then wear a gaudy outfit, weird stockings, a big hat and glasses. Nothing matched! With ten colors and that getup, she made more people look at her.

Paulette Goddard was similar to Greta Garbo in that way. Paulette was the girlfriend of Charlie Chaplin. She would go out wearing purple socks, a green dress, and big earrings while riding a bicycle. She had the worst clothes imaginable. Everybody could see her woolen stockings. It was a show to watch her go down the Champs-Élysées on that bicycle. I thought Charlie Chaplin was rather unusual so I suppose they made a good pair. In any case, one should be able to express oneself without care of judgment.

*One should be able to express oneself without care of judgment.*

Marlene performed for the troops right on the front lines. She was amazing. She and Bing Crosby in the trenches would do all of this good undercover and never talk about it. He would get right in with the soldiers and get dirty. Bing Crosby was different from Bob Hope in that way.

I met Bob Hope first in England. He did a lot in terms of entertaining the troops. He made them laugh which is what they needed. Yet he stayed on the big stage versus getting in the actual trenches like Bing Crosby. Both of them gave the soldiers necessary respite from the stresses of war.

The designer Elsa Schiaparelli gave me my first real modeling job. At one point, she had been more highly regarded by the fashion world than Coco Chanel. She would say, "Le corps marche avec la robe," which meant my body and the clothes were one in the same. She liked the way I modeled.

That led me to be taken to famous French designer Jeanne Lanvin, founder of the Lanvin fashion house, a true couturière making exclusive custom-fitted clothes for the high class. Her fragrance, Arpège, was extremely popular along with Jean Patou's perfume Joy, Coco Chanel's No. 5, and Jacques Guerlain's Shalimar. Those were the first famous fashion houses to have perfume divisions. Jeanne Lanvin and her daughter, Marie-Blanche, both married Counts so they were both known as Comtesse or Countess.

I wasn't a number one model for Lanvin. In fact, they didn't like the idea that I smiled all the time. The Countess was helping another young girl from an island in the Indian Ocean-Arabian Sea area like the l'île Maurice or the Maldives and didn't want me in competition. The girl had much darker skin but I was sort of another species of the same type being from India and always wearing saris. We were both deemed "exotic." So, I wasn't really getting as much attention.

Fortunately, Marlene intervened. She was so extraordinary. She was in her pants and had just arrived in a jeep with Bing Crosby, both covered with mud from their visits to the soldiers in the trenches looking as if they needed to get in a bath immediately. She had no makeup on, hair in a mess. You wouldn't have recognized her as Marlene Dietrich except for her funny laughter and her voice.

When Marlene heard I was a model at Jeanne Lanvin, she went straight to Lanvin saying, "I want a dress and I don't want it on any other model except Täo." Everyone in my family and in France said that Täo was my "real name" and it fit me better than Andrée so I started to use it for everything again.

Marlene wanted a dress for that evening to wear at the Olympia Theatre. When I got there and put on this beautiful yellow dress, I thought I looked like the cat's whiskers. I thought I looked so good.

She liked the dress and took her filthy shoes off asking, "Can I borrow your shoes?"

Of course I said, "Yes."

She cleaned up a bit and put the outfit on. Then, I really understood what "chic" meant. Even without makeup she was incredibly glamorous. I realized that I had a lot to learn and a long way to go to be as enchanting.

That's what you call elegance—coming in right from the trenches with mud on her and transforming right before my eyes. I was just thrilled and learned my first lesson in being a mannequin. I used to try to copy her, everything she did. She was a real sweetheart.

Lanvin was promoting the other girl and I didn't have much success there. Jeanne Lanvin's nephew Maurice, who held sway on the opposite side of the road running the men's department of Lanvin, told the Countess that she was "losing out not using me more."

One day Maurice took action on what he believed and said, "Get your things. Today, I'm taking you to meet Jean Dessès."

I was delighted to be introduced to the very famous and chic couturier who, along with Christian Dior, was bringing his fashions to people from around the world. Immediately, this marvelous Greek fashion designer liked me and made me a number one model of his collection. People would come in from places like Brazil and Alexandria and buy ten dresses at a time to take back.

This brought a new turn in my modeling career and I was enthralled. It took on more importance because Jean Dessès designed the dress that Prince Phillip's mother, Princess Alice of Greece, wore for his marriage to Princess Elizabeth II who is now Queen Elizabeth. That dress was draped on me.

I liked wearing clothes from Jean Dessès and went with him all over the place. That made me famous. He was very charming and he liked me a lot. His clothes were very elegant, just right for me. He would say, "Täo, when you wear something you look like it was made expressly for you. You always make the dress look its value."

Coco Chanel then hired me because of that. France had a history of strong women and Chanel was one of them. Nobody could stand in her way.

*Famous Greek couture designer Jean Dessès is draping a dress on me for Princess Alice of Greece, mother of Prince Phillip for his marriage to Princess Elizabeth II. This was featured in a French newspaper.*

Chanel liked suits and was more mannish in her style. I like feminine clothes. With the tiniest waist, I was considered very glamorous, but it was not ideal for Chanel. She made boyish things very straight up and down. I didn't show her clothes to advantage because I had curves and wasn't that style at all, but she still hired me on several important occasions. I also did work for the design house of Jean Patou.

It was a completely different life for me. Up to that point my life had always been an adventure, whether as a child growing up in India learning about peace or as a young adult in Europe experiencing the war.

*Modeling in Paris in one of my Indian outfits in the late 1940s. It's one of the few pictures I still have where you see my long hair.*

Now, I was discovering how to be sophisticated, learning to walk like a queen. For instance, there was this very famous artist and designer named Christian Bérard. He was an architect for big châteaux and interiors including set designs used in theatre. He also drew for designers such as Jean Patou and Christian Dior. We called him Bébé Bérard. He was in high society in Paris. People fawned on him. What he said was gospel.

*Modeling in Paris in the late 1940s. I'm wearing either Jean Dessès or Jean Patou.*

One day I was walking across the street to see Jean Dessès. He had moved into a new palace-type château on Avenue Montaigne. It was very lovely. I saw Bébé Bérard coming towards me and began to back away slightly. He was somewhat loud which was not really my sensibility. He was a bit obnoxious but everyone in theatre and couture gathered around him.

He saw me and exclaimed so the entire street could hear, "Täo

Cherie, elle marche comme une panthère." He was saying, "You walk like a panther."

Jean Dessès was up in the window in hysterics. He said laughingly, "All of the others would have been delighted to be there with Bébé and Täo you just back up from him!" Modeling brought some humorous encounters.

\*\*\*

The war had ravaged France for six years and now the Nazi oppression was over. A day after Germany surrendered to the Western Allies, General de Gaulle announced the end of World War II to the French. A fête de la victoire, WWII Victory Day, is still celebrated on May 8th each year. When Japan surrendered in September, World War II officially came to an end. It was like a cloud was lifted.

With the weight of war gone, everything seemed lighter. We enjoyed a carefree time for the first year and a half of being in Paris. Yvan and I loved each other very much. He was still determining what to do next and started to look for work.

Yvan was pleased that my modeling career was taking off. I knew I could always go to him for advice or comfort. I wanted so badly for him to find a career or even a job, otherwise we might have to go to the Orient where he grew up.

My modeling was catching the attention of top designers and celebrities, and taking me places like Holland, Norway, Sweden, Morocco and Switzerland. Through modeling I met Louis Vaudable, the owner of the famous Maxim's restaurant on rue Royale. Some of the most fashionable events were held there.

Louis' father Octave Vaudable was known for preferring the most prestigious clientele. Louis knew all the models and they would go to the restaurant with their boyfriends because it was the place to be seen in Paris.

All of the fashion houses wanted their models in their dresses to be photographed at places like Maxim's and the horse races. We would go down the Champs-Élysées in horse and buggies with these exquisite couture hats and dresses. On one modeling assignment for Jean Dessès I was photographed in the middle of the Champs-Élysées.

*On the Champs-Élysées in Paris modeling Jean Dessès dress right after being repatriated around 1946. You can see the Arc de Triomphe in the background and very few cars on the road.*

I even won a contest for "Girl with the Longest Legs" in Europe. I was with Dominique Fournier, a French model who worked at Hermes next door to Lanvin. She was dating and later married Jean Gabin. She even looked a bit like his old love, Marlene Dietrich.

*With Dominique Fournier in Juan-les-Pins in France, late 1940s. She later married Jean Gabin. Some of the pictures back then were tiny!*

There was an international model show in the south of France and I was there with a group of girls. We were right on the beach at Juan-les-Pins in Cap d'Antibes. Dominique came running to get a hold of me for a competition that was going on. All the girls were in their bathing suits standing high on a platform. Seeing what was going on, I told them with a big smile, "I'll go in only if you give me number thirteen."

Shaking her head with surprise, Dominique quickly said, "Oh no, you can't do that."

"Thirteen is unlucky," all the girls seemed to agree as a chorus.

In fun, I countered, "It has always been a good number for me!"

I didn't really want to do it but they dragged me back. They gave me number thirteen and I won the contest!

In retrospect, I recall that I signed the contract for MGM on the thirteenth. On the other hand, the year 2013 was a bad year because I had to have surgery. In any case, I think you make your own luck.

*Voted "Girl with the Longest Legs" in Europe at a contest in Juan-les-Pins, France in 1946. Dominique Fournier encouraged me to enter.*

Dominique introduced me to Prince Kolnoski. I believe he was part of the royal family in Russia. He was apparently very close to Prince Edward from England who was King until he married the American woman, Wallis Simpson.

I never really paid attention to people's titles or jobs. If they were nice, that's what mattered. If they wanted to tell me more about themselves, they could but I wouldn't pry.

Prince Kolnoski said he had escaped from Russia and he had a big home in Antibes. He was quite charming and took a liking to me.

Thinking of Yvan, I said, "I'm married."

His reply was, "That doesn't matter. Just being out with you is such a pleasure."

When I was in Antibes, we would go to dinner. He started sending me flowers, a gesture Yvan didn't like when he found out. Still, we kept in touch when I visited the area.

*Prince Kolnoski from Antibes in France around 1946. He was part of the Russian royal family and quite enamored with me even though I was married. Dominique Fournier introduced us.*

\*\*\*

Even though my life was filled with the glamour of modeling for the top fashion houses, my personal life with my husband and our friends was not neglected.

Some of us from Yvan's Free French Squadron would get together to have fun. We would meet at the commissary on the Champs-Élysées until they closed it. We would convene at the French club in the heart of Paris. On the weekends we would go out into the countryside to relax, usually about nine of us, to Sancerre in the Loire Valley.

The town was on top of a hill and is where the famous Sancerre wine is made. I found out later that it had been a command center for the French Resistance. Yvan still didn't know about my dangerous underground work and I didn't intend on telling him. I wanted to leave wartime behind.

*Yvan walking down the hill in Sancerre, France where we met Ernest Hemingway. We went there to relax on the weekends with some of the other pilots.*

It was spring and the weather was getting warmer. Yvan loved to swim. He would go in the Loire River down below and swim all day with the other boys. At night, they would climb up on top of this hill and we would have dinner. I simply enjoyed being around nature versus the crowded city. The town itself was quaint with a long medieval history.

One evening we were sitting there having dinner and there was a tall rather robust gentleman sitting alone. He had been staying at the same hotel. He came over to our table and speaking slowly in French asked very graciously if he could offer us something to drink.

One of the boys in our group was quick to respond in French, "You're sitting alone. Would you like to join us?"

He did, and we had a great evening laughing, talking and enjoying the fine Sancerre wine.

*Yvan and me in Sancerre.*

This curious man learned that all of the guys were Free French fighter pilots of the No. 340 Ile-de-France Squadron and that we had been in England during the war. Since he was an American, we were impressed that he knew so much about the squadron and its commitment to the liberation of France.

He soon singled me out because I was the only girl with the group of young pilots and I was wearing my sari, which is what I would put on in the evenings. He was intrigued with me and wanted to know about India. Since I left India, my life had been so full of activities that I had not reminisced very much about my childhood home.

In our conversations, he seemed to know how to open me up. I talked about so many wonderful memories growing up under the influence of my gurus, especially my uncle and Gandhi. He seemed to never run out of questions. You always knew he was really listening.

Soon, he even got up early in the morning to have coffee with us. We didn't drink from a cup with a handle. We used big bowls and he'd join us. He told us that he had just spent time in Spain and was in Sancerre writing. He must have learned more about us than we did about him. I gathered that he spoke fluent Spanish because he was in the Spanish war. He had just spent time in Spain and his French was certainly better than my English.

This went on for seven weekends, coffee in the morning, dinner and wine in the evening. Then, we didn't go down to Sancerre for about two weeks. When we came back, the man at the desk said to me, "Oh, Monsieur has been asking about you."

Puzzled, I answered, "Monsieur qui?"

He said, "You know, Monsieur Hemingway."

Still puzzled, I said, "I don't know who that is."

A little surprised, he said, "Yes, you know he is a famous writer. He wrote *Pour qui sonne le glas*. He stayed here an extra week because he wanted to see you again. He liked you and your husband very much."

Remembering our American friend, I answered, "Oh, but of course. He was so much fun to talk with."

The desk clerk lamented, "Yes, he's left now but he was looking for you each weekend you didn't come back."

I learned later that he was the famous writer, Ernest Hemingway who wrote *For Whom The Bells Toll*. He liked France. I did see him once in Paris but I was in a taxi. He was with a group of writers and philosophers like Jean Cocteau who was a French writer with an incredible mind. I liked Hemingway very much. He was so sweet and inquisitive about everything. That time we spent in Sancerre is one of my fondest souvenirs.

As the world around us was calming down, new experiences were around every corner. I was grateful for that. As long as I remained open, interesting things and people would appear. It was yet another reminder of our connectedness. I believe you can draw good to you by thinking good thoughts. It sounds silly but it's true. It's not magic but it can feel magical when it happens. You're tapping into the Eternal Energy. When you feel it inside of you, anything is possible. Let this incredible power sprout in you so you can enjoy its bounty.

*You can draw good to you by thinking good thoughts.*

*Part Two*

# The Real & Unreal

The answers are not in the man-made world,
but in the beauty of nature and if you listen
to your inner self, you will hear the
music of the song of life.

CHAPTER 12

## Change With The Seasons

Life is an unfolding, like the changes of the seasons. Nothing stays the same, Flowers bloom and die. Leaves turn colors. Winter strips many branches. Things are bright and then may seem barren. The cycle continues. The energy is never truly destroyed it simply transforms. In life, these shifts are sometimes uncomfortable because you don't know what is going to happen. In those times, I once again looked to nature, my encyclopedia, knowing that each season has a purpose.

*Life is an unfolding, like the changes of the seasons.*

As my career was growing, Yvan was reaching a low point. It was a hard time for him because he was having difficulty finding work. Bomber pilots were hired immediately into jobs with Air France because they piloted large planes.

The Spitfire fighter pilots were all having trouble. They flew smaller planes and many, including Yvan, suffered long-lasting injuries. There were no jobs left for them and it was very disillusioning. They had survived after doing so much for the war and now couldn't find work.

The tiny fighter planes were always in first to shoot down enemy planes. With a bomb on the nose of the plane, it was extremely dangerous. You can see it now in war movies. For Yvan and the other pilots, it was real.

As they were coming down, they would let the bomb blow up just as the plane was traveling over the target. Sometimes their plane would get hit. Many of our friends were lost in this way. Tragically, about twenty friends died in two weeks.

Yvan was in a lot of these dive-bombing episodes and he was starting to bleed for no reason. Often he would be dripping with blood from his nose. We would be riding a bicycle in Paris or going to meet his mother, and suddenly I'd see blood dripping down.

At that time, all the people who were unsettled from the war were trying to decide where to go. Australia and New Zealand were enticing the French and others to migrate there and work. Certain places in South America were also open such as Paraguay, Uruguay and Chile. Some of the Germans were hiding in Chile. We decided to learn Spanish together and explore opportunities in South America.

Yvan could learn a language very fast. It was amazing. That's one thing that made me fall in love with him. He reminded me of my uncle in that way. He learned Spanish in no time. I was much slower. I tend to ponder over things and I'm inclined to make up words if I don't find them in the book.

Yvan couldn't fly for Air France because he wasn't a bomber pilot. Finally, he was offered a job with Air France but it was based in Uruguay. We didn't have enough money for both of us to go and I was becoming famous as a model. His salary at the end of the war wouldn't even pay for one week where we lived. I didn't speak Spanish that well yet and I didn't know whether I could get a job there myself.

I encouraged him to take the job, "You go. You don't have to worry about me. It's going to take you a little time to get across in the boat. I am earning enough at least to sustain myself."

I figured I could make enough to join him later. Reluctantly, he got on a merchant boat and left. It took him five weeks to get there. Even though Air France was one of the first airlines to do long flights, they were not paying his expense.

In his first letter to me from Montevideo, the capital of Uruguay, Yvan told me that the job was not as fruitful as he had anticipated. I knew he was disappointed again, and felt helpless to support him.

My modeling career continued to blossom with work for Jeanne Lanvin and others designers, but I felt so lonely and alone without Yvan. I tried not to let it affect my mood too much because I knew I had to continue on and make a living.

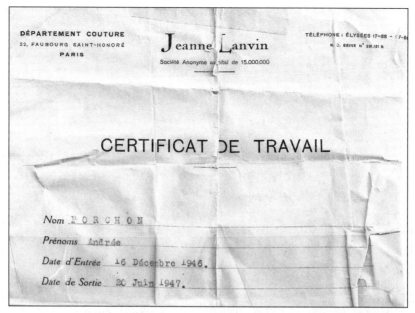

*Work Certificate issued June 30, 1947 for Jeanne Lanvin Couture modeling assignment.*

One modeling show I did in Switzerland in August 1947 was especially memorable. Prince Michael of Yugoslavia was in the audience. The famous American actress Rita Hayworth was there as well with her new boyfriend, the tennis player, not the Indian Maharaja.

Since I could "walk like a panther," Jean Dessès always gave me clothes that nobody else could walk in because they were very tight. The other girls didn't like those types of dresses but I didn't mind.

St. Mortiz was a magical place, very high up. I got a little bit of altitude sickness. Even though we were there to show the new collection, for dinner we had to wear dresses that were from previous shows. In this way, we could showcase the dresses belonging to each of the different fashion years.

Since the dresses for dinner were not from the current show, the models could choose what they would wear. This particular time I wasn't feeling well so I was the last to get dressed. By the time it was my turn, they'd grabbed all of the best dresses so the only one left was much too big for me. They had to sew me into it.

All the other girls had gone downstairs. Everybody was seated and having dinner and I knew I would be making my entrance alone.

*Modeling at the Palace Hotel in St. Moritz, Switzerland in August 1947. I'm on the rostrum and Prince Michael of Yugoslav and Rita Hayworth were in the audience.*

There was a magnificent orchestra playing. As soon as I made an appearance at the top of the stairs to come into the ballroom, the orchestra stopped. As I started to walk down, the whole orchestra turned to face me and started playing, "She's so beautiful..." All the girls, except my best friend Maggy Sarragne, were furious because they had not made an entrée at all, only me.

Later, when they started playing the Viennese waltz, a man came over to me and asked, "Do you like to waltz?"

I didn't really know what he was saying. I just smiled and followed him. I stood out because the dress was so beautiful. It seemed to float around me swishing as I moved. I did the Viennese waltz with him, and then again.

The next day he followed us when we went up in the mountains overlooking Switzerland's Italian side in Pontrasina. He was there the following day, and there were flowers for me.

*In Pontrasina at the Italian Frontier during St. Mortiz modeling trip in August 1947 for Jean Dessès. With Greg, Arlette, Jacqueline, two friends of Greg, journalist Cri-Cri, and "my den mother" Olga. Above: I am on the left at the end. Below: I am second to the left.*

When I got back to Paris I received a big bottle of Shalimar perfume every month. I didn't know it was worth so much and I was giving it away to everyone. I also didn't know who was sending it. The note was written, "To Little Princess Shalimar from your Secret Admirer."

Everybody was teasing me. It was quite amusing. We found out later that my secret admirer was this nice Jewish man who owned a company that made cameras. It was flattering but Yvan had my heart.

On January 30, 1948, I heard news that really shook me. Radios and newspapers were all blasting the headline, "Mahatma Gandhi Assassinated!" He had been shot three times in the chest outside of Birla House in Delhi, India. There had been previous assassination attempts over the years but this one was fatal.

I was so shocked. My mind just went blank like I was in a stupor. I don't remember thinking about anything. I felt like I was stabbed in the heart with a massive icicle. This great friend of my uncle who was a symbol of peace had influenced my life so immensely. He acted on what he believed and his work wasn't just for India. The ordinary man on the street knows of Mahatma Gandhi because he stood for Oneness and freedom throughout the world. I couldn't understand how someone could be so violent toward him. This tragedy added to my sadness of missing Yvan.

\*\*\*

My friend Rita was still in search of Marcel's family and I never gave up looking for his sister on Rita's behalf. I found out that his sister was big with the French Maquis underground and had been captured and put in a German concentration camp.

It was almost two years later after her release that I found her and learned the amazing heroic story of her brother and how he tricked the Germans. The story flashed back to the dangers of wartime and the bravery of so many of the young men.

When he first arrived in England, Marcel was actually fourteen years old, not eighteen as he told authorities. Too young to do anything with the French Maquis, he was still determined to fight for his country. The Nazis had taken over his village and he wanted to find a way to escape from France.

First, he pretended to be younger than his age of fourteen so he could get closer to the German pilots at the air base. By gaining their confidence, he was able to gather pertinent information about flying plans that he passed on to his sister in the French underground.

Even so, his sister wanted him to distance himself from the Germans. She didn't like that he was playing up to them because it was extremely dangerous. Even the villagers were upset with Marcel for hanging around the Nazis. Marcel didn't let any of this deter him.

He became so trusted that they would allow him up close to the planes. He wanted to learn to fly so he asked questions as an innocent child would about their flying techniques and the various airplane controls.

After doing this for several months, he became a sort of mascot to the squadron and was able to go everywhere on the airfield. He wanted them to believe that he was too young to be detrimental to their activities so he treated them like they were his heroes. Marcel would run around cheerfully doing errands, helping them with chores, and even bringing them gifts of Calvados, the French apple brandy.

Watching everything they did very closely, he learned what was happening on the base and how to do certain things. When planes returned to base from an air flight, he would watch the ground crew as they overhauled them and repaired different problems. He was there every day ready to help. He was even allowed to mount into cockpits as they mended the planes.

Marcel knew how to sound so innocent while all the time he was learning first-hand how to repair some of the problems that would pop up. Although they conversed in German, he was quick to understand. He carefully watched what they were doing.

One lucky day by chance he found a small broken-down French plane that had been discarded and put on a junk heap at the far end of the field. Delighted, he started to secretly try to put it together from what he had learned. Slowly, his plan was taking shape. He would help gas up planes and found a way to take some gas each time to his little plane to ready it for an emergency takeoff.

Little by little his work on the plane was falling into place. Some wounded pilots returned in a damaged plane and he was able to find some needed parts. Shortly thereafter, a whole new squadron flew into the base and Marcel could no longer ask questions so easily.

One day, the Gestapo came to the camp and looked at him

suspiciously. The situation was becoming tense. Soon, a German regiment installed itself at a camp near the airport. Now that his village was swarming with soldiers and new German pilots, he realized that it was time to put his escape into practice. Listening to them talk, he decided to prepare for takeoff.

Bringing several bottles of Calvados, Marcel pretended to be joyous about the new regiment that had come. With a big smile for everyone, he encouraged them to drink, happily rejoicing in French, "Grande fête! Grande fête!"

His infectious spirit of celebration caught on and a big party ensued. As the rowdy laughter continued for a couple of hours and dusk started to fall over the airport, a new group flew in and the party started all over again. After he saw that they too were drinking heavily, Marcel just waited.

When they had become drunk and more rowdy than ever, he put his plan into action. Realizing this was the time to make his break, he quietly crept away. The noise from the squadron seemed to show just how much they were inebriated.

As more and more of the boisterous sounds of laughter filled the air, he crept over to his plane. He was feeling good that he had gotten this far without attracting attention. Quietly he made preparations for takeoff trying to remember all of the details of how to fly. Soon, the engine began to purr softly. Filled with anticipation, he carefully followed every maneuver he had heard from the pilots.

Pausing for a silent prayer, he took a few deep breaths knowing that his plan of escape was in action. In the darkness of night, this kid was piloting a plane he put together from scraps and old parts guiding it quietly down the farthest runway from the camp knowing that he could be shot down.

Although he had been studying and carefully gathering information, he still had no real idea about what he was doing. Miraculously, he managed to start up the engine with no problem and get to a takeoff speed moving faster and faster down the runway. Soon, he felt the buoyance of lifting off the ground.

Heart pounding, he found himself airborne within minutes and had hardly any real clue as to whether the direction he was headed was towards the British coast or not. Time passed and everything seemed to be going well, when suddenly the plane engine started to splutter and with a loud breaking sound, he saw that a part of the plane was falling off. Instantly, the plane itself began to plummet and quickly fall apart. Before it hit the water, Marcel managed to dislodge himself from the seat and plunged into the English Channel.

Fortunately, he made it close to the British coast and a small fishing boat was a few yards away. Seeing the plane hit the water, they reached him just in time to drag him into their boat amongst the fish. With a few broken bones, he was quickly taken to shore and carried to the nearest military post. They realized he wasn't German. Hardly able to talk, he eventually gave the British all the vital information about his adventure.

Scared they would not let him fly again, he pretended he was eighteen years old, and was transferred to a military hospital until he had healed. So he found a way to use his age twice to carry out his plan—once making himself younger and then making himself older!

When he was better, Marcel was trained and became a real pilot. That's when we met him. He was then a young well-trained pilot when he was sent to the Ile-de-France Squadron. I never knew whether Yvan had heard the whole story. I thought it was an outstanding display of ingenuity and bravery. We still don't know what happened to him when he disappeared after D-Day but the backstory seemed to give Rita more perspective on her daring love. I think it gave her some peace to be able to move on.

***

Things in France were difficult when Yvan went away. I had been apart from him during the war but this was different. We had experienced a regular life as a married couple and now all of that changed and I was alone again.

Fortunately, I was working a lot. I got a part in *Dr. Knock* with Louis Jouvet. I also did a show with dancing at the Salle de la Chimie. I just made things up like I did in London, some Cambodian dancing and an American Indian drum number.

I was becoming a big star in France and earning enough money so that Yvan didn't have to worry about me, but I really didn't have enough to relocate. Things were in a state of flux. At times I would give things up, modeling and everything, expecting to go to be with him.

Despite all of the glamour, I missed Yvan terribly and would wait in anticipation of his letters. It was extremely hard not to be with him. I needed to find a way to get there.

My friend Maggy was the number one model in the world at the time. She did a lot of work for French designer Christian Dior and was always booked. She came from a very poor family and made it big as a model.

*Left: My best friend Maggy Sarragne who was one of the top models in the world in the 1940s. She recommended me for the tour to America with Lever Brothers after the war. Right: Photo taken of me in Paris for my passport in the Spring of 1948 but they didn't let me use it because my shoulder was nude.*

Maggy had been asked to go to America for a model tour but she had a contract for something else and had to decline.

The tour was apparently a pretty big deal. They were looking specifically for experienced French couture models and asked her, "Who else do you have in mind?"

Right away, she said, "Täo. You should take her. She speaks some English and has a chic smile." So they asked her to see if I would do it.

Immediately I said, "Yes," thinking if I came to America I would be nearer to South America and closer to Yvan. We were talking less and less, and I was getting fewer letters about what was happening. He hardly spoke of what he was doing. My heart was longing to be with him.

I tried to be enthusiastic about the possibility of earning money from a show in America thinking it would bring me closer to him. I didn't realize that from North America to South America, and from France to South America are about the same length of travel. It was just as far away but in a different direction.

I took advantage of the opportunity and was one of the first nine French models to go to America after the war. Lever Brothers chartered two Pan Am planes to fly us all around the country. In those days, Pan Am was a big international airline and would do things with high style.

We had actress Ilka Chase as mistress of ceremony. Her mother was Edna Woolman Chase, the long-time editor-in-chief of *Vogue* magazine. Ilka was known for various roles on Broadway such as *The Red Falcon* and in films such as *No Time For Love*.

A whole production crew came with us for the grand multi-city tour, including the orchestra from the Pierre Hotel, NBC announcer Tony Russo and NBC singer Todd Manners. In addition to the models and these entertainers, there were hairdressers and couturiers of Faubourg St. Honore for promotion of Harriet Hubbard Ayer Hair Style products.

It was May 1948. I remember that it was very warm when we arrived in New York. We didn't stay there long. We went right to Cleveland, Ohio to do a show.

They brought all of the American models to meet us for a welcome lunch. The amount of food was overwhelming, particularly after living on rations during the war.

They came out with big plates, platters really, with a huge sizzling steak dripping with lots of fat. The French models looked at it in shock. None of us ate that much. We asked, "Are you going to cut it up for each of us?"

The girls wanted them to cut the one slab into three pieces and trim all the fat off. We were horrified when we realized that each one of us was getting this big chunk of meat and a huge potato. Our host was going to give me a platter, but I immediately began expressing with my hands and shaking my head "No," trying to indicate, "I don't eat meat."

Looking at me like I was a strange bird, he said, "You don't eat meat. Oh, that's terrible!"

I understood the word "terrible" and was a bit annoyed. I replied using my best English, "No, it's not!"

All the girls were laughing because they had never seen so much meat. I will always remember it. Every time I think of meat, I think of that. I looked at it and was disgusted. I said, "I'll eat the potato." It was the biggest potato I had ever seen.

From Cleveland, we went to the stormy city of Chicago. That's where a radio announcer asked me, "Have you seen the plains?"

I reflected and smiled affably, "Yes, we came over in one."

Confused, he said, "You came over in the plains?"

Comprehending the mistake, he added, "Oh, no I don't mean those planes. You know where we grow all the corn and everything."

Not really understanding him, I said, "Oh, I didn't know."

He then noticed, "You have the tiniest waist I've ever seen. How much is it?"

Being congenial, I said, "About fifty."

All the people started laughing. I gave it in centimeters.

He exclaimed, "Some waist!" demonstrating how hefty that was with his hands. Laughingly, he added, "You can get two of you in that!"

I continued to smile politely as I used my hands to demonstrate my miniscule seventeen-inch waist. I didn't realize how comedic I was. I was the only one of the French models that could say more than two words in English but it still got me in a bit of trouble.

Lever Brothers put on a grandiose event. It was amazing to see. They'd have an immense hall in Macy's stores in different cities and we would do a fashion show. People were wearing big hats in those days in America. They were promoting something to make your own hair curly so the French hairdresser with us demonstrated how to use the product.

There were various people on the program but they liked me mostly because I smiled. Many of the other models didn't smile and they were sort of frightened. They were not used to everything. Since I had traveled with my uncle and throughout the war, I just found new situations interesting. Life should be full of new experiences. That's how you learn and continue to grow.

*Life should be full of new experiences. That's how you learn and continue to grow.*

So, everywhere we went they always featured me and put me in the show. In each city it was a similar setup with Macy's and the demonstrations. I was dressed in clothes from French designer Marcel

Rochas. The clothes weren't made on me as I was used to. They were from an existing collection so they were not the latest but that was fine.

From Chicago we went to San Francisco where they carted me off again to be in a show. There was so much creativity in the air. I would have enjoyed staying there longer but we then went down to Hollywood. The American film producer and director Jack Cummings was there. He had heard about all of the publicity I got from the shows I did in London and then went to see me perform in *Dr. Knock* in Paris.

He gave me his card and said, "I wish I could bring you into MGM but you're not a big enough actress. Still, if you ever come to Hollywood look me up."

People will say to you "give me a call" all the time and you never know if they really mean it, but I kept his card. I found out later that he was the nephew of Louis B. Mayer who co-founded Metro-Goldwyn-Mayer studios or MGM.

*Getting on the plane in Albuquerque, New Mexico as one of the first nine French models brought to the USA for Lever Brothers tour after World War II May–June 1948.*

From Hollywood we went to Albuquerque, New Mexico. From Albuquerque, we went to Boston where I pretty much got kicked out of the city.

Mayor James Michael Curley had just come out of prison. I found out later that he had been convicted of mail fraud. I was hearing all these people talking about him. Since my English was not that good, I didn't really know what they were saying. I understood bits and pieces.

The Americans had packaged the items we were promoting, men's cologne and shaving items from Lever Brothers and Marcel Rochas, with beautiful bows on them. The models were supposed to give these gifts to the Mayor. The Mayor gave the key to the city to Ilka Chase and then waved his hand to dismiss us.

We were standing there with these two packages and I said in the best way I could, "But please Mayor, we're obliged to give you these."

Arrogantly, he asked, "What is it?"

I said, "I think mine is an aftershave lotion from the famous house of Marcel Rochas."

Brashly, he said with a smirk and a chuckle, "Oh, that's that stinking stuff Latin gigolos use!"

I didn't know what he meant. I politely asked, "Won't you accept it?"

People were watching intently. Our exchange was in all the newspapers, "French girl and Mayor…"

The reporters later asked me, "What did you think of the Mayor?"

Since my English was limited, I thought I was safe to repeat what I heard some other press people saying. So I smiled and clearly replied using my best English, "I think he's a 'cinema-beach.'"

Apparently, my statement went on-air throughout the city and other places. I didn't realize that I had made a faux pas nor did I know why they were so worried about me. I kept hearing about him being called a 'cinema-beach.' I thought it was a compliment. They were really calling him a son-of-a-bitch and that's what they thought I said!

Needless to say, they got me out of Boston very fast. I arrived at the Waldorf Astoria Hotel in New York before the others did. We had two days in New York before we left. They took us to a Broadway theatre production and we appeared on a couple of television shows.

We each received $500 for the tour. I left mine with Tony Russo to hold in a bank. The other girls were buying things to take back to France. I figured if I was coming back at some point I would need some dollars here. In those days, it was harder to do a money exchange. Also, I thought I would be able to pay my fare to see Yvan.

From New York, we flew back to France. The entire showcase lasted about three weeks. I didn't make a lot of money but that adventure started me off on a different path.

\*\*\*

The tour in America introduced me to a whole new set of people. I was becoming more known in the U.S. and Europe. After returning home to France, I continued modeling mostly for Jean Dessès, who had become one of my favorite designers. I was still searching for a way to get to Yvan in Uruguay. I missed him terribly. I would earn a little here and there but it never seemed to be enough.

*Back in St. Mortiz, Switzerland in August 1948 with Jean Dessès (far left) and other models. I am fourth from the left.*

*Maggy and me in St. Moritz, August 1948.*

*With friend and fellow model Arianne in St. Moritz.*

*Relaxing in the gardens high up in the mountains at the Palace Hotel in St. Moritz, August 1948.*

I also would spend time in Cap d'Antibes and see my friend, Prince Kolnoski, when I had time.

*The port of Cap d'Antibes, France in August 1948.*

*In Juan-les-Pins in Cap d'Antibes with Prince Kolnoski.*

American actress and producer Lucille Lortel came through Paris. She was married to paper magnate Louis Schweitzer who was also a philanthropist. He had amassed a lot of money making special paper used in the tobacco industry.

Lucille had recently established the White Barn Theatre at their estate in Westport, Connecticut and was looking to help develop young talent. She was intrigued with me and we decided to keep in touch.

Around that time, Lever Brothers invited me back to America. They were planning on doing a television show with Ilka Chase and wanted me to appear in it. I was the only model they asked to come back for the show. It looked like an auspicious opportunity and I learned from my uncle to seize good fortune as it came.

It took me almost a year to get my visa and to get all of the documents needed to work in the country. It was different than coming over on a short tour and there were a lot of underhanded things going on in Paris at the Consulate at the end of the war. Several times when it was my turn to get the visa for America, I didn't get it. People were paying big sums to get them. I finally got my visa and was able to go. It was August 1949.

Soon after arriving, the television show fell through. It was a catastrophe. Ilka Chase didn't test well in the ratings and it all went to pieces. NBC canceled the show.

Once again, I found myself asking, "What would my uncle do?" I was stuck in New York with very little money and no job. I could write English but I still couldn't speak it very well. As I had done before,

I called up my "Inner Diary" for guidance. Worry is not useful. It clouds your mind.

Ilka Chase said, "Oh, you can stay with my secretary."

> *Worry is not useful. It clouds your mind.*

I thought this was a stroke of luck but she ended up being a stout, miserly Scottish woman who wasn't very nice. She gave me a room but she charged me an inordinate amount. The $500 I had given to Tony Russo to hold was pretty much spent and I went through the rest very quickly. Almost every penny was gone within a short time.

This woman charged me for everything! It was $30 a night for the room which was a lot of money at the time. She was charging me for washing the sheets every day but only washed them once a week. She would go shopping and say "this is special food for you" even though it was nothing that I ate. It was a long list of things.

I stayed in her house for a while. Eventually, I didn't have enough to pay her the rent. Here I was stranded in New York. I sent for money that I had in a French bank, but I didn't want to take everything out. It wasn't that much anyway so I was in a bind again.

Even though I had grown up with many luxuries, I had come to realize during the war that I didn't need a lot of things to be happy. I settled into a place for girls on 57th Street for a while. It wasn't very expensive.

I met a lawyer that I had helped in France. He knew some very wealthy people who could use a house sitter. He explained, "These people will let you stay in their apartment. They won't charge you anything. Just keep it nice."

It was a stunning and spacious apartment right opposite the Waldorf Astoria Hotel. I was extremely grateful. Although I was fiercely independent by nature, I had also learned to welcome good fortune.

I got a job modeling but it certainly wasn't like in France. In Europe, you were a big star as a model. You walked and didn't talk to the clients. In America, you almost were the saleslady as well as the model and I wasn't used to that. I remember one girl came in and asked, "What size do you want?"

I said, "What do you mean?"

Pointing to my bust, she said, "What size bust are you going to put in there?"

Surprised, I responded, "I think I have enough in there!" So it was odd for me.

The garment district was a bustling area with a lot of activity. They were probably making a great deal of money but the clothes were not the same quality as the couture I was used to modeling in Europe.

*Modeling in New York in 1949. People raved about my 17-inch waist.*

It was a very different energy and experience than in France. In Paris, I'd been used to being well regarded with royalty coming in to order their dresses. I'd stand like a queen sometimes on a pedestal, literally! Then, in America for them to ask me to talk to the clients and be a saleswoman was in some ways demeaning. It was a step down from the world's top designers personally draping their clothes on me. You must do what you can to live but always retain the highest vision of who you are.

*You must do what you can to live but always remember the highest vision of who you are.*

I did that horrible modeling job for about three weeks. I was at a low point and needed to do something for myself. I was miserable in Manhattan and felt absolutely lost. The city was closing in on me. I needed to be in nature and to be creative again.

I missed Yvan and felt like I couldn't breathe. Breath always is an indicator of life, whether you feel alive or deflated. If it is constrained, then back away to see what's wrong. My breath was telling me I needed a change.

> *Breath always is an indicator of life, whether you feel alive or deflated.*

Thankfully, I saw a flyer with Katherine Dunham's name on it. She went around the world with the first Black ballet troupe. She was very well known and they loved her in France.

I was enthralled with her and thought, "I'm going to go and learn to dance with her." I felt it would lift my spirits. I endured an extra week of modeling just to pay for the classes.

*The wonderful dancer Katherine Dunham. I was delighted to take dance lessons with her.*

She was very sweet. The boys in her troupe were doing tremendous leaps and everything. I went right in and did this flying leap. As I was coming down I twisted my head in one direction and then the other direction. It was what I learned from the Watusi dancers in East Africa when I was a child. Katherine was laughing hilariously and the rest of the group was dazzled. I was probably the first girl, particularly white girl, who had ever done the leaps and flips that the guys in her troupe did.

Katherine said, "We're going to Las Vegas. I wish I could take you but I don't want you to have to sleep on the floor. They won't allow us to sleep in the hotel where we are going to be performing."

I didn't quite understand saying, "What do you mean they won't let you in?"

She explained that there were no Blacks, or Colored people as they said in those days, allowed.

In France, they stayed in the best hotels, the same as everybody else. They didn't discriminate in this way. They loved her and her whole troupe. I was stunned at their treatment in America. Everything I had learned from my uncle and Gandhi welled up in me. I couldn't get over the injustice in what I thought was the "Land of the Free." Like India had been for so long under the British Crown rule, it seemed "free" was just for the chosen.

They left for Las Vegas and I needed to decide what to do. Lucille Lortel, whom I met in Paris, knew that I was in America and invited me to perform at the White Barn Theatre. She was very selective, so I was quite appreciative and accepted. I thought it might be a good respite from my current predicament and a much-needed creative outlet. Nature doesn't stop expressing itself. It simply changes through the seasons.

*Nature doesn't stop expressing itself. It simply changes through the seasons.*

I went up to Connecticut one weekend while I was still in the area. I learned from my uncle to not procrastinate. If there is something in front of you to do, a task or an opportunity, then welcome it right away.

The trip was glorious. The estate was enormous with a man-made lake on it. She had converted an old horse barn into a theatre. She would bring people there every weekend. Her mission was to present experimental works so actors could develop their skills without the financial pressures.

She was very warmhearted and was known for helping young actors and actresses who were just starting out by giving them parts so they could earn some money. I learned later that her husband gave her a theatre in Manhattan where she put on the *Threepenny Opera*. It won several Tony Awards, something unusual for an Off-Broadway show.

I performed an American Indian number with a drum. I still have a photo in full costume with the headdress and everything on. It was great to be in a very supportive environment in the company of other aspiring actors and actresses but I still needed to earn money.

That weekend, Lucille connected me with the writer Polan Banks. He had been married to Amelie Baruch, the niece to the financier Bernard Baruch. Polan wrote novels such as *The Street of Women* and *The Far Horizon*. He had already sold the film rights to at least two of his books. *The Far Horizon* had been made into the movie, *The Great Lie*. He knew a lot of movie people because of that.

His most recent book, *Carriage Entrance*, was going to be made into the film, *My Forbidden Past*, and he was on his way to California. That's when I made up my mind to go to Hollywood. Lucille said to Polan, "When you're out there, you have to help Täo and introduce her to everyone."

\*\*\*

So much was happening. Although some things were going the wrong way, others were working out little by little. Just as I was pondering my next step, my friend from the WACs telephoned. We had been corresponding all along. I had talked to her from Paris. After serving in the war, she settled outside of Los Angeles. She was always saying to me, "If you ever come to California, please call me."

I told her about what happened with the Ilka Chase show and what I was considering. She said, "Look, you're an actress. Why don't you come out to Los Angeles and be closer to where you might find jobs. You have met all these people, such as Jack Cummings, who are interested in you. Maybe it will work out better."

After a couple of months in New York, it was time to make another move. I didn't have very much money, just a couple hundred dollars left, so I decided to journey across the country. It wasn't too expensive and I could see the United States. I got on the Greyhound bus headed to California.

Once again, I confronted the injustice of ignorance. Ignorance not only makes us blind to our true nature, but also it can greatly harm others. By not understanding the Oneness of all, a person can make decisions that go against the principle of *ahimsa*, or nonviolence.

To hurt another—in thoughts, words or actions—is to hurt oneself since we are all a part of the Eternal Energy. Gandhi lived

*By not understanding the Oneness of all, one can make decisions that go against the principle of ahimsa, or nonviolence.*

this principle. More and more, I was starting to understand how that principle was not practiced by so many.

The experience on the Greyhound bus was one of the most upsetting in my entire life. I still can't get over it after all of this time. On the bus, there was a young Black girl standing there with a newborn baby on her shoulder and holding the hand of a little child about three years old. There were some men sitting with their feet across the seat and they wouldn't let her sit down. No one gave her a seat.

In shock, I said in my very best English, "I can't believe what you're doing. You let her sit down."

They didn't budge. I got up horrified and went to the driver. Livid, I insisted, "You tell them to give her a seat. She's been standing for hours. She's going to faint."

The bus driver sheepishly said, "Oh, don't get involved, lady. We don't let niggers sit down."

Again, I didn't understand his language. I repeated louder, "You have to tell them to give her a seat."

He said in a whisper, "No, you can't do that. You better be careful. You'll make them angry and they'll pounce on you. You're in for trouble."

I finally understood something and said even louder, "Good, if they do then I'll have the French Embassy after them and that will give them trouble."

Everyone on the bus seemed to look at me like I was crazy, like I was breaking a cardinal rule.

I said defiantly, "If you won't let her sit there, she can have my place!"

I told the woman, "Take my seat and I'm going to stand." So she did.

After a while, I went over near the guys and sat down myself. Eventually, the guys seemed to back down a bit. They probably didn't know what to think of me with my accent and all.

In the fall of 1949, America had recently come through a heated presidential election. President Harry S. Truman had come to office after President Franklin D. Roosevelt died suddenly. Then, President Truman won the next election. Americans had been pushing for General Eisenhower, who had great support from his successes in the war, to get in the race but he didn't.

World War II had ended but now the so-called "Cold War" had started. As I understood it, the United States and Soviets had diametrically different views. America was built on capitalism and free will, and the USSR believed in Communism where the government owned everything and controlled the society. Communism was supposedly based on sharing things equally which sounds like a good thing but I'm not sure it worked out for the everyday people.

On the other side, even though President Truman was putting forth something called the "Fair Deal" and was talking about civil rights, it wasn't clear how fair it really was going to be for the Black people in America. The actuality of basic liberties for this young girl on the bus was not yet apparent.

The deplorable discord between Whites and Blacks was palpable and hit up against my deep belief in Oneness that I had learned from my uncle and Gandhi. I had survived the Germans and here I see this is America. It was terrible. It was similar to what the Colonial British did to the Indians or the overall degradation of the Jewish people by the Nazis. How could one person believe to be superior over another? Like in nature, all the flowers and trees have different colors and make up the tapestry of the Universe's beauty.

*Like in nature, all the flowers and trees have different colors and make up the tapestry of the Universe's beauty.*

I read later that 1949 was the first year in which no African-American was lynched in the United States. If that is true, I can't determine whether that is a great achievement or simply an indication of how heinous things had been previously. I can't imagine that all of that kind of awful violence was actually reported. It seemed like people just looked the other way like the bus driver. That ride across America opened my eyes to so much.

I tried to get something to eat asking partly in French, "S'il vous plaît, I'd like a glass of wine and a baguette."

Some passengers asked, "You don't want a hot dog at the bus stop?"

I said, "No, I don't eat meat."

They couldn't believe it. In the end, I managed to find some Weetabix and I ate Weetabix all across America.

I'd been traveling a long time and was not accustomed to being so unclean. In India, I was used to taking a bath in the morning, before lunch and before dinner. When we made it to St. Louis, I went to the place that said "showers." They would not let this Black girl go in with the White women to wash her baby and young child. I had her come in with me. The others said, "You're going to have trouble." I didn't care.

I had left most of my things on the bus thinking they would be safe there. When I came back from the shower, all of my things were stolen—my money, my passport, my green card—everything. I think it was the same guys from the bus. They took off with my most important belongings. Now I was traveling with a few quarters in my pocket and no ticket to get my luggage out of the bus.

We continued to roll along, crawling through the dusty roads of Kansas and the open stretches of Colorado. On one of the stops someone helped me call my friend from the WACs. When we arrived in California, I saw all of these policemen waiting at the bus station and I wondered what was happening. I had arrived but now what? I thought I had done something wrong so I started backing up. Perhaps my defiant ways on the bus had caught up with me.

I didn't realize that my friend, after leaving the military, was now a Deputy Sheriff in downtown Los Angeles. I hadn't the faintest idea what that meant.

She had all of these officers come out to meet me and help me get my luggage. They were very nice and couldn't believe that I had everything stolen and had come across America with absolutely nothing. I suppose I looked like a lost soul. Since I had no identification and no money, my Deputy Sheriff friend took me to her home. So much happened in such a short span of time.

My life certainly changed from my peaceful and idyllic childhood in India to the vicissitudes from wartime living. I met and fell in love with the dearest man and now we were apart. It was the first time I felt my heart ache for someone. I knew I had to hold on to the hope of our reunion while living fully in each present moment. Holding on too tight often leads to crushing the natural order of things. Just as spring turns to summer, I had to accept the change in season.

*Holding on too tight often leads to crushing the natural order of things.*

## CHAPTER 13

# Come Back To Center

The English scientist Sir Isaac Newton teaches us that what goes up must come down. It's the basic law of gravity. I liked reading about him because he was inquisitive even as a child. He would make toys and invent things. He was interested in the Universe—the sun, moon and movements of tides.

Knowing that life itself will pull you up and down, it helps to build a solid center. In yoga and dance, your core muscles allow you to do more complex moves. Similarly, a strong spiritual foundation allows you to withstand the roller coaster of life. In my case, I had to figure out how to come back to my center in the midst of trying to make a living.

*A strong spiritual foundation allows you to withstand the roller coaster of life.*

My WAC Deputy Sheriff friend was very sweet. Her home was nice but cramped with loved ones to take care of and it was far away from Hollywood. I had done some research and found that it was about an hour out, a long way from Culver City and even further past Santa Monica. I didn't realize how far apart everything was in the Los Angeles area and Hollywood. Universal Studios was in San Fernando Valley. Twentieth Century Fox was near Culver City, as was MGM. The only studio that was actually in Hollywood was Paramount.

The places I wanted to go were in all directions and since I didn't have any money, I had to get up really early and take buses. The traveling was hard but at least there was a way. Complaining would not help. I had learned that if there is an option that will get you where you want to go, no matter how slow, embrace it. Get started in any way you can.

Just a few days after arriving, I made my way into town and was walking down Hollywood Boulevard. I had a cute dress on from France and was looking at the street trying to find in what direction I should walk. Since I didn't have a car, I really didn't want to get lost.

> *If there is an option that will get you where you want to go, no matter how slow, embrace it. Get started in any way you can.*

Suddenly, I realized there was a man that had been following me. He was right next to me. We were almost shoulder to shoulder. He kept saying something. I didn't really understand and got mad with him when he wouldn't leave me alone. I took my elbow and knocked it out to the side and hit him. People around saw what happened.

There was a policeman standing nearby who came running up asking, "What happened? What happened?"

The man said, "I only said that she was a sight for sore eyes and she hit me!"

I didn't know what that meant and said, "He wouldn't go away."

The policeman said jokingly, "Miss, you keep on hitting them when they bother you like that and you'll have no trouble in Hollywood!"

A bit embarrassed I said, "I am so sorry!"

That was my entrée into Hollywood. I wasn't used to the environment and didn't speak English very well.

In order to be able to work, almost immediately I had to go to the office of the Consulate General of France in Los Angeles. I needed to get my French passport and papers replaced from that ill-fated Greyhound bus ride. The Consul General's name was Raoul Bertrand and he took a liking to me right away. I told him about my situation.

He knew a lot about my family background. The first thing he said was, "Porchon, that's strange. I knew a Porchon de Sanglier when we gave Pondicherry back to India. We represented the French colony." Surprise! He knew my uncle.

After India gained independence from the British in 1947, India and France made an agreement to unite French India with the Indian Union. Even though it wasn't ratified until a few years later, it was still a momentous moment. My uncle, who had been involved in various activities related to India's independence, was there on that historic occasion.

So, Monsieur Bertrand and I instantly had a connection. I was grateful to find some link to both of my homes, France and India. I hadn't known him very long before he began to tell me that he liked my style. He would say, "Täo, you are chic, not like an ordinary model."

He realized that I wasn't like the other girls getting a job here and there modeling in France, but that I was a real couture model who had worked with all of the top designers in Paris. He also liked my background and said, "Täo, you're not like some French girls who have come to try to get into films, but have no substance."

Later, whenever anyone important came through, he would invite me as a French representative. Monsieur Bertrand told me he wanted glamour and someone who could hold a smart conversation, not just a French actress there to be sexy.

Although I enjoyed spending time with my WAC friend's family, I didn't want to stay too long. I didn't like to be dependent on anyone so I knew it was time for me to move on. I'd come to California to work and it would have been ridiculous to stay so far away and find a job without a car.

I told her, "You're a dear friend. Thank you for everything," explaining further that it was time to find work. "I was told about a Girls Club where I think I can stay."

She understood and reminded me that anytime I needed her, she would always be there. That was reassuring and with a warm hug of friendship and thanks, I was on my way closer to Hollywood.

Before making the trip to California, I had written to various people letting them know I was coming. I remembered Jack Cummings' invitation to look him up if I ever came to Hollywood, so I did. He kept his word and made an appointment with me. I was also able to get meetings with Ted Richmond at Universal, and Sol Seigel at Twentieth Century Fox through Lucille Lortel's friend Polan Banks. What I had learned from my uncle and Gandhi about "taking action" was paying off.

My French and English once again got me in trouble. When I was at Ted Richmond's office I didn't know how far the other studio meetings were from each other. So I said to him, "I have a rendezvous with Sol Siegel at Twentieth Century Fox and I don't want to be late."

He said, "Oh, I know Sol. I'll call him."

He got on the phone, "I have a little French girl and she has a rendezvous with you. Is the time still good?"

Sol apparently said yes.

At the same time, I called Jack Cummings at MGM and he was asking me to come straight away to our appointment. I got there and he held me up. I said, "I'm late again. Oh, Monsieur Cummings, I have a rendezvous with Sol Siegel at Twentieth Century Fox. How far away is it?"

With a little smirk on his face, he kindly said, "I'll call him."

He got on the phone and said, "Sol, I have a little French girl and she has a rendezvous with you."

Annoyed at this point, Sol said, "For crying out loud! Everybody in the studio thinks I'm having an affair with a French girl and they want to know who she is. Tell her please to stop saying she has a rendezvous with me!"

In French, a rendezvous simply means a meeting. Apparently, in English, it took on a different meaning.

Well, I didn't get the job at Fox but Sol was very nice. Jack Cummings at MGM was nice to me as well and said, "I want you to come in again so I can introduce you to Eddie Mannix and all the people."

Things were looking up.

I met with Eddie Mannix and he said he would give me some work at MGM. My "rendezvous" became our joke. Whenever I would see him after that he would ask with a grin, "Who do you have a rendezvous with today?"

For a while, I still didn't know what he was talking about and why it was so funny.

\*\*\*

So far my life experiences in India, France and England did not expose me to the names of many of Hollywood's celebrities except at some of my modeling shows. I didn't know that MGM produced movies with the most outstanding stars of the time, names people today would still know. Prominent actresses included Elizabeth Taylor, Judy Garland, Ava Gardner, Katharine Hepburn, Joan Crawford,

Lana Turner, Debbie Reynolds, Janet Leigh, Esther Williams, Kathryn Grayson, Leslie Caron and Barbara Stanwyck.

Some of the dashing men included Clark Gable, Spencer Tracy, Gene Kelly, Fred Astaire, James Stewart, Charles Bronson, Kirk Douglas, Peter Lawford, Mickey Rooney, Burt Lancaster, John Ireland, Lionel Barrymore, Jim Backus, Red Skelton, Van Johnson and Ricardo Montalbán.

MGM Studios fascinated me because it was like a small city. I enjoyed exploring it. Each day, I could find something new and exciting happening. There were multiple expansive lots on the main grounds with sound stages, workshops, even a barbershop. There were sets with homes, swimming pools and stables. They had wide-open areas for Westerns and even a zoo. I was "Täo in Wonderland."

My first job at MGM was in the movie *Show Boat*. I was now "under contract," as they said, with Hollywood's most prestigious studio. Since I spoke very little English, they seemed relieved to find work for me in the New Orleans scenes since I could speak French in it. I heard them saying, "Now we know where we can put her."

The American actress and singer Kathryn Grayson was in the movie along with the beautiful Ava Gardner and actor and singer Howard Keel. He thought every girl was flirting with him. I wasn't, so he commented, "She doesn't like me very much!"

As I remember it, Kathryn had about forty pages with lines. Romanian-born actress Lisa Ferraday had a smaller part in it—eighteen pages. I had only six pages but it didn't matter. I was working and got to experience this magical movie-making environment. Our set had a real boat and a lake, which they made look like the Mississippi River. It was incredible. The boat actually moved along the water.

I would spend a lot of time at the MGM commissary. One day, I was there looking for a place to sit. I saw a man with space at his table. I asked, in not the best English, if I could sit. I hadn't the faintest idea who he was. He wasn't very nice and replied rather ostentatiously, "It's reserved."

I found another place to sit, but noticed later that no one came to join him. I suppose he liked being sequestered. It was the actor Spencer Tracy. As I learned more about the celebrities, I was almost shocked out of my skin when I finally realized who he was. I was not used to being treated like that. He reminded me of the sniffy Colonial British in India and in London during the war.

Around the lot, everybody was saying that he was romantically linked to actress Katharine Hepburn. He had been in movies such as *Boom Town* and *San Francisco* with Clark Gable who himself was famously known for *Gone with the Wind*.

I was still in the commissary that day when I heard all of these voices and people laughing and talking. I looked around and saw a crowd of people. I kept hearing, "Hi, King!" Everything "King."

I naively thought, "Isn't that wonderful that America has kings in the film studio. Who was this King?" When I looked carefully at the person who was being honored, I was surprised to see that it was the incredible actor Clark Gable. I recognized him because I had met him once at a club in London. After that day, I would always observe how people came over to talk with him.

Everybody, even the people who cleaned the room, would sit at his table. He would say, "Oh, sit down, sit down. Have a drink with me." He was so sweet. He had been a major in the U.S. Army Air Force during World War II. I liked him because he was both humorous and humble.

Polan Banks kept his promise to Lucille Lortel and took me to a lavish party in Beverly Hills where I met everybody. The Barrymores, who were like Hollywood royalty, were there. That's where I met Johnnie and Dick, a very flamboyant gay couple who became my dearest friends. At the time, I didn't really understand what gay was. It didn't matter to me. They were so nice.

Johnnie's full name was John Raven. I don't remember Dick's. Johnnie's mother was famous and very wealthy. She was a generous philanthropist, and sponsored arts organizations and a lot of the big award shows. She died in a place crash from Georgia.

Every day Johnnie and Dick made sure I learned a little more about Hollywood and met more people. There was a famous market right where Sunset Strip ends and becomes Beverly Hills. Everybody seemed to gather there at a popular tearoom. It doesn't exist anymore. I looked for it the last time I was visiting.

There was Sunset Blvd and then the area of famous homes where many celebrities lived. Suzanne Allen, who later became a dear friend, lived next to Frank Sinatra's daughter. Liberace's house was further down on the slope, while Dean Martin's house was down the street. George Raft was further along near the Beverly Hills Hotel. Greta Garbo's house was in the area. I went there once and was surprised to see that her ceilings had mirrors so she could always see herself.

From there, you could go straight up the hill to the very top and find where the Barrymores lived, and all of the big homes. Johnnie and Dick's home was up on the hill with all of these famous mansions, right next to the Barrymore Estate. The Australian actor Errol Flynn also lived up near Johnnie and Dick. Flynn was known to be a notorious ladies man and would have a lot of parties.

Johnnie and Dick decided to move down to a magnificent home right opposite Mary Pickford's immense estate in San Ysidro Canyon. It was called Pickfair because she had been married to actor Douglas Fairbanks. Charlie Chaplin lived on the same stretch. It was in the area where there were a lot of actors who were popular in silent movies. Only a few actually made it in talking films. Johnnie and Dick bought the house there because there was hardly anyone around them.

Johnnie was very short and dripping with wealth. He had twelve dogs he fed every day and the largest dog enjoyed his Rolls Royce. Johnnie wanted so badly to be an actor and would put money in various films. Everybody would promise him a part but it never seemed to work out. They really took advantage of him.

I went to a party at the estate of comedian Joe E. Brown, who starred in films such as *Son of a Sailor* and later *Some Like It Hot*. He was the captain in *Show Boat* and also knew Johnnie and Dick. You would get to the big gate at the beginning of the property and then a train would take you down to his stupendous home where he had open-air parties. It was extraordinary. Hollywood was certainly different than any place I'd experienced.

\*\*\*

Change was happening in India and I watched it from afar. Although India received its independence from the British in the summer of 1947, it took almost three years for the new constitution to come into force. On January 26, 1950, Dr. Rajendra Prasad, who had supported Mahatma Gandhi and Prime Minister Jawaharial Nehru, took the oath as the new President.

A public holiday, called Republic Day, was declared throughout the country. After almost a hundred years of British rule, India was fully her own—free and independent. I was thrilled that my wonderful uncle would be there at the celebration. It would have brought me great joy to have been there sharing such a long-fought for event with him and others.

Lord Mountbatten, who had been Viceroy of India after the war and India's first governor general, was at this function representing Great Britain. He was Prince Phillip's great-uncle. Although I didn't go, I collected the news clippings and decided to make a film about it.

Through my uncle, I knew Clement Baptista from Hunnar Films, a production company based in India. With some money I had through my uncle, I had them film it. From that, I made my documentary, *Republic Day Celebrations*. There was a 31-gun salute ushering in this new era. After President Prasad took oath, he gave a short speech in Hindi and then English declaring:

> "Today for the first time in our long and chequered history we find the whole of this vast land from Kashmir in the north to Cape Comorin in the south, from Kathiawad and Kutch in the west Coconada and Kamrup in the east, brought together under the jurisdiction of one Constitution and one Union which takes over the responsibility for the welfare of more than 320 million men and women that inhabit it."

The whole of India with its many languages and cultures was now one. Then, as I later saw from the footage, there was a procession through the streets of Delhi. Millions of people were everywhere, on roofs and even in trees, chanting *jai* which means "victory." It was a grand military parade. You could sense the collective pride hearing the National Anthem and the guns saluting a new flag, a new nation and new hope.

Although this wasn't really a commercial film, I was very proud of being able to tell the story of a free India. The Republic Day Celebrations still take place in August every year.

I realized then that I was a natural storyteller like when I was a child. At that point, I knew that I wanted to write and produce. First, I had to figure out how to make a living as an actress.

*Photos taken soon after I arrived in Hollywood, CA around 1949-1950. A friend gave me my first Hollywood photo shoot as a gift.*

\*\*\*

As *Show Boat* was shooting, I continued to meet people. I saw Fred Astaire there at the commissary. I knew his sister, Lady Cavendish, from London. She told him I was coming. He was not show-offish but somewhat of a shy person. He didn't seem to mix very much with people but he came to life as soon as he started to dance. He was working on another set. I think it was the movie, *Three Little Words* that Jack Cummings was producing. Red Skelton and Arlene Dahl were also in it. I never got to be in the same film as Fred Astaire. I was always on another set.

Once I bumped into the American actress Joan Crawford. She had a little dog that was so cute. I bent down to pet it and she pulled him away and barked, "Leave my dog alone!" She wasn't very nice. I always thought she was tall and slim but she wasn't. I didn't know her but I could imagine how what her daughter later wrote in the exposè *Mommie Dearest* could be true.

There were a lot of different types coming in and out. You would see nice people and well as pretentious personalities.

I started off in Los Angeles with somewhat of a mystique. With the award I had won in France, I became known in Hollywood as the girl with the "Longest Legs in Europe." So right away they were saying, "Oh, no. American girls have longer legs than any European."

This went on for two years. I didn't understand it then, but they were using this for publicity and trying to build me up. I used to get really upset and think, "Why won't they leave me alone!"

It seemed that the only person who had legs as long as mine was the American actress and dancer Cyd Charisse. She was two inches taller than me so she really still didn't have longer legs when it came down to brass tacks. Now I find it interesting how all of these trivial things seemed to matter back then.

*Publicity photo taken in Malibu, CA for MGM around 1950. I'm with dancer Bobby Le House who had a B.A., B.S., D.P and spoke eight languages. We performed for Ethiopian Emperor Haile Selassie when he visited Los Angeles.*

I got to know the society crowd in Hollywood through Ginny Berndt who was one of the founders of a huge organization called the Charity Players. I met Ginny in the San Fernando Valley at a party. She came up to me and said with charming flair, "I love France! I love France! You must meet some people. You have to meet this fabulous man."

It turned out to be her longtime multimillionaire friend, Dr. Elmer Tolman, whom she had known in Chicago before moving to California. I couldn't get over his story. He had gone through a divorce and his wife had received millions and millions of dollars in the settlement. He was dying and decided to take twelve girls around the world and give them an experience of a lifetime—to dress them elegantly and teach them about things and places of which they'd never even dreamt.

Ginny explained that he came to her saying, "My former wife has taken so much and doesn't appreciate anything in life. I would like to take a group of girls who never had opportunities on a world tour for about a year. I want you, Ginny, to come and help me."

Her answer, of course, was "Yes!"

The girls were selected. I do recall that one was a hairdresser. Ginny said she prepared them for the trip taking them around to the best shops for their wardrobe, as well as giving them tips on etiquette and how to behave in different locations.

Once everything was in place, Dr. Tolman took these girls around the world. They stayed at the best hotels in major cities including Paris, Cape Town and Singapore, and had a great time for a year.

When they came back, Dr. Tolman told Ginny, "I'm going to marry the one who was the most loyal and wasn't in it for the money."

He picked Frances Barrett, who became Mrs. Elmer Tolman. It seemed all of the girls would have liked to marry him. He was very nice, thoughtful and very rich. To each of the other girls, he gave a good sum of money and wished them well. Although Ginny was rich, he gave her money too for her help.

Ginny took a liking to me and started to take me everywhere. It was delightful, but I didn't have a big enough wardrobe. When Ginny was doing something for the Girl Scouts, she said, "The girls have to see how chic real French people are." To show them, I would go dressed in my most elegant clothes with hat and gloves.

To expand my clothing options, I started using my saris even more. I remembered how Indian women could transform themselves with a colorful strip of cloth. It wasn't something you saw often in Hollywood at that time so people were enthralled.

Ginny's husband, Eric Berndt, invented some of the early motion picture cameras such as the 16mm sound-on-film camera and ran Auricon with Walter Bach. Eric later invented the tiny 3mm motion picture camera that NASA used in space flights.

Eric and Ginny would pick me up and take me to their home where I would spend the night. I think they were intrigued by both my French and Indian backgrounds. People were not as international as they are today. I was fascinated by Ginny's closet that was a very large room with nothing but clothes in it. You'd think you were in a very fashionable shop. She was very nice. I would go out and socialize with her and Eric. Everybody who was considered anybody would come to their incredible house with its huge swimming pool.

Ginny knew I needed to make money and had a group of friends who were going on a tour to Paris. One day, she said, "Täo, teach them how to say things in French."

Soon, I started giving Ginny and her friends French lessons. They wanted to learn the basics like thank you, please, how to buy a train ticket, how to go shopping, how to order something on the menu, as well as some French customs.

She invited me in as a member of the Charity Players and we would raise money for different causes in Hollywood. Even though I didn't make money from that, I met a lot of people through it, and the money they raised was being used for good.

I was involved with all of these rich people and I had no money. It was kind of funny. I laughed sometimes when I would see myself on the society pages and know that I hardly had a penny in my pocket. I found that many of the society set were not from the film world, but were just extremely wealthy living in huge homes, throwing extravagant parties and raising money for everything.

The Beverly Hills Hotel was the lavish place for many of the events. I remember one show in particular because I kicked higher than anyone in the chorus line.

Ginny introduced me to Frances Tolman who was also a member of the Charity Players. I got to know her a bit better through that. Her husband died from his illness. Sometime later, Frances married Armand Hammer, the chairman of the Occidental Petroleum Corporation who worked to help bring peace between the United States and the Soviet Union, and who financed research for a cancer cure.

*Modeling show to raise funds for the Charity Players in Beverly Hills. We had a huge model of an Air France plane and did a performance at a beautiful home. It was very glamorous! A French film star introduced us. When I started walking down the stairs, the other girls followed.*

Frances often invited me to their magnificent home. They had bought it from the actress Gene Tierney who was in and out of a marriage to designer Oleg Cassini. I also got to know Suzanne Allen and her husband William who was a big architect.

I was finding that one thing would lead to another as I met new people and made myself available for opportunities. Through the Charity Players I connected with a dance troupe that had mainly people from India in it. We put together a big show and performed in places like the University of California in Los Angeles. It was such a delight to be with people from my home and involved in something sharing my Indian heritage.

Even though there was a lot of activity and I was meeting some really nice people, it was hard to make real friends in Hollywood except Johnnie and Dick, and Ginny and Frances. It wasn't like in Europe where I had my clique of people. America was different.

*At the Beverly Hills Hotel in California with Frou-Frou and the Charity Players. The picture was featured on Friday, August 14, 1953 (Sec. II, page 2) in the Los Angeles Examiner as "FRENCH ACCENT": "Mrs. Tao Porchon's poodle seems anxious to alight from his equipage as his mistress and her friends drive about completing plans for the Champagne and Caviar Soiree of the Charity Players. Others in the car, left to right, Mesdames William Hepworth Anderson, Lindsley Parsons (press) and Donald E. Harwood (porter). The event will be held on Sunday in the Beverly Hills home of Mr. and Mrs. Robert J. Corcoran. Hours are 4 to 10 p.m., proceeds to help handicapped children." It was an example of the work I did with the Charity Players.*

When I tried to make friends, particularly male, everything was about sex. People apparently saw me as exotic, as if being French I was ready to have sex with everybody and must do something different, more lewd and kinky.

People also seemed fascinated by the fact that I didn't eat meat. They would say things like, "If you don't eat meat, you won't have good sex."

I would reply, "I do just fine." Yvan was the only man on my mind.

*Performing in an Indian-American Ballet in Hollywood between 1952–1953. I did bharatanatyam with the others in a big outdoor theatre. The image below on the right was featured in the newspaper as "Dance at UCLA Festival."*

It was a very strange time. I moved out of this one building and found a place that was a semi-hotel on Sunset Strip that I really couldn't afford. The entrance and lobby were high up on the roadside. To get to the swimming pool, you had to go downstairs. There were rooms all around the pool. I never let anybody come down to it.

My apartment building was also a gathering place. If you walked into the lobby and went to the left there was a coffee shop where people would meet, particularly those in films or who wanted to be in the Hollywood crowd.

Some of the big actors who worked for Warner Bros lived there or would gather for coffee. I would see people like Rock Hudson. I was never in a film with him but we would see each other and smile. I think he would meet his agent there at the café.

A block from where I lived on the left-hand side of the road was the famous Mocambo Club. Everybody was there such as Lana Turner, Bing Crosby and the tap dancer and singer, Sammy Davis Jr. It was the type of club where you dressed elegantly.

*At the famous Mocambo Club on the Sunset Strip in CA. I'm on the far left. This particular picture is from 1955.*

You could go there and hear big band music. That was real music. I still loved that and jazz from when Yvan introduced me to it. I liked listening to Sammy Davis Jr. or dear Louis Armstrong. I particularly loved listening to him because he made everything flower inside of me. This was real music.

Just on the other side was a Belgium restaurant where many stars would go. Sammy Davis Jr. would often perform there. That's where I would have lunch with the French Consul.

Close by on Sunset near Crescent Heights was Schwab's Pharmacy where celebrities and others used to meet. They were not really buying anything. People would go there just to bump into someone or sit at the counter and buy something to eat or drink.

Near the Mocambo was the street that went down to the big open-air Farmer's Market. Everything was under tents. I think it is still there today.

There was a big strip that went over the hills into the San Fernando Valley and you could see down the hills from Wilshire Blvd. That whole area was the heart of a lot of activity. Now, I can't recognize a lot of things. So much is gone but that was the Hollywood I knew.

***

MGM would often have me "on loan" to other studios. There were all of these small projects being filmed. Universal Studios in San Fernando Valley was huge. When I arrived, they were filming an epic story that had to do with the war and were using some French girls who were not really actresses in the crowd scenes. These girls probably were hoping to get into films and had married American soldiers during the war.

The one studio I didn't have much luck with was Columbia Studios. Somebody who was big in films sent me over there. This was still at the very beginning and my spoken English was really bad. I was sitting there and, because they made me wait a long time, I started getting nervous.

When I finally got in to see the film executive, he was standing there at his desk with what looked like a raggedy man in dirty old blue jeans, weathered shirt, smoking a cigarette. I didn't know who he was.

After my meeting with the film executive, the person who sent me to his office had obviously presumed that I knew who the man in the raggedy dirty jeans was and expected a big response from me when I came out. Since I didn't say anything, she enthusiastically asked, "Wasn't there someone else there?"

Innocently, I responded, "Well, I think the man who cleans the floors was in the room."

They thought that was very funny and got a big laugh out of it.

It turned out that it was the famous film star, Burt Lancaster. He was tall, blond, handsome, athletic leading man adored by many women.

With so much laughter, I just started laughing with them because to me he looked so filthy that I never even thought of him as being an actor. He must have just come in from filming a scene and was still in costume.

I soon learned that at that time he was one of Hollywood's busiest actors making from two to four films a year. In 1946, he made his debut opposite Ava Gardner in *The Killers* based on an Ernest Hemingway short story and he became an instant star.

Burt Lancaster made eighty-eight films in his long movie career. Some of his films include *From Here To Eternity, Sweet Smell of Success* and *Trapeze.*

In later years, I learned that he used his celebrity to speak out frequently in support of racial minorities including speaking at the March on Washington in 1963, which I also attended. He was a vocal supporter of liberal political causes such as opposing the Vietnam War and McCarthyism.

There was another hotshot producer at Columbia Studios, a strange little man who was telling everybody that he was going to make me "the biggest star in Hollywood." He would say, "They have never seen anything like you. It's going to be the best!"

I didn't like him too much.

One day he came calling on me. He was going to take me to lunch and tell me about his plans for my stardom. Unfortunately, they let him come down to my apartment. If anyone ever came to see me, they had to wait in the lobby. I would never allow anybody to come into my space. After all, I was married and still very much in love with Yvan even though we hadn't seen each other for so long.

This producer made his way to my room. As I was getting my bag, he was snooping through my things. I had some photographs and a collection of funny little glass animals, all different kinds. It was a bit crazy. I would use these figurines to help me recall names and pronunciations. If a person reminded me of a bear, I would buy a little bear. That would make me remember. I explained to him what they were.

As we were leaving, he said, "Oh, what do you have for me? You must do one for me!"

So, we went into a shop and I saw a skunk and picked it up. Very insulted, he said, "A skunk?"

I explained, "He has the same hair as you." He had a white strip going across his hair.

Needless to say, he didn't make me a big star. He was very upset. I don't even think we had lunch! I am thankful that I was the type of woman that would speak my mind, even in broken English.

\*\*\*

I was still learning about America and once again met up with ignorance and injustice that shocked me. There was a sign outside a club that read, "No Niggers. No Dogs. No Jews." I had already witnessed the discrimination against the young Black girl on the bus, now the Jews in California. I thought that was over with the war.

On Christmas day, where I was living I saw children that had been playing together now throwing stones at the other children who were Jewish. I couldn't get over it.

That's when the Jewish people started to build their own clubs. So many of the directors and even the musicians in Hollywood were Jewish from places like Hungary. They were earning money and started their own establishments. They were soon so well done that other people wanted to join.

The other thing that struck me was the multitude of churches. Every time I walked down a street I found a new one. I couldn't believe it. I had never seen so many different kinds. There were all these various names. The little church around the corner was the First Baptist Church, and then there was the Second Baptist Church, then the First Presbyterian and the Second Presbyterian. It was a bit confusing.

At that time, I was looking for something that I could believe in. Yet, I couldn't get over the fact that within Christianity there were all of these different types of churches. It was like they couldn't agree amongst themselves. How come? Isn't it one God? I grew up believing in One Truth. God is in everything and everyone in this world. It doesn't matter what you call It. There should not be any disagreement. The world survived before man started labeling things.

> *God is in everything and everyone in this world. It doesn't matter what you call It.*

I found the movie world disquieting and I began searching for more peace. I didn't like gyms. People would come out sweating and out of breath. Instead, I would do yoga that I had learned on the beaches of Pondicherry when I was little. It brought me back to another time and another way of being. Yet, I was still searching. I needed a teacher.

Several weeks later, I found the path that would lead me to what I was searching for—the Ramakrishna Vivekananda Vedanta Society. It was built on the principles I had learned growing up that "Truth is One, sages call it by many names." They believed in universal toleration. It is the essence of the Oneness in all people that says you're not different than me and I'm not different than you. God made both of us.

As the story is told, when the venerable Swami Vivekananda visited Los Angeles in the late 1890s after his famous speech to the Parliament of the World Religions event in Chicago, he stayed at the home of the woman who would decades later provide the land and the house for the Vedanta Society. It was built like a little Taj Mahal with a garden of roses and everything.

*The temple at the Vedanta Society of Southern California. It looks like a mini Taj Mahal.*

My uncle's interest in Swami Vivekananda's teachings of Vedanta formed the foundation of my own belief in Oneness. As Swami Vivekananda had quoted that day from the *Bhagavad Gita*, "Whosoever comes to Me, through whatsoever form, I reach him; all men are struggling through paths which in the end lead to me."

So when I found the Vedanta Society, I found my new home and when I met Swami Prabhavananda, he became my new guru. He had been sent by the Ramakrishna Order of India to establish the Society in Southern California. The Society's mission was to "promote harmony between Eastern and Western thought, and recognition of the truth in all the great religions of the world."

*My dear guru, Swami Prabhavananda.*

Through the Vedanta Society, I began to move deeply into meditation and the Vedanta philosophy. I found a new spiritual home but my whole life still seemed unsettled. There was something missing. I hadn't yet experienced success in Hollywood and in many ways that didn't matter. I was not acting for the fame. I simply wanted a way to get back to Yvan. I was always thinking I was going to make enough money to go and be with him. I was holding on to that hope but time kept going by.

I didn't know how long I would be in Hollywood, whether I would be joining Yvan in Uruguay or going back to France, but I knew I needed to be more grounded. An occasional letter would come from Yvan and I realized that he was also still having a hard time. He would barely tell me what he was doing because he didn't want me to worry.

On the other hand, it wasn't helpful because I was wondering whether he was playing around. A lot of women liked him because he was handsome but he didn't know it and never thought about it that way. Despite being around so many people, I missed him terribly and was trying not to drown in uncertainty.

Unfortunately, the movie *Show Boat* didn't turn out very well for me. After five months of working on the project, just about all of the New

Orleans scenes ended up being cut out. The woman who had thirty-two pages to learn was also cut mostly out.

When the movie was later released, it was a bit embarrassing. Everybody in Paris was waiting and all you could see was the boat arriving in New Orleans and me coming down the gangplank in a costume waving and saying, "Bonjour, bonjour, bonjour." It was so fast nobody in France believed I'd had a part in a Hollywood film.

That seemed indicative of my first year in Hollywood, a series of ups and downs like a roller coaster at the Disneyland amusement park that was to open in a few years. It reminded me of early spring when the sun comes out and then it suddenly rains. I never knew what to expect. I had to keep my head up and wait for the rays to come through. Surely it would because that was my lessons from nature.

Finding the Vedanta Society and getting more serious about my study of meditation and philosophy was fortifying me. My peace wasn't instant but I was on a path back to center. The seeds that had been planted years ago by my uncle were once again being nurtured. Sometimes you may see where you want to go and it seems distant. Be patient and stay on the path. You will find your center of gravity.

> *Sometimes you may see where you want to go and it seems distant. Be patient and stay on the path. You will find your center of gravity.*

*After months of shooting the movie Show Boat, the New Orleans scenes were cut out. My friends sent me this picture. They stuck the Eiffel Tower behind a picture from the film as a joke.*

CHAPTER 14

## Let Go

Letting go is the first step to letting in peace. The ancient *Bhagavad Gita* says, "Renouncing all attachments, you'll enjoy an undisturbed mind in success or failure." In yoga class, that may mean letting go of the "perfect-looking pose" and instead feeling the energy behind it. In meditation, we empty the mind so the balance of the Life Force is awakened within us. It's a similar practice in dance. Once you have a strong center, you can let go allowing the energy to be free. That's when your creativity in expression comes out. When you hold on too tight, you constrain the energy. Philosophically that makes sense but it is much harder to practice in life, particularly with matters of the heart.

*Letting go is the first step to letting in peace.*

One day, I was having lunch at the Beverly Hills Hotel with twelve friends from the Charity Players. My friends, Ginny and Frances, were there. We were sitting and talking, just casually dining when without any warning I saw this vivid image. It was more like a sudden startling vision.

My heart began to beat faster. In an instant, I was struck as if an arrow had hit my heart. I was trying to breathe.

Ginny noticed the change in my demeanor and asked anxiously, "Are you all right, Täo?"

Lost in a daze, I answered, "I don't know."

I fell into a trance-like state, watching Yvan with blood streaming down out of his nostrils, more and more blood dripping and dripping. The blood kept coming the whole time I was sitting at the table. It wouldn't stop. I was seeing Yvan as clearly as when I look at someone right in front of me.

Bewildered, I said, "You have to excuse me." I got up quickly from the table and dashed out. The others didn't know what was going on. I rushed to the hotel lobby looking for a telephone. It seemed hard to find, but they knew me at this hotel.

I tried to call Uruguay, but I couldn't get through to him. I called his mother, but didn't get through. I didn't know anybody else to call. I went back to the table and told my friends, "I've got to go home. I have to send a message."

I've always been intuitive, so having a premonition didn't shock me. It was what I saw that was concerning. I knew how Yvan could bleed suddenly because of his war injuries. It reminded me of what would happen in Paris when we rode our bikes, but perhaps Yvan was terribly hurt from something else. Even today I get choked up thinking about it.

I hurried home and wrote to Yvan's mother expressing my concern. I was very worried. As I was about to mail the letter, I received a somewhat cryptic note from his mother in the same post. She was trying to explain the situation.

She had received a letter in France from a person she didn't recognize, not her son, someone in South America. It was about Yvan and said, "He wants you to know that he's all right. He's been given two quarts of blood but he's going to be fine. He's sort of coming through very slowly because he's weak."

Yvan's mother shared that news in her letter to me. She also wrote: "It's been three years and you're not together. It's time for the two of you to come back to France. You can't live like this separated. Neither one of you is able to make enough money to really live. It's time you come home. Täo, everybody knows you in France. You can get jobs here."

Her short note was filled with anguish and, at the end, she asked me to promise not to leave him. That left me with a feeling that something more was wrong.

A strange heaviness seemed to be in the air. I thought that perhaps I should not let him travel so soon after his sickness, but I was excited about finally being able to see him. I started making plans to meet Yvan in France but I didn't know how I was going to pay for it.

The next day I went to see Ginny. The first thing she asked was, "Are you all right? You look sick."

I confided, "I had a terrible dream and it is true. Yvan has something with bleeding that's been going on with him since the war. His mother wants me to get back to France."

That's when Ginny and Frances decided to have a big bon voyage party for me. My Hollywood friends were very sweet. Frances said, "I was going to buy you a present but I didn't want to get you something you didn't need going back to France." Handing me an envelope, she continued, "So, I thought I would give you a little check."

I thought she meant about twenty dollars. When I went into the dressing room and saw it I was surprised. It was two hundred and fifty dollars—just the amount I needed for my ticket.

That paid for my way to New York and then I got on The Flanders ship to cross over to France. As I'd seen time and time again, when there is a calamity something good also happens if you are present to recognize it.

The people on the boat found out that I was an actress and a dancer and they asked me if I would do a show. Of course I agreed. They put me in first class and I performed on the boat. It was sort of a Cuban number. Days before I had no idea where I was going to get the money to meet Yvan. Now I was traveling first class across the North Atlantic Ocean.

*Performing on board The Flanders ship.*

*Performing a Cuban Ola dance on board The Flanders ship.*

I took the boat from New York to France, and then a train to Paris. When I arrived, Yvan's mother was there to meet me. I could see in her demeanor that something was wrong. She told me, with quite a solemn look, that Yvan was on his way. I didn't know what to think, perhaps his illness was worse than I originally imagined. At least soon we would be together.

I didn't have much money left, so I took a small room just big enough for Yvan and me. It was probably a room they had for the cleaning staff. You could barely turn around in it. Gene Kelly was filming *Singing in the Rain* and was staying in the hotel in one of the big suites.

Yvan's mother told Yvan where I was. I hardly could contain myself waiting. My heart jumped seeing him walk through the door. He looked a little weathered but still so captivating.

Without a word, Yvan took me in his arms and hugged me, both of us holding on tightly. We couldn't talk. We just stayed like that. I felt that at last, "I'm home."

We didn't kiss as I had expected but, rather after hugging me, Yvan sat down with a sinking sigh.

With difficulty, he sort of coughed out the details describing his illness and all the friends who had helped him through it, including a girl in his building who had taken care of him. My flush of joy was short-lived.

He started to explain, "When I was recuperating, I had more time to think and I was missing you more than ever. This girl, who had been living in the same apartment building there, was nice to me and helped me when I was sick. She had become infatuated with me and then one day it came to the point that we slept together, just once."

I paused for a moment and then blurted out, "I can understand this happening. You don't have to worry. We were separated for almost three years and it must have been difficult for you."

A young man who has been away from a woman for so long, how could I blame him?

He shook his head like it was more serious than that, saying something that took my breath away, "When I told her I was going to go back to you, she said that she was pregnant. She was screaming and telling me that I can't abandon her, that I must marry her because the Catholic Church would turn her out for misbehaving. She would be considered evil to bring a baby into the world when she wasn't married."

He then announced that he was obliged to ask me for a divorce, "At first, I told her I couldn't marry her because I was already married to you. Then, she went from begging me to threatening to make a scandal so I ended up marrying her to safeguard us both from slanderous publicity."

To make it worse, he went on and said, "I have to get married again to get it legal for this girl. I wish I hadn't done it but I couldn't leave her stranded." To insure that he got a divorce from me she insisted on traveling with Yvan from Uruguay. She was in Paris.

***

I was shocked and overwhelmed. My heart seemed to have stopped and I couldn't find words. My throat was clogged. I asked him to let me give him an answer later, so he left and I went out for a walk.

The darkest light of my life fell. I struggled within searching for an answer. Tears wouldn't come, neither would anger for why should I blame either one of them. I couldn't blame him for the affair. I was the one who didn't follow him to Uruguay. I was more concerned about him settling there and not worrying about me. I was always thinking I would make enough to go to him or he would call for me but the months turned into years.

I knew that he wanted to do the right thing. He was blaming everything on himself. As a soldier, he would certainly be in a terrible mess for being married to two women. I felt compelled to help. I realized that there was only one answer. I must accept the situation. I let his mother know to call him.

I went back to the hotel and he arrived with his mother. With every bit of strength left in me, I said, "Look, I'll divorce you. I know it's a long time, three years now. I don't blame you, Yvan. That's something that can happen to any of us. It could have happened to me quite a few times in Paris and Hollywood, but I didn't let it."

On hearing this, Yvan's mother was absolutely heartbroken. She couldn't believe what was happening. In tears she avowed, "I will never accept this other girl in my house. You're my daughter. You've waited all these years and you haven't done anything wrong. You are not going to let her get away with this!"

I knew she loved me, but I also knew I had to let Yvan go. Things were happening so fast. Although I was trying to control my emotions, I knew my own heart was breaking. I tried to help Yvan's mother accept what was happening just as I was trying to accept it.

I explained to her, "I can't let him down. I can understand him having an affair. That could happen to any young man."

She paid no attention to what I said, but continued to beg me not to relinquish. She didn't want him to go and leave me alone. Trying to remind her that she must not lose Yvan, I added, "You can't do that to him. You lost your other son in the war. Yvan is all you have left. He was caught in an awful circumstance and things happened."

The following day, Yvan and I went to Versailles to get a divorce. He had to go there because he was military personnel. To my surprise, he came in uniform. I couldn't help just looking at him as we walked into the building.

I thought I could keep my emotions out of this, but as I saw him in that splendid Free French regalia, almost immediately my resolve was weakened. My heart began pounding in my chest as fast as it did each time I waited for him to come home to me after a dangerous flying mission.

Suddenly, my mind became flooded with memories of the unbelievable joy we shared—our long talks and walks, the fun times in Paris and Sancerre, the strange experiences in Scotland, the funny stories he would tell to make me laugh, even the hard times during the war as a pilot's wife.

Then, I thought about the longing and anticipation of our being together when he was in Uruguay. For two people who were so much in love, this whole drama seemed unreal.

I began to breathe slowly and deeply trying to quiet my emotions while telling myself, "I'm trying to do what I think is right."

We stood together, both in silence not letting our eyes meet, waiting to sign the divorce documents. I thought of abruptly walking away, but I didn't. The process began. I answered the questions that I was asked and didn't tell them that he'd remarried. I just signed the papers and that was that.

My marriage was over. It was clear in my mind that I had just gone through the process of releasing my husband to another woman—a man I had never stopped loving. It was clear that I was not ready to let go.

A cold breeze encircled my heart. The struggle to find a way to be with Yvan had ended. I walked under the trees by myself along the Seine trying to breathe. It was as though my whole world had fallen to pieces. Fate had decreed.

An argument was brewing within myself, "Why didn't I hold on to the love story that had helped me through the lonely years without him? Should I have fought for my beloved? Why couldn't I beat the sadness? Was I too understanding?"

In Paris, my friends were happy to see me again and tried to offer distractions. Guimas and Maggy, as well as other friends, tried to cheer me up. Since I was well known as a model and actress, I received a lot of invitations.

I tried to hide my loneliness with party after party. My friends dragged me out to the beautiful beaches of the Cote d'Azur at Juan-les-Pins, but that didn't work. Even Bébé Bérard couldn't make me smile anymore when he told everyone that I "walked like a panther." Nothing worked.

I went to visit my aunt's olive groves just to bring back good memories. Even the publicity I was still getting from winning the "Girl with the Longest Legs" in Europe contest did nothing to cheer me. My whole being seemed to dry up. I thought I might go across to England but there were few of the people from my past around and the dull weather would do nothing for me. My dear friend, Noël Coward, had moved to the Caribbean.

After a few months in France, living almost in a stupor, I had to figure out what to do. I knew I had to continue my life.

Marlene advised, "Forget the past, Täo. You have a new future in front of you. Go back and don't even think about it. Don't let it get you down. Close the book on this chapter and open up your life to a new adventure."

I took that to heart and concluded that it was better that I take the next plane away from Paris and the souvenirs of the past. I had to find a new life so I returned to California. I had some money in a British bank and used all of it. We had a joint account in Paris, but I didn't touch it. I left that with him.

When I arrived back in Hollywood, I was lost. Only my dearest friends there understood. I was thankful to Ginny and Frances and Cesar Romero, whom I met previously at a party. We had done some filming and had become friends. Johnnie and Dick lit up my life and were real sweethearts. They brought levity to my world right when I needed it. They were always there for me.

Johnnie and Dick even took me to the Academy Awards where all the stars came out. It was when it was at the glorious Pantages Theatre at Hollywood and Vine.

To people who didn't know me, it appeared like all was fine. The glamorous actress Lana Turner even fawned over my outfit at the Academy Awards one time asking who designed my dress. Little did she know that I didn't have money for a gown and I was wearing an Indian sari sewn on me. All of that was nice but it still didn't fill the deep hole that had formed inside.

\*\*\*

That's when Indra Devi returned to my life. She knew me when I was a little girl. She was about fifteen years older than me and knew my uncle. She followed the teachings of Ramakrishna, Swami Vivekananda and Sri Aurobindo. Later I realized interestingly enough

*The creative and spiritual realms often meld.*

she was also an actress and dancer before dedicating herself to yoga. The creative and spiritual realms often meld.

Many people, including myself, now referred to her as "Mataji" which means, "respected mother" in Hindi. She was the first person from the West to study with the renowned Sri Krishnamacharya and bring his teachings to the U.S. She was asked to start a new yoga studio in Hollywood.

*My mentor Mataji Indra Devi.*

There was a lot of mixing between the arts and spirituality at the time and someone had brought her to MGM. She was on a trip through California on her way upstate to San Francisco, and was coming through with Swami Prabhavananda and the Vedanta Society. It was in some ways strange to see these hallowed gurus who were teaching about humility and non-attachment in the midst of the MGM world of excess and illusion. Yet, their larger-than-life presence somehow belonged there.

As soon as they said my name Mataji Indra Devi looked at me and said, "I know you."

It was so funny that she recognized me after twenty years. I had been a child when she last saw me. She was often there at the Aurobindo Ashram with The Mother.

She continued with her particular way of saying things, "Vhat you do in films? Why you not teach yoga?"

Somewhat surprised, I conceded, "Because I'm not a teacher. I don't know enough of it."

"Nonsense! You teach yoga. You teach it!"

In weak protest, I said, "I really and truly can't."

She insisted, "Yes, you can. You go out and you do it. They need people like you here. You know a lot about yoga. With your uncle you were brought up with it."

I didn't consider myself a yoga teacher but started to think about what she said.

Then, I saw her at the Vedanta Society saying to Swamiji, "Make her teach yoga."

The people in Hollywood didn't even know that I did any yoga. Gradually I started to teach. For a while, I had a group at MGM including American actress and singer Kathryn Grayson and French actress and dancer Leslie Caron.

Leslie was in the musical *An American in Paris* and had a problem with her foot. After one of our yoga sessions, I suggested that she take a Coca-Cola bottle and roll her foot on it like a foot massage. In India, when women were pregnant they used this to help them balance better before and after the baby was born.

The studio thought Leslie Caron was going to be off for three weeks but she was back very quickly. Someone, who I think was a chiropractor, came up and asked, "What did you do so she could walk?"

"Nothing, I just used a Coke bottle. It has a nice indentation and you can move up and down."

Apparently this person, or someone I had taught, thought it was a good business idea. About three months later, one of the first massage rollers was introduced in a studio on Sunset Strip and they were charging ten dollars for it! I often took for granted my own knowledge and intuitive nature.

\*\*\*

I didn't really do any modeling in America after that horrible early job in New York except for when European designers, like Elsa Schiaparelli, came over and looked me up. They knew I was in California so they would find me and ask me to show their clothes and model for them. I liked that work. Through Ginny, these famous designers would arrange shows that would make money for charity. Louis Vaudable, who had become a good friend over the years, would say, "When you go to Hollywood, just go and see Täo."

All of the stars and wealthy set went to Maxim's restaurant in Paris so Louis knew everyone of note. You could always find people from any government or consulate having lunch there.

Right at that time when I was still really down, Louis came to Hollywood and invited me to a big party in Palm Springs. Like my other friends, he was trying to cheer me up. The party was your usual fare of celebrities and glamour.

Although Palm Springs was only about two hours from Los Angeles, it seemed like it was a world away. Something happened to me in the silent beauty of the desert. It calmed my spirit and awakened a part of me that had been dormant for too long.

Like the Vedanta Society, the beauty of the desert of Palm Springs was calling me back to center. I could no longer hide myself from the superficiality of the Hollywood glitz and the constant fighting against every male friendship that would finish in talk about sex. I wanted to be in nature but couldn't figure out how I was going to travel without money or a car. Johnnie laughingly suggested, "Look at a new Oldsmobile. It's automatic. I will hire it for you."

I had never driven before. The people at the car place showed me how to start it, how to put on the brakes, how to stop it and how to get gasoline. One day, I decided to drive into the desert past the glitter of Las Vegas. Time seemed to stand still.

As I approached the sandstone towers and the wild foliage, I felt tremendous peace wash over me. Fascinated by the brilliant sunset I somehow got off the main road and found myself in a narrow canyon and a really rough road. The sun seemed to drop behind the peaks and I decided it was safer to stop as I could hardly see either side of the canyon.

I had been trying to find a place to stay but there was nothing. It was a muddy path at the time. I parked right in the middle of the canyon in the mud. During the night, someone started banging on the car door. It was a ranger, "What are you doing in Zion?"

A bit startled, I replied, "I was crossing through and couldn't find a hotel or anything."

He laughed, "Miss, you're the first person to come through here in three months. Even the man who delivers me milk only leaves it at the entrance. He has never come in here. Only you."

More seriously, he asked, "Aren't you afraid of the animals?"

"No," I replied, "Why should I be scared of animals? I love them. I like listening to the coyotes."

He couldn't believe me. The ranger shook his head and said, "Well, you know, it's always good to be careful."

He told me he would bring me some tea in the morning. I made it through sleeping in the car. In the middle of the night, I did hear a melodic howling and then another haunting cry from a distant mountainside or rock. It was a true call of the wild.

It might have been frightening but it soothed my spirit like I was in conversation with the forces of nature or eavesdropping on something sacred. It was like the lunar influence had eased my mind and the rising sun was opening my heart.

In that moment, I could feel the sound of the Universe—the sound of OM—enter my being and the feeling of *yug*, the joining of body, mind and Spirit. Nature is the encyclopedia giving us a glimpse of our true nature.

*Nature is the encyclopedia giving us a glimpse of our true nature.*

*The beauty of Zion Canyon.*

In the morning, after the ranger graciously delivered my tea, I headed out through the solitude of the Kaibab Forest all the way down through the east side of the Grand Canyon and down through the center of its southern park. I arrived in Hollywood in time to film that afternoon.

Every weekend, when people thought I was out gallivanting and going to parties, I was actually alone going out into nature. I loved the beauty of the west, so I would take a car and drive out into the desert, the mountains, an Indian reservation, a beach or any other natural reserves I could find.

I would go anywhere. I wasn't afraid because my uncle had taken me everywhere. I was interested in the Native Americans. They were so close to the earth. This was their land yet it was taken away from them.

***

I fled into the great canyons of Bryce and Zion, to where my dreams were packed with the wonders of nature. I was just sort of discovering everything.

The more I moved into the desert, the more fulfilled I was and the more I was able to express myself. It was where I belonged and I needed to get away. It was my way to balance out the craziness of Hollywood. I learned that if there is something that gives you energy, pursue it—even if you have to go out on your own.

*If there is something that gives you energy, pursue it—even if you have to go out on your own.*

I was always alone but in many ways it was beginning to heal my loneliness. I went to the wondrous Goblin Valley which is next to Zion and Bryce going in the opposite direction from the Grand Canyon. It's sort of an outer layer of the Grand Canyon. It's part of Arizona and part of New Mexico.

I didn't want to just go around the outskirts. I really wanted to see things and go deep into this remarkable valley that looked like another planet. As I was walking, I ran into two American Indians who thought I was lost. I saw the kindness in their eyes. They couldn't talk to me and I couldn't talk to them so they took me to the nearest ranger.

Surprised to see a woman, the ranger asked, "What are you doing? Where did you come from?"

I answered, "Hollywood."

Seemingly amazed, he replied, "That's many miles away."

"Well, I drove here," informing him with a smile.

Ever more curious, he asked, "Where is your car?"

I gave him instructions, "Well, if you follow this back you will find my car." Knowing that I had to find my way back, I had put a piece of purple ribbon on the trees at certain points along the way. It sounds so silly but this is what I used to do since I was by myself.

*The wondrous Goblin Valley.*

I went to places where nobody else went. I simply had to get away. Once I was driving and found my way to Borrego Hot Springs. It was untouched and yet to be discovered at the beginning of mountains that separated Mexico from America.

It's about three hours from Los Angeles—an ethereal desert landscape with peaks and valleys, steep canyons and spurts of wildflowers. There was just one little place where you could stop and get some coffee, gas and things.

I took my purple ribbon everywhere I was going so I wouldn't get lost. Like before, I would tie pieces of ribbon along the path so I could follow them back to my car. As I was walking along feeling spiritually connected to nature, I suddenly saw a deer that looked like it was almost pointing up. It was quite strange. There was a big wall of mountainside there. It didn't look like you could go over it or around it. The deer disappeared into it. I thought, "How can it do that?" I had a sense it was directing me. So, I went underneath some branches.

I looked ahead and there was a hollow opening so I crawled through it. Most people probably wouldn't do that, but I felt I was being led. I came through it and then screamed. In that moment, it was the most alarming thing that happened to me. There were all of these creepy skeletons with tattered uniforms.

I must admit that I was a bit scared, so I ran back following every purple ribbon until I was safely in my car. I headed back to Hollywood with my brain ticking away about the sight I had seen.

A few days later a close friend asked, "So, what have you been up to Täo?"

I shared, "I went to Borrego Hot Springs and had a really incredible experience."

She was familiar with the area and said, "There is nothing there."

I confirmed, "There are no houses or anything. It's open." Then, I told her what happened. She was shocked.

She knew someone at *National Geographic Magazine* and asked me, "Can you find it again?"

With assurance, I said, "Yes, you'll have no trouble finding it."

I gave clear directions to where I parked the car and then told her, "Just follow the purple ribbons into the bush." I left so fast I didn't take them away.

So, they found it. They could tell from the uniforms that the skeletons were the Spanish that had come out from Mexico. They must have been ambushed. The earthquakes had likely come together and buried them. It wasn't something terribly exciting, but people were talking about it for a short time.

It was so interesting to see the desert and observe what happens twenty minutes after a rainstorm. After the rain stops, guess what? There are shoots coming up, all kinds of plants starting to grow. It is incredible just to see how everything breathes out of the earth, and how the elements come together. I was hopeful that the pieces of my life would come together. Sometimes you have to let go of the story of what you think your life should be so you can be present with what is. It doesn't mean you give up. Instead, you give in to your true nature and what the Universe is calling you to do. You surrender to the vision and live in Pure Awareness.

> *Sometimes you have to let go of the story of what you think your life should be so you can be present with what is.*

CHAPTER 15

# Begin Where You Are

If soil is dry you water it. If plants need food you feed them. Nature teaches us the basics. The Native Americans and most indigenous cultures use this knowledge. Like my uncle said, "The farmer may not be able to read or write but he knows more about farming and his field than you do. So don't ever think that you're better than him." There is so much we can learn from people who are close to nature and the earth. By observing the natural cycle of things, you can learn a more intuitive way of being such as the simplicity of beginning where you are and using what you have.

*Begin where you are and use what you have.*

My life in Hollywood went on as usual with some bright spots. Johnnie finally got a small part with Marlene in the Western movie, *Rancho Notorious*. He was thrilled and she was as funny as ever. She had these big emeralds. The producer Howard Welsch said, "You can't wear that in a cowboy film."

She replied with her accent and Dietrich-way, "If you have it, you v'ore it!"

She did a couple more films in America after that. When she was not getting such big jobs any more, she got fed up with Hollywood. That's why she kept going back to France. She still was so glamorous and performed in cabarets and at the Olympia Theatre in Paris.

One thing that upset her was when her former lover Jean Gabin married Dominique Fournier, who resembled Marlene. Dominique was the model who talked me into entering the Longest Legs contest and also introduced me to Prince Kolnoski. Even though years had passed since Dominque had married Gabin, it still seemed to bother Marlene.

Although Marlene never discussed it outright with me, I got a sense that she felt unappreciated though she wasn't the type to complain. Everything with Marlene was always about today and what was going to happen tomorrow, not about the past. Her attitude was "Go and do it." We had the same ideas about so many things. We both would say, "Never think negative. Stay away from it." Finally, she went back to France to live.

Guimas would always keep me posted on what Marlene was doing. I still have letters from him before he died about fifteen years ago. We stayed in contact all those decades.

On Marlene, he would write, "Guess what she bought me this time?" She was always doing something for somebody.

He reminded me of something funny that happened a few years earlier. I was in Paris and Guimas called me up. He lived only two blocks away from me. He said with some excitement, "I have a friend here. You should come over and join us."

"Well, who?" I asked very curious.

"No. No. No. Just come over and join us. You'll be happy," he coaxed.

Eager to find out who this surprise person could be, I gathered my things and went right away. When I got to the hotel, there was nobody in the lobby. There was nobody to operate the elevator. Strangely, there was nobody anywhere.

I was listening and could hear people laughing. Elevators at that time had to have someone to operate them. So, I started to climb up the stairs and followed the sound of laughter all the way up to the rooms on the seventh floor. When I reached the top, I was breathless. There I could see all of the people from the lobby including the elevator operators.

Right in the center of it all I saw this little electric train running in and out of the rooms, throughout the floor in and out of the rooms where most of the staff lived. Everybody was having great fun watching.

Suddenly, Marlene turned and I saw her with this magnificent fur draped around her chest, as she said with alluring charisma, "Darling von't you join us!"

I was delighted to see her and we had so much fun together. Marlene had bought Guimas that electric train because she found out that he liked them.

She was great like that. You dared not say to her, "I like that." It probably would be in the post the next day. She was so good-hearted and incredible that way.

***

I liked going down to Mexico. It was like going away from everything. I loved the beach and the big sand dunes.

Once I was in something that was filmed in Acapulco. On our way back to Los Angeles, I kept saying, "You know I have this strange headache. It's usually when there's going to be a storm or maybe an earthquake."

Everybody started to laugh at me. "Don't tell us you can predict earthquakes!"

I said, "I can't tell you what it is but I can tell you when something is going to go wrong, or what the weather will be because I start to get a headache."

Laughing, one friend said, "Oh, come on Täo. You're always making us laugh."

I assured him, "I'm serious. I know that I can feel electrical current in here. Like going down yesterday, I could sense a heavy fog before it came."

I had experienced a big earthquake when I was in India with my uncle. It was a deadly quake that hit Lahore, which is now a part of Pakistan. Lahore was called the "Paris of the Orient."

We were at one of the very chic hotels. I was washing my hair or doing something silly. Suddenly, I had a headache. Then, my bed started to move and everything flew across the room. Things were almost being lifted off the ground.

The headache that I had that day in California was similar. It was very early in the morning. By the time I reached my apartment my headache became more violent. I was concerned that I wasn't going to be able to talk very well because the pounding was hitting me hard.

As soon as I opened the door a bit, my bed went sliding across the room. It hit the other wall and slid back again. I saw the big fan moving and I had this feeling that the floor was also moving. I thought I was going to be lifted off the ground.

A horrible earthquake had hit Bakersfield, which is about a hundred miles or so from Los Angeles. The earth had literally cracked open. I later found out that it measured 7.3 on the magnitude scale. The energy I felt was so strong.

The people who had been with me said, "You predicted that three hours ago. How did you know?"

I could feel it. It reminded me of when I was a child and used to put my ear to the ground listening to the grass grow. We each have a connection to nature if we nurture it.

\*\*\*

With my French accent and limited English, MGM had few films that I could act in. My language mishaps were often humorous. At one point, I was doing a film and the director kept saying, "Turn your face to the camera."

I kept my backside to the camera.

"Please Täo, will you turn your face to the camera!" He seemed to be getting mad.

I was getting frustrated and asked, "How do you spell it?"

Sounding a bit annoyed, he said, "How do you spell face? F-A-C-E."

I said, "Oh, that's it! I thought you meant F-E-S-S-E-S, which in French sounds like "face" and means your buttocks!"

Those were the funny things that would happen and why MGM liked me even though it got me in some trouble. They knew I wasn't sarcastic or trying to be funny. I simply and innocently mixed things up at times.

It was the very beginning of TV and they were trying different things. Westerns were very popular. Working to improve my English, I made several short TV films. Tom Dix was in some of them but they never became big.

Loving the idea of seeing the Great Plains and desert, I was delighted to get a call to be in a Western. Most were being shot out at the Rex Ingram Ranch.

We arrived with many cowboy actors and typical attire, big hats and boots. Hundreds of cattle were assembled. I was introduced to the director who asked, "How do you like the idea of being in a Western?"

Not quite understanding, delightedly I said, "*Formidable!* I want to be a coo-girl."

The director looked at me strangely. Someone else understood and with laughter said, "She wants to be a cowgirl!"

Excitedly, I chimed in, "Yes! Yes! A cowboy. A cowgirl."

Everyone chuckled, smiling at me.

They were getting ready to film the girl who was supposed to do the Indian role, and she didn't turn up. The director turned to me, and asked, "Do you know how to ride a horse?"

I didn't know what he was talking about but anxious to be in the film I replied, "Yes! Yes!"

Nodding and smiling, I was saying "yes" to everything. I still didn't know what he was talking about and had never been on a horse in my life.

Suddenly, I found myself being lifted into the saddle. Wow! I was so thrilled. Little did I know what was going to happen next.

As I waited listening for the cue, the director slapped the hind leg of the horse and it took off like an arrow. Completely unaware of what to do next, I heard the director give the order, "CAMERA... ROLL!"

I hung on for dear life, not knowing how to stop it. I was trying to stay calmly on its back as it galloped after the other horses. The trail of the scene seemed to be known to the horse, because it came back and was brought to a halt.

At that point, I thought, "I must tell the director that I'd never been on a horse." I watched the others dismount and I tried to come down too. The director misconstrued my action and somehow thought it meant that I rode bare back.

As I reached the ground, they quickly unsaddled the horse. Before I could say another word, I found myself on its back. Cautiously, I watched others mount and the camera crew getting ready to shoot the scene.

I decided to use a little yoga and breath. For a few minutes, I breathed deeply with the horse, and then patted him gently. He took off and as though he was aware of the script dashed in the opposite direction to the cowboys and another direction slowly swinging back to camera as they called "ROLL."

Everyone clapped saying "Great job! Where did you learn to ride?"

The director helping me dismount, wrapped his arm around my

shoulder exclaiming, "Great job! You'll make a wonderful Indian girl rider."

His crew all encircled me slapping me on the shoulder praising my riding. How could I ever tell them I'd never been on a horse before, let alone ride one!

The thought I used every day when I wasn't sure of life was ringing in my mind, "This is going to be the best day of my life! And it truly was!"

*Playing a cowgirl ("coogirl" as I called it) in an early TV show in the 1950s. The headdress was originally given to me by a French-Canadian who was helping the Native Americans. I used it initially doing a performance in 1947 for the first big Boy Scouts meeting in France at the end of the war. I made up a dance, tapping my feet like I was playing a drum.*

I continued working as an actress at MGM, this time with Kathryn Grayson, as well as Debbie Reynolds. Debbie was a little blonde girl who was in so many dance films with the actor Mickey Rooney. She was pretty with her own fresh wholesome beauty. She made tons of films for MGM and received a lifetime achievement award in February 2015.

Back then, I went with her for MGM to entertain the Marines in a charity show at the Desert Inn in Las Vegas. We also went just north of San Diego. They wanted me to sing.

I told them, "I don't sing."

They said, "Talk it then. Täo, you've got to be very French."

So I sang: "Darling, Je Vous Aime Beaucoup" which was a popular song at the time. While singing, I sultrily walked out into the audience playfully taking the hand of a young Marine and seductively led him on stage where I sang to him. The Marines loved it and I pulled the house down. The comedians that were there didn't want to follow me afterwards. It reminded me of the response I got from the comedians during the war who didn't want to perform after me.

*About to perform at the Desert Inn in Las Vegas, Nevada in 1954. Actress and friend Debbie Reynolds took the picture with her tiny camera as we were walking into the hotel. She called out at me and I turned around. It was very spontaneous.*

\*\*\*

It was a strange time all around particularly in America. Everywhere in Hollywood people were being persecuted for what they thought and said. I couldn't believe it. Whatever you said that didn't fit in with what people were talking about made you a Communist. It was horrible. This was supposed to be "the Land of the Free."

I said to my friends, "You know something, I've been against Communism for a good part of my life. I believe in freedom but freedom isn't Communism."

They would say to me, "Be careful, Täo. They will throw you out of the country."

Defiantly, I would reply, "Then they would have to pay my fare!"

I had the potential to get in a lot of trouble because I would speak my mind. In this instance, it probably helped that I didn't speak English very well. Many couldn't understand what I was saying so I didn't get so mixed up in it, though I would go out and listen to the craziest things that they were saying.

They were horrible to one man who did so much good. He helped many people, including children. They said that he was trying to form them into Communists so they ruined his career. One of the major directors at MGM was being harassed. They were trying to drag him through the court with a case against him because he didn't have the same thoughts as them. A lot of people rose up and made a big deal about it. It was a weird time. A lot of the stars were on a so-called "Hollywood blacklist."

The marvelous American actor Burgess Meredith was helpful in trying to bolster my acting career. He was a very good friend of Marlene so he tried to push me forward. He remembered me from Le Petit Club Français in London, as well as this members-only club where we would go and eat. He knew a little bit about what I did, and saw me perform back then.

I never stayed long in California without returning to France. I would go for a year and then come back. I had an apartment one block from the Champs-Élysées. Avenue George V is on one side, then Avenue Montaigne near Christian Dior. Right there in Rue Marbeuf, the second block over, was my apartment.

I love the Champs-Élysées with all the trees. I moved over to another place on Avenue Montaigne opposite The Plaza. They all knew me at the hotel so they would be there to open the door to my taxi and I then would cross over to my place. I have some very good memories of Paris and nearly every part of France. The horrific times of war seemed to have been washed away from my mind and the sadness about Yvan didn't sting as much. It's no wonder I didn't stay, but I still thought I could get work in Hollywood.

At one point, when I knew I was going to be in France for a while, I had mailed to my Paris apartment many of my precious items including books I had collected, as well as pictures from when I was younger. There was even a check in there from one of my MGM appearances. The items never arrived. When I returned to California, I found that they had apparently been stolen from the Beverly Hills Post Office.

It was during a time when there were a lot of thefts right in that area. I don't know why they thought my things were of value. To me, they were truly dear including a picture with my uncle, as well as one with Marlene. Since there was nothing I could do about it, I had to simply let it go.

Everything seemed to be changing when I got back from France this time. The agent I was with belonged to a big group called the William Morris Agency. I had been introduced to him originally through Marlene but he now was no longer there. I had to find another agent who would really support me.

*I had an agent at the famous William Morris Agency. This is one of my tax statements from later on in 1956. I made very little that year because I spent most of my time in Paris.*

Burgess Meredith tried to get me into the same talent agency he had, but they wouldn't take me because I wasn't a big enough star. It was also a time when he was being heavily persecuted with all of the talk about Communism. I appreciated his kindness. He liked wine and even started a vineyard a few years later. He would invite me to that restaurant on the Sunset Strip where all the famous people went.

\*\*\*

I was earning money but sometimes it wasn't so much. People thought I was making a lot since I was under contract. MGM was still trying to figure out what to do with me. It wasn't completely their fault because of my English. They continued to hire me out to different places.

They had me work with a coach to get rid of my accent because my English was too French. The lovely Arlene Dahl was also getting coached because her English was too British. Richard Greene, who later starred in the British TV series *The Adventures of Robin Hood*, was being coached because his English was also too British! We would see each other either coming in or going out of the coaching room.

I was looking for another agent and someone introduced me Lou Schnitzer, a sweet little man who had been in the business for years in silent movies. He was a German Jew with a slight accent, and liked me right away. He said, "I want you to be a big star. You really don't understand Hollywood."

When he talked about me to others, he would always say, "She is one of the few real ladies that I've ever had pass through the portals of MGM. She is not only beautiful, but she also writes and does a lot of things. She's lived all over the world."

He would come in and talk about me as if I was a big queen of the day. He liked me for the work I did. One day he even had tears in his eyes talking about me. He was sincere.

Although he wasn't a big agent, he was always working for me. The first few months that I was with him he got me work. I was in some plays in Hollywood so he had a lot of people come and see me in them.

I was trying to do everything to learn better English and taking parts where I could. At one point, I was in a play, *East of Eden*. I had somewhat of a strange part. My character's personality was all over the place.

I played the part of being a frivolous maid, and then I became God-stricken. I had to stand in an altar and repeat things from the Bible like, "To everything there is a season." On the one side, the character behaved in a very devout manner and then she was crazy doing everything against religion. It was an intriguing premise.

*Performing at a Hollywood theater in 1950s.*

Ezra Stone, who was in one of the young kid gangs in the films and then became a director, came and saw me in this play. He liked it and gave me a small part in his TV show, *I Married Joan*, which starred Joan Davis and Jim Backus who was famous for being the voice of Mr. Magoo and later for being the millionaire on the TV show *Gilligan's Island*. Ezra told the others, "She can dance."

My part was to dance the tango with Jim. He could never remember anything so they said to me, "Whatever he says and you don't understand, just say something in French even if you swear at him." They didn't ask me really to speak English.

*With actor Hugh O'Brian for MGM project in Hollywood around 1952. Hugh went on to become a big star in television.*

*With actor Hugh O'Brian.*

I did what work I could and was often paired with wonderful people like Hugh O'Brian who later made it big in the ABC Western television series, *The Life and Legend of Wyatt Earp.*

Through my agent, I also worked with Red Skelton who was a comedian under MGM and then TV with NBC. I had a small part in *The Red Skelton Show.*

*I wore this white stole in Half a Hero with Red Skelton.*

*April 20, 1953. The Los Angeles Herald & Express had the headline "Paris Cutie With Longest Legs Gets Role in Red Skelton's New Comedy." The blurb said: "Tao Porchon, lovely Paris model who has many times been voted as the doll with the longest legs in all France, is trying out for a movie career, and has just landed a role with Red Skelton in M-G-M's 'Half a Hero,' which also features Jean Hagen."*

In the 1950s, television was becoming more popular and the movie studios started testing out new ways to get people to the theatres. That's when 3-D films came out. I was in two of them.

The first was *Sangaree* at Paramount. That's when I met Arlene Dahl again. I walked in and she said, "I know you!"

She had become a big star and didn't have as much accent. She was in the film with the English actress Patricia Medina and the suave Latin actor Fernando Lamas, who later became her husband. I had a small part.

I also did the 3-D film, *House of Wax*, with the eccentric American actor Vincent Price at Warner Bros. It was a Dracula-type horror film. They put special Max Factor makeup on me that they were trying out so that people could see in three dimensions.

The Edington-Cloutman Agency got me a part in the 3-D movie, Sangaree.

Costume for a performance in Hollywood in the early 1950s. It came from Cambodia and I originally wore it performing at the Salle de la Chimie in Paris.

Max Factor was popular for creating creams and what became known as "makeup" for movies and then for everyday people. This experimental 3-D makeup, however, poisoned my skin and made me break out in boils. They kept putting makeup on top of it.

It burned my skin and damaged it for months and months. I even lost work because of it. They apparently hadn't perfected the formula. They had to face me away from the camera. Even to this day I have some holes in my face where they put the makeup.

*\*\*\**

As my life became more chaotic with my divorce and so many of the things that were happening to me at the same time, I turned more and more to the Vedanta Society. When I couldn't get into nature, I would go to the Center. I was searching for a deeper connection. I still had bouts of loneliness.

Listening to great writers and other seekers who surrounded Swami Prabhavananda opened up my life and wove a pattern in my heart. We were not doing the physical practice. We would meditate and discuss spiritual matters. At one point, I would go there almost every night. It seemed to be where I belonged and my life started to blossom with clarity and joy. Had I found the Truth? Would this sense of peace last?

I hesitated for I found myself amidst great writers and scientists like Aldous Huxley, Gerald Heard, Christopher Isherwood, Frederick Manchester and so many others on a similar path searching for the spiritual side of being.

We sat on the ground with Swamiji as they asked the deepest and most fundamental questions. From time to time, I managed with my French accent and imperfect English to come up with a simple question. Swamiji would smile with, "You always hit the nail on the head, Täo."

The others would laugh. Even though I didn't know what it meant, he made me feel I was on the right track. He was such a natural holy man capable of hearty laughter.

One of the first things he saw when he arrived in America as he was driving along was a billboard for toothpaste that said, "Stop decay before it starts." He thought that was funny. Referring to negative thoughts in the mind, he would say, "What do they mean stop it before it starts? We're putting it in our minds. Don't even think about it. Stop decay in your mind before it starts."

It was the time that actors and people in Southern California seemed to be all on a journey of self-discovery. They were becoming interested in Indian philosophy. We hadn't yet come to the blossoming of the 1960s when people were crafting a New Age but the seeds representing the sacredness of life were being planted.

The Vedanta Society was the home to many interesting people. They continually were asking for their names to be changed to an Indian name, something to do with meditation and spirituality. When I asked Swamiji about it he laughed and said, "Don't ask me to change your name. YOU are the TAO of life!"

Little by little, I was drawn into opening the pages of my life. It freed me from thoughts of being without a job and somehow unlatched the door to the wonder of living. With the greatest sense of humor, Swamiji provided the simplest answers to everyone.

We touched upon the infinite questions of spirituality and so many subjects I had pondered since childhood, "What am I doing on this earth and where am I heading?" My aloneness was blossoming into a fulfillment of the story of life, and maybe where I belonged.

I would sometimes bring others with me to the Vedanta Society. I used to meet a young man from Israel at the big Farmer's Market and we would go to the Center. Sometimes, I would arrive there with a few boys who were at Columbia Music doing work for television. They were right in Hollywood on the hill. A couple of them were in a film with me and I used to go out with the whole band of them together. One of them spoke French, so it was easier for me to talk to them.

Once I went with the whole group of them to Yosemite National Park. I slept in the car and they slept outside. The next day some sailors whistled at me. My friends looked around as if they had seen me for the first time. After all, I was a girl with about five boys. None of them was my boyfriend. We were just a group of friends. They had taken me to go where you look into this big tree trunk. It was nice to find other people who appreciated nature and the natural surroundings and were searching for something more.

\*\*\*

I was constantly going in and out of Pure Awareness—the dance of mind, body and Spirit. Sometimes I felt like I had to begin again, to once more come back to center. Nature and the Vedanta Society would pull me in and then Hollywood would draw me out.

I received a small part in the movie, *The Last Time I Saw Paris* that Jack Cummings was producing. I was always grateful to him for giving me my first job in Hollywood.

One day on the MGM set I saw Michael Wilding. He was with his wife Elizabeth Taylor, who was the star of the film along with Donna Reed, Van Johnson and Walter Pidgeon. Liz was then the biggest star in Hollywood. Everyone was raving about her.

During the war in London I used to go out with Michael. We weren't romantically dating. We would go to a couple of clubs together with friends, laugh and simply have fun. I was in the film, *Sailors Three*, with him. I didn't have a big part but I was well known in Europe. Now, he was married to this larger-than-life actress.

I saw Michael standing there with her and he apparently recognized me. He was saying something like, "I know that girl."

I wasn't going to go over there and say, "Do you remember me?" I'm a little thing and he's married to this big personality. I thought that would be rude. So I didn't do it.

Apparently Elizabeth Taylor got jealous anyway. She was mad because he kept talking about me. She wasn't very happy. I didn't get thrown out of the film but the producer said, "I'm sorry Täo. We have to change your role."

Disappointed, I asked, "Why? What did I do wrong? Was I so bad?"

He said, "No, on the contrary. You were typically Parisian. Your dress and everything was wonderful. But we have a very big star and she objects. She doesn't want you in it but you're under contract."

I was supposed to be in this superb sleek French dress and they put me in a matronly-looking dark frock. I looked like I'd just come off the streets. They even put my back to the camera! You couldn't see me. Elizabeth Taylor was so gorgeous. She didn't have anything to worry about from me.

Unfortunately, it didn't last very long with her and Michael. They divorced soon thereafter. Although she was a little difficult then, Liz did a lot of good in the later years of her life.

\*\*\*

I learned early on that Hollywood liked controversy. One newspaper put a photograph of the sensuous actress Marilyn Monroe and me in the paper together with a headline: "Gallic Tao Porchon Calls Marilyn Immature: French Laugh at La Monroe's 'Childish, Ineffectual' Sex Appeal." The article went on to say:

> "Marilyn Monroe's sex appeal got the razz today from a sultry French actress who says her countrymen laugh off Marilyn's attractions as 'childish and ineffectual.' Dark-haired Tao Porchon, in Hollywood to make an American movie, said Frenchmen think most American actresses who try to project sex appeal do not quite know what it's all about. 'An actress,' she asserted, 'must live a little before she can successfully portray a woman of deep emotions.'"

I didn't know what they were talking about. They didn't even ask me! I never said anything like this but it looked as if I had said it. Marilyn heard about it. I was so upset.

She had come back from Japan and had just married the American baseball player Joe DiMaggio. She found my telephone number and got me on the phone. In her sultry voice, she offered advice, "Don't worry. As long as they're talking about you, no matter what they print, you're going to be a star. When they stop talking about you, you're going to be in trouble. So don't worry. You didn't hurt me."

I thought that was very sweet. She didn't have to take the time to do that. Despite what people may think, many of the stars were really nice at least to me.

Many people saw Marilyn as simply a sexy woman, but not very smart. That was not the case. At one point, I bumped into someone who was helping her with a few things. He had a bunch of books he was getting for her. I found out that she had a curiosity for learning that you didn't read about in the tabloid papers.

The Los Angeles newspaper that claimed in 1954 that I called Marilyn Monroe's sex appeal "childish and ineffectual." I never said that at all! Under Monroe's picture it says, "Effective or not in the eyes of Frenchmen, Marilyn Monroe has had no complaints on pictures like this from male Americans."

*This picture is from the same set of photos as the one used in the article with Marilyn Monroe. I'm holding a cigarette but I didn't smoke.*

\*\*\*

I was getting all of these small parts. One was the film, *Jump Into Hell*, starring French actor Jacques Sernas and Austrian actor Kurt Kasznar. It was a war film on the Battle of Dien Bien Phu in Indochina. Since it was based on the French Far East Expeditionary Corps, I fit in being half-French.

Then, when they were doing the film *Escape to Burma*, all of these writers were coming up asking me questions given my travels to Burma with my uncle. They would write down what I said and not pay me or give me credit.

One day, my agent came up to me and said, "Täo, at last it's a nice part that's all for you. It's in your territory. You know it. It's the first time we have this opportunity."

*My different looks in my early Hollywood Days at MGM.
I used to put my hair up and sometimes over to one side in Manipur style like
I used to in India. It worked well for a Spanish dance I did in a TV show.*

That night, one of the writers brought me his script and said, "I've got to have this done by tomorrow. Will you look at it?"

I reviewed it. It was so bad that I rewrote the whole thing, staying up practically all night to get it done. The next morning, my agent came to pick me up. While he was waiting for me to get ready, he saw all of the papers on my table—the ones that were left behind. The writer had come in and picked up my changes. My agent asked, "What are all these papers on the table?"

I said, "I've been writing a bit, helping someone."

"Oh, you know Täo this is your first big break and you don't look yourself. You look a little tired."

I assured him, "It will be fine."

We arrived for my interview and saw the producer and director coming out with the writer praising the work, "This is the best script. It's so realistic. It's a little funny because you used some French words."

My agent suddenly realized what happened and said to the writer a bit sarcastically, "I didn't think you knew French."

Turning to the producer and director, my agent exclaimed, "He didn't write it, she did," pointing to me.

Without me realizing it, he had picked up all the papers from the old script while he was in my apartment. He passed it to them saying, "This is what he wrote."

They compared them and saw the differences. I guess I had a few French words sprinkled throughout the dialogue.

What's ironic was I had written myself out of the movie! The part they had for the girl made no sense in that country. Needless to say, I lost that job. However, my agent started to get me some work writing. There were always plenty of people who wanted to do TV programs at that time since it was new. They needed quality content.

This was the beginning of my screenwriting career. Although I didn't speak English very well, I could write it and had passed the British examination that was used by the universities in India and England.

I really liked to write. I still do. Then, I would write in French and English. It reminded me of when I couldn't stay still as a child and the other children would say, "Come on, tell us a story." That's when I would open up.

My uncle would say, "You're gathering quite a crowd around you. Where do you get all of these ideas from?"

My reply would be simple, "I look around me. Then, suddenly something incredible comes up."

Being in nature helped when editing scripts. I was often being asked to change someone's script and help come up with new stories. There is so much beauty in the world that it is easy to develop stories. When one meditates in the great silence of those fabulous canyons, one becomes aware of the power and energy of nature. It spurs creativity. As I wrote more, I started to feel a new direction unfolding.

All the ideas that we need to live in the world, and even heal this world from our own destruction, are out there in the Universe. If you want peace, start by being peace. If you want love, start by being love. If you are searching for creativity, then witness one of the greatest creations of all—nature. The answers to many of our questions are right there in front of us. Most of all recognize that the Creator of all life is inside of you. Instead of looking to the outside when things go awry, begin right where you are by going within.

*Recognize that the Creator of all life is inside of you.*

# CHAPTER 16

# Tune Into Cosmic Intelligence

Sometimes you know things and don't realize it, and sometimes you can do things and don't realize how until perhaps much later. It was like my "knowing" when I was young in Burma with Ayah. I had never been to Rangoon, but I suddenly knew my way around. I'm sure she thought I was a witch. Now, I realize that I had, through my experiences with my uncle, developed a deep intuition and had an innate openness to the possibilities in nature and the world.

> *Sometimes you know things and don't realize it, and sometimes you can do things and don't realize how until perhaps much later.*

When I was growing up, scientists thought that a bumblebee was built in such a way that it should not possibly be able to fly. They were baffled. Assuming that a bee flew like an airplane, its wings seemed too small for its body mass. People would say, "Since the bumblebee does not know this, it continues to fly in its blessed ignorance." Now, scientists have found that bees don't actually flap their wings. They vibrate a muscle that causes the wings to flap giving them more power. It's more like a helicopter rotor than an airplane. The scientists had their basic assumption wrong. How much do we really know about our world? What assumptions may we have that are untrue?

One of my friends from the Charity Players said, "I have someone coming to my house and I would like you to meet him. He talks very much like you. He predicts everything and what he says comes true."

It was Dr. Roman Ostoja who was Founder of the Institute of Infinite Science. He was a very famous Polish man who was going through America with tens of thousands coming to listen to him talk. I had heard a bit about what he was doing and that he was known for hypnotizing all of these people.

He hypnotized the Chinese actress Anna May Wong who was big in the silent movie era and was very famous at the time. She had been in the 1920s version of *The Thief of Bagdad* with Douglas Fairbanks and in *Shanghai Express* with Marlene Dietrich.

In 1927, Dr. Ostoja had been invited by a Santa Barbara newspaper to hypnotize nine people through the radio. He hypnotized the people and then came to the radio station to wake them up. It was apparently a great success and was the first time such an experiment had worked. Someone at Oxford University had tried it and failed.

He had also been buried alive six feet under the ground for two full weeks. Scientists thought it was impossible for the human body to retain life if deprived of oxygen for more than seven minutes. Dr. Ostoja had all air supply cut off and no food and drink for fourteen days.

It was said that he had put himself in a cataleptic trance and his heart and pulse actions resembled those of a dead man. When he was removed from the grave, he was perfectly well though very hungry. That was in 1932 in California. He had reportedly been buried alive on at least fifteen occasions.

I wasn't too sure about what Dr. Ostoja was doing and said, "I don't believe in all of this stuff of being buried alive and everything."

My friend said, "That's not like you, Täo. This is a man who is also doing a lot of good and he's very well known."

She explained that the police in Los Angeles would call him in on murder cases. He would tell the police what questions to ask the suspect. Being a master of telepathy and apparently able to read the person's mind, Dr. Ostoja would know the answers.

He would then write down the name of the street where the murder happened and the culprit would be shaken asking the police, "How did you know all this?"

Dr. Ostoja solved many cases.

A bit curious, I decided to go to the meeting. When I got to her place it was packed. I sat right at the very back of the room. This lean, yet somewhat muscular, tan man with a cream-colored turban came in. He was apparently in his seventies but looked much younger. I didn't know what to think of him.

I could imagine what my aunt in India would have said most likely admonishing me for hanging around a "fakir," her use of the word being derogatory versus a true holy man. My uncle, though, would have been open to someone exploring the depths of consciousness.

Almost immediately Dr. Ostoja said, "In the back of this room there is a very, very old spirit in a young body."

Everybody was looking in my direction, and I was looking back but there was nobody behind me. I was right at the back of this room. He was talking about me!

His lecture on holistic health and healing was interesting. Afterwards, he came to me and introduced himself. My friend said, "I knew you'd be joining up."

I said, "I don't know this man and he doesn't know me."

She said, "Well, everything he said about you is true. He described you without knowing you."

My interest was piqued so I went to a couple more of his events and started to learn more about him.

***

When Roman Ostoja was in his twenties he left Poland for India. In Calcutta, he heard of a Hindu guru named Yogi Ramata who was being buried alive for three months. Ostoja went to observe it for himself. He said, "I was skeptical. Every day I walked past the sleeping man, seeking to detect some fakery. Had there been any, I'd have found it."

Yogi Ramata, who was supposed to be 250 years old at the time, had been in a state of suspended animation. When the guru came out of his trance, he took on the 25-year-old Ostoja as an apprentice and taught him the ancient yoga secrets. For a year, Ostoja lived with his teacher in a hillside cave near Mount Everest in the Himalayan Mountains.

Ostoja explained, "We lived for one year on goat's milk. He said this was necessary because my system was full of poison and acidity caused by Western foods. We caught and milked wild goats for our food. Sometimes for three or four days we didn't see a goat. Mountain goats are so quick but when we saw one we were faster."

He talked about being "trained in the eternal snow." The old guru taught Ostoja to sit nude in the snow for ten minutes the first night, twenty minutes the next night and so on until he sat out all night.

Ostoja said two things made possible this resistance to cold. One was the fact warm air was breathed, and the other was bodily control. "By sitting in the yoga 'egg' position, fingertips resting on toes and face just at the navel, one breathes warmed air. You do not feel cold."

He learned to will one foot asleep, then the other, then his arms, torso, his head. That was the essence of autohypnosis, "Yoga's purpose is to learn bodily control. The mind is the master. One seeks balance and coordination, physically, mentally, emotionally."

> *Yoga's purpose is to learn bodily control. The mind is the master. One seeks balance and coordination, physically, mentally, emotionally.*

Once immune to cold, he followed his master back to Calcutta. There, in blazing sunlight, the master built a fire and told him to walk in it. According to Ostoja, the guru said, "You think you are not yet ready but I think you are and you will never know until you've tried. If you can will your feet warm, will them cold."

So, Ostoja walked barefoot through fire.

Later, he attended St. John's University in Ambur, India, as well as Francis Joseph University in Vienna and St. Andrews University in London. He came to the United States in 1923 at the invitation of Dr. William McDougall, then a Harvard University psychologist. Ostoja lectured on autosuggestion, hypnosis and telepathy. Herbert Sydney Langfeld, Associate Professor at Harvard and later Professor of Psychology and Director of the Psychological Laboratory at Princeton University, was reportedly there as well.

I was really trying to determine whether Dr. Ostoja was legitimate so I read their commentary of his self-control demonstration and experiment in self-anesthesia. The esteemed professors wrote, "In some way he was able to control his muscles so as to draw back the blood, but we're unable to determine how it was accomplished." These psychologists noted that it was the first time they had ever witnessed a voluntary state of trance.

What made me even more interested was that Paramahansa Yogananda, the founder of the Self-Realization Fellowship, was the person who originally introduced Dr. Ostoja to Los Angeles and sponsored his early events in California in the 1930s.

Yogananda was from Gorakhpur in northern India, near the border with Nepal. He had been a spiritual seeker all of his life and is famously known in the West for his book, *Autobiography of a Yogi*. He had died a couple of years previously in 1952 so I never met him but I knew of his writings.

While Swami Yogananda was still active, Dr. Ostoja had taught an "Advanced Super Cosmic Science Course" alongside the Swami. Yogananda gave a free lecture and Dr. Ostoja gave a demonstration of healing by Divine Power. They had done a series of these events together and that collaboration impressed me. In addition to his lectures on health, yoga and self-mastery, Dr. Ostoja would demonstrate self-hypnosis, telepathy, suspended animation and what he called mental anesthesia.

## Advanced Super Cosmic Science Course

**FOR NEW AND OLD STUDENTS**

**Entire New Lessons, Never Given Before, Taught by both SWAMI YOGANANDA and YOGI OSTOJA**

Those who have witnessed the wonderful healing power of Dr. Ostoja will want to learn these marvelous methods themselves.

1. **Healing by Spiritualizing Affirmations and by Astral Food.**
   The future food—what will be eaten 100 to 600 years hence.
2. **How to Develop Creative Intuition.**
   For correct investments and general guidance in choosing proper friends, business associates, and in solving all problems.
3. **Climbing the Tree of Life to Heaven.**
   Great mystery of Adam and Eve explained. Centuries of wisdom packed in this lesson.
4. **Transmigration of Souls.**
   Were you ever on earth before? Will you return again?
5. **Where are Your Dead, Dear Ones Gone?**
   A unique method of getting in touch with those who are gone.
6. **Cosmic Meditations.**
   Making the Universe your body. Expanding consciousness and mental power limitlessly for all-round permanent success.

New Lessons Never Given Before in This Country.     Printed Notes Given FREE.

The Above Super Cosmic Advanced Science Lessons Begin

**Tuesday Night, Feb. 13th, 7:30 p. m., Continuing Wed., Feb. 14th - Thurs. Feb. 15th - Fri., Feb. 16th**

CLASS LESSONS WILL BE HELD IN

**Assembly Hall, Trinity Auditorium**

*Flyer for Lecture and Demonstration by Swami Yogananda and Dr. Roman Ostoja. Yogananda introduced Dr. Ostoja to Los Angeles. Yogananda died before I could meet him.*

In materials I still have Yogananda had written, "I consider Dr. Roman Ostoja one of the great Divine healers of modern times. I prefer him to ten thousand Spiritual Teachers who can talk but cannot demonstrate Spiritual Truths. He is a westerner who has studied with some of the great Masters of India, and has also re-enforced his studies with me. Yogi Ostoja will prove to you that people of the Occident can also master the Universal Teaching of India."

*Dr. Roman Ostoja giving a lecture on Body and Mind Control.*

\*\*\*

I had become a friend of Mary Ellen Kay, an actress who was in films like *The Last Musketeer* and *Colorado Sundown*—both with Rex Allen. I did work with her in the TV series, *Highway Patrol,* which was filmed at the Rex Ingram Ranch.

*With Mary Ellen Kay (on the right in both pictures) filming Highway Patrol at the Rex Ingram Ranch in California around 1953–1954. She was a Republic Studio star. Fifteen years later she introduced me to my second husband, Bill Lynch, in Brewster, New York.*

At that time Mary Ellen was being sent around the country to represent a film like MGM did with me when I was at the Desert Inn. She was going to all of these churches and places to do publicity. I took her with me to this big event where Dr. Ostoja was going to talk and do some demonstrations. He had become very well known and even Bob Hope had been to the events.

When Dr. Ostoja prepared to do a demonstration using hypnotism, he asked the audience, "Would someone like to come up and be buried alive? Would someone like to come up now?"

Mary Ellen stood and volunteered, "I'll do it."

Then, she looked at me and said as if convincing herself, "I am going to let Dr. Ostoja hypnotize and bury me."

Although I knew Mary Ellen might have seen it as a great opportunity for publicity as an actress, I think it was more than that. To be so daring she obviously believed in what he was doing and wanted to help him show the power of hypnosis. Even though I had started studying his principles, I still thought it was rather crazy.

It was apparently the first time in California, or anywhere in the world, to have a public burial of a woman alive. I was there. Mary Ellen was glamorous as ever, dressed in a satin sleeveless gown and thin silk negligee like she was about to go to bed or have a romantic tryst. She asked me for my handkerchief to take with her when she was buried.

First, two doctors from the Los Angeles Medical Department examined her, and then Dr. Ostoja placed her in a hypnotic trance. Once he determined that the hypnosis reached the desired level and one of the doctors re-examined her, she was placed in an airtight coffin like a dead person on the stage in front of all of the people. The coffin was covered with several layers of bags of soil to make a grave.

There were thousands of people there to watch. It was rather tense. Finally, one hour later, the bags of soil were removed from the coffin and Dr. Ostoja brought her out of the trance. The two doctors examined her again and pronounced her completely normal. She came out as glamorous as she went in. It was really incredible! Everyone was amazed. As astonishing as it was, there seemed to be something to what Dr. Ostoja was teaching.

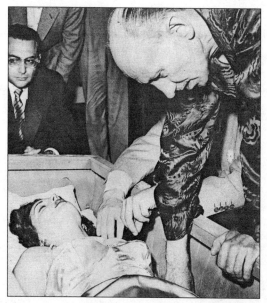

*Mary Ellen Kay, Dr. Roman Ostoja and M.D. examining Mary Ellen just prior to her being buried alive in 1955. I was there. She took my handkerchief with her for the burial. When she came out of the trance she was as glamorous as ever!*

One day, Mary Ellen announced that she met somebody, a big cosmetics executive, and was going to get married. She wanted to do it at my Bastille Day party. She was a bit impulsive like me.

Every year, I had a big Bastille Day party that everyone attended. It was my way to stay in touch with France and commemorate its National

Day, somewhat like the 4th of July in America but on July 14th. My apartment building had a large outside community area with a garden. I'd have easily fifty, sixty people come, sometimes a hundred.

When Mary Ellen asked me this I said, "You can't do that in the middle of a party."

Mary Ellen responded, "Then, we can do it at the start."

I thought it was absurd to get married in the middle of my Bastille Day party. I said, "You can't do that. I've got all of my friends and people from films coming."

"I have to have it at your place because you're my friend."

She sounded so determined, I eventually said, "Yes."

Mary Ellen also wanted Dr. Ostoja to officiate the wedding. He didn't like the idea. Although he had not met her husband-to-be, he felt strongly that she should not marry him.

He said, "I don't think it is the right place for marriage. I'll get somebody else to do it." He went on, "The man you want to marry is not a good man. He's not nice and you're going to have a lot of problems. The marriage will be a disaster. Are you very sure?"

She was insistent and so he finally agreed to marry them. Dr. Ostoja had buried her alive and then later was the official to marry her off! I thought that was such a strange sequence of events.

*Mary Ellen Kay marriage in my apartment courtyard in Hollywood. Dr. Roman Ostoja officiated. I am far right with my head down.*

A lot of what Dr. Ostoja did was hard to believe if you didn't witness it. Once, he did a big demonstration of the powers of hypnosis at Culver City located between MGM and 20th Century Fox. He was to be buried alive for three weeks. He had to sign his own death certificate before he was buried.

When we got there for the demonstration, Dr. Ostoja was already in a trance and had been buried. Hundreds of people were still standing around. A young man and woman from the press were talking.

The man said, "That's the end of him. I'll bet you."

The woman responded, "Sure, I'll bet you that he lives. I don't believe he would do that if he didn't believe he could come back."

Three weeks later, all of the people gathered to witness the outcome. After Dr. Ostoja came out of his trance, people were amazed. He walked right over to the man from the press who had made the bet and said, "You lost your bet!"

Startled, the man asked, "How did you know?"

Dr. Ostoja said, "My body was under the ground, my spirit wasn't." There is so much about the spiritual realm that we don't know about. How can we say what is real and what is unreal?

As I was beginning to study with Dr. Ostoja, I still went to the Vedanta Society. The men who were a part of Vedanta had a place in Capistrano in the south. Capistrano is where they say that the swallows come back every year. It's not too far from San Diego. We used to go down there for the 4th of July, all of us, even though it was usually only for men. They could go and stay there without paying as long as they did some work.

That's when we decided to build a place in Santa Barbara for women who wanted to stay at the Vedanta Society. Swamiji said, "Why should just men be able to go?"

Everybody went to help and did whatever we could do, even carrying bricks and water. We'd drive up to Santa Barbara and work alongside dear Swami Prabhavananda.

Once, Swamiji was coming up the coast and his car started to go over the edge. We asked him, "Were you scared Swamiji?"

He said, "Why should I? If the Lord got me here, he'll get me out of it." He had such a sense of humor.

Every time I arrived, he would say with a smile, "Now don't come and ask me to change your name into something. Your name already recognizes your whole character."

I would still go to the Vedanta Society in Hollywood to help there as well. I would wash windows and talk about the *Upanishads* with Swamiji. The Vedanta Society was really a home for me. It reminded me of the conversations I would have with my uncle.

\*\*\*

More and more I was trying to balance my spiritual exploration with my life as a model and actress. All of these experiences with Swamji and Dr. Ostoja were swirling through my consciousness but I had to go back to France. I had some modeling jobs for Coco Chanel and Jean Patou. Although I was receiving residual checks here and there from some of the television work I'd done, I had to take work where I could. Besides, I missed France.

*Left: Pay note issued November 3, 1955 for modeling assignment for Coco Chanel Couture.*

*Right: Pay note issued May 12, 1956 for modeling assignment for Jean Patou.*

*Screen Actors Guild Residual Payments from various television shows such as I Married Joan, Meet McGraw and Pepsi Cola Playhouse.*

Since I had been in Europe, I hadn't seen Dr. Ostoja for a while. A strange thing happened when a young man and girl picked me up from the airport. The young man who was driving the car kept saying, "You've got to meet my friend Roman."

Trying to be polite I said, "That's very nice, thank you very much."

I was so tired from the trip that I really didn't care who his friend was, but he continued, "You've got to meet my friend Roman."

We got to the house, and the young man went to the front door. Before he could say a word, Dr. Ostoja said, "Oh, Tāo has arrived."

The young man was baffled and asked me, "How did he know?"

I said, "I haven't talked with him for a long time."

Asking Dr. Ostoja, "How did you know she had arrived?"

Dr. Ostoja answered, "The spiritual link is the Oneness behind all things."

> The spiritual link is the Oneness behind all things.

\*\*\*

At one point, Louis Vaudable came to Hollywood and invited me to one of the parties in Palm Springs. He was involved in all of the big events. I liked it when he came around because he was always so gracious. He was married so there was never any affair or anything. He was simply a good friend.

The party was your usual fare of celebrities and glamour. I traveled back to Hollywood with Louis and the Countess Tecla de Volko. The Countess, I think she may have been Swedish, was working for Maxim's. She represented the restaurant in selling their food to a lot of major airlines for first class passengers. Maxim's was big into that kind of high-end catering. The airline industry was just starting to heavily promote catered meals on board with silverware.

The Countess was driving with Louis and me in the car past the palms and canyons back to the roar of Hollywood. The mountainous road was very narrow at a certain point and, to avoid an oncoming car, we swerved and our vehicle stopped with one wheel over the side. It could have been deadly. A policeman in civilian clothes just by chance came by and got us out.

When the officer asked what happened, Louis said lightheartedly, "We were going along 'clopin-clopon' and suddenly the car turned, I was thrown into Täo's breast. It was *fort agréable*." Then, he smiled like a Cheshire cat. There was a pause and then both men started laughing.

Even though the officer didn't speak French, he got the meaning that it was "very agreeable." I think the Countess, who was really uptight, was also grinning in her courtly manner. Louis had a way of turning any situation around.

Still in the car was Louis' precious cowboy hat that was given to him in Palm Springs, so I went back to check into the upside down car and found it. The police took me home and escorted Countess and Louis to the airport. They missed the flight but made a later one. Reporters from around the world had the accident in the papers the next day. It was picked up in places like Texas, Florida and Indiana, and even in papers in Canada and as far away as Germany.

> **Maxim's Owner, Women Safe as Car Overturns**
>
> M. Louis Vaudable, who, as proprietor of the world-famous Maxim's Restaurant of Paris, has an excellent palate, got a taste of the Southland's mountain driving hazards Sunday afternoon, but miraculously escaped unscathed, it was learned yesterday.
>
> With Maxim's executive vice-president, the Countess Tecla de Volko, and Tao Porchon, French actress, the noted restaurateur was traveling the mountain route over Mt. San Jacinto from Palm Springs where the three of them had lunched when their rented convertible overturned.
>
> Although the convertible landed upside down, its wheels spinning in the air, none of the three sustained even a scratch.
>
> According to reports, Countess de Volko was driving at the time. Scene of the accident was near Keen Camp Summit, above Hemet.
>
> After their lucky escape the trio proceeded to Los Angeles where M. Vaudable, missing his scheduled flight by an hour, caught a late plane for New York. Countess de Volko and Mlle. Porchon remained in Los Angeles.

*Newspaper clipping of accident from December 5, 1956.*

The papers made a big deal out of it but we were fine. Despite the mishap, it was nice to get out with a true friend. Now that I was divorced, I tried to go out on dates but so many of the men I seemed to meet were handsome, but vulgar.

Even if I went out with somebody who I thought was going to be nice, it would end in a tussle. I would get in the car, and almost immediately, he would try to make love to me. I was always finding myself having to pull away and stay alone. Sometimes it was really rough. I had never experienced anything like it. Every time something like that happened, I went deeper into myself.

French Consul General Raoul Bertrand was inviting me to more events. Once there was a luncheon at the Beverly Hills Hotel and he asked me to be there to represent France. Lockheed, the company that made all of the big bomber and carrier planes during the war, was trying to sell their aircraft to Air France.

There was a man, one of the heads of Air France, who was

particularly difficult. He was holding up the sale. They were all sitting there trying to figure out how to get this one man to agree on the price and sign the deal.

Raoul decided to sit me next to this man at the table. After we started talking, I noticed that he began to soften. He became interested when he found out that I grew up in India and did yoga. He was curious about meditation and philosophy. We talked about spirituality and different books, as well as the great sage and poet Sri Aurobindo.

After about an hour and a half, he turned around and signed the deal with the others. Air France bought the planes. The man enjoyed our conversation so much that he wanted to sign the papers so we could continue our discussion.

Raoul exclaimed later, "Oh, you see Täo. You did it! It's because of you that he signed the contract."

There was a very interesting man I met through Raoul. He was married to an heiress of the Singer Sewing Machine fortune and loved wine but she told him he couldn't drink it. She had him drinking milk instead. He had a ship line that ran from San Francisco to China and used to bring in various Chinese things including food.

They lived in Santa Barbara and he had an office in downtown Los Angeles. In his office was a large painting of his wife. Much to my surprise, a wine cellar was revealed as he pressed a button behind the painting! I don't think his wife ever knew about it. He used to like sitting with us discussing wine. He and Raoul were buddy-buddy and I was always included.

Raoul would take me everywhere. On one occasion, he took me to San Diego where a grand event was happening on an island with picturesque mansions and enchanting gardens. I was so fortunate to have had those experiences.

My friendship with Raoul was fortuitous. There was no affair or anything. It was just a nice relationship. I met a lot of people through him in America and it opened new doors to use my talents and expertise. Without realizing then, I unwittingly became the liaison in various expanding markets.

When he found out that my aunt had vineyards in the Rhône Valley, he told me, "Don't be a snob. There are some good wines here."

He introduced me to all the great wineries in California. I met Robert Mondavi, who became a wine legend. Robert was making ordinary wine at first but became one of the most revered in the industry when he later started the famous Robert Mondavi Winery. He became a good friend and we kept in touch for many years. Whenever he came to New York, he would ask, "You're coming to tastings, aren't you?"

At the great Consulate affairs, Raoul introduced me to wine of Chile. Always the diplomat, he would have as many American wines as French at the functions. In many ways, it contributed to my wine education.

My aunt in France laid the foundation. She knew so much about the "nectar of the gods" and taught me about all the wine regions of France. Rhône Valley wines have always been special for connoisseurs and my aunt's teachings became the path to my knowledge of wine and the great vineyards of the world. She taught me first to appreciate nature's wonderful fruit—grapes. Next, I learned to appreciate wine as a delightful drink that has migrated across the globe with mankind surviving in so many countries for so many centuries. The history of wine teaches us a lot about mankind.

That is why I enjoyed learning more about the American vineyards while living in California. Raoul sparked my interest and prompted me to get involved again in the wine industry.

Some of these winemaking people I met said, "Täo, you know so many important people in Europe and you also know so much about wine. Can you help us?"

Soon, I was taking people from America to all of the famous wine and beer trade companies, such as John Bull Malt out of Cambridge, England. California's new wine and beer entrepreneurs were able to get more knowledge about production pitfalls and other interesting ideas. In addition to England, we traveled to Italy, France, and Germany to know more about what was happening in these wine regions.

I made that trip on several occasions taking the Americans and introducing them to the right people. It was a lot of fun. Home winemaking was spreading across the country and California was developing a booming world-class industry.

On yet another occasion, Raoul invited me to a big Jewish affair. It was a celebration recognizing the two thousandth year of Jewish people in France. They were there during the time of the Romans. As opposed to other places in the world, France was not creating problems for them. Raoul insisted I join him, "Because you're such a lady." I was honored to be there. I could remember arriving in France for the first time knowing nothing about Jewish people.

\*\*\*

At this point, I was more seriously studying parapsychology and "cosmic intelligence" with Dr. Ostoja. To demonstrate the triumph of mind over matter and convince skeptics of this type of practical metaphysics, he would often perform death-defying feats putting himself in a trance. He would perform these mental miracles to prove that a Westerner was capable of controlling the Infinite forces.

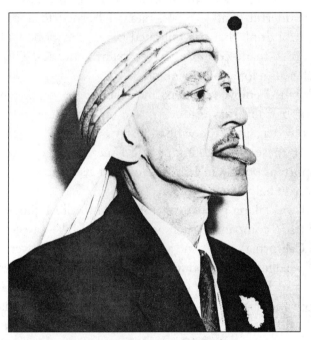

*Dr. Roman Ostoja and his famous ladies' hatpin through the tongue demonstration.*

When they started to ban burial demonstrations, he focused on showing superhuman achievement in other ways including lying on a bed of nails, eating glass, walking barefooted on broken glass and reclining on two sharp swords while somebody smashed a concrete panel on his chest with a sledge-hammer. He also would thrust an eight-inch ladies' hatpin into his tongue and stick another into a bone in his hand. He would close his eyes, breathe deeply and tell himself not to bleed or feel pain. It was shocking yet quite extraordinary.

Despite all of these feats, he was really a yogi and one of the first non-Indians to teach the techniques. He would say, "Yoga is more than a spectacular demonstration. It is a philosophy, a science through which anyone can attain glowing physical health. The yoga system is based on concentration of will. It attunes those who use it with the universal law of growth and, properly mastered, enables the individual to achieve immunity from mental, emotional and physical stress."

Dr. Ostoja recommended meditation and concentration for the mind and breathing exercises for the body. He said that proper breathing stimulates circulation, "The body is fed mostly by the bloodstream. The blood is purified by oxygen in breathing. Anyone can learn to breathe the Yoga way." He shared, "There was a time, when I was in training, when I could make a single inhale last five minutes, a single exhale last ten minutes."

He taught that yoga is based on self-mastery, "At first this seemed selfish to me. Yogis should be able to help others, I thought. But today I understand. How can I help you if I cannot first help myself? If I can help myself first, then I can help you in a greater way."

He said the good life is not a fat bankroll and tranquilizer pills, but "blissful vibrations" which can be attained by anyone, "One need only inform oneself about the laws of the Universe and work with them, not against them or independently as most people are doing. When you reach this blissful state you're in harmony with the Universe and in tune with cosmic vibrations. At one time or another, we all experience this 'cosmic harmony.' The trick is to become 'aware' and learn how to put yourself in 'permanent harmony.'"

*At one time or another, we all experience this 'cosmic harmony.' The trick is to become 'aware' and learn how to put yourself in 'permanent harmony.'*

About practicing yoga for fifty years, he said, "All I have to show for it is great health and peace of mind." He was incredible and gave me his book, *A Pictorial Half Century In The Life of A White Yogi*, which included all the famous people he knew. Joan Davis, who I worked with in the TV show *I Married Joan*, was in it. She had a lot of stress and he taught her how to obtain relaxation. He also cured film director Lloyd Bacon of insomnia.

Other prominent students included British conductor Leopold Stokowski, American composer and conductor Leonard Bernstein, and American pianist Van Cliburn, as well as a long list of actors and actresses such as John Barrymore, Ginger Rogers, Lana Turner, Dick Powell, Joan Blondell, Marilyn Maxwell, Paulette Goddard and Margaret Lindsay.

In his book, he has pictures with people like Russian writer Count Lev Nikolayevich Tolstoy, Russian composer Alexander Glazunov, German-born conductor Walter Damrosch, President of the UN General Assembly Eelco Nicolaas van Kleffens, General Carlos Peña Rómulo, former wartime chancellor of Austria Dr. Kurt Von Schuschnigg and former Governor of New York Averill Harriman.

He has a picture sharing his private thoughts with the Honorable Nelson Rockefeller about his candidacy in the New York Governorship election. He even demonstrated his techniques to esteemed scientist Dr. Albert Einstein.

Dr. Ostoja liked me because he said, "I can hypnotize 10,000 people but I can't hypnotize you because you're an old, old spirit in a very young body."

He liked when I worked with him. I wanted to know more about this practice he was doing and see what it was about. I wanted to see for myself that it wasn't black magic or someone else's theories. He wanted me to "tune in" to special exercises, not just read about them but also to find myself from within.

I would go and meditate in front of a mirror. He had this technique of putting blue light behind you. It was used to try to enhance what you could do with the mind. I'd see all sorts of weird forms come up in meditation while cleansing my mind.

I studied with Dr. Ostoja for three years and then he went to New York to spend time lecturing at Columbia University and offering demonstrations there. He even did two events at Carnegie Hall.

***

One day, seemingly out of nowhere, the incredible Maharishi Mahesh Yogi appeared in my life. A disciple of Swami Brahmananda Saraswati, he had been given the honorific title "Maharishi" meaning "Great Seer" and had just started to teach Transcendental Deep Meditation in India. He was beginning to share it in America.

He was in San Francisco teaching and by strange coincidence talked to the concierge of my building who was also visiting. Not having met or seen the concierge or me previously, the Maharishi said to him, "In your building, you will find someone there whom I want to meet."

Upon returning to Hollywood, the concierge serendipitously bumped into me and told me about his peculiar encounter. With a bit of curiosity he said, "I'm certain he means you, Miss Porchon. There is no one else here that it could be."

Hardly any time passed and the Maharishi seemed to simply materialize. With him was a group of people. I had my back to them as I was walking to my apartment. Then, I heard someone say, "I told him I'd find you here. I've come to meet you."

I turned around, but didn't know who he was.

He got rid of everybody and then said to me with an amazing infectious smile, "Come, we talk."

So, we sat. After a brief discussion about India, he said with a magical charm, "You and I are going to meditate."

*My dear teacher Maharishi Mahesh Yogi who taught Transcendental Meditation which has become popular around the world. He was such a joyful and kind spirit.*

I had a long day and was just sitting there so tired, not really meditating. Then, he tapped me on the shoulder. I looked up at him and saw a big playful smile on his face as he said to me in a teasing tone, "You think you're fooling me, don't you?"

I was ashamed of myself and confessed, "I'm so tired. I just did theatre and after the show I had to clean up."

That evening I had performed a drama on the Hindu goddess Kali at the theatre with the Indian-American dance troupe. I resisted doing anything else saying, "I'm not ready to meditate."

His eyes twinkled with an inner mirthful light as he warmly insisted, "Nonsense."

He held my hand for a moment and said in a voice very soothing and captivating, "We're going to meditate."

Without knowing what had happened, we silently entered into a deep meditation. I felt like I wasn't on this earth at all. When I came to, it was as though I didn't hit the ground. I was floating. It was like I was walking on air the whole week. I didn't know what happened to me.

That night he told me he was going to be on a TV show with Eva Gabor. I didn't like it because they sometimes made people look like fools on the show. I didn't want that to happen to him, and so I said, "Don't go. She will make fun of you."

With his contagious giggle, he said, "Don't worry, Täo. If it is meant to be, it will be."

I saw him again and when he was leaving California, he held my hand and said, "I'm going to England now, but our paths are going to cross again. I want to do some things with you. Keep doing. There is something about you."

He stopped talking for a second or two, and then said, "Well, I don't need to explain that."

I informed him, "I'm going back to France soon." Then we bid goodbye.

The Maharishi's emphasis on the energy within us was very similar to what I had learned as a child and my studies at the Vedanta Society. He had a joyous spirit that was infectious. Having searched so long to find the inner road, how did he know I needed his thoughts and his presence at that moment?

That stillness of meditation helped me find some of the answers. I had traveled the world searching and, like the rays of the sun at dawn lighten up the sky, in an instant I knew. I felt like he was reaching outwards to answer my inner quest. He seemed to have known me forever and understood my search. I didn't have all of the answers, but I once again felt I was on the right path.

It seemed like the beauty of life opened up from the darkest quarter and I moved into an ethereal new chapter. All of these gurus had appeared in my life at this time—Swami Prabhavananda, Dr. Roman Ostoja and now dear Maharishi. Like in Pondicherry, where I had access to the teachings of Swami Vivekananda, Sri Aurobindo and Mahatma Gandhi, I once again had a spiritual community of venerable teachers.

I was attracting extraordinary people into my life. I now realize it was a Universal principle in action—the more you focus on something, the more you attract towards yourself something of the same essence, whether it is good or bad. Through the influence of these great teachers, I was focusing on the expansiveness of the Universe and my own abilities. I was coming back to my Self.

Meditation opens you up. In its simplest form, meditation is focusing the mind on one thing such as breath. When the mind and senses are isolated, then all becomes Absolute Consciousness, for there is not beginning and not end. That is the path to recognizing our Oneness and tapping into Cosmic Intelligence. It is of vital importance to let go to tune deep inside. When you can find stillness in your everyday life, you can start the process and then find at least some moments of blissful vibrations.

> *When the mind and senses are isolated then all becomes Absolute Consciousness, for there is not beginning and not end.*

CHAPTER 17

Say Yes!

In reflecting on my life, there was this intermingling of people and experiences from seemingly different worlds all coming together introducing me to what it means to live life on so many levels. Each situation opened a new door of understanding that I didn't know was even there for me. I had learned from my uncle to be open to new circumstances and not be afraid. Saying "yes" to new things can expand your thinking and enrich your life.

*Saying "yes" to new things can expand your thinking and enrich your life.*

I was still going back and forth to France. Most of my modeling was in Paris and I kept my apartment on Avenue Montaigne. I considered Paris to be my home despite my work in Hollywood.

It seemed like my two worlds of France and India were intersecting. I knew the Bhavagarty family in India. One day I was delighted when I ran into Mr. Bhavagarty in Paris. He was now working with UNESCO, the United Nations Educational, Scientific and Cultural Organization, which was created right after the war.

He was part of the film department of what he and the Indian Ambassador laughingly called "The Marching Nations," all of the small nations that were not seen as important. They were fighting for a place with the others. India, for example, wasn't considered a big power at that time.

Since Mr. Bhavagarty knew that I had been making films in India and had been working in Hollywood, he said, "We need someone with our film department. Will you come and join us?"

Everybody had gone on holiday either back to India or someplace else. So I said, "Yes."

I believed in what they were doing in trying to promote peace and intercultural understanding through educational efforts. Their headquarters was right on Place de Fontenoy in a grand building with majestic columns. From one view, you could see the Eiffel Tower in the background. The film department was in the basement.

*When I worked at UNESCO in Paris in 1959.*

My work with UNESCO was interesting. We were making films about different countries that were members of the United Nations. Over the nine months I was there, I gained a greater knowledge of the world and had the opportunity to expand my filmmaking skills. Since I didn't have to be there every day, I had time to do other things.

I was starting to write again. My thirst for a deeper understanding of words and language was growing more intense. When I was young, I was very interested in the similarities between languages and the original meaning and intention of a word. For instance, the word "atonement" was originally written "at-one" and is similar to contentment. It means that in this moment you're at one with everything around you. That is union.

I was so fascinated with words and how they came about that I even started learning about Aramaic, one of the Semitic languages used in ancient texts. I learned early on from my uncle to respect all people and languages. Now that interest in words and language was becoming all consuming.

I read great books as well as some weird ones. I think I ruined my eyesight because I would read just about anything I could get. I found a Hindi book and thought reading it would do me good.

When I was writing, I would become so immersed that time would just go by without my realizing it. Anything that came in my mind, I wrote down. I still do that at all hours of the day and night.

Sometimes I burned all the pans because I'd be writing and forget about what I was cooking. It seemed like I could go a week without thinking about eating.

There was this little lady who lived on the seventh floor of my place in Paris. She had to carry everything up since there was no elevator. She worked as a maid and used to clean all of the apartments. She'd come to clean my place and see that I'd started making some food. I'd either burned it or had forgotten about it. It was really awful.

She would make me little meals and put them right at my door with a sign saying, "Mangez-moi!" which means "Eat me!" It was really kind. I had all of these guardian angels some more obvious than others.

Although there were branches of the Vedanta Society in other places outside of Los Angeles, there was not one in Paris. It was outside of the city. In India, there were plenty of these gatherings to do with Hinduism and spirituality. It was harder to find elsewhere.

Someone I knew heard me say, "I miss that there is nobody here" referring to a place for spiritual study.

He offered, "There is a place not far from where you live."

There was a woman who had started a sort of study group just off the Champs-Élysées about four blocks from where I lived. It was based on the work of Madame Blavatsky. They had apparently been gathering there for a long time.

Helena Petrovna Blavatsky, who had died decades earlier, had written a lot about spirituality. I still have *Les Rêves*, one of her books in French. It explained her teachings on dreams and esoteric philosophy.

This group of people at Loge Unie Des Theosophes, or the United Lodge of Theosophists, was studying about her. I went to several of their events every week.

We would also study the *Bhagavad Gita*. We would go through different chapters and could ask questions like "Who is Krishna?" I had nobody to discuss these things with in France before and was pleased that I had something to go to that I believed in.

*Consistent spiritual study, or abhyasa, is important to hone your thinking and help you discover your beliefs and Ultimate Reality.*

There are still two Vedanta places I go to in New York—the Vedanta Society of New York at 34 West 71st Street and the Ramakrishna Vivekananda Center of New York at 17 East 94th Street. Consistent spiritual study, or *abhyasa*, is important to hone your thinking and help you discover your beliefs and Ultimate Reality.

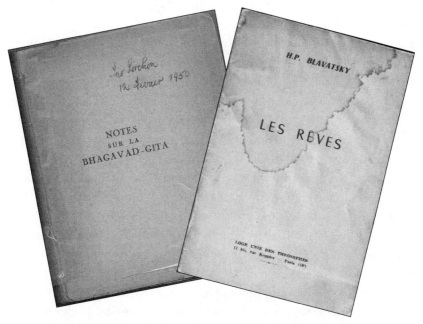

*Two of my dear (and somewhat worn) books for spiritual study, Notes on the Bhagavad Gita and Les Rêves by Helena Petrovna Blavatsky.*

\*\*\*

When it was time to go back to Hollywood, I needed to figure out what I was really doing. My acting career had not taken off and I was now yearning to produce films. The volunteer work I did with the Charity Players didn't bring in any money but I kept meeting new people.

A woman I met when I first arrived, one of the ladies from the Charity Players, was always inviting me to dinner at her home. She was a very sweet person who had a terrific education. She had spent some time in Switzerland for her schooling.

One day her son came back from college and she introduced me to him. We started to go out quite a bit even to one of the Academy Awards. His mother said, "You really should meet his aunt because she loved India and was with Gandhi."

I didn't know who the aunt was at the time or what she had done but the mention of Gandhi made me curious. So I said that I would like to meet her. It ended up being Dr. Welthy Fisher. I didn't meet her for about a year or two later in person but I first heard about her through the mother of this young man.

The connection with this family was fortuitous. I met Bill Halstead, another nephew of Dr. Fisher who was visiting Hollywood. He was President of Unitel and a true pioneer. He wrote in *Reader's Digest* in the 1950s that there was going to be global TV. The concept was revolutionary at the time. He told me what he had done with TV in Japan, that he was instrumental in the development of the Nippon Television Network or NTV.

This was the first time they had TV and a full-fledged TV station in Japan. When they demonstrated it people were everywhere, even sitting on shoulders to watch the three big screens across the stations and parks in Tokyo. They sold about a thousand television sets in one night.

I thought what he was doing was great but why should it all be in English? Why couldn't it be in other languages? We were talking about working something out so that everybody could understand the different languages. Now you can see films that are dubbed or in closed captioning. In that day, there was nothing like that.

Halstead was very intrigued with me. I'd done so many things and was international. I was also interested in what he was doing. We were talking so intensely about what he was doing that time just went on late into the night. I thought working with him had a lot of potential.

Then, we started talking about India. He said, "You know something, Dr. Welthy Fisher is my aunt. She is so crazy about India and would love you. She is working on something called World Education."

*With Bill Halstead, President of Unitel in Beverly Hills around 1959. Bill was a talented engineer and visionary. He helped to develop Nippon TV in Japan.*

I didn't know it was the same person I had marched with as a child. As I had come to know, everything is connected and comes back around. After leaving Hollywood he kept in touch with me.

I had been going back to India all the time making films there. I had made the documentary on the Republic Day Celebrations with the Hunnars a few years before. I still have a newspaper clipping from when I was interviewed. I was honored to have met Prime Minister Nehru before he died. My uncle knew a lot of notable people.

When I came to New York, I saw Halstead again and he said, "I must have you be a part of this work."

He asked me to go to India and use my contacts there to help put TV in India. He was also curious about my connections in France and wanted to try and set up TV with the French government. Having been in the French Resistance and being a top couture model, I knew many people including General de Gaulle and some people at the banks. He thought those relationships could help.

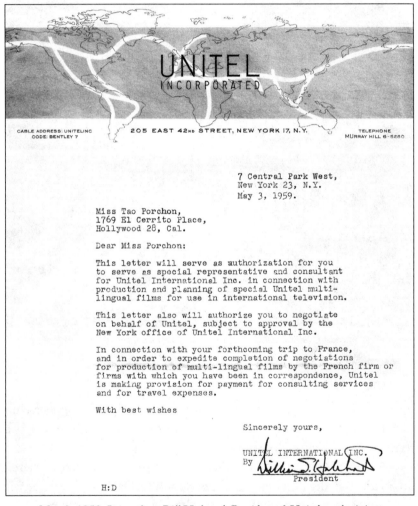

*May 3, 1959. Letter from Bill Halstead, President of Unitel, authorizing me to serve as special representative and consultant for Unitel International, Inc. Later, I was named Vice President of Unitel.*

I was on my way back to Paris. I had to stay there some time to renew my visa and to feel that I was still part of France. Halstead talked me into introducing him to people in France and using my apartment in Paris as an office. He was on his way to Russia so he paid me for the first two months for the use of my place.

In essence, I opened up an office for Unitel in Paris. I introduced Bill directly to key people. However, he talked so much about himself and going to Russia that my French contacts began to back off. I continued to try to make it work in France while he was in Russia.

My friend Maggy was back in Europe at that time and was sweet to look out for me. She was still modeling and trying to start a singing career. She would say, "Täo, you don't eat enough. I'm sending my brother to you and he is going to make you go out."

She would instruct him, "Go and take her out. I'm afraid she is going to end up in a convent or we're going to walk in and she hasn't eaten for a month." So she made him go and pick me up.

*Maggy starting her singing career.*

Bob Hope was also doing a TV film in London and all of the famous French models were in it so I was included. I had met him when I was doing cabaret performances in London and had seen him when I came to America with the first French models after the war. Now, they were filming at the Dorchester Hotel in Hyde Park.

*With Bob Hope at the Dorchester Hotel in London to film The Bob Hope Show in 1959. I wore a gorgeous Jean Patou dress.*

The couture house of Jean Patou designed a luxurious dress for the program. The dress was exquisitely feminine and I was the model who met the requirements with the necessary glamour.

When the British built the hotel they had these big steps coming down for grand entrances. The dress was so wide with its sweeping elegance that I couldn't come down the steps like the other models. With Bob Hope so handsomely dressed and looking very formal, I felt like a queen floating across the stage on his arm. I also spoke more English than the other models so he liked me.

*Hyde Park, London in November 1960.*

I worked with Bob Hope on a few occasions. He used to call me Ta-O—like Lake Tahoe. I don't know where he got that. I think it was his way of having fun.

In California, Bob Hope had invited me to his home in Palm Desert, which is right next to Palm Springs. I loved that area so I would go. He would invite us all over, models and actresses, to listen to him practice his jokes. He said he would buy them cheaply from students at Princeton University in New Jersey. I thought that was kind of funny. Mary Ellen Kay joined me on one occasion.

Being around Bob Hope in London for the show reminded me in some ways of my time in Europe during the war. I knew Bob before Bing Crosby. There were all these interconnections. I knew Bing because he was with Marlene performing in the trenches. She had known me through Noël Coward. Guimas was a friend of Noël as well. I missed my clique.

Those reminders of the fun and friendships in Europe highlighted the fact that my experience in Hollywood was so different. Besides Ginny, Frances, Johnnie and Dick and some nice people like Cesar Romero, it was emotionally desolate despite the constant activity. I would get invitations to parties and such but they were often big, impersonal events.

In the meantime, I was building up a terrific bill in Paris for this office I was maintaining. After being paid for the first two months, I didn't get any more money from Halstead and I was putting out all of my own. I received no salary.

Knowing Bill Halstead had stopped paying me, Maggy insisted, "You've got to get out of this thing." She was a good friend trying to make sure I wasn't being taken advantage of.

He owed me for at least six months of pay and I was silly enough not to think about it until I was down to my last franc and dollar. Now, I had to come back to America otherwise I would lose my green card. I still had the possibility of doing some scripts in Hollywood and so I thought I better come back.

I was already ten days overdue for my visa and I didn't have enough money to get an airplane ticket, but I don't believe in worrying. Even if I was broke, I would sit there and say, "Now I'm going to meditate on this and I'm going to find a way." The answer soon came.

I received a call from Louis. Once again, he showed himself to be a good friend. He always used to look me up. He said, "I thought you were in America?"

I explained, "I'm supposed to go back but I have to get a seat on a plane."

"I'll get you on Pan Am. We're doing all of the food for them." Maxim's restaurant was catering for Pan Am.

I said, "Well, it's a little more difficult than that. Louis, I don't have the money for it. I have some money owed to me, more than $10,000, but I have to pick it up."

So he offered, "Oh, don't worry. I will fix it with Pan Am that you'll pay when you get to the United States. They'll give you things on my behalf."

Grateful, I said, "Okay and thank you." I prepared to leave that night.

*My dear friend Louis Vaudable, owner of Maxim's restaurant in Paris, sent me this letter on July 19, 1960. We met in the 1940s and remained good friends for decades.*

\*\*\*

Even more doors opened that very day. Before I left Paris, I received two calls. The first was from people in Texas who knew me from Hollywood. "We want to see you Tāo, and we want you to do something for us in France."

I said, "But I'm coming to America."

"Oh well, go to American Express on 5th Avenue in New York City. We'll leave some money for you and a ticket to Dallas."

Of course, needing the money, I said, "I'll be there."

The other call that night was from my friend Mary Ellen Kay. She had married the man Dr. Ostoja warned her against. He was big in cosmetics doing "Make Yourself Lovely" and "Your Chance to Be Lovely" hair products. She had moved to his home in Brewster, New

York with his children from a previous marriage. They recently had a baby girl together.

She said, "I wish you were here. I want you to come up for this big party. We are going to welcome the Jewish Synagogue into our community." She wasn't Jewish, but they were opening up a Synagogue in her area. She said, "I'm singing one of your songs that you did with Debbie." She was going to sing "Darling, Je Vous Aime Beaucoup" that I did for MGM with Debbie Reynolds.

I said, "That's funny. I'm supposed to leave tonight for New York but I don't have any money. I just have a ticket that I got from Louis Vaudable."

She offered, "I'll send my chauffeur for you." Then, sounding a bit desperate, she said, "Please come and see me. Besides, I really need you. I'm in such a bad state. I have a baby and I'm scared."

With that, I figured I'd better see her so I gave her the number to Halstead's office in New York so we could connect.

My flight was a little late. As I was going through customs, they decided to hold me up. Finally, they deemed that I was okay. When I finally got through, I was relieved to see Halstead waiting for me at the airport.

As we drove from Idlewild Airport, which later became John F. Kennedy International Airport, Halstead informed me that he was taking off for India the next day and then to Africa. He took me to the hotel that was right by the side of the east river on Third Avenue around 47th Street facing the United Nations. Then he left and didn't pay for it. I only had ten dollars in my pocket. Here I was stuck again in America. Everywhere I seemed to be having trouble.

Now, I was checked in this hotel with my luggage and I couldn't even pay for the room. Fortunately, I was able to pick up the ticket to Texas and a check for $200 from the people in Dallas. With that, I paid what I owed Pan Am and the hotel.

Mary Ellen sent her chauffeur for me, which was good since I really didn't have money to spare. The estate was huge with acres and acres. They had big bulldogs that would bark at you. They were so vicious that you had to be careful or they would bite you.

Even though her husband was extremely wealthy, she was not very happy and was so pleased that I had come. She needed a friend. It was so wonderful for me to see Mary Ellen and her precious baby girl Molly.

After we talked, it seemed like everything Dr. Ostoja said was coming true and they actually divorced soon thereafter.

In any case, it was on that visit with my friend that I met William J. Lynch, or Bill. His father was well known in insurance and had several homes including one near Saratoga Springs and another in Florida. He seemed nice enough. I didn't realize then how much Bill Lynch was going to affect the course of my life.

After visiting Mary Ellen, I went to Dallas and was able to do the work that the Texas people wanted me to do for them in Paris. They were buying a painting and I knew who could help. At that time, there weren't as many people who had international contacts as I did.

The Dallas folks were funny and had taken a liking to me. When I was in Paris I was getting letters from them and one of them wrote "Ass ever" because of the way I pronounced Dall-ass with two s'. When I sent a note back to him I thought I must have made a mistake so I wrote Dall-ass with two s', and Tex-ass with two s'.

I got a letter from the post office in Dallas saying, "We know you are a foreigner. We'd like to bring to your attention that Dallas is written with one 's' as is Texas." Well, while I was in Dallas everybody was laughing at this. They all were taking copies of my letter and sharing it with everyone. They thought it was funny and so did I.

After my work was completed in Dallas, I returned to New York. I still didn't have enough money to get back out to California. I was trying to get there to see if my agent could get me some work. After some thought, I decided not to move out to Hollywood without any money.

I always thought Halstead was going to pay me so I stayed in New York. Everything seemed to be going off course. Halstead's secretary Harriet said, "He hasn't paid me either. Come and stay with me."

So, I was able to go there for a bit. She lived on 52nd Street right near 3rd Avenue in one of those old buildings.

Halstead was what I would call a "dream" man. All he could think about was what he was working on. He had all these creative ideas and would avidly pursue them. He was the one who suggested putting in the lights to give the information about traffic and everything on the New Jersey Turnpike. He did the same thing at the Los Angeles airport. He put in early LED signs for the World's Fair on Long Island in 1964.

He was an incredible man. It seems that whatever thoughts came to his mind, he used. Sometimes be would let me do the work and not give me credit which was typical of many men in that day. Nevertheless, I met a lot of people through him.

Things were happening so fast from all directions. Halstead said that I could use his office in New York for my films but I didn't really take advantage of that. I was meeting the people from Japan who were always coming in there. Even so, I felt I was getting away from films and I even stopped acting for a long time doing this work with Unitel.

\*\*\*

Suddenly, Bill Lynch started showing up everywhere. I guess he got my information from Mary Ellen. He was even at the building on 52nd Street. He kept coming down there and calling all the time.

I went to India to get them interested in TV. In those days some of my uncle's important friends and contacts were still alive. I knew the very wealthy Motwani family. They were ready to put money in television development. The great microphone in front of Gandhi in the various pictures came from the famous Motwanis.

The Mayor of Bombay had recently received David Sarnoff from NBC, but said, "Oh, I don't believe in all of that. It's all nonsense talking about TV."

My friends in India from Behrhor, a big finance group, were ready to finance it, but warned me, "He may kick you out, Täo. First he doesn't really like that women do anything. He doesn't think they are capable. He's also just been quite rude to David Sarnoff. "

Instead of dismissing me, the Mayor spent three hours with me and when he came out he said, "I've always believed in what TV would do for Bombay. It will bring in new jobs." He said all of this as if it was his idea.

My friends were chuckling, "Look what you did, Täo. You turned him around. You made him do it."

In the middle of talking with the Mayor of Bombay, I got a call from Bill Lynch. They thought that he was some big person related to TV. He was actively pursuing me and calling me all over the place.

I didn't want to get involved with him because I knew he was in the throes of a divorce. He had two young children, a girl who was three and a boy who was five. I didn't know what to think of him. I had never met anyone so persistent.

There had been conflict between the Chinese army and the Tibetans for a few years but now it was heating up. The Dalai Lama fled Tibet to avoid persecution. The fighting seemed to be getting worse and many thought the Chinese were going to invade India.

```
                    No. 12(6)/64-B(D)
                   GOVERNMENT OF INDIA
            MINISTRY OF INFORMATION AND BROADCASTING

                          New Delhi(2), the 16 September, 1964
To
      Shri T.K. Menon, & Tao Porchon,
      C/o Messrs United Overseas, INC,
      C-261, Defence Colony,
      NEW DELHI.

Subject:- Expansion of Television in India.

Dear Sirs,
           I am directed to refer to your Literature
(Unitel Plan for Development of Television Broadcasting
in India) received here on 27th August, 1964 and to request
that the firm may be asked to give us the best possible terms
and make a concrete offer in regard to deferred payment
arrangements on as long term a basis as possible and on
lowest possible rate of interest on outstanding amounts.

                              Yours faithfully,
                                  s/ Shri
                                (Shri Bhagwan)
                      Under Secretary to the Government of India
```

*Letter we later received from the Government of India regarding TV in India.*

The government had already approved the deal to bring television to India. The investors were in the process of drawing up the papers and Westinghouse was going to be one of the partners. A family from Madison, Wisconsin who owned something like thirteen radio stations in America was also going to join in, along with the Motwanis in India. They were all going to put money in it, and then they simply pulled out when they heard about the potential for war coming to India. So TV in India at that time didn't go through but we laid the groundwork.

A lot happened during that trip to India. I was able to meet with Dr.

Welthy Fisher, Bill Halstead's aunt. That's how I made the connection with her again after not seeing her since we marched with Mahatma Gandhi when I was young.

She was originally from Rome, New York. After graduating from Syracuse University in 1900, she had studied opera at Carnegie Hall. With the curiosity of a cat and a very big heart, she disappointed her parents by deciding to go into missionary work. In 1906, she went to China. She traveled alone to Nanchang, six hundred miles up the Yangtze River from Shanghai.

For eleven years she was headmistress of the Bao Lin School, the only school for girls in the province of forty-five million people. She later said, "It was especially hard on women to assert their rights. Yet I found many girls who were determined to guide their own fortunes."

When World War I broke out, she turned the administration of the school over to the Chinese and returned to America, where she did welfare work for the YWCA. She worked in Europe as a member of the War Work Council and after the war an aunt gave her $5,000 to travel and study the rest of the world. She then edited the Methodist magazine, *World Neighbors*, in New York.

Her husband, Bishop Frederick Bohn Fisher, died before I met her again as an adult but he was said to be quite committed to education and speaking out against poverty. She married him at the age of forty-four considered rather late for women of that day. She said, "I tell each generation of girls I meet not to fear leading independent lives. I generalize, of course, from me. The gamble was whether I could have my cake and eat it too. I wanted to do the work I did and in the end I found the man who loved me for this."

Although Welthy was Methodist, she embraced all religions and cultures and that is why I think Gandhi liked her so much. She and her husband had become friends with Gandhiji and supporters of India's struggle for independence. Welthy once said, "I can't believe in any one government any more than I can put all my faith in any one race or one language or one religion. The World is one reality and I belong to it."

She was described as having "spiritual color-blindness" and said, "I consider, following Christ and Confucius, that all men are brothers within the four seas."

Gandhiji was also impressed with her work in women's literacy in various places. She even lived for a while in Central India at his "village of service," Sevagram, in Wardha. After her husband died, she had been traveling and working all around the world—South America, China, and The Middle East. Right before Gandhiji was assassinated in 1948, he requested that she come back to India to work with women and education.

He said, "Go to the villages. If you do not help the villages, you do not help India because India is the village."

Gandhiji told her to teach the adult villagers to read materials about things that concerned them—their work and their land—so they could stand on their own. He didn't want them to be compelled to go into the cities where there was nothing for them. At that time, India had an illiterate population of about 400 million and cities were starting the slums that were collecting rural people.

This is how Literacy House came about with a focus on "functional literacy." Adults were equipped to face up to the responsibilities of living and learned subjects pertinent to their day-to-day rural life such as agriculture.

Welthy recruited educated Indians and gave them practical experience in teaching illiterate villagers using techniques such as word-picture association. She said, "No democracy can long flourish where only a thin top layer of the population is literate and educated."

They would write plays and use puppets to teach in Hindi and other Indian languages. It would draw big crowds. Welthy said, "Ideas expressed by these puppets in Indian dress and in Indian languages seem to have far more impact than if they were conveyed by live actors."

She went back to America and raised enough money to buy ten acres of land on the outskirts of Lucknow, the capital of Uttar Pradesh—one of the largest States in North India. The site of the school was surrounded by nature and away from the activity of the big city. I got a chance to spend time with her there as she was building it. It began as a small classroom and grew into a campus with redbrick classrooms, workshops, a library, staff residences, and hostels for male and female students.

There was even a beautiful octagonal shaped hall, the House of Prayer for All Peoples, where Hindu, Sikh, Muslim, Parsi, Christian or anyone could enter for prayer and contemplation. They published a weekly news report in Hindi called *UJALA* and created over fifty-five easy-to-read books covering subjects such as hygiene, health and sanitation, farming and citizenship.

It was tremendous to see what one dedicated woman in her seventies could do. Welthy was simply following Gandhiji's wishes.

Once someone said, "Like a stone thrown into a pond, her efforts have multiplied in benefits." She would often get up at 4:30 a.m. because her days and evenings were too full. Dr. Welthy Fisher became one of my heroes and mentors.

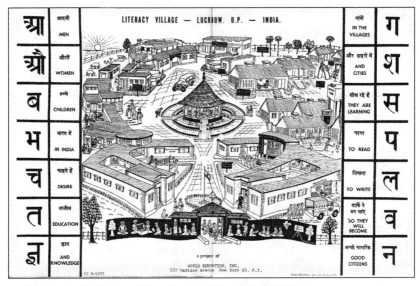

*Literacy House materials from World Education.*

Whenever I was in India, I would take yoga classes. They weren't taught by the big names, just teachers who were offering the practice. I needed something to help me feel connected. The first major teacher I truly studied asana with, besides my play on the beach in Pondicherry, was B.K.S. Iyengar.

I was actually older than him by a few months, and even though I was introduced to yoga asana when I was eight years old and he started when he was sixteen, he continued learning and teaching it all of his life. Iyengar was introduced to yoga by his brother-in-law and guru Sri T. Krishnamacharya who was one of the most known and influential yoga masters. Mataiji Indra Devi was the first woman and Westerner to study with Krishnamacharya. K. Pattabhi Jois studied with him and later Krishnamacharya's son T.K.V. Desikachar.

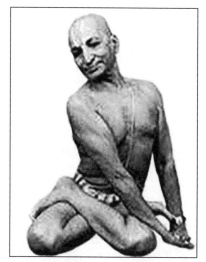
*Tirumalai Krishnamacharya*

*Bellur Krishnamachar Sundararaja Iyengar*     *Krishna Pattabhi Jois*

I was one of the first women to study with Iyengar around 1957, long before he opened the place in Pune. I actually helped convince him to take women. He was reluctant at first since it was traditionally a practice for men. I think my boldness and persistence surprised him.

We were in a small school and would stand on wooden benches. He would order us, "Touch the ground!" There would be three of us girls on one side—Dona Holleman, another Indian girl and me. Years later, Patricia Walden would come to study usually the month after me.

Iyengar was very precise in his teaching on alignment. It felt good to be able to put the pieces of the practice together—things I knew intuitively and learned from my uncle with lessons from such a dedicated master. Now Iyengar's style of teaching is studied around the world and has influenced many younger teachers who have become popular. I was delighted to study with him again.

I thought I may see my uncle on that trip to India but I kept missing him. It's a big continent and he was never in one place for long. He was always out working on the railroads in Africa and other places but we continued to write to each other.

I was always concerned about finding Ayah. After she went to stay with the British family in Devonshire during the bombings, we didn't communicate. At the end of the war, I couldn't locate her before repatriating to France. I have a feeling she went back to India. Sadly, I never saw her again.

When I returned from India, Bill Lynch was waiting at the airport to meet me. He had started contacting the Unitel office to find out my whereabouts. I really didn't know what to think of him. I had only met him briefly.

Since I thought I might stay in New York for a while, I decided to go to California to pick up some of my belongings. I didn't want to mail things since so many of my most precious items had been stolen at the Beverly Hills Post Office years before. When I returned to New York, Bill was there waiting. He seemed to be embedding himself into my life.

It was a strange time of many new experiences. I didn't know what was to come of it all. So much was in flux. I liked the promise of television with Unitel and the work I had been doing with UNESCO. I knew that storytelling was something that had always been a part of me and moving in the direction of producing was what I wanted. It was a delight to see Dr. Welthy Fisher and have yet another strong woman mentor. The one thing I wasn't too sure about was this new person in my life—Bill. Sometimes you have to say "yes" to something new and simply see where it takes you. It may turn out to be a stumbling block or a stepping stone.

> *Sometimes you have to say "yes" to something new and simply see where it takes you. It may turn out to be a stumbling block or a stepping stone.*

CHAPTER 18

# Let Trials Strengthen You

In some faith traditions there is a belief that the more spiritual you are the more roadblocks come up by no fault of your own. It's like there is an invisible battle between the forces of good and evil. Sometimes life can certainly seem that way. I've learned that if you face trials head on, you can find more strength. Don't run away from what looks like a challenge. It may be an important part of your path. You have to be persistent and follow what you believe.

*Don't run away from what looks like a challenge. It may be an important part of your path.*

When I went back to France for Unitel, I saw the Maharishi again. He was traveling throughout Asia, Europe and Africa teaching Transcendental Meditation.

He wanted me to put together a meeting at my place in Paris. I said to him, "You know, the people here have a different way of thinking from those in America and apartments here are not quite the same as there. I don't think I can fit too many people. I really don't know if I will be able to set up a meeting for you."

In his irresistible way, he replied, "If it is supposed to be, it will."

Curious, I asked, "What are you doing?"

Showing anticipation, he answered, "I am looking to open up an ashram and need people going different places to look for a location for me. We've been to Japan and China, but I haven't yet found exactly the right place."

"You know, Maharishi, I don't think you will find it in France."

"Well, I'm supposed to be meeting up with some people who found a place."

He came with a group of English people. I didn't know from where they all materialized. It seemed that suddenly I had all of these people squeezed into my little apartment. I don't know how they fit.

They enjoyed him talking about meditation and everything. I was just delighted to have the Maharishi's light shine in my small space. It was around 1960, and the teachings he learned from his guru, Swami Brahmananda Saraswati, were beginning to catch on.

After the gathering, Maharishi was on his way to meet somebody in Switzerland. I was really worried about him being on the train by himself with no guide. He simply had a ticket for a sleeper car on the train. I walked through the streets of Paris with him. I wasn't sure he had food for the trip so I stopped to get some fruit and yogurt.

When we got to the station, the man in charge of the sleeping cars came up and tapped me on the shoulder and said in French, "He's a holy man, isn't he?"

I said, "Yes."

"Where is he going?"

We showed him the ticket.

He graciously offered, "I am supposed to get off when we arrive at the frontier. I will stay on the train until he finds his people."

Without Maharishi completely knowing what this man was saying, he said with a quiet surety, "You see, Täo, everything is going to be all right."

I thought that was funny. He seemed to have no worries. Usually, I tend to not worry. I don't believe in it. It's an unnecessary block to positive energy flow.

*Worry is an unnecessary block to positive energy flow.*

Right after that, Maharishi would send people to me in Paris. A couple of months went by and I received another call from Maharishi who had gone back to England. With laughter in his voice, he said, "Täo, there's a gentleman who has found a place for me in India. We are going to build it and I had to tell you. I told this man, 'You can't go back to America without going to Paris among the beautiful trees to see Täo.' Will you see him?"

The man arrived and I could tell that he was a very nice person. We began to talk and he told me the story of how they found the place for the Maharishi's ashram.

He had been with a group traveling around looking at different places. They couldn't seem to find anything they liked. He was getting a little sick from traveling. When they got to the Himalayas, suddenly he couldn't go any further. He was too tired and sick. He told the rest of the party, "You continue up the mountain."

Concerned, they asked, "Will you be all right?"

He assured them, "Yes, you pick me up on your way down."

He continued telling me the story, "After they left, I instantly started to dance. I thought I was going mental. I was jumping up and down and singing to myself. When the others came back they thought I'd gone mad."

The man said he told the others, "We've found the place!"

The energy there absolutely enthralled him. He had to tell me about it. He said, "The spiritual energy seemed to ooze out of the ground. It was exactly what I was looking for."

That is where the Maharishi built the ashram.

As I had learned when I was a child, if you are in tune with all that is within you, you can feel what is right.

\*\*\*

Despite that delightful experience with the Maharishi and this man in Paris, I didn't stay much longer in France. It was now almost ten years after the war and it wasn't the same. I wasn't as well known and the people I knew were gone. I didn't know the people in Parliament. Most of the pilots had broken up with their families or could not be found. It was hard to be alone again there because there were a lot of memories but no real help at all. I decided it was best to go back to New York.

Halstead's secretary was nice but I couldn't continue living in her place. The lawyer who was working with us said to Halstead, "You can't do this to this girl. You're using her. She's got to live. She's put you in contact with everybody in India and you've got to give her something."

Halstead made me Vice President of Unitel and started paying me again. He didn't pay me what was owed but at least it was something. He also gave me the first few months of rent to get my own little apartment on 47th Street right by the United Nations. I remember the bank on the corner.

I was still using the Unitel office. We started working on TV in Uganda and Jordan. Then, a big conflict broke out in the Middle East. With the trouble there, they canceled the TV in Jordan. I still didn't have enough to live on and was wondering what to do.

Bill Lynch had been pursuing me for a long time, calling me everywhere I went. Without realizing what was happening, I found myself involved with someone with whom I really wasn't looking to get involved. I was intrigued with a person who would be so persistent and we started dating even though I didn't feel it was a big love affair like Yvan.

Right at that time I was looking to make a big film, *Two Worlds, Two Loves*, in India. It was about an American who comes to India on a visit and falls in love with the country. It was my attempt to interpret India, her people and their warmth to the rest of the world through a commercial feature film versus a documentary. We were going to do it through the eyes of a small Indian boy and this American.

I agreed to do the film through Unitel Productions. It was a way for me to pursue my film ideas, look for films to distribute internationally, and identify international films to distribute in America. I wrote the script, which I still have, and was going to be director on the American side and wanted to identify an Indian co-director. I was becoming much more interested in directing than acting and the years I spent acting were great training.

The plan was to shoot in Bombay, Kerala and around Mysore and so I went to India to set things up. It was to be a true Indo-American co-production done in English and Hindi. I was working once again with Clement in Bombay and we had to get the proper approvals from the Indian government, as well as raise the money. The total budget was 55 lakhs, which would be equivalent to about 5.5 million rupees or about $92,000 today. Indian participation was about a third of the budget. I was also beginning pre-production and looking at who we were going to cast for the film.

## Plan For A Hindi-English, Indo-American Co-Production

AN Indo-American co-production film, "Two Worlds, Two Loves," to be entirely "shot" on locations in South India and Bombay, has been planned by Unitel Productions, of New York, on the American side and Hunnar Films, of Bombay, on the Indian side.

Details of the project were worked out by Miss Tao Prochon, vice-president of Unitel Productions, and Mr. C. T. Baptista, of Hunnar Films. "Shooting" of the film to be made in English and Hindi is expected to commence in late November this year and end after a 14-week schedule.

Planned for world-wide distribution, the film will feature one known American male star. The rest of the cast will comprise Indian artistes, who will be professionals but not the top or very well-known ones, it was explained. A key character in the movie, a small boy, will be played by an Indian child. Technicians associated with the project will also be Indians.

"Two Worlds, Two Loves," to be "shot" in Eastman Color, has been scripted by Miss Tao, who will also be the co-director of the film on the American side. The Indian co-director has not yet been named.

### INTERPRETING INDIA

Miss Tao, who visited Delhi and Bombay and flew off to Paris on Wednesday, told "Screen" in an interview that "Two Worlds, Two Loves" was an attempt to interpret India, her people and their warmth to the rest of the world.

"It is difficult to give an idea of the story in a nutshell," she said. "One can say it is about an American trying to understand India and her people and, the best way to achieve such understanding being through children, his effort to do so through the agency of a small Indian boy."

"This is a feature film and a cent per cent commercial proposition," Miss Tao explained and added that the movie would, incidentally, promote better understanding about India.

### IN THEATRICAL GROUP

In the French capital, with Louis Jouvet, she played in "Doctor Knock" on the stage for eight months and also featured in the film version of the same drama. Also made films with Vivian Romance and Pierre Fresny.

### Co-Production Plans

(Continued from Page 1)

She visited America for the first time in 1949 and, a year later, through the good offices of Jack Cummings, secured an acting contract with M-G-M and acted in films like "The Last Time I Saw Paris," "Jump Into Hell," "Half a Hero" (with Red Skelton), "Sangaree" (the first 3-D film), "Show Boat" and "The Long Walt."

Miss Tao acted in nearly 200 television films in America, also appeared in the Bob Hope show in London.

She turned to direction in 1956, taking up an assignment as assistant director. Also commenced writing in 1959.

As writer and director, she has made such television film series as "Illicit Cargo" and "This Is Paris."

The last time she visited India was in 1956.

### MET MINISTERS

During the present visit, besides finalising the details of the co-production, Miss Tao met Ministers of the Government of India in Delhi as well as Ministers of the Government of Maharashtra in Bombay. She saw a number of films, features as well as documentaries, with a view to ascertaining if any of them could be distributed in the United States.

"Unitel looks after distribution, too," she explained, in regular cinema houses or on television.

(Through her offices, a half-hour film, called "The Face of India" made by Hunnar Films, has already been shown on television in the United States).

Miss Tao has been particularly impressed by some of the documentaries and plans to secure them for television showing in America under a series called "Jewels of India." A feature film called "Andolan," also touched her deeply and she held out hopes of securing a commercial release for it in the States, "with suitable clippings and effective editing."

*September 23, 1962 article about my plans for my film, Two Worlds, Two Loves*

When I got back to America, I continued looking for money to make it. One day, some people came into the office offering me a big sum. I didn't really know how they found out about the project, though I had been featured in various articles. They were saying that since the film would be shot in different places, they could gather money from those places. They were looking to attract foreign money but I didn't really understand the details.

Bill Lynch, who always seemed to be around, said to me, "Täo, don't get mixed up with those people. I don't like the looks of them."

I thought that he was just trying to get into my business affairs so I didn't pay too much attention to him. One day a very handsome young man came in from Uganda. He was well educated and really sweet.

The lawyer for these people who were interested in financing my film was sitting there and turned to me, "You let niggers into your office?"

Stunned, I asked, "What do you mean?"

He said, "You know they've got purple blood. They should be put in pig pens."

Shocked at what I was hearing, I exclaimed, "What? You're a lawyer. Haven't you been educated?"

Really mad, I stood up and said, "If that's the case then a good third of the boys that were in France during the war have the same blood. Those that had transfusions from these Black boys didn't mind. So half of your people in this country have that blood."

Then, I added emphatically, "Well, if you feel that way you can't work with me either because I'm half and half too!"

He looked at me and stamped out of the place. Needless to say, I never got the money. How completely stupid can people be? Ignorance like that makes me so mad. You have to speak up for what you believe in even if you have to make a sacrifice.

*You have to speak up for what you believe in even if you have to make a sacrifice.*

I believe that if you were born with a mix of ethnicities, it can really be a gift. It gives you a window into various cultures and hopefully makes you more open and tolerant.

As I continued to pursue funding for *Two Worlds, Two Loves*, other projects came up. I started working with a man that I thought would be helpful. He was a dreamer like Halstead with all of these ideas.

He wanted to make a film like Disney and he was talking about me being involved. He made the British version of *Alice in Wonderland*. It wasn't as beautiful as Disney's version of the film. It was more strident, not so pretty.

He now was going to make a film with Ben Lucien Burman who wrote *High Water Catfish Bend*. Hitler destroyed two of Burman's books when they burned all of the books. They said that *High Water* was "bringing people together" and they didn't like that. They only wanted Germany to exist. Those were strange times.

Since this man had some experience and was working on this film with Ben Lucien Burman, I assumed he knew what he was doing. Someone introduced me to the great jazz musician Duke Ellington and he agreed to do the music. He was intrigued by the concept. It was going to be one of those fantasy-type films with puppets and everything in it like *Alice in Wonderland*.

Ellington was really so sweet and such a charming gentleman. I think "Duke" was the perfect name for him. He had one of my favorite bands and played the most beautiful music. We used to sit and talk. I asked him about the inspiration for *Deep Purple*. He told me that it was the Caribbean sunset. Nature is the ultimate muse.

*Nature is the ultimate muse.*

Unfortunately, once again, the other money people for the film pulled out. They didn't like the man with whom I was working. I had everything going and then this man was becoming a bit difficult. He was using me. It was always about what he did and this was "his film." It sounded almost as if I was just his secretary even though it was partly my money. Finally, I pulled out as well. It seemed like I had one disappointment after the other.

\*\*\*

Apparently, people in the movie business were beginning to hear about my ability to get films for distribution. America wasn't as involved in international films at that time. One day a Greek gentleman walked in and said, "We want to work with you and set up an arrangement."

I thought anything would help. I knew films and had contacts in various places. I began to work with them and managed to get them films from France, England and even Hollywood to distribute. It appeared to be going fine and then once again, after I had done the work, they ended up owing me.

That's when I met Irving Feld. He was a real go-getter. I was able to get him films from various places around the world to distribute, and he was helpful to me. I managed to get a film that John Brom made on the Belgium Congo. I still have a painting of the Congo in my apartment today. Since Irving was able to distribute that film to this country, he started giving me some money.

We moved to an office on the 42nd floor in the tallest building in Manhattan located on 34th Street—the Empire State Building. Soon, all these people from Japan were coming to the office to do things. Hidetoshi Shibata, the head of Nippon TV, was meeting with Walt Disney who was developing a couple of golf courses in Japan. I would see Hidetoshi all the time in the office and got to know him very well. At every turn it seemed like something was going to happen and then I would realize that it wasn't really going anywhere.

I was still trying to produce my film, *Two Worlds, Two Loves*. I had received the okay from the Indian government, which was a big accomplishment. In those days, you had to have the approval from the Indian government to film anything. The country was just in its first years of being free.

With the approval secured, I was still trying to find investors but was not having any luck. Irving Feld was having financial challenges and we had to move out of the office on the 42nd floor. Everywhere I turned things seemed to be falling through.

That's when I met the King Brothers—Frank, Maurice and Herman. They ran King Brothers Productions and did films like *Gun Crazy* and *Carnival Story*. One of their films, *The Brave One*, earned an Academy Award for Best Screenplay.

They knew that I was making films in India and they wanted to do a project there. They wanted me to go there and do all of the work for them—get the okay from the Indian government to shoot, introduce them to people and such. I still knew a lot of people through my uncle and my films.

They saw that I had all of these films for distribution that didn't cost anybody any money. People had given them to me to distribute. So these brothers said they would back me but they didn't really. I gave them some tips and that was all. They didn't do anything for me.

I finally realized that wherever I was working, nobody was paying me. Everybody was using me and I was allowing it to happen. I wasn't the best at business and it was tough as a woman in those days. Many men felt like they could take advantage of my kindness.

Irving was constantly trying to make things happen. On one occasion, he was on the plane coming from his office in Los Angeles and was chatting with the person sitting next to him. He was from American National Films talking about a movie they wanted to do in India. Irving said, "Oh, you should really meet Täo."

Everyone thought that this was wonderful and we decided to go ahead with it. Even if I couldn't get my own film done, at least I could be involved in another feature film in India. I started to do some work on it but in came someone from the finance department to ruin it!

He said, "We've got *Caravans* written by the man who wrote *Hawaii*. He's a famous writer. If we're putting money into anything, it should be in *Caravans*."

James A. Michener had written *Tales of the South Pacific* and many other books. Needless to say, my project fell through.

By this time, I was fed up not being able to do what I wanted to do.

***

Bill Lynch was still in hot pursuit of me. He seemed to show up no matter where I was or what I was working on. During our encounters, I learned more about him.

One thing we came together on was our stance on justice. We shared similar views. Right around that time, Dr. Martin Luther King, Jr. was speaking out on civil rights and poverty, and Bill was interested in it. I found out later that Bill's father was really against everybody particularly "these handsome dirty kids" as he called them. I think that fueled an even deeper sense of justice in Bill. He didn't want to be like his father.

What I found fascinating was Bill's approach to things. He wanted us to go and learn about something before getting into it. He was learning all the time. He said, "You believe in Gandhi and freedom. This man stands for freedom, but I don't just want to follow him without knowing more about the history."

We actually took night classes at Woodlands High School to learn about the slave trade and problems in America about which Dr. King was talking. I liked Bill's commitment on this. In 1963, we went to the March on Washington to hear Dr. King.

It reminded me of my times with Mahatma Gandhi. There were long stretches of people—thousands coming together to follow Dr. King and make a statement to the world. There were people from all over. He was talking about basic rights for people, not just Blacks. Like Gandhi, Dr. King stood up for what he believed in.

*Bill Lynch and I attended the March on Washington in 1963.*

Even though it wasn't a big love affair, I liked Bill's attitude on equality. It had been about two years since I first met Bill and his son was now around seven years old, and his little girl was about five. Their mother was taking care of them and Bill used to go back to Brewster to see them. When the divorce came through, Bill thought he was going to get custody of the children, but he didn't. He had them on weekends, but didn't have money to do anything with them.

To make it easier for Bill, I told him, "You can have my apartment on weekends to be with your children. I'll go stay with Harriet."

I used to lend my apartment to him so that he could see his children there on certain weekends. I would let them stay in my place even though it was small. It was a bit complicated but I was trying to help him. When he saw me in New York, he would stay with friends in Hartsdale close to his insurance office.

Looking back, I suppose my choice to be with Bill was odd. We had different sensibilities. He drank scotch and gin, while I enjoyed a glass of wine.

One day I told him, "I'm sorry. I don't like these heavy drinks and I don't want to go out with you when you're like that."

Instead of getting upset he said, "Täo, what wine do you like?"

Pleasantly surprised, I replied, "Pinot Noir."

Smiling expectantly, he asked, "Will you go on a picnic with me tomorrow?"

I looked him in the eyes for just a second and could see that it meant a lot to him so I answered, "Yes, that should be nice."

Apparently, he went all over looking for the wine I liked and preparing for our rendezvous.

The next day he showed up with a beautifully prepared picnic basket with fruits, cheeses, sandwiches, sweets and two bottles of Pinot Noir. I had never gone on a picnic and it seemed that he had thought of everything to make it enjoyable for my first one.

We were on the Manhattan side of the Hudson River. The only problem was that it was winter and it seemed like one of the coldest days ever! We sat by the side of the river which was completely iced over to have a glass of wine. It was a nice thought but a little strange in that weather.

Nevertheless, it was really good to get away from the hustle and bustle of the city for a while. Despite the cold, I enjoyed relaxing in the open air with the sounds of nature and life around us as we talked and savored the food and wine.

I experienced seeing my first ice floats and marveled at their beauty. The only thing I didn't really like was his little German Volkswagen bug car. It reminded me of all of my friends I lost in the war. I know that probably sounds odd. In any case, I could see that he was really trying. It was quite a day and Bill was very charming.

*On a picnic in New York when Bill and I were dating around 1961–1962. This is in warmer weather, not like my first picnic by the Hudson in winter!*

All of the pieces seemed to be falling into place for my film, *Two Worlds, Two Loves*. I had money in India and thought this would help get more on the American side. The script passed the Indian Film Censor Board and had passed all the approvals from the Indian government. They were even going to let the Indian military be in a scene when they were building the dam. I was going to give them publicity and some financial participation in the film.

Irving connected me with the head of Cinerama who thought the film was perfect for them. They knew that I could access money in India and they were bringing in money from some Texas people, not the ones I knew. I was so happy something was finally moving forward. We were ready to close the deal.

It was a big day. We went to the Cinerama office on Park Avenue preparing to sign the mounds of papers. We were sitting there waiting and my lawyer hadn't come yet. An hour went by and I tried to call him. Nobody answered. We waited and waited. These people from Texas were getting angry because they had flown in especially for this meeting.

Finally, we sent somebody over to my lawyer's office and there was a notice on the door that read, "Closed for Death." I learned later that my lawyer had gone to the hospital for a check-up, and as he was being brought out in a wheelchair, as they often do, he had a stroke and died immediately right on the hospital steps! He had just been checked out and deemed to be all right.

I was shocked and then disappointed again because the Cinerama people withdrew from the project. The Texans left right away with their money. It was so disheartening. I had been working on this film project already for quite awhile. Each time it seemed like we were close to making it happen something would go wrong.

Irving said, "From now on Tāo, consult me. You've been taken so many times. It's time now that you did something."

He was really very sweet and supportive. Even though I didn't make a lot of money through him, he was always trying to sincerely be helpful. Irving was very enthusiastic about me but he wasn't able to raise the money that he said he was pursuing. He would give me money from some of the films that he distributed. He helped distribute some of the documentaries that I made and had relationships with some schools and libraries as well.

I made one documentary with people from Morocco. I made another film with John Brom who did the piece on the Belgium Congo. He had a lot of films that we distributed. I was helping filmmakers in Europe and America, getting to know more and more people.

There was activity with Bill Halstead still trying to push TV in India, TV in Uganda, and all of the people coming in from TV in Japan. I had the office but I didn't have any money. Here I was committed to all of these people and nothing was working out. Wherever I was working nobody was paying me. Everybody was using me whether they intended to or not.

All of this was going on with my work and then there was Bill and his children. Everything was happening at the same time and yet nothing happened.

I continued to allow Bill to use my apartment to see his kids. Bill's children were there at my place when the Maharishi came through New York. It was my last encounter with him. I remember it because it was right before The Beatles came to America for first the time. They were already popular in Europe. They later spent time with the Maharishi studying meditation.

The Maharishi was at the Ritz Hotel and I wanted to call up and see him. I couldn't invite him to my place because things were a bit chaotic. When I went down to the hotel, the Maharishi was surrounded by people and it was impossible to get in to see him given his growing popularity.

I think the Maharishi had captured people's attention by both his teachings and his presence. America was in the throes of change. There was talk about civil rights but there was still a lot of injustice. Rising discontent with the war in Vietnam was causing tension. It seemed like everyday people were searching for more spirituality and peace.

My life seemed more and more unsettled. I was getting frustrated with my various projects that would start and then not work. Bill wanted me to marry him but I really wasn't in love with him.

Yvan still occupied my heart. I was in love with him despite everything that happened. I didn't have that same kind of thing with Bill. It wasn't a love affair. I think I was just so fed up with what was going on in my life that I eventually said yes to marrying him.

Right after that last encounter with the Maharishi, Bill and I began preparing for the wedding. I didn't quite understand the details of his custody situation with his children. They had been staying with their mother but I found out that she had personal problems.

We were days away from getting married and Bill asked me if I would come with him to talk about the children. I knew he was worried about them but I didn't quite comprehend what was going on. Again, my English was okay but not the best.

There was a man, Mr. Cohen, whom I later found out was an attorney representing the interests of the children. He asked, "How do you feel about children?"

I said, "You know something, there are so many in this world. I don't have to have my own because I am older now."

Then, he asked the kids, "What do you think about being with somebody other than your mother?"

The little boy said, "I stand on the fifth amendment."

He was such a little tough guy even at seven years old.

I didn't realize the implications of my statements that day. I thought I was just helping Bill get more time with his children. I later realized that this was part of their custody case.

Our wedding date was set for late on the day of November 22, 1963. I remember it so clearly. It was in the afternoon and I was going across Central Park to the French Consulate. That's when I heard the news on the radio—"President John F. Kennedy has been assassinated." Somebody had turned the volume up and I found out he had been shot.

Everything seemed to stop. It was devastating to everyone. He was so young and had done so much. His wife Jacqueline was genuinely elegant and dignified with the two young children. We put the wedding off. Exactly one week later, we got married.

Since Bill had already been divorced twice, we couldn't get married in New York State at that time, and so, he made arrangements to go to the Justice of the Peace in Connecticut. The man who officiated even had champagne there for us. A lot of friends had fun laughing because we were to meet on a corner at a parking lot in Stratford, Connecticut to go to our celebration. A friend of mine who was an engineer at NBC gave us a big party.

My friends from India decided that it would be fun for me to have an Indian ceremony as well. So we planned it at the United Nations. My friend from the Indian Consul brought a Swami to officiate. After a beautiful ceremony, they gave us a great party. It was wonderful. People came from all around the world including India, France and Africa. Mr. Bhavagarty from UNESCO was even there.

Bill moved into my Manhattan apartment. It was cute but very small with only one room. It was my bedroom as well as my sitting room. I thought it was fine for the two of us at least for now. Bill bought me a fish tank with fish, but a plant would have been better.

I had been surrounded by all of the great spiritual teachers such as Swami Prabhavananda, Dr. Roman Ostoja and the Maharishi, and now my life seemed to be taking a different course. I felt my energy being scattered. So much was going on and yet so little was really accomplished. When you are distracted, it is hard to focus on what really matters. I woke up one day and my situation had completely changed. My work seemed to be at a standstill. I had a new husband and his children. I didn't recognize my life. Despite some trepidation, I decided to press forward hopeful that the challenges of the recent years were behind me and that this season would bring a sense of completion and new adventures.

*When you are distracted, it is hard to focus on what really matters.*

*November 29, 1963. My wedding to Bill Lynch at the United Nations in New York. It took place after our marriage at the Justice of the Peace in Connecticut. We're with the Swami from the Indian Consulate who officiated at the UN ceremony and various friends including Shri Vasudev from the United Nations.*

CHAPTER 19

Honor Human Nature

Even things that are beautiful, like roses with their sweet fragrance and intense colors, can have thorns. How do you enjoy the beauty and not get pricked? If you do, how do you heal the cuts? You can go into the market today and buy organic fruit. It's often not as pretty as the other fruit. However, if you can look past the visible flaws and bruises, it is delicious. Mother Nature gives us clues about how to appreciate and honor human nature.

*Even things that are beautiful, like roses with their sweet fragrance and intense colors, can have thorns.*

When Bill and I first got married, I didn't realize the entire situation. He finally told me that his wife had taken everything from him in the divorce—the house, furniture, everything and had even run up enormous bills that he had to pay. He had grown up with money and now had none left. With a wry sense of humor, Bill smiled and remarked, "At least I got a stool that I ended up giving to a friend."

Trying to look at the bright side and offer some encouragement, I said, "At least you are still in the insurance business and you're very good at that. We can continue to live in my apartment until we can do better."

That thought didn't last very long. A few days later, as I walked by Bill in the apartment, he stopped me abruptly and with an overwhelming urgency insisted, "We've got to get something bigger."

I stared at him thinking, "This doesn't make any sense. What is happening here? I don't understand."

From all that Bill had told me about his financial situation, and knowing my own, I didn't know why he was pressing for us to move. I didn't think we could afford it.

Looking up at Bill's strained face and hearing how adamant he was, I agreed, "Okay, we'll look for a larger apartment."

As a newlywed, I wanted things to be peaceful. I never experienced anyone like Bill and was trying to understand him. Although I didn't grasp the urgency of having to move immediately, I began to think, "Well, if we can afford it, a larger place would be good for us as we begin our life together. We can have a nice bedroom, sitting room and even a view."

We soon found another place on Third Avenue in the sixties. I was pleased because it had space enough to even invite friends over from time to time.

Two weeks later, Bill came home with his children. I thought they had come for a visit but surprisingly he announced, "Kevin and Tracy are here to live with us." They dropped their little suitcases at the door.

Bill's behavior began to make sense to me. He knew even before we were married that he was getting full custody. I didn't. He never told me.

I was shocked but tried not to show it. My life changed in an instant, more so than I could have ever imagined. Seven-year-old Kevin and five-year-old Tracy were quite rambunctious—running around, fighting over toys, throwing things at each other, screaming very loudly. I was not used to any of this. The kids were young and I thought the divorce must have been tough on them, so I tried to be compassionate.

In our new apartment, the room that was supposed to be our bedroom was given to the children. We had part of the sitting room as our bedroom. The apartment I thought was spacious felt more like a closet. I tried my best to make personal adjustments and get to know them. As soon as possible, I began to plan activities I thought the children would enjoy.

When The Beatles came through, I went all over New York looking for Beatle boots. Eventually, someone suggested I go to a place where they made boots for dwarfs and have them made. That's what I did even though I didn't have much money. The next day, after Kevin wore the boots to school, all the mothers were calling me asking, "Where did you get them from?" Apparently, Kevin had given them our phone number.

The children's mother sold the house in Brewster and moved to Pleasantville. It was about forty-five minutes from Manhattan. Bill was now driving the children back and forth to visit. Since his office was in Hartsdale, he would drive the twenty minutes from there to pick them up and then bring them back to me in Manhattan.

Kevin and Tracy had been with us for the first winter months of our marriage and I had turned my life around totally. In the two years that I had known Bill, the children lived with their mother. Now, Bill and I both were adjusting to having them with us full-time. It was complicated.

In the midst of all of these life-altering adjustments, I discovered I was pregnant. I guess it happened pretty much right away. I was quite surprised since I was forty-five years old. So much was changing at once. My many experiences around the world had not prepared me for this. It was like nothing I had ever known.

I tried my best to make our home pleasant despite the fact that I was having complications with my pregnancy and had some bleeding. Sadly, Bill was not very helpful. Perhaps he simply wasn't good with things like that.

When I got to five months, I felt that something was terribly wrong. I was bleeding all the time. I went to the hospital there on the Westside Highway. I think nuns ran it. After checking me out, they advised me to go home but said, "Stay off your feet. You may lose the baby." That was heartbreaking to hear.

On top of that, I caught a cold. The children had been visiting their mother so Bill left me in the apartment and went to pick them up. I had been bleeding all night. I knew I needed help, so I called a doctor myself. When I told him what was happening and that I could hardly stand up, he came over with the emergency services and they immediately took me to the hospital. I think it was Lenox Hill—the one on the East Side past 70th Street.

As soon as we arrived, I was rushed to a room for the doctor to examine me. He quickly called all of these doctor-students in like this was going to be some big event. It seemed the doctor pressed my stomach and all of this blood flew out of me like a bunch of grapes. It was all a mess. The physical pain was gone but I began to feel the pain of losing my baby.

A nurse was finally able to reach Bill. He had just come back from picking up the children. When he walked in my room, I was so glad he was there. Showing some impatience, he simply said, "I can't stay. I have the children in the car."

I didn't know what the nurse told him so I tearfully shared that we had lost our baby. I told him everything that happened. I thought he would be comforting, but instead he made an offhanded remark. He shrugged, then left and went downstairs.

I practically fainted. I had a traumatic experience and Bill was not very sensitive. I thought, "What have I done to get married?"

I made it through the war and the dangerous missions in the underground with the French Resistance. I remained strong as a pilot's wife during the war. I even sustained myself in Hollywood with its twists and turns. Now, I found myself in the fight of my life. It was the first time I felt totally abandoned and adrift. I had strayed off my path of peace and being spiritually grounded.

***

After losing the baby, we simply went on like nothing happened. As I was rebuilding my body, I noticed that Bill seemed restless again. Surely enough, he came to me with another demand, "Tāo, we have to move up near my office." He didn't ask me or discuss it. He simply made the declaration and I suppose, in retrospect, I just accepted it.

Living in Manhattan was important to me. I still believed in my film projects. I wanted to be able to quickly take the bus to meetings. It gave me a sense of freedom to do what I wanted. I thought, "How can I do this from Hartsdale especially since I have to be there for the children?"

Without any fuss from me, we moved into a big apartment building not far from his office. It was right on the hill. You can still see it today. It was a nice size and that was good. Unfortunately, I did not like that it was facing the north. We never got any sun. I couldn't stand that. I loved the sun and the feeling of nature coming inside. I needed to feel that kind of warmth. I also didn't know anyone.

Although Bill's office was there and the children were also starting school in the area, Hartsdale was new to me. I had visited my friend

Mary Ellen Kay in Brewster where I met Bill. Hartsdale was located in Westchester County, an upscale suburb of Manhattan. With the train station right across from our apartment, I began to feel more comfortable about the move knowing that in less than an hour I could go into Manhattan for meetings.

Much to my dismay, Bill gave me another jolt, "You'll have to give up your film business and everything."

Not being used to hearing something like that, I said, "What do you mean?"

He simply replied, "The children are starting school."

I didn't know what to think about that. I was so used to being independent even when I was married to Yvan. Now, there were all of these changes.

There had been a fire in Bill's office so they moved to another one on Central Avenue. Soon thereafter, he came home with an unusual look on his face and announced with enthusiasm, "My partners have decided to retire. They feel they are getting too old for the business. So I'll be getting full control."

"That's great. Let's celebrate with a nice glass of wine."

I was happy for him since he worked so hard. I also felt excitement thinking that Bill would ease up on what he said to me about working.

After we were both more relaxed, I broached the subject again. Instead of the response I expected, he mocked me, "Film is a waste of time. You've had all of these things go wrong since I've known you so you have to give it up. We've got the children here now."

I simply did not know how to respond.

Since his divorce left him with nothing, we had to make a home from scratch and in many ways, scraps. I decided to make the best home we could have with our resources. As they say, I rolled up my sleeves and dug in. My gums were even hurting and I couldn't go to the dentist because all the money was being spent on the children.

Each child had a room. I painted Tracy's all white and actually painted everything in her room since there was no real furniture. Then, I got pink and white polka dot fabric and made a design all around one of the chairs and even covered the cushion to make it pretty. All of her friends said to her, "Oh, it's as if you're a princess sitting there."

I made Kevin everything to do with the American Civil War. I gathered all of these pictures and things to make him feel that he had a boy's room. I made everything, even curtains, and I couldn't even sew properly. I smile sometimes and think, "It was lucky that they stayed together."

The children had everything—music, a recording device, including a TV. Bill and I didn't even have furniture for our own bedroom. All of my things, including my clothes, were in cases for at least a year. We didn't have money to buy furniture or new clothes. Nearly ninety percent of the time I wore saris. Everything was for Kevin and Tracy.

I thought if I could show the children love and do nice things, it would work out particularly since it was tough for them before. No matter what I did they seemed determined not to accept me. I suppose many women who have been in this situation of families coming together have experienced it. I thought that perhaps the children were rebelling and it would pass.

Kevin and Tracy taunted and made fun of me because of my French accent. Bill didn't help because he always took their side thinking it was funny. I think he was trying to be giving to them and didn't realize it was hard on me.

Their teasing made me even more determined to learn English without an accent. I would get hold of anybody and make the person say certain words. Then, I would try to pronounce the words that way. I would keep on doing it until I didn't hear too much of an accent myself.

Even though I was trying to perfect my English, I didn't want to lose my French. I was not going anywhere I could speak it. No one I knew in Hartsdale spoke it and I was getting more and more alone in a strange village without a friend.

It was difficult all around. Everything became dependent on the children. Bill let them have their own way all the time. I had no say at all. It was almost unbelievable to me that I was caught in this strange situation. It was beyond anything I could ever have imagined in my life. Bill was at work and I was left with these kids who seemed to enjoy making my life unpleasant.

I tried my best to be a good stepmother. As we settled in, they started to have friends over. The friends liked me and delighted in what I did, like the chair I made for Tracy or the birthday parties I would give. We would have over twenty children there enjoying themselves. They would be all excited and say, "Oh, Mrs. Lynch will you make that wonderful meal for us? You make the best food." Kevin and Tracy never thanked me.

Bill was rather intolerant. He didn't seem to want me to do anything outside the home, not even drive the car although I had driven in California. In New York over the previous months, I had started to earn $750 every week for two scripts, and now he wouldn't let me write or work. I was hiding nearly all the things I started in France because he demanded that I give up my job.

Some women might not have minded being taken care of, but I had been fiercely independent. What was I going to do without earning my own money? I had taken care of myself all of my adult life. I had used up most of my money trying to help Bill. Now, I was almost like a prisoner. I was ready to run away.

Bill certainly didn't want me to go back to Hollywood. He gave me just enough to pay for food in the market. He made sure that I didn't have money to take off anywhere. Later on, one of his friends told me, "Täo, he is scared you are going to leave him." People deal with fear in different ways, but it was difficult to comprehend.

I had already learned that I couldn't argue with him. He would turn into an absolute frozen thing. I couldn't even get near him. Once he didn't talk to me for three weeks. He just came in and out. He was having problems with his insurance company.

I thought, "You're supposed to be able to give and take. Maybe I should to be able to cope with it all but I can't live like this!"

I decided to pack my things and just move out. I went down to the train station with three dollars in my pocket. Once Bill found out, he rushed to the station, grabbed me and brought me back. I couldn't get anywhere with him and thought, "What am I doing here?" This was a dismal part of my life. I felt I wasn't me.

I don't know if I could totally blame Bill because he had such a rough time as a child. Although his father was very successful, he was said to be quite a character. Bill didn't even let me meet him when we got married. He said, "He will change everything as soon as he walks in including the furniture, what you're wearing and everything. He will find something wrong with it." Both of Bill's parents had been married and divorced multiple times. I was Bill's third wife.

Things really weren't going very well at first. Bill was working hard with his insurance business but we still had no money. He would get up early in the morning to go out. He was doing a lot of work with one of the big insurance companies as a broker and even gave courses for them. He called them "Fort Knox" because they made so much money.

At one point, he got really mad with the company because they were canceling people's policies. People may have had the insurance for twenty-four years and then something would happen that was not their fault, a fire or something, and the company would cancel their insurance. It wasn't fair so Bill put up a fight saying, "This is wrong. They can't do this to people. These people have been paying the company for years and now they cancel on them!"

With about three or four people with trouble like that, he tried, to no avail, to get this big insurance company to make it right. They had famous lawyers who kept preventing him from taking it to court. They were really nasty to Bill. Other insurance brokers were scared to join him. This big company was able to get away with it so he ended up turning in all of our insurance policies except for the kids. Despite all of our issues, I admired Bill for standing up for his beliefs.

\*\*\*

Fortunately, one thing Bill and I shared was a love of wine. Bill was intrigued by my knowledge of it and impressed by my family history and the fact that we had a vineyard in the Rhône Valley for so many generations. He didn't mind me doing work related to wine since it was an interest of his as well.

A new craze was becoming a number one hobby—home winemaking. Popular in Britain, a place without vineyards, it had caught on as being one of the most fruitful hobbies they had ever known. In less than ten years, it had spread throughout Canada and the United States. It was becoming as popular as football and other games.

Making wine and beer brought a new wave of appreciation of drinking it. Rather than drinking it to get drunk, the notion of savoring the nuances of taste and flavor was catching on. It made people aware of the incredible beauty of nature and these beautiful drinks from the fruit of the earth.

Home winemaking needed products and knowledge. It brought into existence products that set the stage for new industries needed to make this "elixir of the gods" such as wine concentrates, corks, oak barrels and equipment. Multiple stores opened up providing equipment and a blooming industry spread. But where could you find these products? Germany, Holland, France, Spain and Italy were key places.

With this new market, magazines and newspapers on where to find the best products to make wine and beer, and the needed education, became important. People were hungry for information, so I started the *Beverage Communicator*. It was one of only three wine appreciation newspapers in America at the time. There was one called *Wines and Vines* out of San Francisco and *Wine Spectator*, which is still around.

*The Beverage Communicator newspaper I published for over thirty years.*

The interest in home winemaking had grown so much that soon there were perhaps a thousand stores across the United States, and within eighteen months these three newspapers became famous. I started mine because people couldn't find places to buy ingredients or anything. I supplied information and the addresses to find these tools

If I was going to do something, it had to be of high quality. Luckily, I found a girl in the Bronx who worked for a big newspaper. She thought what I was doing was great and helped me make my paper professional.

Grape growing for a wine industry in America was still relatively new except for the pockets of early experimentation. Spanish missionaries growing grapes made the first wine in California in the late 1700s. North Carolina had the Scuppernong grapes grown in Tyrrell and Washington counties and wine was made from them. Virginia and Long Island became other states that were growing grapes at that time.

Thomas Jefferson was U.S. Minister to France in 1785, a long time before he became President in America. He spent five years in Paris and became enamored with European wines. When he returned, he started testing out grape growing for wine in Virginia. In the 1800s, the first grapevines were planted in New York in the Finger Lakes region, which is now known for its wineries.

In the 1960s, there seemed to be a surge of interest in wine in the United States. People like Robert Mondavi, whom I had met a decade earlier, were experimenting with different grape varieties and becoming popular. Many people started buying pieces of land on Long Island to grow grapes.

In fact, Long Island was doing some of the best wines in New York State. The Finger Lakes region was also still quite popular, with a lot of research on grapes being done with the New York State Agricultural Experiment Station at Cornell University in Geneva, New York. Cornell's main campus is in Ithaca, New York, and people still go up to the Finger Lakes area for wine tours.

American wineries on the West Coast started working with France. I had a little bit to do with that. I would get involved everywhere. It wasn't intentional. People came to me asking if I would help them here and help them there. I kept saying yes. If you have something to share, then share it. Charles Fournier had already introduced French-American hybrid grapes to New York and now there was a renewed interest in a deeper connection with Europe.

*If you have something to share, then share it.*

My newspaper covered everything for people who made wine and beer. It was international because I knew people from everywhere. I had articles on India in it. I wrote about meeting Ernest Hemingway after the war in Sancerre where many of the wonderful wines came from. That area is known for its Sauvignon Blanc and some Pinot Noir.

Hemingway was a wine connoisseur and people seemed to enjoy my writing about him and other wine experiences, such as my early Napa Valley stories.

One of the heads of a big wine and beer organization, the Home Wine and Beer Association, lived in Westport, Connecticut. She would keep me updated on what was happening in the industry to put in my newspaper. When she received information, she would immediately redirect it to me.

I was getting news from all over. Since everybody wanted to sell to America, they were advertising in the *Beverage Communicator* because it was the only newspaper doing that. I knew so many people and therefore it was distributed in at least forty-seven countries in addition to the United States and Canada.

Bill was interested in making wine for fun and actually started making it in our apartment in the cupboards! Canada was much further advanced in terms of home winemaking so nearly every weekend he would drive us up to Montreal to get supplies. That was good because I'd see my Indian friends who lived there and I could hear and speak French.

We'd go to Beaconsfield to buy products and come back loaded with different things. Bill had a "Going to Canada" hat. He didn't really care what he wore. The things I didn't want him to wear, I would send to the cleaners so he couldn't find them.

Bill decided to start a wine-related shop so he would have everything close by. He took a place on Central Avenue across from his office right behind the Italian restaurant called Sergio's.

The shop had everything to do with wine but we didn't actually sell wine. Instead, we were selling books and things to make wine and beer. I wasn't into beer but there were a lot of people looking for products to make it.

We focused on carrying only quality products. I bought corks from Portugal and some oak wine barrels and wine concentrates from Spain.

Bill replaced all of the windows to make a huge window and started growing grape vines in front of the shop. He took two big barrels to make a counter and cut off cognac bottles that he made into lamps. It was creative and since the wine shop was very close to his office, Bill was delighted designing the store. He did everything to glamorize the shop but then never joined me to talk to clients. He only wanted to make the wine.

The store drew people from miles around. People were putting samples of the wine and beer they made right inside the door. They wanted to know if it was good. They would leave notes saying, "Please tell me what is wrong with my wine."

*In front of our car ready for a roadtrip.*

Bill had these great ideas, but didn't want to put the work in so I found myself to be a sales girl in this shop along with being publisher of my newspaper. Bill didn't really want me to do anything else except be there. He thought that if I got involved in this little shop, I would be content.

People were coming to me from all over the area with questions trying to sell or buy products. In addition, more people were advertising in my newspaper. However, as the shop became known and the newspaper expanded, I had very little time to devote to my creative work.

The *Beverage Communicator* was bringing wine and beer people to advertise their products from Great Britain, Germany and other countries. The British were the foremost in making home wine and beer products and about three-quarters of the space in advertising was bought by those from Great Britain.

Soon, I got to know huge beer brands like John Bull in Cambridgeshire and the head director, Lance Middleton, became a good friend. Later, in the 1970s, there was a John Bull Home Beer Kit that was promoted with, "So good, it could put pubs out of business!"

During that time, wine was like ballroom dancing now. There was a certain kind of enthusiasm in the air for something that was new. The fun of this new experience seemed to flow across the United States and Canada at full speed capturing everyone's interest. It was one of the things that kept me from going mad during this period.

As the children got older, they seemed to be more difficult to manage. The apartment seemed smaller and smaller. The first three years of the marriage were really hard. When we finally moved into a beautiful house in Hartsdale, it got a little better. It was near Bill's insurance office and was very spacious, and so we added dogs to our family.

*Our house on Findlay Avenue in Hartsdale.*

*Our dogs Pep and Penny.*

At least, now there was room enough for me to sneak away and write when nobody was looking. In between running the newspaper and the shop, I did nothing else but write whenever I could. I was able to escape to my own fantasy world where I wrote many film scripts behind Bill's back.

I literally had to steal moments because I was not often alone. I found it interesting that in Hollywood I was on my own and so lonely, and now I had a family and felt even more alone. Bill was fine with me getting involved with the wine culture, but he liked to be in control. He listened to everything about the children who still came first in our lives.

I had been quietly saving money. With some of it, I started collecting bulbs from Holland. Bill didn't know so I hid them. I didn't really know how to plant them. When he found them, to my delight, he was very interested and helpful. He showed me how to cut the little stems so I could get the roots into the ground.

When spring came, I had flowers everywhere. Everybody was coming to see the spectacular colors of the tulips. It was funny to me because they didn't understand the role the garden played in my life. To them, it probably seemed like something that was simply pretty. To me, it was my return to nature and once again my saving grace.

Touching the soil is like a spiritual awakening. It is healing and makes me feel my connection to the Oneness of life and the Creator of all things. It brought me back to myself. It became my sanctuary. When I had trouble, I would run out in the garden just to plant more flowers. It made me feel like I was breaking out of prison.

> *Touching the soil is like a spiritual awakening.*

I was thinking that there must be a way to make my marriage work. I kept hearing my uncle's voice saying, "Never ask anyone to understand you, always try to understand them. If you don't like them it's not their fault, it's yours." I had to do something to bring more peace but what? I also thought of my friend the Maharishi and began to meditate on it.

During my meditations, I was able to call up my "Inner Diary"—the voice within and the lessons I'd learned from my many teachers. In the stillness, I felt more peace and gained clarity. All of my life when I wanted to do something, I just went on and did it. I told myself that I was not going to have the children's voices drive me crazy with Bill saying, "They're only children."

The next time we had a fight, I decided to take a more yogic approach. When I was in bed that night I put my hand on Bill's heart. He didn't move. He didn't pay any attention to me. So I breathed at the same time as his heartbeat, making sure we were in synch—his heartbeat and my heartbeat. It's similar to what I did in Hollywood when I rode the horse bareback for the first time. I synched our breath and we were one.

I began to remember all of the things I learned from my three years of study with Dr. Ostoja. He would stress that we could all tap into

Universal Intelligence through breath and our thoughts. By tuning our mental vibrations we could experience cosmic harmony. I decided to put this into practice. With Bill, I visualized what I wanted and then I transferred my thoughts mentally. I know it must sound silly to some people, but it achieved results.

Bill went into a deep sleep. He had worked late and would be going to his office at five in the morning. To my satisfaction, when he got out of bed the next day he was nicer. To resolve our argument, he used my words as if they were his own.

After that, rather than engage in a disagreement with him, I would be quiet and do my inner work. I'd just hug him a little bit, put my hand on his heart, breathe with him at the same time and get the answer I wanted. It began to ease things up with us. Breath is the one thing we all share. If we can breathe together, we can be together.

> *Breath is the one thing we all share. If we can breathe together, we can be together.*

I learned that you have to make a personal commitment to peace. Peace comes from inside. If you find yourself getting out of synch, make a conscious effort to reconnect to your own center and it may help you determine how to connect with others. Like the contrasting aspects of a rose, human nature is complex. A person can be creative and engaging yet that same person may be difficult and controlling. Is that person a bad person? How do you love the good and release the bad? I learned from my uncle to always look for the good even in seemingly bad situations. I think we are all good at heart.

*Left: New Year's Party with Bill. Right: My friend Harriet.*

CHAPTER 20

# Seek Common Ground

If you choose to grow a relationship, then it's important to seek common ground. On the surface it may seem like you are very different but you probably have more similarities than you think. If you dig deep enough, you may find you share the same roots. Once you discover the link, strengthen it. Water it with kindness and compassion. Sometimes it may take time but you will be amazed at how it blossoms. That's what was happening with Bill and me.

*If you dig deep enough, you may find you share the same roots.*

Bill had many admirable qualities and I started to see more of them. He had a great sense of humor but he couldn't tell a joke. He would start laughing before he got to the end!

I found that he was at his best when he was helping others. When he joined the Rotary Club in Hartsdale, he became very active. If he saw something that needed to be done in the community, he simply would do it. I admired this about him. Bill didn't think they were doing enough and would say, "A dollar here and a dollar there is nothing when we could do things."

He was right. It is easy for each of us to do little things to make the world around us better. When he saw people standing along Central Avenue waiting for a bus during the winter months with snow and rain coming down on them, he right away wanted to do something to fix it. He said, "I can't see them standing like this on the roadside."

He wanted to build something they could stand under. There were no bus shelters at that time and so he went to another person in the Rotary Club and offered to provide all of the materials if he would help construct them. Together they built several covered bus stop shelters along the way. They were not the greatest looking structures but at least they were something. He found an architect who had designed a hotel in White Plains to help.

*It's easy for each of us to do little things to make the world around us better.*

People began to know that Bill was a man of action when he learned of a need. Someone came to him and said, "You know it's a shame that these older women and men want to have a garden but they can't bend over."

Bill suggested, "Let's make raised up gardens."

Up here on the hill in Hartsdale there are still twenty-four raised garden beds in Woodlands High School for people to grow plants and food. He built them so that older people would not have to bend over to plant flowers and vegetables. Someone from the Rotary Club helped design and raise them up.

Bill was always doing things for people and as soon as the press would come to film it, he would fade in the background. He would say, "I didn't do it for the publicity." He didn't want his name in the papers for the things he did even though he was president of the Hartsdale Rotary.

He even planted the first trees along the avenue there in front of the school. Every year, the Rotary Club still plants a tree so it can be a nice place to play. The Club flies a flag outside of the railway station in his honor.

Bill was earning a little more money from his insurance business so we were doing more fun things. He wanted a place to store his wine so he built an extra garage. Over it, he built a place where we could go outside and have parties on the roof. I could get a hundred people on it so we began to entertain, which I liked.

I saved all of the labels from the wines we used and from the shop, and put them together on the wall in the kitchen. Everyone who came by would say, "Where did you get that wonderful wallpaper?"

With a sense of pride, Bill would reply, "She put them on there." There were several thousand labels.

The Rotary Club would sometimes host people from other parts of the world. One year Rotary was hosting a girl from Colombia. She was supposed to stay at several places during the year but she stayed with us the whole time. My friends from various countries would come and stay with us—people from India, the United Nations, UNESCO in Paris, and even people I knew from the brewery business.

Whenever anybody from a different country would come, Bill would go out and get the flag and put it up to make them feel welcome. Outside of our house right across the veranda were different flags, including the American flag, Indian flag, and French flag. He was wonderful for that.

One time, he had some people fly to New York Rotary from Bermuda for a big gathering, including the very British governor of Rotary from Bermuda. Bill put on each table a Bermuda onion. That might sound strange but he researched their culture and found that Mark Twain wrote, "The onion is the pride and joy of Bermuda. It is her jewel, her gem of gems." Bill would do thoughtful things like that. The layers of his personality were revealing themselves to me like peeling away the layers of an onion.

*I would often wear my saris for various events.*

Bill and I also came together around our love for nature and protecting the environment. Our huge lawn allowed us to do much more. He even went out and bought three beehives. He then went around looking for people who had beehives so he could find out how to maintain them. That was his type of character. He would investigate things to make sure he knew about the history of them.

*Bill with his bird house and setting up one of his three beehives in our yard.*

He was also big into recycling. Even in our garden he made a mulching bend. He put anything like food or stuff in a special issue fenced-in container to make sure that it would be recycled.

Even in the wealthier sections of town, people threw garbage and plastics on the streets and the lack of maintenance made the area look awful. People were living in these homes, some were even millionaires, but that didn't stop them from throwing the stuff in the streets. I didn't understand that. Bill would get up in the morning before going to his office and collect garbage. He would come back with a big bag of garbage. I would ask, "Why are you bringing it to our house?" In retrospect, some of the things that happened were really funny.

Once a cat climbed up a tree hiding from a dog and nobody could get the cat down. It had been there for a couple of days and was probably too frightened to come down on its own. Tracy was beside herself. It was a sight to see right opposite Bill's office. He told the fire department that he would give a reward if they got it down. They said, "We can't do anything about it." So, he put it on the media and everyone flocked around it with ladders and steps to try to retrieve it. Eventually, the fire department got the cat down and Bill kept his word by giving them the reward.

An old Jewish gentleman who had worked with Bill in insurance had to go into a nursing home. He had a cat that had been with him all his life. Bill kept the man's cat there at the office and it would sit in the window. We couldn't take it home because we had the dogs.

Bill's involvement in various things gave me a little more time. Even though I was still consumed with him and the children, and keeping up with the newspaper and wine shop, I was stealing moments to write.

Soon I realized that I had written many scripts, including a television series called *The Ambassador's Son*. It's amazing what you can get done when you work consistently at it. It's like water wearing away rock.

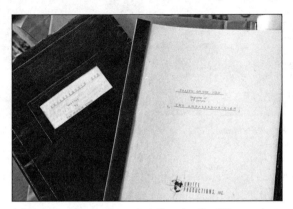

*Scripts for The Ambassador's Son that I still have today.*

My series was about a little boy and his journeys and unusual experiences around the world. I began to try and market it. I wrote to people in countries that were relevant to the stories. I had people in Egypt interested, as well as Thailand.

The story that was based in Iran attracted the most interest. Without Bill knowing, I had worked out a business arrangement and had even gone through the Iranian government in preparation for filming. We were at the point of closing the deal with people coming over from Iran to see me.

Right around that time, Bill had to go into the hospital for an operation on his throat. I was relieved for two reasons. One was that it wasn't serious and the other was that I could go to my meeting without him knowing.

I went to the Essex House on Central Park South to meet the two men who had come to finalize the deal and bring me the check. I was sitting alone for a while anxiously waiting and yet extremely excited knowing that I was back in the business.

Finally, one of the men arrived. He was white as death. In disbelief, I listened as he told me that on that very day the Ayatollah had invaded their film department and everyone had been shot. His partner had taken off and I never got the check and thus could not make the film.

I was not only shaken by what had happened but I was also very disappointed because I had planned to go to the hospital that day and say to Bill triumphantly, "See, I did it!" But, it didn't work out.

Even though Bill didn't want me to work, people were still asking me to do things. The King Brothers were developing a TV series in Rajasthan and they asked me to help them set it up for them.

---

**KING BROS. PRODUCTIONS · INC.**
c/o Metro-Goldwyn-Mayer, Inc.
Culver City, Calif.

Mr. Toa Porchon
229 West 42nd Street
New York, New York

November 14, 1966

Dear Toa:

As you know, we here at King Brothers Productions are preparing to leave for Bombay, India, where we will commence shooting in December, 26 hour-long color Television films to be aired on NBC next year.

Since you are familiar with the enormous production problems you run into in a situation of this kind and as you have lived for several years in India, I would appreciate it very much if you could give me the names of anyone you know in India that could be of help to us, primarily anyone that could help us in expediting our equipment in and out of India.

MGM, NBC and we here at King Brothers Productions have great expectations for this exciting series. We will be spending within a period of one year over four million dollars there. I am sure you are aware of the importance and urgency of this matter.

I would like to thank you in advance for your help.

Sincerely yours,

Del Tenney

DT:kt
cc: Frank and Maurice King

*Letter from the King Brothers requesting my assistance with a film in India.*

---

Surprisingly, Bill was actually fine with me going to India. I was shocked. He met some of my Indian friends and liked them. He liked the way they thought. They were kind to each other.

I tried to help the King Brothers but it was hard keeping up with everything. I spent a lot of my own money, the little I had left, and then they hardly paid me. Even so, I was happy once again to be working at all and hopeful that Bill would continue to ease up.

Some of the work I had started with my company Ciné Universal Ltd. was beginning to materialize. A project I had started a few years earlier producing and distributing the English version of the *Face of the Sahara* was released by Sterling Education Films. It was nice to see the result of some of my work. The film chronicles the first expedition into the Sahara to map the only uncharted region and to search for proof that the Sahara had once been green.

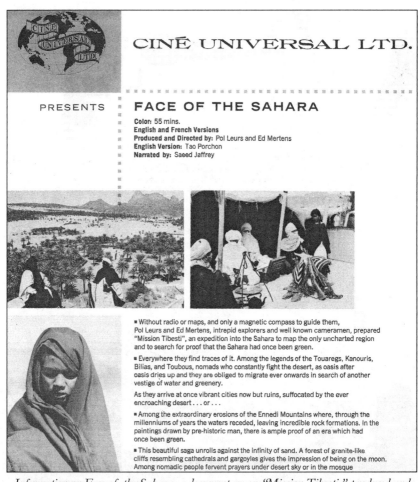

*Information on Face of the Sahara, a documentary on "Mission Tibesti," produced and directed by Pol Leurs and Ed Mertens. I produced the English version.*

I was also able to distribute another part of that same series. This time it was the film *Face of India*. It had been filmed almost two decades earlier in New Delhi on India's National Independence Day on August 15, 1947 when India attained independence from the British. In the documentary, you can see how it was such a joyful and exciting day. Indians proudly witnessed the raising of the saffron, white and green Indian national flag and Jawaharial Nehru becoming the first Prime Minister of India. The spirit of India shines with powerful images of grandeur of the people. This is the kind of story that made me want to be a filmmaker.

*Information on Face of India, a documentary on India's National Independence Day. Clement Baptista and Vijay Vijayakar filmed it and I wrote and directed.*

Things in my life seemed to come in waves. As things were easing up with Bill, more good was coming back in terms of my work. As part of this wave, much to my delight and surprise, I received a call from Dr. Welthy Fisher. I had not spoken to her in ten years since spending time in India when she was still building Literacy House.

Early on, Welthy expanded the work outside of India and created World Education with an office on Madison Avenue in New York City. The saying printed on their pamphlets was, "Literacy makes a man aware of his world and gives him the tools to play his part in it."

Since they had an office in New York, Welthy was urging me to be a part of it, "Come and work with me Täo. We need someone like you."

Not seeing how I could do that, I responded while searching my mind for creative ideas to offer, "I don't know enough on literacy to be able to help you. My English is still not good enough. It's all right writing—talking it's not the same."

Then, an idea came to me, "I'll tell you what Welthy, I'll make a film you can use to go out and raise money." She loved it.

She had lived up to what Mahatma Gandhi suggested when she asked him, "What can I do to help when India gets its freedom?"

Gandhi told her, "Go into the villages and teach them to read and write." And Welthy did that. I believed that with a film, people could learn about her work and help to continue it.

Welthy was already 90 and had done so much. One of her mottos was, "It's better to light one candle than to curse the darkness of ignorance," so we called the film, *To Light A Candle*. Surprisingly, Bill let me make the documentary. He said, "This woman is really worthwhile."

So I set out to make the film. I worked with the Consul General of India in New York to obtain permission from the government to shoot the documentary and clear the necessary camera equipment through customs. I decided it was best to shoot the footage and then write the script.

I didn't have enough money to use Americans. One of the people I was working with was coaxed to make another more risqué film with the money. Clement was interested and supplied me with a cameraman.

Vimal Ahuja, an actor and producer who had won the Gandhi Award for the Best Film at the Indian Film Festival for his production *Five After Five*, was going to be the production manager in India.

Again surprising me, Bill said, "We have three thousand dollars in the bank. You need to buy film to take over there and you'll need it for editing and everything. Use it along with the money you have in India. Go and do the documentary with Welthy Fisher."

*With dear friend and esteemed documentary filmmaker Clement Baptista of Hunnars Films.*

I went to India and started to make the film through a joint-production entity called White Tiger Productions.

Literacy House had grown. Welthy had even incorporated family planning into the literacy training with puppet plays such as "Small Family, Happy Family."

The many refugees from Pakistan, Afghanistan and China flocking into India created unchecked population growth making it impossible to build enough schools, train enough teachers, or produce enough textbooks. The programs of Literacy House were needed.

Welthy had attracted international organizations such as CARE and the Ford Foundation. People were coming from all over the world —Afghanistan, the Philippines, Thailand, Turkey, Iran, Tibet—to be trained to teach and write for adult learners. Literacy House was becoming so well regarded that it was invited by the Indian government to conduct orientation training for elected chairmen of the village councils on the new responsibilities of their office. They also had a program offering courses for women to become rural teachers, village workers, midwives or other types of specialties.

I spent about three weeks in India capturing incredible footage and then began to edit the film back in New York. I named Bill as the producer since he put in some of the money. I was honored to be able to showcase all of what Welthy was doing. I knew that if people could see her good work they would want to help support what she had built.

\*\*\*

Almost as soon as I got back from India, I was sitting in the kitchen and suddenly heard "pop, pop, pop, pop." Bill had taken all of my things out of the cupboards and was aging wine in there. He bottled it too fast and it was blowing up in the cupboards, splattering all over the place.

I had chosen our particular house in Hartsdale because it had a big cellar. Bill had about two hundred gallons of wine at one time. He had put five gallon wine barrels all over the place. We even started growing grape vines across the kitchen window and then in the back. Now, he was obviously also using the cupboards.

Before I could react to the wine blowing up all over the cupboards, Bill said with some excitement, "Don't unpack. We're leaving right now. We're going up near Lake Erie. There's going to be a big conference there of people in the wine business."

It was a meeting at a vineyard near Hammondsport in upstate New York. Grape growers and winemakers from various places were coming to discuss the start of the American Wine Society so we went up there and were among the founders.

The American Wine Society came into existence on October 7, 1967 with around 200 grape growers, home winemakers, and wine lovers including Bill and me. Well known viticulturist and winemaker Dr. Konstantin Frank hosted the meeting at his vineyard on Keuka Lake. His wines are even more popular today, particularly the Riesling.

Given my family background and wine connections, they were interested in my opinion. I eventually became the Vice President of the American Wine Society for Southern New York, from Albany down to New York City and Long Island.

So, all of these things were happening. I never seemed to stop moving with the winemaking, the films, and the children.

*Well known viticulturist and winemaker Dr. Konstantin Frank from the Finger Lakes region showing us the Geneva Experimental Station vineyard at Cornell University. The grapes on the bottom left are Pinot Chardonnay being processed at The Findlay Vineyard.*

\*\*\*

It was the evening of April 4, 1968 and I was preparing dinner while listening to music on the radio. Suddenly, there was a broadcast interruption and the words I heard stunned me: "Dr. Martin Luther King, Jr. has been assassinated!"

I sat in disbelief listening to the details that had become available.

I thought, "How can someone so vital to bringing about change be gone?" My mind was racing with all kinds of thoughts. My heart was going out to his wife and small children. I began thinking about how the world needed this great man who believed in the Oneness of all people.

Bill came in and had heard the news. We were both devastated and it all seemed unreal. It was like all of these good men were being killed —Mahatma Gandhi, President Kennedy and now Dr. King.

We felt it was important to go to the funeral. Dr. King had been speaking out for justice for all people, not just Blacks. He was so young and brave. Like Gandhi, he was vital in transforming people's perspectives and bringing about nonviolent change.

We flew to Atlanta, Georgia with the children because we wanted them to understand the significance of this great man. Tracy was around ten and Kevin was twelve. I thought it was good that they were with us, but Kevin was running all over the place and getting into everything. We stayed at a school with so many others who loved Dr. King and felt they had to be there. They put the men in one room and the women in another. Tracy and I were there together, and Kevin went with Bill.

The next morning, April 9, 1968, there was a bus at the school to take people to the funeral. We boarded the bus and waited, but nobody came to drive it, so Bill drove it.

Two funeral services were held on that day, the first was for family, dignitaries, celebrities and close friends at Ebenezer Baptist Church, where Dr. King and his father had both served as senior pastors.

Following the private service, Dr. King's casket was loaded onto a simple wooden farm wagon pulled by two mules to go to the second service. We marched slowly behind Dr. King's casket for the three-mile procession from Ebenezer to Morehouse College where Dr. King had gone to school.

The procession was silent except for the occasional singing of freedom songs that were sung during the marches with Dr. King. At the college, there was a heartfelt public service. Later, I learned that there were about 150,000 people from around the nation and the world who marched in that procession or watched in reverence on the sidelines.

As the ceremony came to a conclusion, the handsome young singer Harry Belafonte urged the crowd to hold hands and we began chanting and singing, "We Shall Overcome," the song of freedom. The action of its meaning seemed to spread across the whole Universe. Even Tracy, as she held hands with a little gentleman, became part of the power that pervaded the whole scene. Thousands of people joined hands and chanted as we walked in the blazing sun.

Then the crowds mingled with famous people, as well as government officials. I noticed that New York City's Mayor John Lindsay and Robert Kennedy mixed with the poorest. They created an intense atmosphere as they solemnly shook hands without any ceremony or trying to stand out as important.

With the heat, many in the crowd drank from the same paper cup that was passed from hand to hand. It was so hot we got sunburned. All of us there together represented the message of freedom and Oneness both Mahatma Gandhi and Dr. Martin Luther King, Jr. stood for. The whole experience was very moving. I will always remember it.

At the end of the march we tried to get a taxi. Incapable of finding any transportation, I saw a lone car surrounded by police and dashed over to try to find out if it was free to take us to the airport. A policeman said that it was for the wife of Senator Eugene McCarthy, who was running for President. Trying to appeal to them I said, "I'm with my husband and two children. Can you help us get to the airport?"

The policeman said, "We don't know whether this important woman will share the car with you."

As we talked near the car, Mrs. Abigail McCarthy heard us and we could almost hear a sigh of relief when she spoke to the policeman and asked, "Will you be escorting me to the airport?"

The police escort was confirmed. Then she said to me, "We can take you and your family. There is enough room to squeeze in."

It seemed like this somber occasion brought people together. The police asked Bill if he would drive the car to the airport to get her out of this place where very large crowds of people were standing everywhere. The policeman added, "We also need someone to take her into the airport."

Bill responded, "I will take her in."

So a calamity was wiped out as he drove Mrs. McCarthy and our family to the airport. Bill escorted her into the airport and made sure she had appropriate security there. He was so tall that he looked like her security guard. The fact that we were escorted to the airport with armed police on motorcycles was thrilling for the children.

When we returned to Hartsdale some people from the Rotary Club said to Bill, "We know where you've been" looking at his sunburn. They knew how deeply he believed in justice. Whatever he stood for, he stood for with a vengeance.

He was so angry at what was going on. He would say, "How do we dare write 'freedom' on the Lincoln Memorial if it's only for a select group of people?"

Bill was a strange and complicated person. He was good at the center of his whole being. I recognized that I wasn't always easy myself. He would say, "You're very difficult because when you don't like something you come straight out and tell everybody."

I would say, "Well, why shouldn't I say what I believe in?"

Then, I would add, "I'm half-Indian, I may not look it but I am."

Thinking about Dr. King's message and fight for civil rights took me back to the discrimination I endured by the Colonial British when I was growing up in India, when people would call me a "half-breed." That put a fire in me. Gandhi also instilled in me an unwavering belief in equality for all. I felt strongly that we all could work to break the boundaries of ignorance.

At the time of Dr. King and all that was going on in the America, if anybody said anything that I felt was wrong I would strike out. I was rather outspoken about issues I believed in but I didn't like strife on personal matters.

I was seeing Bill in a different light. I thought he was beginning to respect my opinion and realized how much we believed in some of the same things. We came together around wine, justice and the environment. We got off to a rocky start but were able to find common ground. There is always something to come together around. If you remain open and actively seek Oneness with another, it will reveal itself.

*There is always something to come together around. If you remain open and actively seek Oneness with another, it will reveal itself.*

*Part Three*

# Living Light & Truth

Yoga is a *darsana*—a mirror to look at ourselves from within. It helps you find that union within yourself no matter what your path. It helps you see the Light and can lead you to Absolute Truth.

CHAPTER 21

# Feed Your Soul

It's interesting how the things you need present themselves to you. If you are aware, then you will recognize them and take action. If you let your spirit lead, you will naturally gravitate to that which feeds you—a deep passion or something that gives you energy and speaks to your soul. At first, it may seem like you're stumbling upon it, and then seemingly all at once clarity comes. This is how yoga became a more conscious path for me. It was there all along but had to be fed.

*If you let your spirit lead, you will naturally gravitate to that which feeds you.*

Tracy was always on some kind of diet or exercise program. I tried to teach her the things I learned from my aunt in India about good manners. I did everything I could to help her build her self-esteem in every way I knew how.

First, she wanted to play tennis. I tried to play with her but when I hit the ball it went in the other direction like when I was playing table tennis with Lord Tennyson's cricket team. I was not very good. So she gave up on me there.

Next Tracy announced, "I want to do yoga."

Delighted, thinking this was something we could finally connect on, I said, "I'll help you. I'll teach you."

Defiantly she responded, "No, no, I want a real teacher!"

Clearly, she didn't want me as a teacher, and so we searched in the Hartsdale area and found a yoga class at the White Plains Public

Library. We went there together and discovered this tiny woman named Cecelia Leiseroff teaching. Everyone called her "Chicky." I decided to take the class with Tracy and afterwards Chicky came to me and said, "I've never seen yoga done like that. You really and truly are wonderful. Would you give a class for us?"

Tracy looked at me making a funny face. She didn't really like that I would be involved in it. She wanted to be as slim as I was but didn't want me to have anything to do with it. I taught a class but Tracy then asked to go someplace else and study gymnastics.

We found a place on Central Avenue. I was surprised to see this unusual glass circular building. It had a big statute of the Greek mythological figure Atlas with his arms upstretched holding a globe. Inside, we found everything—a gym, pool, massage room and even a place to eat. It was very European like a big spa. The building itself is still there but Atlas does not have his globe.

Soon I began taking Tracy there for gymnastics. One day, I walked into a yoga class and saw a girl teaching with a book by her side. Looking down at the book, she was saying, "Well, now you stand on your head."

In disbelief, I immediately reacted, "What do you mean? You can't just tell people to stand on their heads like that. You'll hurt them. Aren't you going to show them how?"

The surprised girl responded, "I'm taking it from the book. Do you mean you know how?"

Realizing that yoga was not well known in many places, I suppose I couldn't blame her for wanting to share the practice. However, what she was doing was dangerous. She needed more hands-on knowledge so I taught the class. She went and told the Director and they asked me to take it over.

We got home and shortly thereafter Bill came to me, "Tracy says you've signed up to give four classes a week there. How much are they paying you?"

Surprised that Tracy even mentioned it, I replied, "You can't take money for yoga."

A bit annoyed, he said, "What do you mean you can't take money for yoga?"

"You're not supposed to get paid for teaching yoga. Yoga is something you give to people. It has to come from you."

Not too keen on me working for free, he replied rather sarcastically,

"Oh, you're not? That's typically you. You're going to take all the week away teaching yoga even on a Saturday when we usually go out."

I responded, "Well, yes."

So I started to teach. I felt myself opening up a little bit like strength was coming back to my spirit.

At this point, fitness was a big thing. Jack LaLanne, whose parents were originally from the southwest of France, was really known with a television show. He had been doing all of these athletic feats like a thousand jumping jacks at one time and swimming while pulling a large boat. It was extraordinary.

He had opened up several fitness clubs throughout America and came to Hartsdale to open one there. One day, he came to the place where I was teaching on Central Avenue. He looked in on my class and was shocked, saying to the manager, "I've never seen so many people doing yoga!"

*Fitness pioneer Jack LaLanne hired me for my first paying yoga teaching job. Right: I'm demonstrating Tree Pose at age 57. I was getting used to being a "real" yoga teacher.*

I had developed a loyal following. One of the girls in the class was even a successful tennis player who had gone all around the world.

Looking to buy the place, Jack LaLanne asked the manager, "How much do you pay her?"

He replied, "Nothing."

I had been teaching there for two years without getting paid. After Jack LaLanne took over the place and transformed it into the European Health Spa, he offered me $15 a week to teach four classes. Though it certainly wasn't a lot, it was my first paying yoga job.

I did it for a little while but got somewhat annoyed when he started telling me that the students had to wear sneakers.

I couldn't believe it and so I told him, "You can't do yoga with sneakers on! That's ridiculous. Besides there is so much dirt on the floor and so much of what we do in yoga is on the floor. You should have some mats."

He insisted, "No, no, when you do anything you must wear sneakers." He apparently knew a lot about fitness, but obviously not as much about yoga at that time.

So I left, moving across the road to a big cellar. He was surprised because most of the people left with me. They wanted to continue my class. That's when I truly started teaching yoga on my own. I was becoming known everywhere. I remembered what dear Mataiji Indra Devi said, "Teach yoga. They need people like you."

I might never have thought myself as a yoga teacher if it hadn't been for her. I didn't think I was good enough. My confidence in teaching was growing.

The image of that girl teaching yoga from a book stuck with me. Even though I had knowledge of yoga from growing up and studying philosophy with Sri Aurobindo in Pondicherry and Swami Prabhavananda in Los Angeles, I wanted to be more perfect in what I did in terms of the physical practice. When Bill would go to a big insurance convention and the children were in summer camp, I would go to India and study with some of the masters of yoga.

My students in New York were quite funny. The first time I left, they made me a big card with a huge plane on it saying, "Direction, New York. Please come back." They wanted to make sure I was coming back to teach my class with them.

I had already been studying with B.K.S. Iyengar for many years.

Still, there was something else I was looking for and I went to ask the advice of the Maharaja of Mysore who was part of the royal family. He sponsored Sri Krishnamacharya who had a yoga school in the palace for many years and spurred so much of the yoga that was happening in Mysore. When I was in Bangalore, I would go down to Mysore and take classes.

Since Mr. Iyengar and K. Pattabhi Jois were primary pupils of Krishnamacharya, the Maharaja in essence had been a sponsor of them as well helping to spread yoga in that area. There was a big yoga group there. It seemed like everybody was in Mysore. The Maharaja was wonderful about helping those who were interested.

So, I went to see him. He was the last actual prince of Mysore before India's independence and then became Governor of Mysore State. He said, "I'm glad you're not sticking only to one path."

He knew Iyengar was great but he thought it was good to be exposed to various teachers. Each guru has a personality and certain things, obvious and subtle, that they impart.

> *Each guru has a personality and certain things, obvious and subtle, that they impart.*

I decided to spend time studying with master teacher K. Pattabhi Jois. I'd go over for a month at a time. He was an extraordinary man, strong and yet so quiet. He didn't seem to give much instruction but you could almost hear the walls breathe. There was so much energy there. I was enthralled with him. I thought his technique was very good, so I kept going back whenever I could.

I was still trying to push forward with my film, *Two Worlds, Two Loves*. It had been a decade since I started working on it. I still believed it was a worthwhile project and had been somewhat secretly putting the pieces together without Bill knowing. I really wanted to make this happen.

I had commitments from two big stars. We secured German actress Elke Sommer who won the Golden Globe Award as Most Promising Newcomer Actress for the movie, *The Prize* with Paul Newman, and we had American actor James MacArthur, who was known internationally for the popular television series *Hawaii Five-O*.

This time in India I was able to work out the details with Hunnar Films and I did a couple of newspaper interviews to drum up interest. Given my Hollywood work and modeling in Europe, I was somewhat of a star when I went to India. I also did some yoga. I kept up with everybody and the teachings. I inquired about my uncle but he was off traveling. We had written each other but I missed seeing him in person.

```
              MEMORANDUM REGARDING CO-PRODUCTION OF FILM
                       TWO WORLDS .... TWO LOVES

To be filmed in Widescreen in Eastman color
Length 100 minutes
Shooting schedule:    4 weeks pre-production, 12 weeks physical production
August 25th, 74       8 weeks Post-production

With the exception of 2 scenes, the entire film will be produced entirely
in India.

The script has passed the Indian Film Censor Board.

A certain amount of pre-production work has already been accomplished
saving a great deal of time and money.

STARS: Elke Somers & James MacArthur, the latter star of the Internationally
           reknowned Television Series Hawaii 5.

BUDGET
The Budget has been slightly raised due to the higher costs of production
in the past 6 months.
Total Budget                      55 lakhs.
American Participation            37 Lakhs
Indian Participation              18 Lakhs

AMERICAN PARTICIPATION
Will include the following: STARS, PRODUCER, EDITOR, SCREEN RIGHTS,
COLOR RAWSTOCK AND US LAB COSTS. LOCATION SHOOTING OF TWO SCENES
WITHIN THE USA. CAMERA CREW AND STUDIO WITHIN THE U.S.A.: THEME SONG
& ITS COMPOSER, ORCHESTRA, RECORDING OF SAME WITH WELLKNOWN ARTIST,
U.S. P.R. WORK TO PUBLICISE FILM, INTERNATIONAL SOUND TRACK FOR FOREIGN
DISTRIBUTION, AIR FARES FROM N.Y.-BOMBAY & RETURN. SPECIAL EQUIPMENT
NOT AVAILABLE IN INDIA
INDIAN PARTICIPATION
Will include: INDIAN TECHNICIANS, STUDIO COSTS, EQUIPMENT, TRAVEL WITHIN
INDIA. INDIAN STARS, ANIMALS AND TRAINERS, MOBILE UNITS, STAFF, HOTEL
FOR STARS AND INDIAN STARS WHEN ON LOCATION, MISCELLANEOUS GOVERNMENT
CLEARANCES AND STAFF.
```

*Memorandum Regarding Co-Production of my film, Two Worlds, Two Loves*

My marriage seemed to find its own rhythm. Bill was always finding something to protest or a march to go on. That's when we really connected. He was on a rampage about people in the government spending huge sums of money. He got so mad saying, "They're together at restaurants spending all this money on food when really and truly there are so many people starving." We even marched against Vice President Spiro Agnew because Bill was against so much of what he was doing.

The kids at this point were teenagers. We were still living in our house in Hartsdale and they were running the place. People say the teenage years are rebellious and this was certainly the case in our family.

One year around Christmas time, Tracy was working in a pet store. She must have been around sixteen years old and came home exclaiming about a little dog that was just right for me. I thought it was a nice gesture but we already had our two dogs, Pep and Penny. She begged us anyway to go down to the store to see it.

The store had brought in two little Shih Tzu puppies. One was found a home and the other one, because it had one tooth missing, was left behind. Tracy was upset because she thought the dog was lonely without its sister, which I thought was very compassionate.

We went down to the store and Bill picked this little dog up to look at it. It immediately scrambled to get inside his jacket and went to sleep like it was saying, "I'm home."

We resolved, "Well, that's done. We've got to take it with us."

We called her "Maharani," which is a title used for the wife of the Maharaja. Her full name was "Maharani Roodle Doodle Love Bug Lynch." If I said just Maharani she knew she was in trouble.

She was so cute. She would come by my bed, even when she was tiny, and try to climb up the steps. Every morning, I'd wake up and she would come and grab my sheet and pull it. She wanted to do yoga with me. She would go and do Downward Dog pose looking at me, getting into the most perfect posture.

If I didn't get out of bed she would growl at me. Then, she would come back really annoyed and pull the sheet more. Finally, I would get up and both of us would do yoga together. This was our ritual. She also loved to go back in the yard and just run.

*Just picked Bill's tomatoes with the help of Maharani Roodle Doodle Love Bug Lynch.*

Since the kids were a little older, I had been trying to convince Bill to come to India. I had been talking about it for years. Unless it had to do with the Rotary Club or insurance, he had a way of putting things off. It was the opposite of the way I thought about things. There was so much in life to see and do. Just as I was as a child, I didn't want to miss a moment.

Finally, Bill came with me to India and we stayed with my friend, Clement. Bill really enjoyed it. Perhaps it helped him to better understand me as well because his spirit seemed to be getting lighter. He wasn't so rigid and controlling. Clement came and stayed with us in New York several times.

When Tracy was having a really hard time in school and everything, she went to India for six months and stayed with my friends. They treated her like a princess. She enjoyed it so much that she didn't want to come back home.

One day my students said, "Can we go with you somewhere?" So, I took twenty-four students to Bali. We had a good time. They gave us a big welcome at the hotel with a sign, "Welcome to Täo's group." It was sweet.

Bali is a place like India that gives you a direct connection to nature and Oneness. There are these incredible mountain peaks, so many species of birds and of course the aqua water and coral all around. Bali in those days was quite fabulous. There was an ashram run by a woman. She kept talking about this incredible courageous American woman who had visited. She said it was Hillary Clinton.

I went to India and had twenty-four people join me. Some of them were really serious about yoga, not just doing the physical practice but getting more into the spiritual side as well. I took them to meet K. Pattabhi Jois and we sat on a big windowsill because the room was packed.

He wasn't giving an asana class. That time, he was giving a class on breathing. You could almost hear vibrations of the walls from the breath. He was teaching different techniques. It was very interesting.

When in India, I once again inquired about my uncle. I missed seeing him the last couple of times I came through. He was always off traveling. My aunt had died and I wanted to see him. All I could think about was that I just had to reach him. I had missed him so much.

A friend tried to explain why my uncle wasn't there, saying, "He left at 82 years old and said it was time for him to go up in the Himalayans to be in touch with nature and pureness."

My uncle was renouncing the world to live a more spiritual life and to put into reality the

*Everybody has his or her own path. What's important is that you live in Truth. Ultimately, we are all a part of the Great Oneness.*

Truth he had always lived and believed in that "Truth is One; sages call it by many names." Everybody has his or her own path. What's important is that you live in Truth. Ultimately, we are all a part of the Great Oneness.

My uncle had lived his role on earth and now he had to finish it. He didn't want me to try to look after him. Since my aunt was no longer living, I guess he felt that it was time for him to be alone. When a spiritual person decides to do that, you're not supposed to try to connect with them.

Everything in my life seemed to be changing. I learned from my uncle though, instead of being good or bad "some things just are." If you believe that everything is energy, then my uncle's energy was still there simply in another form.

He was as spiritual as any Swami. He just lived it. He didn't just talk about it. He was the epitome of the philosophy "Truth is One" in everything. It didn't matter if the person was the most important on earth or the little boy running on the street, he treated them with the same respect. He was always helping somebody. I think that is why Gandhi liked him. He didn't make a big fuss. My uncle just gave him a chair. If you open up to help people, don't do it for the glory. Do it from your heart. In yoga philosophy, it is the principle of *seva*, or selfless service.

> *If you open up to help people, don't do it for the glory. Do it from the heart. In yoga philosophy, it is the principle of seva, or selfless service.*

Instead of feeling sad, I felt grateful that I had such a loving person in my life. His studies of Swami Vivekananda influenced me deeply and he introduced me to the great soul Mohandas Gandhi. My uncle laid the foundation for my spiritual journey by planting the seeds of Vedanta in me and nurturing my innate curiosity. On the railroads and in everyday life, he gave me experiences that helped me see and feel the Oneness in everything. Over the years, I had studied with so many great masters but my uncle was my first guru.

I smiled at all of our great memories and my wonderful childhood filled with love and adventure. It would have been nice to see his face again but I knew his spirit would always be with me. Since Bill liked my Indian friends, he would have certainly loved my uncle. They would have come together on their shared sense of justice and love of nature.

Bill and I were traveling more together since the children were older and Kevin had gone into the Marines. At one point, we took a trip out to California to a wine convention and to visit some friends in the San Fernando Valley. We went to a party at the house of my longtime friend Ginny Berndt. It was such a delight to see her.

*On our roadtrip to California and then at Ginny Berndt's house with Bill.*

Even though Bill was sort of an agnostic, he drove me out to the 4th of July party given by the Vedanta Society. It was so nice to be there with everybody. I had studied with Swamiji for a long time. I belonged to the Society since 1950 so I had come to know a lot of people who came through.

Since it is a temple, people often offer donations. When you put money in the till you have to put it in an envelope. Swami Prabhavananda never allowed anyone to put money in front of people just in case they didn't have any money to offer. He didn't want anyone feeling badly. He would say, "If you don't have money, put your love in it." He was so extraordinary.

I still have some of the letters Swamiji wrote to Christopher Isherwood before he died. Christopher went back to England and Swamiji would write to him. Things like:

"One day you will look at someone and suddenly you'll think: There is a presence of God! One can do this when one begins to fall in love with God. Mere human love wears out, but love of God grows. You do not get tired of it. It gains in intensity."

It was quite beautiful. I still buy books and things from the Vedanta Society for inspiration.

A few years later, we went to Bermuda with the Rotary Club, which was really nice. Bill and I were enjoying our time together.

*Bill and I at the Bermuda Conference for the Rotary Club in 1979.*

All this time, I was still working on the documentary, *To Light A Candle,* on Dr. Welthy Fisher. We were almost through with the editing and found out that Welthy was going to receive a Humanitarian Award, which was to be presented at Caesar's Palace in Las Vegas. I didn't have much money left but I got a cameraman from Hollywood and went there. Adding that footage, I finished off the project.

Welthy continued to amaze me. If she wanted to do something, she went ahead and did it. When she received the Literacy Award from the President of India she said: "In the autumn of your life you are still announcing the dawn." I was fortunate to have come in contact with strong women like her and Indra Devi.

At 99 years old, with a broken knee and subzero temperatures, Welthy went to China to visit old friends who shared her interest in education of women. She said, "I could never manage to feel as I was supposed to about my chronological age. Maybe I was too busy. The future always seemed limitless and I have never stopped expecting something to happen, some invitation for another adventure."

On Welthy's 100th birthday, they had a party at the United Nations. I let the organizers use the film, though they edited it significantly. I told them, "I made it for Welthy to be able to make some money from it."

*Letter from Admiral Leroy Vernon Honsinger, Trustee and Vice Chairman of World Education and Welthy's nephew. I received it a few years earlier in 1973 praising the documentary I produced and directed, To Light A Candle.*

Bill and I went to the event and we were delighted as we stayed in the background and watched as so many people surrounded her. She died the next year at 101. I was thankful to have known her and for having Bill's support in my making the film.

*Dr. Welthy Fisher, at 90 years old, receiving the Nehru Literacy Award from the President of India.*

*Welthy with Mrs. Indira Gandhi, Prime Minister of India.*

*Welthy is greeting me at the United Nations during her 100th birthday celebration on September 18, 1979.*

Around this time we also had a party at our house for Ben Lucien Burman. I tried as much as I could to stay in touch with friends over the years. Mary Ellen wrote updating me on her life. At one point, she included pictures with her beautiful daughter Molly.

*With Ben Lucien Burman.*

*Mary Ellen Kay with her daughter Molly.*

Yoga was becoming popular in the United States. All of the known masters, such as Swami Satchidananda, B.K.S. Iyengar, and K. Pattabhi Jois had visited America and created a presence. Television shows like Lilias Folan's series on PBS and magazines such as *Yoga Journal* were popping up.

I was beginning to see more of a need for better trained teachers in my area so I got together with Barbara Kestenbaum, Mary Karis and a couple of other people, somebody from South Africa and another person who danced. At that time, we called ourselves the Yoga Teacher's Alliance and started offering teacher trainings. Mary was a very sweet Greek woman who was big into Kundalini Yoga. All of them have since died except Barbara who was in Florida the last time I spoke with her.

I knew a lot of people so we brought in guests to do workshops even though it cost a good deal of money. We decided we would only have outstanding teachers who had real training and experience such as Rodney Yee, David Swenson and Beryl Bender Birch all of whom are still very popular now. Beryl is an extraordinarily good teacher, particularly in training other teachers.

I believe Rodney Yee and David Swenson are two of the most outstanding yoga teachers in the whole world today. David belongs to the very essence of life like a true angel. He is so humble and when he does yoga he seems to cross the earth without even touching the ground. Douglas Swenson is also fabulous as a person and teacher. Both David and Doug have been dear friends for years.

Rodney really stands out in the energy he gives and the ability to make students feel that there is nothing they can't do. Now, Rodney and Colleen Saidman Yee both bring such skill and joy to their joint offerings. Colleen is a sweet person and wonderful teacher.

All of these incredible teachers seem to open the door to show students the way and that was the intention with our YTA programs. I was president of the Alliance for many years. A girl in Nyack took over from me as president. She didn't manage the books well even though it was getting packed and the training had become popular. I decided that I better take it over from her again but didn't know what to do.

One of my students, Cyndi Warbi, was married to a successful lawyer. He suggested that we change the name and start fresh. That's when we changed it to Yoga Teacher's Association to keep the YTA initials. At this point, it was around 1979.

We wanted to create a community of people interested in yoga and offer ongoing affordable learning opportunities. Part of the goal was to improve the quality of Hatha Yoga teaching in accordance with the high standards laid out in the classic *Hatha Yoga Pradipika* and as developed by great yoga masters.

This was about twenty years before Yoga Alliance came into existence. They now set the standards for yoga teaching in America. Ironically, when I went to register my training program, the first thing they did was ask, "Who did you train under? How many teaching hours do you have?"

I said, "I've got so many hours, about 35,000 I think!"

The registry agent said, "Oh, but you only have to have 200 or 500 hours of training to be a Registered Yoga Teacher."

They were not going to approve me to train other teachers because I didn't go through one of their registered schools. It was really strange. Years later, I received an honor from Yoga Alliance through my dear student, Terri Kennedy who was Chairwoman of their Board at that time and knew my teachings. She recognized that I had been trained by true masters and was teaching long before their organization was even in existence.

In addition to having the YTA community, I felt strongly that a more formal training program for teachers was necessary so I founded the first Yoga Teacher Training Program in Nyack in 1980. One of my students, who had become a very good teacher and even trained with K. Pattabhi Jois in India, was with me when I started it. Somebody had to show people that yoga does not involve jumping around to make you perspire and choke because you're not breathing correctly. That's what was going on in so many of the yoga classes.

Yoga had always been a part of my life. The seeds had been planted long ago on the beaches of Pondicherry. Little did I know that game that fascinated me when I was eight years old would be the center of my life decades later. I learned how to "live" yoga from my uncle. It was more than what I could have received from a book. Then, my many great teachers added subtleties of understanding. Look deeply for the seeds that have been planted in you. Nurture them so they can fully take root. The thing that will feed your soul is right inside of you.

> *Look deeply for the seeds that have been planted in you. Nurture them so they can fully take root. The thing that will feed your soul is right inside.*

*With Doug Swenson over the years.*

CHAPTER 22

Do It Today

If you want something to happen, see that it happens. You have the ability to achieve what you believe if you don't procrastinate. As my uncle taught me, "If you believe in something, do it if it's good." If it has caught fire in your mind and feeds your spirit, then take action. "Tomorrow" never comes. One minute after midnight is already today.

> *"Tomorrow" never comes. One minute after midnight is already today.*

With all of my new activity with yoga and more travels to India, Bill may have sensed that he was losing me. One day he announced with unusual enthusiasm, "I'm going to take you to Paris!"

I was so stunned that I just stared at him for a moment. Then, I realized he was serious and answered, "I'll start packing." For so long we had been talking about going to France together. I was delighted even though it was just for an extended weekend.

Bill had been working really hard and was very tired. Our flight was leaving New York Wednesday night and arriving in Paris Thursday morning. By the time we got there he was sick. He had been a paratrooper during the war and his feet had been frozen when he was dropped over in France. This experience continued to affect him. He got sick very quickly. We finally made it to Paris but he wasn't in the best of spirits.

At that time, they used to have something called a teleprinter. It was a bit like email today. It was a phone link of sorts, a way to send and receive typed messages. You could put a message on the phone and it linked up anywhere to get hold of people. Then, they could phone you back.

As soon as we got to the hotel, I left a message for my dear friend Louis letting him know we were in France and where we were staying. Almost immediately, the phone rang and it was Louis, "Täo, cherie. You're finally back in Paris. I want you and your husband to come to dinner tonight at a very special place."

Special indeed! It was a famous private club that was only for royalty and heads of government. It was so exclusive someone had to die before another person could become a member.

I was excited to get dressed for dinner. It reminded me of my former, more glamorous, lifestyle. Paris had been my home and in many ways my heart.

Knowing how elegant and well dressed everyone would be at the club, I became nervous when I realized that Bill didn't even bring a tie. He didn't really care so much about what he wore.

Very calmly I said, "Why don't you get in the bed? You'll feel better later."

I was sending him good energy to make sure he would be up for our evening. Then, I immediately dashed out searching for something decent for him to wear. It was late in the afternoon and just about every place was closed. Finally, I got him sort of a scarf tie, a cravat, and rushed back to the hotel.

Even though he was sick and tired when I left, I found him invigorated when I returned. Once we were dressed, I looked at Bill and was very pleased. It's amazing what a touch of elegance can do.

We arrived at the club, and had to press a bell. A man appeared at the door and took our names looking us over carefully. Then, after seeing we checked out, he permitted us in making a sign indicating we could enter. It was all very ritzy.

I had talked to Bill about eating these huge mushrooms in France and he always wanted to taste them. So, that was one of the things he asked to eat. It was a treat—really all so wonderful.

Louis was going off to Austria and said, "You know Täo I've made arrangements for you and your husband to have dinner at Maxim's. It's all paid for. I want you to enjoy your time at home."

That was sweet. That's how he was, always a good friend. Friendship is a jewel, something to treasure and hold dear.

The following day was simply divine. I had fun showing Bill some of Paris and just relaxing at an outdoor café with a nice glass of wine. I could see that he was beginning to unwind. We topped off our trip with a beautiful dinner at Maxim's, which was still the most famous restaurant in the world. Our short holiday was eventful and exciting. It was good for both of us. Getting away from your everyday circumstances can refresh your mind and spirit. For me, it was a homecoming.

*Friendship is a jewel, something to treasure and hold dear.*

I think the Paris trip helped Bill to see new possibilities. He started looking to sell his insurance office and do more international things. I was elated.

My friend Lance Middleton from John Bull helped me greatly. In 1982, we set up a big Wine & Beer Conference at the prestigious Cambridge University in England. It was successful and brought people from around the world. Wine and beer conferences had started to become popular.

*Above: Wine & Beer Conference held at Cambridge University in Great Britain in 1982. I'm with the owner of Britain's main wine and beer magazine. Left: I received The 1981 Instone Trophy from the Home Wine & Beer Trade Association in April 1982 for outstanding service to the industry.*

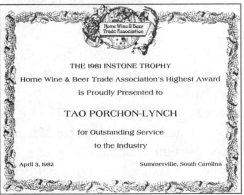

*My dear friends in India, Kumkum and Susheel Somani. On the right is Kumkum's brother, Rahul Sood. He stayed with us when he was studying in New York.*

My dear friend, Susheel Somani, offered to work with Bill in India to introduce him to the right people and to help with whatever he wanted to do such as start a vineyard. The family was very well off. One of their brothers was Mayor of Bombay and the other had been the Governor of the state of the Maharaja. Kumkum, Susheel's wife, is so creative. She writes children's books based on the ideals of Gandhi. Her mother, Kamini Kaushal, is an acclaimed Indian actress. She used to pick up girls on the streets, give them showers and show them how to make puppets to earn money.

*Acclaimed actress Kamini Kaushal making puppets.*

Until Bill met my Indian friends, getting out of the insurance business was not something he had considered since it had been his whole life. But he fell in love with India. I never saw him having so much fun as when we were there. We even started considering living part-time in India, perhaps even retiring there. Tracy and Kevin were in their mid-twenties and both out of the house.

We were going to accept the invitation of my friends to go there for a month. The beauty of friendship swelled in my heart. I couldn't believe how happy and excited I was.

Bill made the decision to definitely sell his insurance business and even had someone ready to buy it. He was making a few arrangements so that the sale of his business would be smooth when we returned.

I was ecstatic as I thought, "I'll be able to go and study with Mr. Iyengar. Bill can stay with Sushell and perhaps figure out his new business. How wonderful it will be to spend Christmas with my friends and start living anew!"

Bill made a very strange remark that took me by surprise, "Do you realize we never had a honeymoon? We are going to have one now."

India was like the promise of a new life surrounded by people who adored us. He would have fun doing something he loved and I would continue teaching yoga and deepening my studies with Iyengar.

We started preparing for the trip. Bill had to renew his passport and get his visa. One week before we were supposed to leave, he left early in the morning to pick up his passport in Manhattan. I was busy running around and getting things together for our trip. I came home from teaching yoga and was surprised he wasn't there.

Hours went by and I was very concerned. The phone rang and I rushed to get the call thinking it had to be Bill. Instead, it was the hospital. The voice on the phone said, "Your husband has had an accident and is in the hospital."

Stunned, I found out where he was and rushed to him. It seems he was coming back from the passport office and he passed out which caused the accident. They rushed him to the hospital but there were only cards and his passport on him. They did not initially know how to contact me.

The doctors informed me that he had a stroke. They had been trying to bring him out of it, but he had not yet come through. He was in a coma.

Seeing him there all stretched out I tried taking his hand and imparting a little of my own energy into his body, but he didn't stir. Desperately wanting his eyes to open, I clasped his feet and tried to use some massage and yogic energy. Nothing worked. Seven days later Bill died. I was in a state of shock and disbelief. How could this happen to us? Our life together was finally opening up.

With all of my experiences, I was unprepared for this one. Things happened so quickly. We were looking forward to a new phase in our lives together. We had been talking about this for a long time and Bill kept putting it off. He was always putting things off. My Indian friends had been coming to our house for years and he liked them. He kept saying, "Maybe next year... maybe next year we'll go to India."

That is another reason why I say don't procrastinate. If you procrastinate, something can go wrong.

Bill wanted to be cremated. Even though I felt numb from the shock, I put my mind to preparing a small goodbye ceremony. It was comforting to hear from so many people Bill had touched. His friends from the Rotary Club, such as Ron Tvert, were especially helpful.

We had been married almost twenty years. Although it had its rocky times, Bill and I had found a deeper Oneness. There were funny times, such as the winemaking in the cupboard and I appreciated his strong sense of justice. It wasn't perfect, but he was really a good person.

My friends in India didn't want me to be alone so they encouraged me to come anyway. They lived in Mumbai, so I spent some time there. Then they decided that we should go to Goa for Christmas. They thought that environment would breathe life into me. It was about an hour south on the west side of India, known for its white sandy beaches and gloriously blue waters.

At dawn on the first morning, I decided to go along the beach. I walked and walked about five miles in sort of a daze. I knew I must be careful because I heard barking. I thought it was dogs from the villages I was passing. Suddenly, I realized it was not coming from the earth. As I turned, I saw that it was coming from the ocean. It was incredible! Traveling side by side with me were two dolphins, and then they leaped happily high up in the air and swam away. I believe they almost sensed my sadness and had followed me like they were protecting me.

Every morning I would walk on the beach. It was nice to feel the sand between my toes. That brought me back to my youth on the

Pondicherry. It helped me think. I knew I must figure out my life. What am I going to do next? I spent three weeks reflecting. In a more relaxed state, I began to consider what I should do to move forward.

Should I just shake off the past? A sudden wave was gathering force, clearing my mind of those ideas that had been restricting my life. Like Marlene had advised years ago, something was telling me it was time to start anew. The passing of Bill brought to the forefront again my continuous search for Truth.

Each day seemed a renewal of my quest since childhood to find that hidden knowledge. I needed confirmation that what I believed in could be accomplished. I didn't want to sit around reading what others deemed the Truth. I wanted to put my own beliefs into practice.

I was searching for that road to the true destiny of life. In the beauty of nature is where I had always discovered the answers. As I thought about letting go of the past, I decided to sell my house, gather a few souvenirs, take Maharani, shake off the dust and face the world.

\*\*\*

When I returned to New York, there was still so much to take care of. Bill left pretty much everything to the children. When he had the problem with that big insurance company he had canceled our policies but not the children's. Ironically, I didn't even have insurance money. I had to determine what to do with his business. I decided to close it.

I was alone again with not much money. I had been in this situation before. Now, at 64 years old, I knew that I had to reorganize my life and once again reclaim myself. I realized that, in all the years that I was married to Bill, I spent maybe ten days in France. I could hardly speak French anymore. My Hindi was a little better. So much of who I was had slipped away.

I felt that delving deeper into yoga was the path I wanted to take. I was Program Director and President Emeritus of the Yoga Teacher's Association. I was in charge of putting together and organizing a variety of workshops for teachers and students of yoga. They were well attended but I still thought there was a need for high quality Teacher Training in the area.

The program I did in Nyack was good, but I decided to create something a little closer to home so I started the Westchester Institute of Yoga.

By this point, it was the spring of 1983 and yoga was becoming even more popular. Teaching yoga was the answer for me and I was asked to hold additional classes. Students were coming to learn about the practice and be trained as teachers.

I was beginning to realize that the foundation of my own yoga philosophy went back to the Oneness I learned from nature as a child and my early insights on Vedanta from the teachings of Swami Vivekananda.

I loved the poetic voice of Sri Aurobindo and his perspective on Integral Yoga. He expressed things in such a beautiful way such as, "Inspiration is a slender river of brightness leaping from a vast and eternal knowledge, it exceeds reason more perfectly than reason exceeds the knowledge of the senses." That was one of the many aphorisms, or statements, he wrote that influenced so many.

Then, there was Mahatma Gandhi. He had been a constant voice in my head and my heart—my "Inner Diary." He was my compass guiding me to always stand up for equality and justice. He inspired me to take action and do my own "experiments with Truth" as he called it.

I had a strong foundation in meditation and spiritual study from Swami Prabhavananda and the Maharishi. Dr. Roman Ostoja opened my eyes to the world of metaphysics and had talked a lot about yoga and healing.

Although I had studied with many teachers in India over the years, I wanted to adopt a more in-depth spiritual understanding rather than just the physical. Still, I wondered how I was going to find my own style and if I would ever be able to do really good yoga. I had studied asana with B.K.S. Iyengar and K. Pattabhi Jois, and wanted to initiate a deeper practice.

We graduated our first class of new yoga teachers from the Westchester Institute of Yoga and I decided to go back to India to study with Mr. Iyengar. I also wanted to explore yoga from all regions of India and see how the value of the different styles of yoga came together.

From my first paying yoga-teaching job for Jack LaLanne to now training teachers, I had come a long way but I was just finding the time to delve into my own being and develop my own consistent asana practice.

\*\*\*

Iyengar's Institute in Pune had become popular. It was dedicated to his late wife, Ramamani, and his son and daughter were teaching with him. It was much more established than the little school in Mumbai where we attended classes sixteen or seventeen years earlier.

While studying with Iyengar, I met a very tall charming German girl who was also his student. She had been to India many times to study yet had never been outside the hotel or the studio to do anything. She had never really seen India at all.

"Please come to Germany. I'd like to work with you. Come over and see me because I have more fun with you than anybody," she would say.

I made her laugh. She was very particular and everything had to be so perfect. She used to arrive with her silk sheets and drive me completely crazy. Can you imagine going to India not knowing where you're going to be staying and taking your own silk sheets with you?

One day, she came up with a flash of inspiration, "I want to go to Pondicherry."

I thought, "This is strange. I have been thinking about Pondicherry." I smiled and was curious about her request, "What do you want to do in Pondicherry?"

With an air of excited anticipation, she said, "Well, there's an Indian man there who came from Africa. He predicted the death of Holy Mother. He's very famous. I want him to talk about me and my boyfriend."

She told me that he was a Vedic astrologer named Indu Patel, Founder and Director of the Planet Center in Pondicherry.

Not being very much into astrology, I shook my head with some doubt in my mind as I inquired, "You don't believe in all of that, do you?"

She responded, still filled with excitement, "Yes, but in any case, I want to go."

Without further hesitation, I agreed, "Well, I'll take you then."

With a childlike joy, she said, "Would you? I don't want to go with a travel agent."

In the midst of my own thoughts, I blurted out, "I haven't been back to Pondicherry since I left."

Astonished, she said, "You haven't? How long ago has it been?"

A bit surprised by my own calculation, I said, "A long time, over forty years. I'll take you there."

The reality of what I had just agreed to do gripped me for a moment because although I'd come back to India many times, I had not been back to Pondicherry. Most of my trips in the past, for films and such, were to the big cities like Delhi, the capital in North India, or Mumbai on the west coast.

By train, Pondicherry is as least a full day, if not two days, of travel from these cities and there wasn't a way to take a flight there. The closest big city is Chennai, which is about four hours away.

Before my uncle went up in the Himalayas, I would always inquire with him about the best travel route home. However, in the midst of everything that was going on in my life, it was a challenge to get there easily and see things for myself. This is why I probably said yes so quickly. I had someone with whom to take the journey.

So, I made us an impromptu plan, "We'll meet in Delhi and take the train down and then the bus."

Delighted she said, "Oh, that's wonderful Täo, you'll love this man."

With that, we were off.

I brought two shawls, a turquoise one and then added a purple one. I was glad because the train ride was cold. I wanted my new friend to understand upfront how I felt and so I said, "I'm not too big on someone telling fortunes. I'm not going to say anything so he doesn't hear my accent."

She hadn't told him about me and I didn't want him to put things together. I wanted to see if he was real. She agreed but still thought it would be interesting, "He's bound to say something about you anyway."

I hadn't been on a long train ride like this for a while. It took me back to when I would ride the rails with my uncle. The trains in India give you a glimpse of everyday life. We were passing through so many cities and little villages. This was India. As Gandhi said to Dr. Welthy Fisher, "Go to the villages. If you do not help the villages, you do not help India because India is the village."

After the train, we took a bus into what used to be French India. I was getting excited about seeing Pondicherry and curious to see how it had changed. There had been a few big storms that probably took away some of the beach. I was looking forward to walking on the coast as I did when I was a child, pressing my feet into the sand. My childhood there was so incredibly special.

Between chats with my friend, I found myself lost in these memories. My whole being felt renewed, alive and connected to the Oneness of all things as we came closer.

Stepping foot in Pondicherry was incredible. The spirit of this place and what my uncle taught me sustained me in the worst of times. This was home. My family had lived in the French quarter with its beautiful gardens, French windows, and European-style buildings with tall pillars. It was like a little slice of France, a town by the sea that made you feel like you were in the Mediterranean glamorized with a touch of the local Tamil culture.

After our long journey we got to the hotel and almost right away Mr. Patel came to meet us. He'd never seen me before, or the shawls that I had brought. I smiled but didn't say anything. The first thing he said to me was, "Your favorite colors are purple and blue. It shines out of you."

Curious, I remained silent. A few moments later, without speaking a word, I left the room so he could talk with my friend privately.

I wanted to go and visit the Sri Aurobindo Ashram. I had grown up with the philosophy and teachings of Sri Aurobindo and was interested in this astrologer's association with The Mother. She had been leading the ashram since Sri Aurobindo went into seclusion in the late 1920s. She was beloved and had many disciples, and had run the ashram until her own death in 1973.

***

After my friend's astrology reading, we decided to go to the ashram. As we are leaving, Mr. Patel gave me a folder saying, "I thought you might like to have this. I know you don't believe me."

It was my astrological reading. My friend had given him my birth date so he had created my chart. I took a quick look at it. It had some typed pages. He wrote about the placement of the Moon and something called a Jupiter-Pluto conjunction. I didn't really understand it all but it was interesting:

### TAO LYNCH

This is a **very powerful horoscope** from many respects. There is a **great potentiality** in the individual for

1) Spiritual development,
2) Material balance & Popularity & opportunities in life,
3) Achievement in Arts & Literature & drama.

One of the most important & close aspect of the horoscope is the trine of Moon with the Jupiter-Pluto conjunction. Mars is in conjunction with Moon and the trine with pluto-Jupiter conjunction. This gives great drive specially in striving for highest spiritual knowledge and understanding of esoteric knowledge and the occult forces working around. The awarness will come by itself. She will meet right persons in material life as well as spiritual life and progress. This is the bases of a successfull life specially in worldly career.

Moon in square with Neptune gives great sensitivene A sense in Art, poetry, litterature; drama, show, show business; popularity, travels. It is probable that Neptune is in conjunction with part of fortunue and that makes her very lucky and unexpected opportunities will come up in career.

The <u>Venus</u> square <u>Mars</u> and quincux <u>Uranus</u> and the interplenatary aspects of these three planets indicate the study of various systems of yoga, also the Technical insight in the methods of show and the drama presentati Also these aspects combine with Moon's various aspects indicate the founding and running of spiritual institut as well as institutions connected with drama.

*Vedic horoscope from Indu Patel.*

There were many typed pages of comments. At the very end he handwrote a few things:

> The colours liked, which would also be lucky colours are Mauve, Turquoise, Pale shades every pale Orange and white.
> The last dates of July and August beginning would be the lucky dates. Oct end/Nov. beginning, are another set of lucky days.

*Handwritten astrology comments from Indu Patel.*

That was a bit funny highlighting mauve and turquoise since he didn't see my shawls. In any case, I didn't pay too much attention to the reading at that time. It was a fun experience but we wanted to get going. There was a bad storm coming to Pondicherry.

We went to the Sri Aurobindo Ashram. It had been so long and I had learned so much there. But it was not the same as I remembered. It was nice to visit but our thoughts of staying there were quickly erased. The bed was too hard for my German friend and she had a fit trying to get her silk sheets on it!

Seeing how flustered she was, I offered, "Don't worry. It will be all right. Let's go back to the hotel."

We got there just in time. She was feeling sick and the storm had started. It lasted three days. It was huge with high winds. The seawater came up past the third floor where we were staying and was splashing into our bedroom. My friend didn't want to go out, so I wandered off around the beaches where I played as a child. I wasn't afraid. Storms are just nature showing her power.

*Storms are just nature showing her power.*

I went out to where the fishermen gathered so I could find a lobster. I thought that some food would do her good. Just as when I was little, the fishermen looked like they were walking on water with these large baskets to catch fish. After all of that work, there was just one lobster in there. I took it back to the restaurant and asked them to cook it for her. She was grateful and it seemed to give her more energy.

After Pondicherry, we went back to see Mr. Iyengar. My friend was a little scared of traveling alone so I took the train with her despite the long ride.

Iyengar was very funny. He had his own way of doing things. Since my friend had a heart problem he had her hanging from ropes. I don't even know how good she was at asana because I never really saw her do any yoga on the mat at all. He had her in her own little studio.

At the time, I couldn't figure out what he was doing. I understood later that Iyengar was using props and tools to get better alignment. Given my friend's ailments and needs, Iyengar devised a special program for her. He was a master at that kind of modification. That is the beauty of yoga—it really is for everybody regardless of ability.

People are getting hurt nowadays because they are treating yoga like gymnastics and are losing the foundation of breath. Americans, in particular, like to do everything fast. They come out of fitness classes out of breath, "Oh, what a class! What a workout!"

I'm not against the idea of exercise but I do think people can benefit from a greater understanding of breath. You don't have to be panting or nearly passed out to feel you've had a good yoga class.

The *Hatha Yoga Pradipika* states, "An undisturbed breath leads to an undisturbed mind." That's really the essence of the practice. Yoga is an exact science and the goal is the union of the individual soul, the *Jivatma*, with the Universal Soul. Breath is a gateway to this union.

I was so happy to have yoga more present in my life. It was my anchor in a sea of changes and helped me get through the loss of Bill. Studying with B.K.S. Iyengar again fortified me and going back to Pondicherry after so many years filled my spirit. It was the place of my beginnings in yoga and spiritual seeking. I was grateful for my uncle's teachings and knew it was time to do those things I really wanted to do. As the astrologer wrote, "unexpected opportunities will come up" and I was ready to experience them!

> *Yoga can be an anchor in a sea of changes.*

CHAPTER 23

# Let Your Spirit Soar

I love watching birds soar across the sky. They can go where they want, when they want, solo or in unison. It's their choice. I had always been an independent spirit. Now, I felt a wonderful sense of freedom I hadn't felt for a very long time. Freedom is the ability to do what's in your heart.

*Freedom is the ability to do what's in your heart.*

When I got back to New York, I tucked the folder from Mr. Patel away in a drawer and didn't really think about it. I was thrown back into all of the things I needed to do. I was alone again and on my own to make decisions about my path. I was clear to go in any direction and I naturally went to where my spirit could connect with the Oneness in all. I was happy to get back into teaching yoga and offering retreats for my students.

Soon I began to laugh to myself when I would think back to when Tracy scowled at me, saying she wanted "a real yoga teacher." This memory would bring a smile to my face and a twinkle in my eyes because finally I was beginning to feel like a real teacher.

In 1983, I took a group to Morocco, and did more trips to Bali and India in the following years. My dear friends Johnnie and Dick were once again so sweet to me. We went on a couple of European cruises and kept in touch for many years. At one point, they moved to Rhode Island. I also saw Guimas after many years. We visited an ancient wine cave within the walls of Paris and the grave of General Charles de Gaulle.

*Left: On the Golden Odyssey Piraeus cruise through the Mediterranean including Yalta in August 1983 with dear friends Johnnie and Dick. Right: With dear friend Guimas.*

*With Guimas in the 1980s at an ancient wine cave within the walls of Paris, dating back to 2005 BC (left) and visiting General Charles de Gaulle grave in France (right).*

India kept calling me back. It invigorated me every time I went there. I decided to spend time studying with K. Pattabhi Jois. He was very different in style and energy than Iyengar. As a teacher, Iyengar often pushed you to reach a certain pose—sometimes literally! Even though it was not the way I teach, I learned a lot from him.

K. Pattabhi Jois was very strong but softer in approach. You could feel the energy emanating from him and the Truth coming out of him. He was so engrossed in breathing and what it meant. I enjoyed spending time at his home.

Yoga is not a physical thing. You may look good, but if you're really doing yoga an aura shines through you and it makes you feel that everything in the world shines. It reminds us of our Oneness. It makes us whole. I was beginning to feel more of that wholeness within myself.

> *Yoga is not a physical thing. You may look good, but if you're really doing yoga an aura shines through you and it makes you feel that everything in the world shines.*

Just as Sister Ignatius predicted, travel was once again becoming a key part of my life. I wanted to share more of the world, and places that were special to me, with my students.

*I took students on a retreat to the South of France around 1983 when I was 65 years old. There was a road being made through mountains and we discovered Greek remains. We stopped and did yoga amongst the ruins. This is my favorite Peacock Pose, a posture as old as the remains.*

I led a series of trips to France—Juan-les-Pins, Dordogne and Montpellier in the south where I had been aiding people in escaping during the war. We visited vineyards and practiced yoga in an incredible château. More and more I was feeling right on my path.

Back in New York, I continued to publish my wine newspaper four times a year. I wasn't making a lot of money from it but it was reaching more people. I would usually write the feature and then have articles from other people. I had a whole range of national and international advertisers. I was still Vice President of the American Wine Society for Southern New York and would often host wine appreciation events.

*I was pleased to be able to give back to the wine industry through my newspaper.*

I enjoyed combining yoga teaching with my love of wine in retreats to France so my students could experience both. It was creative and great fun for all. I started offering yoga and wine workshops at Elizabeth Seton College in Yonkers. It was consistently booked with at least twenty-four students each.

Since I was living alone, I sometimes had problems when I went away and even when I was at home. Boys in the neighborhood would try to break in my house and cause problems. Little Maharani was certainly not a guard dog. She was so naturally friendly. Finally, I decided to move. It was too much for me to take care of that big house and I didn't feel safe.

In 1989, I sold my house and moved to Lake Isle in Eastchester, New York. It was a nice area but they were working a lot on a big highway so there was a lot of noise. I had all of Bill's bottles of wine in the cellar, as well as many of my films but the dampness in the air from the nearby lake caused them to rust over. I ended up having to throw them out. With all of these issues and nobody to help me, I stayed for just about a year.

Then, I moved into where I'm living now in White Plains, New York. I chose this place because they let me have Maharani. Everyone in the building loved her because she was so intelligent.

At first, I bought two places in the building, one for me to live in and the other was a studio for me to teach yoga. When I would teach yoga, Maharani would often be with me. During the relaxation at the end, I'd shake my finger and head "No" saying, "Maharani, you can't come in." I'd turn off the lights.

Suddenly, in the midst of everybody, she was right in the center on her back with her feet up. What would give her away was her tail swishing backwards and forwards. She would have a big smile on her face like she was saying, "You can't move me. I'm right in the center."

It was so funny with her one tooth missing and all. The students loved her and wouldn't let me take her away. She would stay right there to the very end of relaxation in the center of everybody. Animals are so wonderful.

We used to enjoy walking around the neighborhood. Even the bird in the tree would talk to her and follow us. I had to let Maharani go in the end because she had become sick from a horrible infection on her skin she had caught in the dog hospital. Afterwards, that bird stayed there for days and days looking for her. I think animals have a connection to life and an innate intuitive nature, something humans could learn a lot from.

As I was shifting the furniture around, settling into the apartment, I found the folder from the Vedic astrologer I met in Pondicherry. I kept it tucked away all those years. I opened it up and looked at it in more detail. It was the most extraordinary thing, astonishing really. I look at it now and so much of it is true. It made me feel like I was once again moving in the right direction. It spoke to my true nature and what was to come. The planet alignment for me was favorable:

> TAO LYNCH
>
> <u>Comming Time</u>
>
> In the recent past Pluto and Jupiter combine transited over Mars. This must have thrown her since the begining of 1980 in the occult/spiritual world and practices. The movement continues further and Pluto transit over Moon will take her to further spiritual progress - may be under some strain. Also Pluto the planet of highest yoga is still within orb of progress/sun conjuncte progress/ Mercury which denotes further interest and efforts for spiritual rise.
>
> Again, the sun progress Uranus Radicul trine, will take her to the Psycho-occult studies in comming years and its a good sign for the spiritual development. May continue during whole of eighties.
>
> Mercury radical and progress are in very closely aspects of secondary Mars and radical Mars respectively. It indicating lot of activities in writting small and big travels, Ambassadorial work and this xis a very good omen. The progress-sun is in square with birth venus and it is a good sign for association with show business. The Neptune-Jupiter transit opposite birth Pluto-Jupiter, would indicate excellent development in the career (worldly) and in spiritual progress.
>
> — x —
>
> *During the coming years there will be much self-confidence and quick action. Originality and leadership qualities will be witnessed.*

*Vedic horoscope from Indu Patel.*

This was indeed the heart of what I love—writing, producing and teaching yoga. I had studied various systems of yoga as the horoscope had indicated and was now running a spiritual institution of sorts. He ended it with a hand-written note that said, "During the coming years there will be much self-confidence and quick action. Originality and leadership qualities will be witnessed."

Although I didn't live by astrology, I began to see it from a different perspective. Just as farmers plant by the cycles of the Moon, there is wisdom in being able to read the language of the planets. There was so much there that I didn't understand but the reading somehow made me feel that I was moving into an exciting, and yet perhaps even more spiritually grounded phase in my life. I was in my seventies and, as it said, I was becoming an ambassador for yoga as well as wine.

***

In 1995, along with 400 teachers, spiritual and yogic masters, I was invited to participate in Yoga for Peace, an International Peace Conference in Israel. It was a time of peace talks. Israel and the Palestinian Liberation Organization had just signed an agreement with the goal of getting to a peace treaty after so many years of discord. Right after that, the Israel-Jordan Treaty of Peace had been signed, so there seemed to be a force driving for peace in that region.

*In Jerusalem with other yoga teachers for the Yoga for Peace Conference in 1995.*

*Cover of the Yoga For Peace Conference Pamphlet. It was a tremendous trip to Israel with 400 yoga and spiritual teachers coming together to help bring peace to the Middle East. A special yantra, or symbol, was created for the Conference.*

When we went to Bethlehem, we arrived at one o'clock in the morning. The sky was filled with stars and it felt like you could grab every star in the sky. It was gorgeous. We sat there looking at this wonder. It reminded me of when I was a little girl up in Darjeeling talking to the stars which added to the beauty and spiritual atmosphere of the scene.

Suddenly, Jesse Kalu brought out his flute and began to play. I had one of my silly ideas and said, "This is incredible. All we need to do to make this picture perfect is to salute it with a glass of wine!"

A few days later I received a call, "Täo, do you know something about wine? Do you have time? Can you come with us?"

One of the men explained what happened, "We were excavating a cave and got to what we thought was a back wall. It was the back of a mountainside and behind there was another cave. Behind that were huge carboys that looked like they were filled with dust."

I remember those big containers my aunt used on her vineyard. They helped her hide people.

He continued, "We brought the carboys outside and it started to rain. We quickly took them inside. When the rain stopped, we took them out again and then there was a tiny little shoot in one of them. We didn't know what to think. There must have been grapes in them."

Now I was quite curious. The area they were excavating was very old.

He said, "We had a feeling that these were Roman, so they must be about 5,000 years old. Would you know what was in them? What kind of grapes do you think they are?"

That was a very exciting discovery—dust and now a little shoot. I said, "I think it must be a Shiraz because this is close to Iran."

They decided to get it tested to determine where the grape variety originated. They had to be very careful since it was so fragile. It was amazing. A few drops of rain can suddenly make something grow. It shows that nothing ever really dies.

*It was incredible to feel the energy of so many yoga and spiritual teachers coming together for peace in Israel.*

The Peace Conference was extraordinary. All of these teachers from around the world came in for the week to help bring peace to the Middle East through yogic principles. It was sponsored by The Israeli Yoga Teacher's Association, Unity in Yoga International, Swiss Association for the Study of Yoga, and The Center for International Dialogue.

That's when I saw Mataji Indra Devi again. At that point, I was 77 years old and she was around 95. It was good to spend time with her. For me, she was a connection to India and my beginnings in yoga. She was the one who initially gave me the vision of being a yoga teacher. I was grateful for her inspiration.

*Mataji Indra Devi at 95 years old teaching at the Yoga for Peace Conference in Israel in 1995. It was amazing to see her again.*

The event itself was a tremendous coming together. In addition to Indra Devi, I saw T.K.V. Desikachar. He was the son, and later student, of the famous Krishnamacharya who taught Indra Devi, K. Pattabhi Jois and B.K.S. Iyengar who was Desikachar's brother-in-law.

Desikachar had been encouraged to take a modern path of education and studied engineering. Then, one day in visiting his parent's house in Madras, he witnessed the power and influence of his father's teachings. A Western woman had come to visit exclaiming how Krishnamacharya had healed her insomnia. Soon thereafter he gave up his engineering path and devoted his time to studying with his father. It's funny how everything seems to be related. Now we were together in Israel.

One newspaper clipping had the headline, "Mideast Peace Sought by Spiritual Means." Another said, "Yogis From Around the World Meditate for Peace. Hindu chants mixed with Hebrew prayers in a week-long meeting of yoga devotees intended to help the peace process."

Rama Jyoti Vernon, President of the Center for International Dialogue and Founder of Unity In Yoga said:

> "As Yoga continually reflects, if we truly want to change the world into an evolutionary construct, we have to change ourselves. The healing of the Nations begins within ourselves."

This was Oneness. With people from different traditions and nations all in Jerusalem, the event confirmed the power of yoga to bring people together. Yoga is accessible to everybody and is a gift to share. Rama Jyoti Vernon still to this day does an incredible job in using yoga and a gateway to peace around the world. Everything she has planted has been for the good of mankind.

*Press coverage from The Jerusalem Post on Feburary 3, 1995.*

## The Healing of Nations

Patanjali in the Yoga Sutras refers to the darkness or the invisible having to rise to the surface to become visible before it can be eradicated. We are witnessing this phenomenon personally and collectively throughout the world. Global unrest reveals what has been lying unresolved in the collective psyche. As Yoga continually reflects, if we truly want to change the world into an evolutionary construct, we have to change ourselves. The healing of the Nations begins within ourselves.

The Venerable Thich Nhat Hanh has said, "To practice peace, we must be peace." The word peace has many meanings. To one, Peace may represent a quietness. To another, complacency and boredom. To yet another, it may mean absence of pain and suffering. Peace to one nation may appear as oppression to another.

If Yoga is the realization of the oneness of the individual with the universal, then the true sense of "Oneness" begins by seeing no distinction between our internal process and the world process. The borders we have established within ourselves are the same borders that divide people, states and nations.

Do we have the courage to demonstrate Unity with each other? Can we see our brothers and sisters as ourselves? Can we feel the pain of others as we would our own? Can we feel the joy of their successes as the joy of our own? Can we heal our past would so that war torn countries can heal theirs? Can we rise above the judgements and criticisms that bind our minds in separation to support, love and honor others as the Self? Can we hold love for people of All Nations? Can we practice Yoga as a state of being to effect the peace and healing we would like to see within the world? J. Krishnamurti in one of his last talks repeated three times, "Each one of us is all of humankind."

Let us welcome each other in the spirit of unity as we gather here in Jerusalem. Let us honor our diversity. Let us honor all teachers of peace who have walked the path before us bringing light to the darkened corners of the world. May the future generations of light bearers of all nations, all traditions, continue to keep the eternal flame of Yoga, *the remembrance of oneness*, burning brightly within the hearts of humankind as we cross the threshold of the new millennium.

Rama Jyoti Vernon, President
Center for International Dialogue
Founder, Unity In Yoga

### SPONSORS
*The Israeli Yoga Teacher's Association*
*Unity in Yoga, International*
*Swiss Association for the Study of Yoga*
*The Center for International Dialogue*

### ADVISORS

**ISRAELI YOGA TEACHER'S ASSOCIATION BOARD OF ADVISORS**
Eddie Behor
Shlomit Brug
Shmalzer Izzhar
Ziva Kinrot, Chair
Rina Tawil

**UNITY IN YOGA INTERNATIONAL ADVISORY COUNCIL**
Linda Cogozzo
  *Rodmell Press*
Joseph Dugan
  *Consultant, Canada*
Angela Farmer
  *Yoga Teachers, England*
David Frawley
  *Institute of Vedic Studies*
Lilias Folan
  *TV Personality & Author*
Joan Giguiere
  *Past President, CYTA*
Michael Gliksohn
  *Publisher, Yoga Journal*
Vyaas Houston
  *American Sanskrit Institute*
Eveline Idanova
  *Healthy Family Club, Russia*
Howard Kent
  *Yoga for Health, England*
Prudence Kestner
  *Pres. (US) IYTA*
Gary Kraftsow
  *Maui Yoga Therapy*
Dr. Vasant Lad
  *Ayurvedic Institute*
Laureen MacLeod
  *Liaison\**
Dr. Robin Monro
  *Biomedical Trust, England*
Nischala Devi
  *Dean Ornish Program*
Sylvia Klein Olkin
  *Positive Pregnancy*
Aadil Palkhivala
  *"Yoga Centers"*
Dr. Manny Patel
  *L.I.F.E. Foundation, England*
Larry Payne
  *Int'l Assoc. Yoga Therapists*
Prof. Jorge Quiros
  *Costa Rican University*
Kali Ray
  *Tri Yoga Centers*
Jeane Rhodes
  *Aquarian Yoga*
Bruce Rogel
  *Business Consultant*
John Schumacher
  *Unity Woods, Yoga Center*
Dr. William Wulsin
  *Self Health Services*

**EXECUTIVE COUNCIL**
Patricia M. Hansen
  *President*
Leslie Kaminoff
  *Vice President*
Sandra L. Kozak
  *Vice President*
Irene Beer
  *Secretary*
Judith Hein
  *Treasurer*
Mukunda T. Stiles
  *Member-at-Large*
Nancy Ford-Kohne
  *President Emeritus*

**FOUNDER**
Rama Jyoti Vernon

*Rama Jyoti Vernon's beautiful overview of our intention for the Yoga for Peace Conference, "The Healing of Nations." Rama is still leading peace initiatives around the world. The list of advisors include many friends and notable yoga teachers.*

I've had all kinds of people in my yoga classes—Christian, Jewish, Muslim, Hindu and Buddhist. All people are at the same level. All of them pulse with the same heartbeat. I think we have to get over boundaries, frontiers and even passports. We must combat ignorance in people thinking that they're better than another because they're from this place or that place. It's simply not true.

Mahatma Gandhi had it right when he said, "Hate the sin, not the sinner." We can all have our own ideas and talk about them in a different way. I may not like your principles, but that has nothing to do with you as a person. Everyone is entitled to his or her way of thinking as long as you are not harming another. We don't have to agree but we should respect each other since we are all a part of the One.

> *We don't have to agree but we should respect each other since we are all a part of the One.*

After the Yoga for Peace Conference, yoga and travel became more prominent in my life. I particularly love taking my students on retreats. I've since led almost thirty trips to places like Bali, Bucharest, Morocco, France and India. I believe such visits offer a nice escape from a person's everyday circumstances and, in certain environments, can open the path to understanding. I've been invited to teach programs in Sri Lanka, Budapest, and even Moscow. In many ways, yoga can be a gateway to cultural exchange.

*One of my trips to India with students in January 1996. I'm in an arm balancing pose. I was 78 years old. Yoga can be done at any age!*

*We usually go to the Taj Mahal during our yoga retreats.*

> हिन्दी . HINDI
> महात्मा गां
> I WOULD LIKE TO SEE INDIA FREE AND STRONG SO THA
> SHE MAY OFFER HERSELF AS A WILLING AND PURE
> SACRIFICE FOR THE BETTERMENT OF THE WORLD. THE
> INDIVIDUAL, BEING PURE, SACRIFICES HIMSELF FOR THE
> FAMILY, THE LATTER FOR THE VILLAGE, THE VILLAGE
> FOR THE DISTRICT, THE DISTRICT FOR THE PROVINCE, THE
> PROVINCE FOR THE NATION, THE NATION FOR ALL.
> I WANT KHUDAI RAJ, WHICH IS THE SAME THING AS THE
> KINGDOM OF GOD ON EARTH, THE ESTABLISHMENT OF
> SUCH A RAJYA WOULD NOT ONLY MEAN WELFARE OF
> THE WHOLE OF THE INDIAN PEOPLE BUT OF THE
> WHOLE WORLD.                    MAHATMA GANDHI
> अंग्रेजी . ENGLISH

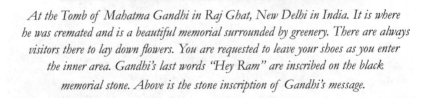

*At the Tomb of Mahatma Gandhi in Raj Ghat, New Delhi in India. It is where he was cremated and is a beautiful memorial surrounded by greenery. There are always visitors there to lay down flowers. You are requested to leave your shoes as you enter the inner area. Gandhi's last words "Hey Ram" are inscribed on the black memorial stone. Above is the stone inscription of Gandhi's message.*

Going to India, in particular, offers enlightenment about the true spirit of yoga. It's nice to see the sights like the Taj Mahal and visit the shops in Jaipur and Mumbai. When we get to Kerala, in the south of India, we slow down and can make a deeper connection. This beautiful locale is the birthplace of doing Ashtanga yoga and the first medicine of the world, Ayurvedic medicine. It's where it all started. You can witness nature coming alive. Doing yoga while watching the sunrise or sunset over the backwaters, you feel the link between the very essence and beauty of the Life Force within you.

*In Kerala, India with students. We always go down the backwaters and do yoga in the open air. It is one of my favorite trips. I love sharing the beauty and history of the birthplace of Yoga and Ayurveda.*

When I get on an elevator in big cities, I say, "Good morning!" and ninety percent of the people look at me like I'm crazy. They seem to be thinking, "Why are you talking to me? I don't know you." It's like they've forgotten how to smile. Yoga helps us open up so we can smile and get rid of fear. Then, all of the world will smile with us. Wine also opens us up, not to drink to get drunk but to connect and socialize.

*Yoga helps us open up so we can smile and get rid of fear. Then, all of the world will smile with us.*

*In France with students June 1998.*

*In France. In the top picture I'm with the owner of one of the oldest restaurants in Beaune, Burgundy. In the middle, I'm at Château Haut-Brion in Bordeaux. On the bottom, I'm receiving a trophy and being shown how to open a Champagne bottle with a sword.*

I made a point to stay close to my sister, Kaye. She moved to Wales and I would visit her until she died just a couple of years ago. She also loved nature and had such beautiful gardens. I was grateful to have her in my life for so long. We each have the power to shape our own lives, choose our activities, and create our own *sangha*, or community of like-minded people. Don't just think about it. Enjoy the life you want today!

> *We each have the power to shape our own lives, choose our activities, and create our own sangha, or community of like-minded people.*

*With my sister Kaye.*

*In Australia.*

*My yoga practice was blossoming. Here I am in my eighties.*

CHAPTER 24

## Dance To Your Own Rhythm

The music of the soul is a sweet sound to behold. It comes through when we fully embody our passions and follow our heart's desires. Like in dance, we each have a different rhythm and set of steps to express ourselves. If you want to do something that will bring you joy, just start. It's never too late. With anything, as you practice you get better. That's how I became a competitive ballroom dancer at the age of 87.

*Like in dance, we each have a different rhythm and set of steps to express ourselves.*

I've rented a room for my yoga classes at the Fred Astaire Dance Studio in Hartsdale for many years. One blustery winter day in 2005, I was there waiting for my Teacher Training students to arrive and the dance teachers, Alex and Irina Vasendin, were also waiting for their students. None of our students braved the snow to come to class.

While we waited, I was intrigued by the gracefulness of Alex and Irina doing a waltz. Then, they began to do the tango. Enthralled by the music and captivated by their playful yet sensual rhythmic movements, I could not hold it inside, "It's so wonderful to watch you. I love the music and everything."

Alex asked, "Do you dance?"

I answered somewhat apologetically, "I can jitterbug, if you call that dancing." I added, "Before I die I want to go to Argentina and dance the tango."

As if trying to entice me Alex responded, "Why don't you start tonight?"

Irina enthusiastically chimed in saying, "Yes, you should begin right now."

So I did and I haven't stopped dancing since.

*Dance teachers Alex and Irina Vasendin who encouraged me to start ballroom dancing at the Fred Astaire Studios in Hartsdale, October 2005. I was 87 years old and I've been dancing ever since!*

That very evening I knew that I wanted to dance forever. It wasn't very long before those at the Fred Astaire Dance Studios became a part of my family and some of my teachers became my dance partners. Soon, we began to practice every week. We not only danced the tango, but added several other categories—mamba, samba, cha cha cha, waltz, foxtrot, Viennese waltz, quickstep, jive, and paso doble. They encouraged me to enter dance competitions. Practicing and competing makes me better.

One time I was doing a competition in Puerto Rico and my flight was terribly delayed. I got to the hotel and they didn't even have my room available. I had to get dressed and ready for the competition in the bathroom. I made it to the dance floor just in time. When you are in a competition, you have to be ready to dance the dance at a moment's notice.

*One of my early dance costumes and competitions with Alex.*
*I was almost 90 years old and felt younger than ever!*

Looking back, I realize that dance has always been a part of my life. Like yoga, it has been a *sutra*, or thread. When my uncle took me to French Somaliland, the Watusi put me on their shoulders and taught me African dance—how to swing my head around and feel the rhythm. In Pondicherry, I learned *bharatanatyam*—a classical Indian dance with the stylized hand and eye movements. It is very dramatic and quite graceful. It goes back to ancient times as a form of devotion.

Dance helped me to survive when I escaped to England from France. During the war, dance led to my first job in the nightclubs when I bumped into Surah walking down Shaftesbury Avenue. I will always remember that day. I had one bar of chocolate, a shilling in my pocket and no money to pay my rent. Surah remembered seeing me dance *bharatanatyam* with my uncle at the Oberoi Grand Hotel in Calcutta. It was the energy and beauty of the dance she recalled. Things began to turn around because of that encounter.

*With Armando Martin, a senior executive at Fred Astaire Dance Studios, and Alex.*

*With other students and teachers at the Fred Astaire Dance Studios after a competition.*

Dance eventually made me famous in the cabarets. Fearless during the bombing Blitz in London, I danced every night at five of the most popular clubs. With limited English, dancing led to movie and television parts in Hollywood such as doing the tango with Jim Backus in *I Married Joan*.

Over the years, dance gave me inspiration and brought me back to myself when I felt lost. When I was in New York and at a low point in my career after the NBC show with Ilka Chase fell through, dance rescued me. I saw the flyer with Katherine Dunham's name on it. I endured an extra week of that horrible modeling job just to pay for classes with her. It was incredible to do flying leaps with the guys in her troupe. Dancing like that lifted my spirits.

Now, dance has given me new life yet again. Everyone wants to know the secret behind my dancing. All I have to say is, at this age, I dance for the love of dancing. I breathe dancing. I'd rather dance than eat and I dance as much as I can afford to. Dancing with someone who likes to dance can make you feel at one. It turns on the energy and lights up your body.

For me, the foundation of dancing is getting to the beauty inside of it. When you go to Africa and see those people dancing, they light up with every fiber of their body. That can teach us something about beauty. The beauty is that they are in touch with the rhythm of life.

*The foundation of dancing is getting to the beauty inside of it.*

My dance partners are seventy years my junior. Vard Margaryan swings me around, flips me upside down and picks me up as I kick my feet in the air. Once I kicked so high I made a hole in the ceiling! I feel I'm a totally different person when I'm dancing. He makes me feel free and definitely keeps me young. He doesn't mind my age. He twirls me around like I'm in my twenties. We even danced together on the television show *America's Got Talent* in June 2015, I was 96 and he was 26. It surprised the judges and the audience, and we received a standing ovation.

Each one of my dance teachers and partners have brought joy to my life. Hayk Balasanyan is very special. He doesn't dance just for himself—he dances to make me look good. We've done many competitions together and he joined me when dear photographer Robert Sturman took pictures of me dancing in nature. Robert's pictures, including the red dress photo on the cover of this book, have been seen around the world.

When I compete, I dance often in up to thirteen categories. Sometimes we do two of each dance so I may do up to thirty dances in one day. There are thirty-six categories. It may seem tiring but it gives me energy.

I like the gracefulness of the waltz, and the smooth steps of a foxtrot. I love the fun and energy of swing, jitterbug and quickstep. I find that Latin dances fire up my spirit as I get inside of the rhythms of the paso doble, bolero, tango, rumba, samba, and cha cha cha. I like to do what I believe is beautiful.

I've had exquisite gowns and dresses made for each dance category. It's expensive but it is something that brings me joy. In a recent Fred Astaire Dance Competition, I had five dress changes. They wanted me to wear one dress for all of the dances. I said, "No. Dresses have to represent what you're dancing. If you're dancing a tango, you don't want to be in the same kind of dress as when you're doing the swing."

I design my dresses and then have them made by design genius Ishitobi. A lot of the fabrics we use are from the over two hundred saris I own.

With my high heels and multiple dress changes in a competition, I try to make my performances professional and beautiful. I get lost in the joy of it all. For one competition in White Plains, I arrived there at 9:30 a.m. after teaching my morning yoga class. I didn't get home until after 11:30 p.m. I had been up since 5 a.m. and still wasn't tired. After the competition, I danced just for fun with the other dancers as we ended the day's competition with a delightful reception. Music makes you come alive, like a flower opening its petals to nature.

> *Music makes you come alive, like a flower opening its petals to nature.*

There are many similarities between dance and yoga. When you are working on yoga, you're working from your inner self and moving into this wonderful energy that's inside of you. When you are working on dancing, it has to come from that inner self and then it's like opening a bottle of Champagne—it swishes around and then pops with energy. You actually feel the joy of it and the wonder that's inside that says, "I can do it!" It's amazing.

**Entries for Porchon-Lynch, Tao**

**With Bilozorov, Anton**

| Session@Time | Number | Heat | Event |
|---|---|---|---|
| 1@10:50AM Sunday | 150 | Heat 66 | L-C3 Full Bronze Open Argentine Tango |
| 1@10:57AM Sunday | 150 | Heat 71 | L-C3 Full Silver Open Argentine Tango |

**With Vasendin, Alex**

| Session@Time | Number | Heat | Event |
|---|---|---|---|
| 1@11:25AM Sunday | 198 | Heat 84 | L-C3 Full Silver Open American Waltz |
| 1@11:27AM Sunday | 198 | Heat 85 | L-C3 Full Silver Open American Tango |
| 1@11:28AM Sunday | 198 | Heat 86 | L-C3 Full Silver Open American Foxtrot |
| 1@12:24PM Sunday | 198 | Heat 106 | L-C3 Silver Open Int'l Waltz |
| 1@12:26PM Sunday | 198 | Heat 107 | L-C3 Silver Open Int'l Tango |
| 1@12:27PM Sunday | 198 | Heat 108 | L-C3 Silver Open Int'l Viennese Waltz |
| 1@12:28PM Sunday | 198 | Heat 109 | L-C3 Silver Open Int'l Foxtrot |
| 1@12:30PM Sunday | 198 | Heat 110 | L-C3 Silver Open Int'l Quickstep |

**With Bilozorov, Anton**

| Session@Time | Number | Heat | Event |
|---|---|---|---|
| 1@12:53PM Sunday | 150 | Solo 6 | L- "Viva Los Toreadores" |

**With Styran, Olexii**

| Session@Time | Number | Heat | Event |
|---|---|---|---|
| 1@02:03PM Sunday | 195 | Heat 143 | L-C2 Bronze Open Int'l Cha Cha |
| 1@02:05PM Sunday | 195 | Heat 145 | L-C3 Bronze Open Int'l Cha Cha |

**With Vasendin, Alex**

| Session@Time | Number | Heat | Event |
|---|---|---|---|
| 1@04:46PM Sunday | 198 | Heat 244 | L-C2 Full Silver Open American Samba |
| 1@05:11PM Sunday | 198 | Heat 262 | L-C3 Full Silver Open American Cha Cha |
| 1@05:12PM Sunday | 198 | Heat 263 | L-C3 Full Silver Open American Rumba |
| 1@05:13PM Sunday | 198 | Heat 264 | L-C3 Full Silver Open East Coast Swing |
| 1@05:23PM Sunday | 198 | Heat 271 | L-C2 Full Silver Open American Cha Cha |
| 1@05:25PM Sunday | 198 | Heat 272 | L-C2 Full Silver Open American Rumba |
| 1@05:31PM Sunday | 198 | Heat 277 | L-C3 Full Silver Open American Samba |

*Typical schedule for a dance competition. This one is from a competition in June 2015. I danced with Alex Vasendin, Anton Bilozorov and Olexii Styran, and I did a solo. I won multiple First Place Awards that day.*

*With Alex Vasendin. The pictures are from live Fred Astaire Dance competitions. I am grateful to Alex for encouraging me to learn how to ballroom dance.*

*With Hayk Balasanyan. The picture above is part of a beautiful series taken by dear friend and photographer Robert Sturman. The images below are from live Fred Astaire Dance competitions.*

*With Vard Margaryan. The pictures are from live Fred Astaire Dance competitions. On June 9, 2015, I appeared with Vard on the NBC television show, America's Got Talent and received a standing ovation from the audience and all four judges including Howard Stern, Heidi Klum, Mel B, Howie Mandel.*

Like yoga, dance can bring about a feeling of Oneness. In January 2014, after I led a yoga retreat throughout India with a group of my students, I danced with famous dancer and actor Sandip Soparrkar in Mumbai. We performed together in a program called "Inspire to Dance" in front of an audience of over 5,000 at Phoenix Marketcity in Kurla, a suburb of Mumbai. It was absolutely incredible! People were everywhere enjoying the festivities.

Sandip exudes love in all he does. Other beautiful Indian celebrities joined us afterwards including Hema Malini, Zeenat Aman, Madhoo Shah, Hasleen Kaur, Shiv Darshan, Amy Billimoria, Sushmita Sen and Sandip's talented wife Jesse Randhawa. All of them with their warmth and boundless smiles reminded me of why I love India so much.

If I could start and delve into a passion at 87, anyone can. I believe it is important to learn something new. Seize the moment like I did. I've won over 700 First Place Awards for dancing and I'm still competing at age 97 against people who are 50 years old and above.

I've danced and done yoga through three hip replacements and a broken wrist. I don't often get sick but I have injured parts of my body. Each time, I'm determined to come back and prove to the doctors that nothing is impossible! Live with a sense of fearlessness. Do your dance in life, whatever that is, and don't give up.

*Live with a sense of fearlessness. Do your dance in life, whatever that is, and don't give up.*

*With famous dancer and actor Sandip Soparrkar in India. We danced together in a program called "Inspire to Dance" in front of an audience of over 5,000 on January 19, 2014.*

With Indian celebrities including actress-politician Hema Malini, actress Madhoo Shah, former Miss Universe Sushmita Sen, former Miss Asia Pacific Zeenat Aman, model Hasleen Kaur, actor Shiv Darshan, fashion designer Amy Billimoria, model-actress Jesse Randhawa and, of course, Sandip Soparrkar who helped to make it all happen.

CHAPTER 25

# Live Light & Truth

My life has been a vast quest of trying to understand the Truth. Why am I here? What am I supposed to be doing? What is the reason for so much sadness in the world? Why are we on various levels of consciousness? I turned to my teachers and other famous seekers of Truth from Mahatma Gandhi and Indra Devi to the incredible Swami Prabhavananda and Maharishi. I reached out to nature and to the Infinite to discover a new source of understanding. I now realize that the path to finding Truth is to pass through the cycles of life with wonder and a sense of exploration. It is then that you can really experience the essence of *yug*—the joining of body, mind and Spirit.

*The path to finding Truth is to pass through the cycles of life with wonder and a sense of exploration.*

At 97 years old, do I know the secrets of life? Have I found the answers to the many questions I asked as a child? I think by living fully in the world I found some of the answers. Who I am today is made up of pieces of insights from my many teachers and experiences like a jigsaw puzzle fitting together and exposing the full picture.

You too can find the answers by observing nature and life itself. You will feel what is right intuitively and develop your own "Inner Diary." Take time to find your own practice of stillness and your own gurus, or teachers. They will help you break through the *Avidya*, or ignorance. They will help shed light on the darkness in your mind and open your eyes to what's inside of you.

Once you find the light, that center of who you are, it may flicker like a candle in the wind. This is the dance—weaving in and out of spiritual awareness. You may seem to go back and forth, up and down, even sometimes spinning around, but always seek to come back to center.

> *Sometimes you will be present with life and sometimees not. No matter how dizzying the situation, remember to keep practicing. Keep dancing to your own rhythm.*

Sometimes you will be present with life and sometimes not. No matter how dizzying the situation, remember to keep practicing. Keep dancing to your own rhythm. As Vedanta says, "Truth is One, sages call it by many names." Walk your own path and we'll meet on the top of the mountain.

People often ask me about my key to longevity and vitality. I think it goes back to yoga and the simple things I learned as a child about honoring nature and the connection between the mind, body and Spirit. I seek to capture the fullness of life and be in harmony with the Universe. You can too! Here are some thoughts from my life's journey to perhaps enhance your current experience:

**1. Recognize that everything is Energy and we are One here and now.** *Satya* is a Sanskrit word that means "Absolute Truth" and "that which is unchangeable." It is the true reality, not the veil we often perceive.

The Truth I've come to believe is that Oneness is right here. It is not out in space but deep within us. As my uncle said, "Every blade of grass has a heartbeat." Otherwise, how could it push through the earth? Every single thing has a heartbeat that is the essence and energy behind it all.

In certain places you can really feel this energy. In 2008, I was in Peru with my students. I climbed Machu Picchu with heels and everyone thought I was nuts. It was incredible to feel the energy of that special place. It is said to be an energy vortex coming from deep within the earth. I felt a sense of magic and reverence for the ancient Incas. Like the energy chakras in the body, we are all a part of this Force that may not be seen but can be felt.

One time I was in India at The Casino Hotel in Cochin with my students for a yoga retreat and something extraordinary happened. Since we had a few hours to spare before taking our flight back to the U.S., I suggested we do an early morning yoga class in the hotel's beautiful garden. I arrived first. As I waited, I started to practice some yoga asanas. Suddenly, I heard a shriek of laughter and looked up from balancing in the Peacock Pose. Nose to nose, I faced a real peacock that had crossed the garden. It was staring at me as to say, "That's not the way to do the peacock!" In that moment, I could feel our connection.

One of my dearest students Lori Schulman saw what happened and had started to laugh. Other students heard and came running just in time to see the peacock turn in disgust and move a few feet away, opening its wings royally. It fluttered them and then took off. Everyone was in hysterics. We share an unspoken language with all living things and yoga helps you tune into that energy.

I believe this Divine Force is within all of us and in everything in this world. It doesn't matter what you call It. I really truly believe with every bit of my heart that THAT is the Lord of Creation—the essence and energy I learned about and felt when I was a child. The veil, which is ignorance to our true nature, is the perception that we are separate.

*This Divine Force is within us and in everything in this world.*

*Feeling the energy in the tree (left) and the energy at Machu Picchu in Peru (right).*

**2. Tune into breath which IS the Life Force and gateway to peace.** It all starts with breath, the energy within us and the power behind all things. Your breath doesn't know how old you are. It doesn't know what you can't do. It's important to learn how to tune into your breath and inner self. It can tell you a lot about yourself. Proper breathing is the power that opens many doors including longevity, vitality and tranquility.

In 2011, I taught yoga to almost ninety people through the Department of Defense at the Pentagon. These are the people who really need the practice for they are responsible for making decisions about war and peace that are affecting all of our lives. It's helpful if they make those important decisions from a place of inner calm. Some of it was to aid young men who had lived the horrors of war and help in making their lives normal. No matter what their individual physical capacity, every person there could take a breath. As I had learned in trying to find harmony with my husband Bill, if we can breathe together we can be together. This is the essence of peace.

> *Proper breathing is the power that opens many doors including longevity, vitality and tranquility.*

That same year, I participated in the Newark Peace Education Summit and shared the stage for the Opening Panel on Peace with His Holiness the 14th Dalai Lama, two other Nobel Laureates Jody Williams and Shirin Ebadi, and other notable people including moderator Dr. Robert Thurman who founded Tibet House in New York and Dr. Deepak Chopra. Deepak's work, inspired in many ways by our dear teacher the Maharishi, has shed light on the consciousness of so many around the world.

On the panel, we talked about how peace starts within—with personal transformation. That's how we can start to have peace in the world. The Dalai Lama is an example. He had a smile that lit up the entire place! The next day, I led a workshop with my dear student Terri Kennedy called "The Gandhi Effect." She facilitated my involvement in the Summit. Our program together was tremendous with standing room only. We talked about social change and my beloved guru and world master of peace Mahatma Gandhi. Climaxing it, we taught a sequence of breathing and meditation techniques. Once again breath was our starting point, something we each share.

DANCING LIGHT | 413

*At the Newark Peace Education Summit in May 2011. Honorary Host was Mayor Cory Booker and the Co-Conveners were Dr. Robert Thurman and Drew Katz. I shared the opening panel with His Holiness the 14th Dalai Lama, Dr. Deepak Chopra, Nobel Laureate Jody Williams and other notables. I also led a workshop with Terri Kennedy.*

*"The Gandhi Effect" workshop I co-led with Terri Kennedy in May 2011 as part of the Newark Peace Education Summit. We had a standing room only audience.*

This is why I often finish my yoga classes in a circle. We hold hands palm to palm. I send the heat and Life Force from my hand to yours. By the time it comes back around, you can actually feel that power within you. Then, we send out energy. We take a breath and we send out this breath to people that suffer and even to people we don't like as well, unclogging what is in that person we may not like. We are no more right than the other person is and if we can become one with that person, it's better. Then, we are "living yoga" and experiencing Oneness throughout the world. To seal this intention, together we say, "May peace be unto you and to every living creature."

The end of the class takes us to the true practice of yoga when the mind is controlled, stilled and silenced. What remains is the soul or inner self. In the Universe there is no higher or lower self, they must be equal. Only then, can you become a yogi. Only experience and expression of the self become awakened when body, mind and Spirit become one. The quest of the Self is to light a spark of Divinity, the very essence of *yug*, and then you can Live Light and Truth. The song of the soul is the breath of Eternal Life flowing through you.

*Closing circle after class. We send breath and energy to each other.*

**3. Focus your mind on positive thoughts for what you put in your mind materializes.** Some people are stricken with fears that vibrate through their thoughts, deteriorating their lives and bodies, creating decay. This shuts down their experiencing the magnificent pulse beat of their heart and the wonders of life. While others dwell in the tomorrow, hoping things will open up the way. Then, they sink back into an abyss of darkness, unable to see through the clouds of ignorance or watch the perfect blueness of the sky and the sun lighting up the heavens.

I don't believe in fear and don't allow my mind to dwell on the negative. Instead, I focus on positive thoughts that open my mind to solutions. I mentally visualize opening the door to that which is good. I breathe in and know

*Mentally visualize opening the door to that which is good.*

that good things are happening. That's when you can relax and feel that power within you.

Just as we put junk in our bodies, we put junk in our minds through television and other media particularly commercials telling us what we can't do or what medicine we must take. Don't let fear into your mind. I don't fill my mind with what I cannot do, or more importantly, allow the anguish of fear to penetrate my life. I may encounter some problems but I know that with every breath I take I can consciously make the adventure good or bad—both with the promise of enlightenment.

If you're told you have an illness, start off right away knowing that it won't get a real hold on you. Then, you can start to heal yourself. Look for the good. Stay away from violence coming into your mind and don't let the world pull you down. Always focus on the good and know that good will come to you.

**4. Live in meditation.** People often ask if I do a seated meditation at a certain time each day. My life is my meditation. As I awaken to the dawn, I smell the perfume of the flowers and take in the beautiful shades of green of the leaves on the trees and the grass below. All the incredible colors that flow with the earth penetrate my being.

I feel the beauty coming out of the earth, the incredible beauty and wonder of it. Where did it come from? What does it do that can help me survive? I learn everything from nature. It is so important that I have experienced this power. Since the time I was a child, nature has been my encyclopedia. Everywhere there is something that seems to show me the purity and the innocence of nature and the power behind that.

I'll stop on the road if I see a whole little group of sparrows pecking in the garden. Often the grass is taller than they are. It's so beautiful. The song of the birds enters my heart and opens the door to the mirror of my soul. I am immersed in the music of the Universe and start to feel and live the dance of joy and wonder of Eternal Life. I witness the energy of the tiniest creatures.

I also get asked about my "typical day." I don't have a typical day. Each moment is special. When I wake up in the morning, I always look forward to each day and say joyfully, "This is going to be the BEST day of my life!" That way I can face anything and smile at the world. Every day, the dawn of life starts again, and so, I live better each day.

> *Every day, the dawn of life starts again, and so, I live better each day.*

**5. Feed your body to fuel your spirit.** How you feed your body can affect the vibrancy of your life and the ability to express your true spirit. Be in touch with nature and the fruits of life. That will keep you healthy. I love mostly fruit, especially mangoes and fruit juices. The juices of fruit cleanse my blood stream. I always have fruit at night to cleanse my system. I enjoy green vegetables both cooked or as a salad, particularly spinach, which is my favorite food. Sometimes I'll have soup for dinner.

I've never eaten animal meat or poultry. I have been a lifelong vegetarian, however recently, I occasionally eat a little bit of fish, lobster and shrimp. I'm very much into "save everything"—save the whales, save the wolves, save this, save that. I know it's a bit crazy. We don't have to kill things to eat. Most animals only kill something when they are really very hungry. They don't usually do it just for the sake of it. But many people eat all the time and it is usually what is called "junk food."

I don't eat just to eat, and I usually eat lightly and slowly. My uncle never would force me to eat a lot of food. I took just what I needed, not more or less. He didn't want us to waste food because somebody else could use it. Every time I see people in restaurants with their plates piled high, I feel a little sad because millions of people are starving. There's so much left over and so many people could benefit from it.

I don't eat much and I don't get tired. I never take large portions of any food. People say I eat like a bird. That's a good example how to feed the body. When you eat too much it creates heaviness in the body and it stifles the energy. No one should eat huge quantities of food. Just take a little. If you want a little more, take a little more but don't fill your stomach up more than is necessary. It makes it hard to get rid of. It's silly but it's true.

*I love fruits and vegetables, yet I will also treat myself to ice cream and chocolate!*

Some people find it funny that I also enjoy milk chocolate and wine. Sometimes I'll eat a whole bar of chocolate and then I won't have any for another year. I enjoy it in that moment. I've always believed that wine is good for the blood. I like a glass of wine with my food but I don't like to drink alone. I also don't drink water except in my tea and that often shocks people. Too much water washes out the good nutrients and often water nowadays is not pure. The chemicals that are in it can move into our systems.

After becoming a vegetarian, Dr. Ostoja said, "Sometimes I have an urge for meat so I will eat some but I don't want to get into it. If I have an urge, I will eat it. Then, I realize that I really don't like it that much." Using Dr. Ostoja as an example, I would say that you can train yourself to be healthy but it doesn't have to be in a rigid way.

*You can train yourself to be healthy but it doesn't have to be in a rigid way.*

**6. Respect and honor our planet.** The song of the birds can lift your spirit and, yet we make noise by putting tons of machines together. Then, when they're done, we throw them away to let them contaminate the soil. We need to learn to live with the beauty of this earth and not put garbage in it. We're pulling down trees and killing off everything. There was something like a billion butterflies and now they're hardly seen. We're killing off the fish and the whales. We're killing the earth.

Soon we'll have nothing except cellophane to eat. It will all be junk. I look in the market, go down one aisle and everything is fabricated. Except for the produce, there is nothing that is real. Everything else is dead from an energy standpoint. There is no *prana*, or Life Force, left.

*Enjoying coconut with my students in Kerala, India.*

The earth gives us so much. How can we truly believe we can take over nature? We can learn so much from it. Every season, it renews. Every season something comes from it. Coconut is an example. I simply love coconut. There are so many things you can do with it. You don't have to kill the tree to get it. It produces more. You get oil out of it, you get juice out of it and the pulp. You can even make mats from it without destroying the tree. We have to realize that the beauty of this Universe is being destroyed by our own actions.

**7. Keep the energy in your body flowing.** Nature is constantly recycling itself and it's telling us something. We can learn that we can recycle ourselves. We don't have to fade. If I'm tuning into the Creator of life with every breath I take, I'm actually staying about the same. I'm recycling my body.

Usually at night, I have a lot on my mind before I go to bed. To get rid of it, I do Shoulder Stands with about fifty Leg Lifts up and down and side to side. All day long your blood has been moving downwards with gravity so I do the opposite. It clears the brain and helps me sleep. I also massage my hands and feet to keep everything flowing.

*Nature is constantly recycling itself and it's telling us something. We don't have to fade.*

*Shoulder Stand in Montego Bay, Jamaica at 96 years old.*

*Yoga in Montego Bay, Jamaica at 96 years old. I was there with Janie and Terri (co-authors of this book) and the rest of the Kennedy family to work on editing this book.*

Yoga is an elixir for the mind, body and spirit. When I'm doing yoga, I try to immerse myself in the power within me, which in turn becomes less physical and more spiritual.

People truly can renew all aspects of themselves. Look at my life. I had seasons of turbulence and darkness. Then, I found renewal through nature and spiritual study. Even in a calamity, if I remained calm, I would find an answer and even moments of laughter. Whatever problem and seeming calamity faces you, know that the answer will be a better solution than you expected.

\*\*\*

Even if you feel you're in harmony with the spiritual of side of being, life won't always turn out the way you want it to but you have to move on and live. When I divorced my first husband Yvan, I was so heartbroken. My dear friend Marlene Dietrich told me to let it go and "close the book."

Life is funny. At one point, I got a call from a man in the Rotary Club saying that a card from France had come addressed to me. It was from a woman who had apparently seen me on a television program and she wanted me to contact her. It said, "There are not many Täo's in the world. I would like to find out whether there is a link here." She left her information.

I wrote back and it was the daughter of Yvan and the woman with whom he had the affair. This was many years later and she had children. I learned from her that she was born eleven months after Yvan and I divorced. It turned out that her mother was not pregnant as she claimed but became pregnant a couple of months after they married. If she hadn't said she was pregnant, it is possible that Yvan and I may have stayed together.

Apparently, as soon as Yvan found out that she had lied, he left her. Since he could learn languages so quickly, he got a job with Air France and went to Russia leaving the woman and the baby in Uruguay. At some point, he died and was buried back in France.

The daughter never knew her father, and her mother would never talk about him. This young lady contacted me because she wanted to know her background. I understood her need to know and got together many of the photographs I had left of Yvan and sent them to her.

I never saw Yvan after we divorced but he has always remained in my heart. That's the power of love.

Disappointments can make you bitter. Instead of dwelling on them, I learned to close the book and move on. The way to have no regrets is to take action. Don't dwell on the past. Close the book on disappointments. By not dwelling on what could have been, you can live a present, hopeful life.

> *Close the book on disappointments. By not dwelling on what could have been, you can live a present, hopeful life.*

\*\*\*

When my uncle retired in his 80s, he decided to finish his years in meditation in a remote part of the Himalayas. Everyone has his or her own energy and path. I don't believe in age. Instead of slowing down, I seem to be busier than ever. It's a feeling of knowing that there's so much to do in this world and so little time to do it. I'm still learning and growing. I'm always preparing for my next dance.

This is why Vinyasa in yoga is not just linking up physical movements, but it is also linking up from within—from our Life Force that is the Creator. Even when I pass on, Spirit never dies. My body will go back to the earth, it's made of the earth. Spirit is within me, around me and through me. It will just go on. All I need to know is that I lived in Truth and that can be helpful while I'm here.

There are so many billions of stars up there in the Universe. You can't tell me that our tiny little planet is the only place with life on it. It doesn't seem right. It's all a part of the Eternal Energy. I think we keep going on in another form—cycling and cycling. I just have a feeling that this is not the end of it. It may be the end of this world but it's not the end of what is life. It may sound crazy to some.

This I believe. Not just in words but in my actions in facing a new dawn. I am OM—One without a second with the whole planet within this Universe. I think I've always had this feeling from when I was a little girl in Darjeeling looking up at the stars. Sister Ignatius said, "It's T for Truth, T for Travel and T for Täo, and you'll be doing it all! You're going to be doing everything you want to do in life."

I've experienced so much, yet I'm just as inquisitive as I was when I was young. I was teaching a charming class in Manhattan run by Karate Sensei John Mirrione. The children were from three to five and six to twelve years old. As I sat on the floor surrounded by twenty-four of these young spirits, they wanted to know if they could ask me some things. They asked me a load of questions but the one I shall cherish all of my life made this an incredible souvenir.

A little six-year-old girl suddenly asked in a very serious tone, "Täo, what are you going to do when you retire?"

I replied, "I'm not going to retire."

With resistance she said, "But what are you going to do?"

"I'm going to dance my way to the next planet!"

"Oh, goodie!" she said enthusiastically. "That's great! We've put a man on the moon and maybe we can go to the stars." Still completely serious, she added, "So when I'm your age, I will be able to find you!"

This beautiful soul of a child showed me she was already opening the door to the wonder of life just as I did when I was her age. So you see, the cycle continues like a river flowing into the ocean of Cosmic Consciousness with everything on this earth.

THAT I AM...
*Neti neti*... you are "Neither this, Nor That," but
ONE with the whole Universe.
All the answers are there
As you go through the sacred Dance of Life,
Not the judgment lived by others,
But the deep richness of Truth,
Let us know and explore the Eternal Energy,
ONE WITHOUT A SECOND.

Stay curious and remember...
There is nothing you cannot do if you harness the power within,
For you are not the doer, you are the instrument!

YOU ARE THE LIGHT AND THE TRUTH.
YOU ARE ONE WITH ALL THAT IS.

It's a beautiful day, isn't it?

*This poem, I still know by heart, expresses my philosophy so beautifully—that you can go through rivers and depths of problems in your life slipping between the ridges but can always come up again. Like the brook, Spirit continues to flow....*

I come from haunts of coot and hern,
I make a sudden sally,
And sparkle out among the fern,
To bicker down a valley.

By thirty hills I hurry down,
Or slip between the ridges,
By twenty thorps, a little town,
And half a hundred bridges.

Till last by Philip's farm I flow
To join the brimming river,
For men may come and men may go,
But I go on forever.

I chatter over stony ways,
In little sharps and trebles,
I bubble into eddying bays,
I babble on the pebbles.

With many a curve my banks I fret
by many a field and fallow,
And many a fairy foreland set
With willow-weed and mallow.

I chatter, chatter, as I flow
To join the brimming river,
For men may come and men may go,
But I go on forever.

'

I wind about, and in and out,
with here a blossom sailing,
And here and there a lusty trout,
And here and there a grayling,

And here and there a foamy flake
Upon me, as I travel
With many a silver water-break
Above the golden gravel,

And draw them all along, and flow
To join the brimming river,
For men may come and men may go,
But I go on forever.

I steal by lawns and grassy plots,
I slide by hazel covers;
I move the sweet forget-me-nots
That grow for happy lovers.

I slip, I slide, I gloom, I glance,
Among my skimming swallows;
I make the netted sunbeam dance
Against my sandy shallows.

I murmur under moon and stars
In brambly wildernesses;
I linger by my shingly bars;
I loiter round my cresses;

And out again I curve and flow
To join the brimming river,
For men may come and men may go,
But I go on forever.

—Alfred, Lord Tennyson
*The Brook*

# PHOTO ALBUM

My life is very rich with experiences and people.
I thank all who have traveled with me on this path
and those who continue to teach me and bring me great joy.
You are all my family. May peace be unto you and all living things.

*With Robert Sturman. From the first time we met in the Spring of 2012, Robert has taken beautiful pictures of me including the red dress photo on the cover of this book.*

*With fitness trainer Jeannette Jenkins, acclaimed actress and fitness pioneer Jane Fonda and yoga teacher Tara Stiles. Tara and I filmed a yoga program together.*

*With Valerie Romanoff, a wonderful composer and musician who wrote special music for my "Reflections: The Yogic Journey of Life" CD. Jesse Kalu is playing the flute. We were together in 1995 for the Yoga for Peace International Conference in Israel.*

*With fabulous singer-songwriter John Guth. We did a CD together called "The Rhythm of Stillness." It offers guided meditations and relaxation. He plays the Hang, a very special instrument that looks a bit like a steel drum and has a very ethereal sound.*

## Yoga Alliance
is pleased to pay tribute to the lifetime achievement of
## Tao Porchon-Lynch, E-RYT 500

An Elder in the American Yoga Community,
as she celebrates her 90th birthday

Founder of the Westchester Institute of Yoga and one of the first
women to study under Indian master B.K.S. Iyengar,
Tao is the living embodiment of one of her favorite sayings,

*"There is nothing we cannot do if we harness the power within us."*

An accomplished ballroom dancer and former actress and model,
Tao has trained and certified hundreds of yoga instructors in the United States.

*Jai! Victory to the light in you Tao!*

August 16, 2008

R. Mark Davis
President & CEO
Yoga Alliance

Dr. Terri Kennedy, Ph. D
Chair of the Board
Yoga Alliance

*A tribute from Yoga Alliance presented to me at my 90th birthday event on August 16, 2008 by Terri Kennedy (below)—my dear student and co-author of this book. She is an Integral Yoga Teacher and was Chair of the Board of Yoga Alliance at that time.*

*Right: With Swami Ramananda of Integral Yoga Institute where I've taught many times. He is a senior disciple of Sri Swami Satchidananda, the founder of Integral Yoga.*

*I received an honor from Camus Cognac in France, May 2009.*

*Guinness World Records named me "Oldest Yoga Teacher" in May 2012. Thank you to Joyce Pines, Sherri Holman and Karen Young for nominating me. So many came out to celebrate. I received a Proclamation from the City of White Plains. It was quite an honor.*

*Yoga Journal Conference in May 2012. I saw many dear friends such as David Swenson, Rodney Yee and Colleen Saidman Yee. They are all such beautiful yoga teachers.*

*With John P. Mirrione, Founder of Harmony by Karate, and his class after I taught a workshop in New York. I serve on the Board of his National Stop Bullying Campaign.*

*Above Left: May 8, 2014. TEDx talk I gave hosted by Columbia University School of International and Public Affairs (SIPA). Above Right: August 4, 2013. Speaking about Swami Vivekananda at the 14th Annual Heritage of India Festival in Westchester, NY on the 150th Anniversary of Vivekananda's birth.*

*I was delighted by the illustration by New York artist/cartoonist, Connie Sun.*

*July 2014 at the Nantucket Yoga Festival, co-founded by Joann and Ted Burnham.*

*Left: With Duilia Mora after teaching yoga at the Pentagon.*
*Right: Teaching at Kripalu Center for Yoga & Health in Stockbridge, Massachusetts.*

At the American Heart Association Go Red Luncheon in New York on March 3, 2015 with Terri Kennedy, Dr. Suzanne Steinbaum, Dr. Icilma Fergus, Agapi Stassinopoulos and MaryAnn Browning.

I received a Special Tribute Award from the Women's Research and Education Fund at the 31st Annual Women's Hall of Fame Awards and Scholarship Luncheon on March 27, 2015 in Tarrytown, New York. Carolyn Glickstein (bottom right) nominated me and presented the award.

*I spoke at the JCC Mid-Westchester in Scarsdale, New York on April 27, 2015.*

*Talk at Wainwright House in Rye, New York on June 18, 2015.*

*Yoga workshop at the Integral Yoga Institute in New York City on June 27, 2015.*

*Top Left: At the Iowa Yoga Festival with longtime student and teacher Susan Douglass. Top Right: At the Global Mala Yoga event in New Jersey. Bottom Left: With Cyndi Weis and her daughters Carly and Abby of Breathe Yoga. Right: With musician Matt Venuti.*

*At the home of Arun Gandhi, Mahatma Gandhi's grandson, in July 2015. This was one of the most special experiences in my recent years. He was instantly like family. We exchanged memories and insights from his grandfather's teachings that have influenced both of us profoundly. There are very few people I can talk with who have this shared perspective.*

*Left: With Gurmukh Kaur Khalsa, co-founder/director of Golden Bridge Yoga Center in Los Angeles. Right: With Louise Hay, founder of Hay House.*

*Preparing to lead a meditation in Times Square for the summer solstice.*

*With Suzanne Roberts, TV host and philanthropist.*   *Eu-nah Lee after filming Tao in Jamaica.*

Left: With professional boxer Laila Ali, daughter of boxing legend Muhammad Ali.
Right: With Traditional Healer Doña Leova and yoga teacher Robert Carris.

Filming a yoga program with Suzanne Jackson and her daughter Rebecca Jackson (on the right) who was Miss Delaware 2013.

*Students from the class I teach at the Jewish Community Center (JCC) Mid-Westchester in Scarsdale. I've taught there since the early 1980s.*

*Some of my regular students at the Fred Astaire Dance Studio in Hartsdale.*

*I've taught at the Hudson Medical Center for a number of years. It's been a delight to bring yoga into that environment.*

*Class at Athleta in Scarsdale. I was named an Athleta Sponsored Athlete in 2013.*

*I've taught yoga at the University of Delaware a few times. It's usually a very big group. This is from May 2015. We split the photo in two parts to get as many students in as possible. Their Yoga Club has over 800 members.*

*Terri Kennedy hosted me in Harlem for the first time on November 5, 2011. It was at The Dwyer Cultural Center. In 2002, Terri founded the Ta Yoga House, the first yoga studio in Harlem.*

*A yoga workshop in Harlem at the Urban Yoga Foundation founded by Ghylian Bell.*

*My most recent yoga retreat to India with my students in January 2014.*

*Recent trips to Jamaica in December 2014 and May 2015. There is such warmth in the community there and beautiful yoga being practiced.*

*Having fun "flying" in AcroYoga with Chris Loebsack and Brian Davis.*

*Women's Wellness & Yoga Class at Converse College, the first college class to study this book as part of their course thanks to Professor and Iynegar Yoga Teacher Janet LeFrancois.*

## How do you craft an amazing life?

*My life is more full and fulfilled now than it's ever been. Instead of slowing down, it feels like it's speeding up with a host of delightful experiences and people.*

Discover what you love and do it...

*I spend my time teaching yoga, dancing, traveling the world, enjoying good wine and learning from all who cross my path.*

# DANCING LIGHT | 449

Gather with friends as often as you can...

*I spend special occasions and holidays with friends such as Joyce Pines, Baiju Mehta, Susan Douglass and Ron Tvert. All these people, and their families, are my family.*

## Celebrate milestones and achievements...

*Every year I have a big birthday bash. We eat, have fun and dance! We often have it at the Taj Palace Indian Restaurant in White Plains. The owners are like family.*

# DANCING LIGHT | 453

## Give and receive lots of hugs...

*Hugs are a wonderful way to exchange positive energy.*

## Give back and nurture the next generation...

*I was delighted that Joanna and Mike Rajendran named their precious daughter Natasha Tao (above left) after me. It's important to nurture the innate curiosity in young people.*

DANCING LIGHT | 457

## Remember, you can make the sun come out...

*Smile and don't give into negativity. You can choose to see the good and make good things happen in your life.*

# DANCING LIGHT | 459

Thank you to my collaborators on this book!

*I consider all of the Kennedys—Janie, Terri, James, Sheila and Daniel—my family.*

# Author Bios

This book focuses on storytelling using Täo's own voice based on over 75 hours of interviews conducted by a mother-daughter writing team.

**Janie Sykes Kennedy** is a 45-year veteran of international relations, media and culture, and an early advocate of integrative health. Having studied writing at the New School for Social Research in the late 1950s under Don Wolf, she always found a way to keep writing in her life. She used her background in business and the arts to undergird her spiritual search that led her to found a school called "Inner Dignity" focusing on building self-esteem in inner city girls. With a BA degree from Howard University in Economics and Accounting, she stayed close to the arts by running an art gallery in New York City in the late 1950s—about the same time she and her late husband, Dr. James Scott Kennedy, operated one of the first multicultural theatre companies in New York. They worked as a team on many international assignments. She has worked in the U.S., Africa, Australia, Europe, Asia and the Middle East. Later she received a MS degree from the Graduate School of Journalism—Columbia University where she also studied with Samson Raphaelson who wrote *The Jazz Singer*, the first talking movie. World highlights include: The First World Festival of Negro Arts in Dakar Senegal (1966); University of Ghana for nearly three years; the First Pan African Cultural Festival in Algiers, Algeria (1968); invited to introduce "new concepts of people—African American and African"—to the continent of Australia (1973-1974); produced plays for the Papua, New Guinea Independence Arts Festival; invited by HUD and the U.S. Department of Commerce as one of 14 delegates to go on the first-ever trade mission of American women to the Peoples Republic of China in 1987; invited by the President of Senegal to participate in the Third World Festival of Black Arts & Culture in Dakar, Senegal (2010) and spoke to thousands before an Akon concert. Throughout the years, she has continued to write including the *Excel* series with over one million in print. For more, go to www.janieskennedy.com.

*Täo and Janie*

*Täo and Terri*

**Teresa Kay-Aba Kennedy** began writing little books when she was three years old and never really stopped. Born in Africa, she started school in Australia and studied design in Italy giving her an unusual introduction to the world. She has blended her spiritual and creative soul with the full spectrum of training and life experiences. A Harvard-trained strategist, she has over 25 years of experience as an executive, entrepreneur, academic, writer, producer and yoga teacher. As President of Power Living Enterprises, Inc., she focuses on inspiring minds and empowering success through media (print, video, audio), training and events. A Certified Professional Coach, she has led programs for hundreds of organizations and coached thousands of client-hours, including teaching yoga to executives on the Great Wall of China. She is also creator of "The Gandhi Effect®" which teaches tools for personal transformation and social change. She started her career as a Research Associate at Harvard Business School, and founded VH1 Interactive and VH1@Work radio. As VP of Business Development & Operations for MTV Networks, she managed a 200-person operation, negotiated landmark deals, managed partnerships, and helped launch six digital cable channels. She also was Creative Consultant to Universal Studios, working with the legendary Lew Wasserman. Inspired by her mother, she started yoga at four years old. Her primary professional training is from the Integral Yoga Institute, Täo Porchon-Lynch and Sri Dharma Mittra. In 2002, she founded the Ta Yoga House, the first yoga studio in Harlem, and also served six years on the Board of Yoga Alliance, including Chair of the Board. A sought-after moderator and speaker, she is a National Spokesperson for the American Heart Association. In 2009, she was named a World Economic Forum Young Global Leader and has been a discussion leader for the Annual Meeting in Davos, Switzerland. She has a dual BA in Sociology and Studio Art from Wellesley College, an MBA from Harvard, a Ph.D. in World Religions and Executive Education in Global Leadership & Public Policy. She has been featured in various media from CNN and the cover of *Yoga Journal* to Oprah's book *Live Your Best Life!* For more, go to www.terrik.tv.

# Glossary & Notes

Below are terms used in the text that may not be familiar to the general reader. Most of the words are Sanskrit and some Hindi.

**abhyasa**—spiritual practice that is regular and consistent over a long period of time; in the *Yoga Sutras* and *Bhagavad Gita*, it is one of the essential ways to control the mind
**agni**—digestive fire; a concept used in Ayurveda related to our ability to process all aspects of life from food to experiences
**ahimsa**—nonviolence towards all living things in our thought, words and actions
**Ardha Chandrasana**—Half Moon posture
**asanas**—body postures, physical practice of Hatha Yoga; the third limb of Ashtanga Yoga
**Ashtanga Yoga**—the Yoga of eight limbs, also known as Raja Yoga
**avidya**—ignorance of the identity of oneself, delusion or lack of self-knowledge which leads to ego consciousness
**ayah**—nursemaid
**Ayurveda**—Indian system of medicine
**Bhagavad Gita**—sacred Hindu text in 700 verses; a portion of the Sanskrit epic Mahabharata in the form of a dialogue between the hero Arjuna and his charioteer, the avatar Krishna
**bharatanatyam**—a classical Indian dance that combines graceful and dramatic movements, including those of the hands and eyes
**citta**—mind or consciousness
**dharana**—concentration and cultivating inner perceptual awareness; the sixth of the eight limbs of Asthanga Yoga
**dharma**—essential duty or path, destiny, work, natural role to play in life
**dhoti**—garment or loincloth worn by male Hindus, consisting of a piece of material tied around the waist
**dhyana**—meditation on the Divine; the seventh of the eight limbs of Ashtanga Yoga
**drishti**—focused gaze, a way to develop concentration; relates to pratyahara, the fifth limb of Ashtanta Yoga and dharana, the sixth limb
**darsana**—auspicious sight, perception of ultimate Truth
**fakir**—a religious ascetic or holy person who lives solely on alms, or money and food given to poor people; also one who performs feats of magic
**Ganesh**—remover of obstacles and provider of prosperity and good fortune of both material and spiritual kinds
**gunas**—one of the three interdependent qualities of prakriti which includes sattva, rajas and tamas
**guru**—spiritual teacher, imparter of knowledge and remover of the darkness of ignorance
**Hatha Yoga**—a system of physical postures and breathing control
**Hatha Yoga Pradipika**—classic Sanskrit manual on Hatha Yoga written around the 15th century CE by Swami Svatmarama, a disciple of Swami Gorakhnath
**jai**—victory
**jivatman**—individual soul
**jnana**—knowledge or higher wisdom
**kundalini**—latent primal energy believed to be stored at the base of the spine
**namaskar**—to bow to; to adore
**neti neti**—not this, not that; the method of Vedic analysis of negation and inquiry
**niyama**—positive duties or observances; the second of the eight limbs of Asthanga Yoga
**OM**—the first sound of the Universe, containing all other sounds, words and languages
**prakriti**—the prime material energy of which all matter is composed as recognized in Vedanta, the nature of intelligence by which the Universe exists
**prana**—vital energy or Life Force
**pranayama**—breathing exercises and control of prana or the vital energy; the fourth of the eight limbs of Ashtanga Yoga

**pratyahara**—Sensory control and withdrawal; the fifth limb of Ashtanga Yoga
**Raja Yoga**—the royal path of Yoga intended to achieve control over the mind and emotions
**rajas**—the element of prakriti associated with activity, energy and passion
**samadhi**—superconsciousness or union with the Divine; the eighth and final limb of Ashtanga Yoga
**sangha**—a community; referring to the monastic life as well as lay spiritual seekers
**sattva**—luminosity or quality of light, the element of prakriti associated with purity; one of the three gunas
**satya**—Absolute Truth, that which is unchangeable, being truthful in one's thought, words and actions; one of the five Yamas
**satyagraha**—passive political resistance practiced by Mahatma Gandhi; it translates loosely as "insistence on truth"
**seva**—selfless service, work performed without any thought of reward
**Surya Namaskar**—Sun Salutation (sequence of yoga postures)
**svadhyaya**—introspection and self-study; one of the five Niyamas
**tamas**—the element of prakriti associated with ignorance, lethargy and darkness
**Upanishads**—a series of Hindu sacred treatises written in Sanskrit elaborating on the Vedas written probably between c. 800 BCE and c. 500 BCE
**Vedas**—the most ancient Hindu scriptures
**Vedanta**—Hindu philosophy based on the ancient Upanishads; it teaches to transcend the limitations of self-identify and realize one's unity with Brahman, or the ultimate divine reality
**vidya**—right knowledge or clarity
**Vinyasa**—linking and union of breath and movements
**Virabhadrasana II**—Warrior II (yoga pose)
**vritti**—whirl-pool referring to mental fluctuations and disturbances
**yama**—self-control or restraint whether on a bodily or psychic level; the first of the eight limbs of Ashtanga Yoga
**Yoga**—union of the individual with the Absolute
**Yoga Sutras of Patanjali**—196 Indian sutras compiled around 400 CE by Patanjali; one of the core texts on Yoga
**yug (yuj)**—state of union, to join or unite

## NOTES:

The following texts were referenced and/or cited:

xvi, 25. *The Yoga Sutras of Patanjali* (ancient text).

xviii, 263. *Autobiography of a Yogi*, Paramahansa Yogananda.

27. *Raja Yoga*, Swami Vivekananda.

27. "Swami Vivekananda Parliament Addresses," www.ramakrishna.org.

27, 218, 221, 283-284. *Bhagavad Gita* (ancient text).

28, 371. *Thoughts and Aphorisms*, Sri Aurobindo.

260-268, 275-277. *A Pictorial Half Century In The Life of A White Yogi*, Dr. Roman Ostoja.

269. *The Upanishads* (ancient text).

283-284. *Les Rêves*, Helena Petrovna Blatvatsky.

371. *Gandhi: An Autobiography-The Story of My Experiments With Truth*, Mohandas Gandhi.

362, 377. *Hatha Yoga Pradipika* (ancient text), Swami Svatmarama.

# Index

**A**

abhayasa (spiritual practice) 283
Academy Awards 228, 284
Africa 14-15, 41, 43, 52-54, 149, 193, 292, 300-301, 315, 361, 372, 401, 461-462
    Abyssinia (Ethiopia) 15
    Addis Ababa 15
    French Somaliland 15, 40, 43, 399
    Massawa 15
    Morocco 52, 165, 313, 378, 390
agni (digestive fire) 49
ahimsa (nonviolence) 30, 195-196
Ahuja, Vimal 340
Air France 173-174, 211, 271-272, 421
alcohol *See also* wine
    Calvados 62, 179, 180
    Pimm's 96
Alfassa, Mirra *See* The Mother
Ali, Laila 438
Allen, Rex 263
Allen, Suzanne 204, 211, 263
Aman, Zeenat v, xiv, 407-408
American Heart Association 434
American National Films 309
American Wine Society xviii, xx, 342, 381
*America's Got Talent* (TV show) xv, 401, 406
Anderson, William Hepworth 212
Andhra Mahila Sabha (school) 35
*A Pictorial Half Century In The Life of A White Yogi* (book) 275
Ardha Chandrasana (yoga pose) 128
asana (postures) 298, 355, 371-372, 377
Astaire, Adele *See* Lady Cavendish
Astaire, Fred 207
astrology 9, 372, 374, 376, 384
Athleta (clothing) 440
Aurobindo, Sri xix, 24, 27-29, 34, 228-229, 272, 279, 351, 371, 374, 376
Aurobindoville (Auroville) 29
*Autobiography of a Yogi* (book) xviii, 262
avidya (ignorance) 24, 409
awakening xvii, 330
awareness iii, xvi, 410
    Pure Awareness 235, 252
Ayah 9-10, 15-17, 21, 42-43, 45-46, 52-53, 55, 59-60, 62-64, 66-78, 84, 258, 300

Ayurveda 393

**B**

Bach, Walter 210
Backus, Jim 203, 246, 401
Bacon, Lloyd 276
Bad Gastein 157
Bakersfield 1952 Earthquake 239
Balasanyan, Hayk 401, 405
Bali 355, 378, 390
Banks, Polan 194, 201, 204
Bao Lin School 296
Baptista, Clement 33, 206, 304, 339, 340-341, 355
Barrett, Frances *See* Frances Hammer
Barrymore, John 276
Barrymore, Lionel 203
Barrymore Estate 204-205
Baruch, Amelie 195
Baruch, Bernard 195
Battle of Dien Bien Phu 255
Bérard, Christian (Bébé) 163-164, 227
Behrhor 294
Belafonte, Harry 344
Bell, Ghylian 442
Berkeley Hotel 101
Bermuda 334, 358
Berndt, Eric 209
Berndt, Ginny xxi, 208-210, 212, 221, 223, 228, 230, 357
Bertrand, Raoul (French Consul General) 200-201, 215, 271, 273
*Beverage Communicator* (newspaper) xx, 325, 327-328
Beverly Hills Hotel 205, 210, 212, 221, 271
*Bhagavad Gita* (book) xx, 27, 218, 221, 282-283
bharatanatyam (Indian dance) 79, 213, 399
Bhavagarty, Mr. 280, 315
Biggin Hill 129, 140-141
Billimoria, Amy 407-408
Bilozorov, Anton 403
Birch, Beryl Bender iv, xiv, xxi, 361
Blavatsky, Helena Petrovna 282-283
Blitz (bombing) xv, 86-87, 90, 92, 95, 98, 101-102, 109, 129, 401

Booker, Cory  413
Boots Cash Chemist  90
Borrego Hot Springs  234-235
Boy Scouts  241
breath (pranayama) iv, xv, xvi, 4-5, 8, 18, 49, 53, 65, 70, 83-84, 87, 89, 96, 98, 109, 119, 121, 144-145, 150, 157, 193, 218, 221, 225, 227, 240, 275, 279, 330-331, 352, 355, 363, 369, 377, 401, 412, 414-415, 419
Breathe Yoga (yoga center)  436
Brighter London (Darker London)  95, 97
British Expeditionary Forces  77
Brom, John  307, 313
Browning, MaryAnn  434
Brown, Joe E.  205
Bucharest (Romania)  390
Budapest (Hungary)  390
burial demonstrations  274
Burma (Myanmar)  15, 255, 258
Burman, Ben Lucien  306-307, 361
Burnham, Joann and Ted  433

## C

Caesar's Palace  358
Cambridge University  43, 366
Canada  4-5, 271, 324, 327, 329
    Beaconsfield  327
    Saskatchewan  4-5
Canada House  72-73, 75-78, 82-83, 93, 128
canyons (Bryce, Grand, Zion)  231-233
*Caravans* (film)  309
CARE  341
Carlton Gardens  110-112, 126
Carnegie Hall  276, 296
*Carnival Story* (film)  308
Caron, Leslie  203, 230
Carris, Robert  438
Cavendish, Lady (Adele Astaire)  96-97, 207
Cavendish, Lord Charles  97
Center for International Dialogue  viii, 387-388
Chanel, Coco  xxi, 160-162, 268
Charing Cross Hospital  87
Charisse, Cyd  208
Charity Players  xxi, 208, 210-212, 221, 258, 283-284
Chase, Edna Woolman  183
Chase, Ilka  183, 186, 190-191, 195, 401
Château Haut-Brion  395
China  14-15, 133, 272, 296-297, 301, 341, 358
*Chinese Follies* (performance)  122-123
chocolate  79, 399, 417
Chopra, Dr. Deepak  iii, xiv, xxi, 413
Churchill, Winston  50, 129
Cinerama  312-313
Ciné Universal  338
clarity  250, 330, 348
Clinton, Hillary  355
Corcoran, Robert J.  212
Cocteau, Jean  171
Cold War  196
Colonial British  xxi, 27, 33, 197, 204
Columbia Studios  215-216
Columbia University  276, 432
Communism  197, 243-244
compassion  iv, xvi, 9, 332
consciousness  xvii, 24, 49, 260, 268, 409, 412, 423
Consulate General of France  *See* Raoul Bertrand
Converse College  xiv, 445
Copacabana  82, 95, 102
Cornell University  326, 343
cosmic harmony  275, 331
Cosmic Intelligence (Cosmic Consciousness)  xii, 258, 274, 279, 423
Covent Gardens  76, 78
Coward, Noël  xviii, xxi, 100-101, 151, 228, 289
Crawford, Joan  202, 207
Creator  257, 330, 419, 422  *See also* God
cricket  41, 43, 348
Crosby, Bing  159-160, 214, 289
Cross of Lorraine  110-111
Cummings, Jack  185, 195, 201-202, 207, 252
Curley, Mayor James Michael  186
Czechoslovak Republic  40

## D

Dahl, Arlene  207, 245, 248
Dalai Lama, the 14th  xiii, xxi, 295, 412-413
dance  iv, v, x, xv, xvi, xxii, 11-12, 24, 80-81, 87, 90, 104, 122, 124-125, 129, 144, 149, 152, 154, 193, 199, 207, 211, 221, 224, 241, 246-247, 252, 256, 278, 303, 397-399, 401-404, 407, 410, 416, 422-423, 425, 452
Dance of Life  xv, xvii, xxii, 19, 423
Darjeeling Himalayan Railway  19-20
Darker London  *See* Brighter London

*Darling, Je Vous Aime Beaucoup* (song) 242, 292
darsana 347
Darshan, Shiv 407-408
Davis, Joan 246, 275
Davis, Sammy Jr. 214
D-Day xv, 145-147, 149, 181, 466
*Deep Purple* (song) 307
de Gaulle, General Charles xx, 57-58, 94, 110, 127, 129-130, 134-135, 144, 146-148, 165, 286, 379
Desert Inn 242, 264
Deshmukh, Durgabai 35
Desikachar, T.K.V. 298, 387
Devi, Indra xx, 228-229, 298, 351, 358, 387, 409
dharma 3
dhoti 29, 35
Dietrich, Marlene xvi, xxi, 100-101, 151, 159-161, 166, 228, 236-237, 243-244, 259, 289, 370, 421
DiMaggio, Joe 253
Dior, Christian 161, 163, 182, 243
disappointments xv, 422
discrimination 36, 217, 346
Dix, Tom 239
dogs 46, 116, 118, 121, 205, 329, 335, 354, 369
dolphins 369
Dorchester Hotel 287-288
Douglass, Susan viii, xiv, 436, 450, 467
Dover 50, 72-73, 86, 103-105, 109, 114, 124-125, 133, 151-152
Doyle, Jack 107
Doyle, Michael 107
drishti (gaze) 109
*Dr. Knock* (play) 181, 185
Duchess of Gloucester 112
Dunham, Katherine 193, 401
Dunkirk 50, 73, 77, 83, 103
Dwyer Cultural Center 442

**E**

*East of Eden* (play) 245
Ebadi, Shirin xxi, 412
Ebenezer Baptist Church 344
Edington-Cloutman Agency 249
Einstein, Albert 276
Eisenhower, General Dwight D. 144-145, 147, 196

Elizabeth Seton College 381
Ellington, Duke 307
Elstree Studios 93, 103
energy iii, iv, xiii, xvii, xxii, 2, 8, 10-11, 13, 15, 20, 23, 49, 62-63, 73, 76, 85, 98, 103, 109, 125, 128, 136, 138, 142, 149-150, 171, 173, 192, 195, 221, 233, 239, 257, 278, 302-303, 315, 348, 352, 356, 362, 365, 369, 377, 379-380, 386, 399, 401-402, 410-411, 414-418, 422-423, 454
energy vortex 410
English Channel xv, 4, 50-51, 59, 61, 70, 125, 129, 135, 141, 145, 147-148, 181
enlightenment xix, xxi, 3, 25, 392, 415
equality 36, 309-310, 344, 346, 356, 369, 371
Essex House 336
European Health Spa 351

**F**

*Face of India* (film) 339
*Face of the Sahara* (film) 338
Fair Deal 197
fakir 29, 260
Farmer's Market (famous market in Los Angeles) 215, 251
Faubourg St. Honore 183
fear xvi, xx, 7, 48, 51-53, 56, 59, 66-67, 70, 74, 77, 87, 95-97, 103, 105, 108, 117-118, 127, 133, 140, 145, 147, 296, 323, 394, 415
Feld, Irving 307-308
Fergus, Ilcima 434
Ferraday, Lisa 203
Findlay Vinyards 329, 343, 467
Finger Lakes xviii, 326, 343
Fisher, Bishop Frederick Bohn 296
Fisher, Welthy xx, 35, 284, 296, 298, 300, 340-341, 358, 360, 373
Folan, Lilias 361
Fonda, Jane 427
Fonteyn, Margot 99
Ford Foundation 341
*For Whom The Bells Toll* (book) 171
Fournier, Charles 326
Fournier, Dominique 166-168, 236
France ix, xv, xx, 4, 10, 18, 37, 40-42, 44-45, 50-52, 56-60, 74, 77, 79, 81, 103, 108, 111, 114, 119, 122, 126, 129-136, 138-141, 143-144, 146-151, 155, 160-161, 165-174, 178, 181, 183, 186-187, 189, 191-194, 200-202, 207, 209, 211, 219-220, 222-224, 228, 236-

237, 241, 243-244, 248, 265, 268, 271-274, 278, 280, 283, 286-287, 291, 300-303, 306-307, 315, 323, 325-326, 350, 364-365, 370, 374, 379-381, 390, 394-395, 399, 421, 430
    Cap d'Antibes 46-47, 54, 167, 189-190
    Carpentras 46
    Châteauneuf-du-Pape 46
    Dordogne 56, 381
    Juan-les-Pins 166-167, 190, 227, 381
    Loire Valley 169
    Marseille 45, 47, 52-55, 59, 96, 136
    Montpellier 47, 54, 381
    Rhône Valley xx, 42, 46, 112, 114, 272-273, 324
    Saint-Jean-de-Luz 59, 114, 116, 149
Francis Joseph University 261
Frank, Dr. Konstantin xviii, 342-343
Fred Astaire Dance Studio 97, 397-406, 439
freedom xx, 10, 14, 19, 27, 30, 34, 36-37, 39, 52, 67, 117, 178, 243, 309, 320, 340, 344-346, 378
Free French 56-57, 94, 110-111, 131, 134, 136, 146, 148, 159, 169-170, 226
French Can-Can (performance) 122
French Far East Expeditionary Corps 255
French Indochina 15
French Resistance (underground) 4, 52, 54-59, 86, 92, 103, 113-117, 119-120, 122, 125, 127, 140, 151, 156, 169, 178-179, 286, 320
*French Without Tears* (performance) 94, 100
Fresnay, Pierre 152
friendship xx, 201, 231, 272, 365-366, 368

### G

Gabin, Jean 159, 166, 236
Gable, Clark 112, 203, 204
Gabor, Eva 278
Gandhi, Arun 436
Gandhi, Indira 360, 467
Gandhi, Mohandas (Mahatma) xv, xvi, xx, 24, 27, 30, 32-39, 41, 50, 108, 117, 127, 170, 178, 201, 194-195, 197, 205, 279, 284, 294-296, 309-310, 340, 344-346, 356, 360, 367, 371, 373, 390, 392, 409, 412, 414
Ganesh 47
Ava Gardner 202-203, 216
gaze (dristi) 109
Krupa, Gene 112, 148

Girl Scouts 209
Girl with the Longest Legs (contest) 166-167, 208, 227, 237, 248
Glazunov, Alexander 276
Glickstein, Carolyn 434
Global Mala (event) 436
Goblin Valley 233-234
God 8, 22, 26, 32, 46, 217-218, 245, 357
    Divine xvii, xxi, xxii, 13, 25, 28, 142, 262-263, 411, 414
    Great One 13, 19
    Infinite xix, 127, 259, 274, 409
    Lord of Creation 411
    Universal Soul or Reality 283, 377
Goddard, Paulette 159, 276
Golden Age of India 3
Golden Bridge Yoga Center 437
Grand Canyon 233 *See also* canyons
Grayson, Kathryn 203, 230, 241
Greene, Richard 245
Grappelli, Stephane 112
Greyhound bus 195-196, 200
Guimas xxi, 94, 99-100, 110, 129, 146-147, 151, 227, 237-238, 289, 378-379
Guinness World Records xxii
guru 24, 38, 219, 260-261, 298, 302, 352, 356, 412
Guth, John 428

### H

Hagen, Jean 248
*Half a Hero* (TV show) 247-248
Hall, Francis de Salva 76
Halstead, William (Bill) 284-287, 290, 292-294, 296, 303, 306, 313
Hamilton House 99, 129, 134
Lady Hamilton 99
Hammer, Armand 210
Hammer, Frances (Tolman) xxi, 209-210
Hang (instrumen) 428
Harlem xiii, 442, 464
harmony v, xvii, xxii, 21, 28, 128, 219, 275, 331
Harmony by Karate (school) 431
Harriet Hubbard Ayer 183
Harriman, Averill 276
Hartsdale 311, 319-322, 329, 332-333, 342, 346, 348, 350, 353, 397-398, 439
Harvard University 261
Harwood, Donald E. 212

*Hatha Yoga Pradipika* (book) 362, 377
Havana Club 81
*Hawaii* (film) 309, 352
*Hawaii Five-O* (TV show) 352
Hay House 437
Hay, Louise 437
Hayworth, Rita 175-176
Heard, Gerald xxi, 250
Helpmann, Sir Robert (Bobby) 99-100, 151, 208
Hemingway, Ernest xxi, 169, 171, 216, 326-327
*High Water Catfish Bend* (book) 306
*Highway Patrol* (TV show) 263-264
Himalayas 21, 260, 303, 355, 373, 422
Hinduism 20, 26-27, 282
Hitler, Adolf 40, 52, 54, 86, 306
Holland 50, 150, 165, 325, 330
Holleman, Dona 299
Hollywood xv, xvii, xxi, 37, 93, 97, 159, 185-186, 195, 199, 200-204, 207-220, 223, 226, 228-231, 233, 235-236, 242-246, 249, 251-253, 256, 266, 268, 270, 277, 280-281, 283-285, 290-291, 293, 307, 320, 323, 329-330, 352, 358, 401
Holman, Sherri 430
Holy Mother (Sri Sarada Devi) 25, 28, 372
Home Wine & Beer Association 327, 366
home winemaking 324-325
Hope, Bob xviii, 160, 264, 287-289
*House of Wax* (film) 248
Hudson Medical Center 440
Hudson, Rock 214
Hulbert, Claude 94
Hunnar Films 285, 341, 352
Huxley, Aldous xxi, 250
Hyde Park 99, 129, 287, 289
hypnosis 259, 262-262, 264-265, 276
 trance 84, 221, 259-261, 265, 267, 274

# I

ignorance xvii, xi, xxi, 24, 37, 38, 195, 217, 258, 306, 340, 346, 390, 409, 415
Ile-de-France 340 Squadron 129-131, 134-136, 139-141, 148, 170, 181, 340
*Images of Israel* (performance) 156
*I Married Joan* (TV show) 246, 269, 275, 401
Incas 410
India ix, xvi, xvii, xix, 3, 5-6, 9, 10, 15, 18, 21, 26-28, 30-31, 33-37, 39, 41-44, 48, 50, 52, 59-60, 63, 66, 68-69, 71, 75-81, 85, 90-91, 93, 124, 133, 148, 160, 162, 170, 178, 194, 197-198, 200-202, 204-206, 211, 219, 230, 238, 256-257, 260-263, 272, 277, 280-282, 284-286, 292, 294-298, 300, 302-304, 308-309, 312-313, 315, 326, 334, 337, 339, 340-342, 346, 348, 351-352, 354-355, 358, 360, 363-364, 367-369, 371-373, 378-379, 387, 390, 392-393, 407, 410, 418, 432, 443
 Ahmedabad 34, 39
 Bay of Bengal 6, 17
 Bihar 3
 Calcutta 15-17, 44, 79, 93, 260-261, 399
 Cochin 410
 Darjeeling 19-21, 385, 422
 Goa 369
 Gujarat 31, 34
 Jaipur 392
 Kerala 304, 392-393, 418
 Kurla 407
 Lahore (now part of Pakistan) 31, 238
 Lucknow 297
 Mumbai 33, 369, 372-373, 392, 407
 Mysore 93, 304, 352
 Pondicherry xx, 3, 5-6, 14-15, 17-18, 24, 28-31, 37-38, 72, 125, 133, 143, 200, 218, 279, 298, 351, 363, 370, 372-374, 376-377, 382, 399
 Pune 299, 372
Indian-American dance troupe 213, 278
Indian Film Festival 340
Indochina 15, 133, 146, 255
Inner Diary xxii, 152, 191, 330, 371, 409
Institute of Infinite Science 259
Instone Trophy 366
Integral Yoga xiii, 28, 371, 429, 435, 462
intention xvii, 281, 362, 389, 414
intuition 15, 222, 230, 236, 382
Iowa Yoga Festival 436
Isherwood, Christopher xxi, 250, 357
Israel 156, 251, 384-385, 387, 428
*I Wandered Lonely As A Cloud* (poem) x
Iyengar, B.K.S. xx, 298-299, 351-352, 361, 368, 371-372, 377, 379, 387

# J

Jackson, Rebecca 438
Jackson, Suzaane 438
Jallianwala Bagh massacre 36

Jamaica xiii, 419-420, 444
JCC Mid-Westchester 435
Dessès. Jean xv, xxi, 161-162, 164-166, 175, 177, 187
Jefferson, Thomas 326
Jenkins, Jeannette 427
Jews (Jewish) xx, 44, 48, 54- 55, 119-120, 156, 178, 197, 217, 273-274, 292, 335, 390, 439
Jivatma (individual soul) 377
jnana (wisdom) 85
John Bull 273, 328, 366
Jois, K. Pattabhi xx, 298, 299, 352, 355, 361, 363, 371, 379-380 387
Jouvet, Louis 181
joy xxi, 4, 7, 12, 18, 21, 27, 66, 84, 92, 106, 108, 154, 206, 224, 226, 250, 334, 362, 372, 401-402, 416
*Jump Into Hell* (film) 255

**K**

Kaibab Forest 232
Kali 278
Kalu, Jesse 385
Karis, Mary 361
Katz, Drew 413
Kaur, Hasleen 407-408
Kaushal, Kamini 367
Kaye 128-129, 144-145, 396
Kay, Mary Ellen xxi, 263-264, 266, 289, 291, 321, 361
Kennedy, President John F. 315, 344
Kennedy, Janie Sykes vii, viii, xiii, xviii, 461
Kennedy, Robert 345
Kennedy, Teresa Kay-Aba (Terri) vii, viii, xiii, xviii, 362, 412, 413-414, 434, 442
Kestenbaum, Barbara 361
Khalsa, Gurmukh Kaur 437
King Brothers 308, 337-338
King Jr., Dr. Martin Luther xiv, xvi, 34, 205, 309-310, 343-346, 400
Klum, Heidi xv, 406
Kolnoski, Prince 168, 189-190, 237
Korda, Alexander 93
Korda, Vincent 93
Kripalu Center for Yoga & Health 433
Krishnamacharya 229, 298-299, 352, 387
kundalini 49

**L**

La Côte d'Azur de l'Est 3
Lafayette Flying Corps 96, 97
LaLanne, Jack 350-351, 371
Lamas, Fernando 248
Lancaster, Burt 203, 216
Langfeld, Herbert Sydney 261
Lanvin, Jeanne xxi, 160-161, 166, 174-175
Lanvin, Marie-Blanche 160
*La Terre est ronte* (performance) 152
Lavarre, Hélène (Foufounis) 96-97, 104
Lee, Eu-nah 437
LeFrancois, Janet xiv, 445
Leiseroff, Cecelia 349
Lenox Hill Hospital 319
Leova, Doña 438
Le Petit Club Français 110-113, 117, 134, 243
*Les Rêves* (book) 282-283
Le Tac, Joel xx, 110, 113-115, 126-127
Leurs, Pol 338
Lever Brothers 182-186, 190
Life Force (prana) xxi, 2, 13, 26, 221, 393, 414-415, 418, 422
    Eternal Energy xxii, 150, 171, 195, 423
    Light iii, xii, xvi, xvii, xviii, 340, 347, 358-359, 409, 414
Lindsay, Mayor John 345
Literacy House 35, 297, 298, 340, 341
Lockheed 271
Loebsack, Chris 444
Loge Unie Des Theosophes 282
London Underground (subway) 86, 90
longevity 410, 412
Lortel, Lucille 190, 194-195, 201, 204, 469
Lynch, William J. 264, 293, 294, 300, 304, 305, 309, 316
Lyons Corner House 78, 102, 108-109

**M**

MacArthur, James 352
Machu Picchu 410
Macy's 184
Madame Tussauds 91, 99
Maginot Line 41, 44, 50-51, 59, 77
Maharaja 94, 175, 352, 367
Maharani (dog) 354, 370, 381-382
Maharishi Maheshi Yogi xx, 276-279, 301 303, 313-315, 371, 409, 412
Malini, Hema v, xiv, 407-408

Manchester, Frederick xxi, 250
Mandel, Howie xv, 406
Manners, Todd 183
Mannix, Eddie 202
Marceau, Marcel 120
March on Washington 216, 309-310
Margaryan, Vard xv, 401, 406
Marines 104, 242, 357
Martin, Dean 205
Max Factor 248, 249
Maxim's xxi, 165, 231, 270, 290, 365-366
Mayor of Bombay 294, 367
Mayer, Louis B. 185
McCarthy, Abigail and Eugene 345
McCarthyism 216
McDougall, William 261
Medina, Patricia 248
meditation xxiii, 25, 38, 219-221, 250-251, 272, 275-279, 290, 302, 313, 330, 371, 412, 416, 422, 437
*Meet McGraw* (TV show) 269
Mehta, Baiju 450
Mel B xv, 406
mental anesthesia *See* hypnosis
Meredith, Burgess 110, 243-244
Mertens, Ed 338
Metro-Goldwyn-Mayer (MGM) xv, 167, 185, 199, 202-203, 208, 215, 229-230, 239, 241-242, 244, 245-247, 252, 256, 264, 267, 292
Michener, James A. 309
Middleton, Lance 366
Miller, Glenn 112, 148
mind control (telepathy) 259, 261-263
mindfulness xvi
Mirrione, John P. v, xiv, 423, 431
Miss Asia Pacific v, 408
Miss Delaware 438
Mission Tibesti 338
Miss Universe iv, 408
Mocambo Club 214
modeling xvii, xxi, 157, 160, 165-166, 169, 174-175, 177, 181, 187, 191-193, 201-202, 230, 268, 280, 287, 352, 401
Mondavi, Robert xx, 272-273, 326
Monroe, Marilyn 253-255
Moore, Mr. 81, 89-92
Mora, Duila 433
Morehouse College 344
Moscow (Russia) 390
Motwani (family) 294

Mouchotte, René 131
Moynet, Yvan 132-144, 146, 148-153, 155-158, 165, 168-170, 173-174, 178, 181-182, 187, 193, 212, 214, 216, 219, 221-227, 243, 304, 314, 321, 421-422
Mt. Kanchenjunga 21
Mussolini, Benito 40, 52, 56

## N

Nantucket Yoga Festival 433
Napa Valley 327
NASA 210
National Bank of Scotland 42
*National Geographic Magazine* 235
National Stop Bullying Campaign v, 431
Native Americans 233, 236, 241
nature iv, x, xv, xvi, xviii, xix, xxi, xxii, xxiii, 7-8, 10-11, 13, 17-19, 21, 24, 28, 31, 37-39, 90, 108, 122, 141-143, 149, 151-152, 169, 172-173, 191-192, 195, 197, 220, 228, 230-236, 239, 250-252, 257-258, 273, 297, 307, 311, 317, 320, 324, 330-331, 334, 355-356, 370-371, 376, 382, 393, 396, 401-402, 409-410, 416, 419, 421
Navel Officers 105
Nazis xv, xx, 59, 135, 145, 148, 156, 178-179, 197
NBC 183, 190, 247, 294, 315, 401, 406
Nehru, Jawaharial 39, 205, 285, 339, 360
Nelson, Lord 99
neti neti 423
Newark Peace Education Summit xiii, 412-414
Newton, Sir Isaac 199
New York State Agricultural Experiment Station 326
Nippon Television Network (NTV) 284-285, 308
non-attachment 229
nonviolence *See* ahimsa
Norway 165
Notre Dame Cathedral 118, 147

## O

Oberoi Grand Hotel 79, 399
O'Brian, Hugh 246-247
Occidental Petroleum Corporation 210
ocean 17, 32, 64, 67, 69, 369, 423
olive grove 45-47
Olympia Theatre 161, 236

OM xvii, 13, 232, 422
Oneness xvii, xviii, xix, xx, xxi, xxii, 5, 13-15, 23-24, 26-27, 29-30, 32, 37, 142, 178, 195, 197, 218, 270, 279, 330, 344-346, 355-356, 369, 371, 374, 378, 380, 388, 407, 414
Operation Dynamo 73
Ostoja, Dr. Roman viii, xx, 259-270, 274-276, 279, 291, 293, 315, 330, 371, 418
Oxford University 259

**P**

Palace Hotel 176, 189
Palestinian Liberation Organization 384
Pan Am (airline) 183, 290, 292
Pantages Theatre 228
Paramahamsa, Sri Ramakrishna 25
Paramount Pictures 199, 248
parapsychology 274
Parliament of the World Religions 26, 218
Parsons, Lindsley 212
Patel, Indu 372, 375-376, 383
Patou, Jean xviii, xxi, 160, 162-164, 268, 288
Peacock (yoga pose) ii, 380, 411
Pentagon xiii, 412, 433
Pepsi Cola Playhouse 269
Peru 410, 411
Phoenix Marketcity 407
Pidgeon, Walter 252
Pierre Hotel 183
Pines, Joyce xiv, 430, 450
Pontrasina 176, 177
Porchon de Sanglier 10, 113, 200
Porchon, Vital xx, 3, 5-7, 14-15, 17-18, 24, 28-31, 37-38, 72, 125, 133, 143, 200, 218, 279, 298, 352, 354, 371, 374-375, 378-379, 384, 404
Port Said 44
Potter & Moore's Powder Cream 81
Prabhavananda, Swami xx, 38, 219, 229, 250, 267, 279, 315, 351, 357, 371, 409
Prasad, Rajendra 205
Price, Vincent 248
Prince Edward 168
Prince Michael of Yugoslavia 175
Prince Phillip 161, 162, 206
Princess Alice of Greece 162
Princess Elizabeth II 161
Princess Marina 112
procrastination xxiii, 39, 194, 364, 369

Prunier's (restaraunt) 133
Puerto Rico 398

**R**

Raft, George 205
railroads 13, 23, 140, 300, 356
Raja Yoga 27
Rajendran (Joanna, Mike, Natasha Tao) 456
Ramakrishna 25, 218-219, 228
Ramakrishna Vivekananda Vedanta Society 218
Ramamani 372
Ramananda, Swami 429
Randhawa, Jesse 407-408
Raven, John (Johnnie) xxi, 204-205, 212, 228, 231, 236, 290, 378-379
*Reader's Digest* (magazine) 284
Skelton, Red 203, 207, 247-248
Reinhardt, Django 112
Reinhardt, Max 156
Republic Day Celebrations 206, 285
respect 14, 16, 18, 32, 120, 131, 282, 346, 356, 390
retreats (yoga) 378, 381, 390-391
Rex Ingram Ranch 239, 263-264
Reynolds, Debbie 203, 241-242, 292
Reynolds, Quentin 95
Richmond, Ted 201
Roberts, Suzanne 437
Rochas, Marcel xxi, 184, 186
Rockefeller, Nelson 276
Romanoff, Valerie v, xiv, 428
Romero, Cesar xxi, 228, 290
Rómulo, General Carlos Peña 276
Rooney, Mickey 203, 241
Roosevelt, President Franklen D. 196
Ros, Edmundo 125
Rotary Club 332-334, 346, 354, 358, 421
Round Table Conference 35
Royal Air Force (RAF) Drem 135
Royal Ballet 99
Russo, Tony 183, 186, 191

**S**

Sabarmati Ashram 34
Sabu 93
Sadler's Wells Ballet 99
*Sailors Three* (film) 94, 252
Salle de la Chimie 181, 249
Salle Pleyel 156

Salt March xx, 33, 34, 35, 36
salt tax 31, 34
Salzburg Festival Hall 155
Samadhi (self-realization) xxi, 25
Sancerre xxi, 169-171, 226, 327
*Sangaree* (film) 248-249
sangha 396
Saraswati, Swami Brahmananda 276, 302
saris 42, 55 56, 59, 71, 160, 209, 322, 334, 402
Sarnoff, David 294
Sarragne, Maggy xxi, 176, 182, 188, 227, 287, 290
Satchidananda, Swami 361, 429
satyagraha 34
Savile Row 131
Schiaparelli, Elsa xv, xxi, 160, 230
Schulman, Lori xiv, 411
Schwab's Pharmacy 215
Schweitzer, Louis 190
Schnitzer, Lou 245
Scotland 42, 44-45, 135, 137-138, 144, 151, 158, 226
Selassie, Haile 208
self-control (self-mastery) 261-262, 275
Self-Realization Fellowship 261
Sen, Sushmita iv, xiv, 408
Sergio's (restaurant) 327
Sernas, Jacques 255
seva (selfless service) 356
Shah, Madhoo 407-408
Shibata, Hidetoshi 308
Shoulder Stand (yoga posture) 419
*Show Boat* (film) 203, 205, 207, 219-220
Sieber, Rudolf 159
Siegel, Sol 201-202
Sommer, Elke 352
Somani, Kumkum and Susheel 367
*Son of a Sailor* (film) 205
Sood, Rahul 367
Soparrkar, Sandip iv, v, viii, xiv, 407-408
Special Service Company 155-156
Spirit xii, xv, xvii, xx, xxii, 98, 232, 252, 348, 363, 409-410, 414, 422, 424
spiritual study 282-283, 371, 421, 472
Sri Lanka 390
St. Andrews University 261
Stassinopoulos, Agapi iii, xiv, 434
statue of Gandhi 37
Steinbaum, Dr. Suzanne iii, xiv, 434
Sterling Education Films 338

Stern, Howard xv, 406
Stiles, Tara 427
stillness 85, 278-279, 330, 409
Stone, Ezra 246
Sturman, Robert v, viii, xiv, 401, 405, 427
Styran, Olexi 403
Suez Canal 40, 43-44
Sun, Connie 432
Sun Salutation (Surya Namaskar) 85
Surah 80-81, 95, 151, 399
Sweden 165
Swenson, David iv, xiv, xxi, 361, 431
Swenson, Douglas 362-363
Switzerland 165, 175-176, 187, 284, 302, 462
   St. Mortiz 175, 177, 187

**T**

Tagore, Rabindranath 36
Taj Mahal 218, 391-392
Taj Palace Indian Restaurant 452
Taylor, Elizabeth 94, 202, 252
Ta Yoga House 442, 462
Tecla de Volko, Countess 270
TEDx talk 432
Tennyson, Alfred Lord viii, 93, 425
Tennyson, Lionel Lord 41, 43, 203, 348
*The Ambassador's Son* (TV series) 336
The Beatles 313, 318
The Cabaret Club 95
The Casino Hotel 410
The Coconut Grove 95
The Dwyer Cultural Center 442
The Flanders 223, 224
The Gandhi Effect 412, 414
*The Last Time I Saw Paris* (film) 252
The Marching Nations 280
The Mother (Mirra Alfassa) 28-29, 374
The Nut House 95
The Quintette of the Hot Club of France 112
*The Thief of Bagdad* (film) 93, 259
*The World is Round* (performance) 117
Thurman, Dr. Robert 412-413, 472
Tibet House 412, 472, 482
tidal bore 17, 18
Tierney, Gene 211
*To Light A Candle* (film) 340, 358-359
Tolman, Dr. Elmer 209
Tolman, Frances *See* Frances Hammer
Tolstoy, Lev Nikolayevich 276

Toscanini, Arturo 156
Tracy, Spencer 203
Transcendental Meditation 277, 301
Trans-Siberian railroad 15
trees x, 12, 13, 38, 141, 197, 206, 227, 234, 243, 302, 333, 416, 418
Trinder, Tommy 94
Truman, President Harry S. 196
Truth xii, xvi, xvii, xix, xx, xxi, xxii, 10, 20, 22, 26, 27, 30, 34, 217, 218, 250, 347, 356, 370, 371, 380, 409, 410, 414, 422, 423
Turner, Lana 203, 214, 228, 276
Tvert, Ron 369, 450
Twain, Mark 334
Twentieth Century Fox 199, 201-202
*Two Worlds, Two Loves* (film) 304, 306, 308, 312, 352
typhoid fever 41-42, 89

## U

UCLA 213
UJALA 297
UNESCO 20, 280, 281, 300, 315, 334
union xxii, 281, 347, 377
United Lodge of Theosophists *See* Loge Unie Des Theosophes
United Nations 128, 145, 280-281, 292, 304, 315-316, 334, 359-360
United Service Organizations (USOs) 156
United States Army Air Force Band 148
United States Relief and Rehabilitation Administration (UNRRA) 145
Unitel 284-287, 294, 300-301, 303-304
Unity In Yoga 388
Universal Studios 199, 215, 462
Universe iv, xvii, 4, 5, 13, 23, 97, 150, 197, 199, 232, 235, 257, 279, 345, 408, 414, 416, 419, 422, 423
University of Delaware 441
*Upanishads* (book) 268
Urban Yoga Foundation 442
Uruguay 174, 187, 219, 222, 225, 227, 421
USSR 197

## V

Vasendin, Alex 397-400, 403-404
Vasendin, Irina 397-400
Vaudable, Louis xxi, 165, 270, 290-292, 365
Vaudable, Octave 165
Vaughan, Olwen 110, 112-113, 157

Vedanta viii, xix, xxi, 26-27, 218-220, 229-231, 250-252, 267-268, 278, 282-283, 356-358, 371, 410
Vedanta Society viii, xxi, 218-220, 229-231, 250-252, 267-268, 278, 282, 357-358
*Vedas* (ancient text) 28
vegetarian 93, 133, 417
Veidt, Conrad 93
Venuti, Matt 436
Vernon, Rama Jyoti iv, xiv, xxi, 388
Victoria of the Lloyd Treistino Line 40, 114
Vietnam 147, 216, 314
    Hanoi 14, 15, 133
Vijayakar, Vijay 339
vineyard xx, 42, 45-47, 53-55, 116-117, 149, 156, 244, 324, 342-343, 367, 385
Vinyasa (yoga) 422, 464
Virabhadrasana II (Warrior II) 109
vitality xvii, 410, 412
Vivekananda, Swami xix, 24, 26, 38, 218, 228, 279, 356, 371, 432
*Vogue* (magazine) 183

## W

Wainwright House 435
Walden, Patricia 299
Waldorf Astoria Hotel 186, 191
Wales 396
Warbi, Cyndi 362
Warner Bros 214, 248
Watusi 15, 193, 399
Weeping Willie 74, 86, 104
Weis, Cyndi 436
Wellesley, Gordon 93
Wellington Club 40, 95, 131, 148
Wellington Night Club 129
Westchester Institute of Yoga 371
Westinghouse 295
White Barn Theatre 190, 194
White Cliffs of Dover 73, 103-104, 109, 152
White Plains 333, 348, 382, 402, 430
White Plains Public Library 348
White Tiger Productions 341
Wilding, Michael 94, 252
William Morris Agency 244
Williams, Esther 203
Williams, Jody xxi, 412, 413
Windmill Theatre 110
wine xvii, xviii, xx, 46, 53-56, 66, 68-69, 96, 122, 169-171, 197, 244, 272-273, 311, 321,

324-328, 330, 333, 335, 342, 346, 357, 366, 378-379, 381-382, 384-385, 417-418, 448
    Pinot Noir  311, 327
    Sauvignon Blanc  327
    Scuppernong grapes  326
    Shiraz  386
winemaking  53, 273, 324, 325, 342, 369
*Wines and Vines* (magazine)  325
*Wine Spectator* (magazine)  325
wisdom  iii, v, xviii, xx, 8, 13, 24, 47, 85, 109, 384
Women's Auxiliary Corps (WACs)  152-153, 155-156, 195, 198-199, 201
Women's Research and Education Fund  434
Wong, Anna May  259
Woodlands High School  309, 333
World Economic Forum  462
World Education  viii, 35, 284, 298, 340, 359
World War I  3, 41, 96, 296
World War II  xv, xvii, xx, 82, 87, 92, 110-111, 165, 185, 196, 204
WWII Victory Day  165

# Y

Yan'an  14-15, 133
Yee, Colleen Saidman  iii, xiv, 362, 431
Yee, Rodney  iii, xiv, xvi, xxi, 361, 431
Yoga  iii, iv, v, vii, xiii, xiv, xxi, xxii, 18, 25-28, 261, 275, 347, 349, 361-363, 370-371, 377-378, 380, 384-385, 387-388, 390, 393-394, 412, 419, 428-430, 433, 435-437, 441-442, 445, 462
Yoga Alliance  362, 429, 462
Yoga for Peace (event)  384, 387, 390, 428
*Yoga Journal* (magazine)  361
Yogananda, Paramahansa  261-263
*Yoga Sutras of Patanjali* (book)  25
Yoga Teacher's Association (YTA)  xxi, 362, 370, 387
Yogi Ramata  260
Young, Karen  430
yug (yuj)  xxii, 232, 409, 414
YWCA  296